THE POLICE AND SOCIETY:

AN ENVIRONMENT FOR COLLABORATION AND CONFRONTATION

Thomas A. Johnson
Washington State University

Gordon E. Misner
University of Illinois-Chicago Circle

Lee P. Brown
Atlanta Department of Public Safety

Prentice-Hall, Inc., Englewood Cliffs, New Jersey   07632

Library of Congress Cataloging in Publication Data

Johnson, Thomas Alfred.
  The police and society.

  Includes bibliographical references and index.
    1. Public relations—Police. 2. Police—United
States. I, Misner, Gordon E. II. Brown, Lee P.
III. Title.
HV7936.P8J63   363.2'0973   81–5133
ISBN 0–13–684076–0   AACR2

Editorial production/supervision and interior design by Natalie Krivanek.
Cover design by Dawn L. Stanley
Manufacturing buyer: Edward O'Dougherty.

Prentice-Hall Series in Criminal Justice
James D. Stinchcomb, Editor

To Joseph D. Lohman

Printed in the United States of America

10 9 8 7 6 5 4 3 2 1

Prentice-Hall International, Inc., *London*
Prentice-Hall of Australia Pty. Limited, *Sydney*
Prentice-Hall of Canada, Ltd., *Toronto*
Prentice-Hall of India Private Limited, *New Delhi*
Prentice-Hall of Japan, Inc., *Tokyo*
Prentice-Hall of Southeast Asia Pte. Ltd., *Singapore*
Whitehall Books Limited, *Wellington, New Zealand*

CONTENTS

PREFACE

We originally assumed the task of writing this book precisely because we desired to communicate our ideas and the ideas of others on the subject of police-community relations. As the book progressed, it was apparent that we were not only addressing some of the most difficult social and political problems confronting both the community and its police organizations, but we were also discussing the police as an institution, and much of what we discovered will have great applicability to assessing the police organization from a managerial perspective. Since our research has focused on historical and contemporary police practices and issues, the book has, therefore, become as much a statement on "policing conditions" as it is a statement on a particularly troublesome aspect of that condition. In short, policing in a democratic society such as ours provides inevitable opportunities for collaboration and confrontation, and we hope that we have illustrated the manner in which these confrontations occur and how a collaboration between our police and society might be initiated.

The three authors come from diverse backgrounds and experiences, and each has different vantage points from which they observe policing in a democratic society. At the same time, the authors share many common experiences and perspectives, and this book represents a culmination of these.

One of the many commonalities which we as authors share is our great and good fortune to have been associated with the late Joseph D. Lohman, Dean of the School of Criminology at the University of California-Berkeley. We were privileged to have had the opportunity of working with this gifted, outstanding scholar and humanitarian; and our personal and collective indebtedness is expressed through our dedication of this book to him.

We, of course, are deeply indebted to others who have assisted or inspired us over the years, and we wish to acknowledge our appreciation to each of them.

Finally, we thank our families for sharing with us in the many sacrifices that inevitably occur during the process of writing a book. Their words of encouragement, support, and assistance have made this book possible, and we are grateful for their love, patience, and inspiration which has permitted this book to come to fruition.

Thomas A. Johnson

Gordon E. Misner

Lee P. Brown

ACKNOWLEDGMENTS

Quotations from the works of other authors have been reprinted or adapted in this book with the consent of the following publishers whose kind permission is herewith acknowledged:

American Bar Association for excerpts from *ABA'S Standards for Criminal Justice Relating to the Urban Police Function* by the American Bar Association, Copyright © 1973. A revised version of the American Bar Association *Standards Relating to the Administration of Criminal Justice* is now available in a three volume second edition by the Law Division of Little, Brown and Company, Boston, Massachusetts.

American Society For Public Administration for excerpts from "Citizens and the Administrative State: From Participation to Power" by Carl W. Stenberg; "Neighborhoods and Citizen Involvement" by Joseph F. Zimmerman; and "Citizen Participation: Myths and Realities" by James A. Riedel, *Public Administration Review*, Vol. 32, No. 3, Copyright © 1972; and for excerpts from "Dilemmas of Police Administration" by James Q. Wilson, *Public Administration Review*, Vol. 28, No. 5, Copyright © 1968; and for excerpts from "Police Response to Urban Crisis" by Herman Goldstein, *Public Administration Review*, Vol. 27, Copyright ©

1968; and for excerpts from "Full Enforcement vs. Police Discretion Not to Invoke Criminal Process" by Herman Goldstein, *Public Administration Review*, Vol. 23, No. 3, Copyright © 1963, by the American Society for Public Administration, Washington, D.C.

American Society for Testing Materials for material adapted from "Issues of Community Control in the Administration of Justice" by T. A. Johnson, *Journal of Forensic Science*, Vol. 18, No. 3, Copyright © 1973; and for material adapted from "Police Resistance to Police Community Relations: The Emergence of the Patrolman Subculture" by T. A. Johnson, *Journal of Forensic Science*, Vol. 17, No. 3, Copyright © 1972 by ASTM, 1916 Race Street, Philadelphia, PA.

Basic Books, Inc., for passages from *The Policeman in the Community* by Michael Banton Copyright © 1964 by Basic Books, Inc., Publishers, New York.

The Bobbs-Merrill Co., Inc., for excerpts from *Community Control: The Black Demand for Participation in Large American Cities* by Alan A. Altshuler, Copyright © 1970 by Western Publishing Co., Inc., a Division of The Bobbs-Merrill Co., Inc.

The Brookings Institution for excerpts from *Upgrading the American Police: Education and Training for Better Law Enforcement* by Charles B. Saunders, Jr., Copyright © 1970 by the Brookings Institution, Washington, D.C.

Crime and Social Justice for material adapted from "Police-Citizen Encounters and the Importance of Role Conceptualization for Police Community Relations" by Thomas A. Johnson, *Issues in Criminology*, Vol. 7, No. 1, Copyright © 1972 by Crime and Social Justice: Issues in Criminology, P. O. Box 4373, Berkeley, California.

Follett Publishing Company for excerpts from *Confronting Organizational Change* by Ray Johns, Copyright © 1963 by Association Press a division of Follett Publishing Company.

Holt, Rinehart and Winston, Inc., for excerpts from *Social Psychology: The Study of Human Interaction*, Second Edition, by Theodore M. Newcomb, Ralph H. Turner, and Philip E. Converse, Copyright 1950 © 1965 by Holt, Rinehart and Winston, Inc.

International Association of Chiefs of Police, Inc., for material adapted from "The Application of Organizational Theory to the Problem of Police Resistance to Police-Community Relations" by Thomas Alfred Johnson, *Journal of Police Science and Administration*, Vol. 3, No. 1, Copyright © 1975 by Northwestern University School of Law.

Macmillan Publishing Co., Inc. for excerpts from *Minorities and the Police: Confrontation in America* by David E. Bayley and Harold Mendelsohn, Copyright © 1968 by The Free Press, a division of Macmillan Publishing Co., Inc.

Macmillan Publishing Co., Inc. for the passage from *Social Theory and Social Structure* by Robert K. Merton, Copyright © 1968, 1967 by Robert K. Merton.

Macmillan Publishing Co., Inc., for excerpts from *Police and Community Relations: A Sourcebook* by Arthur F. Brandstatter and Louis A. Radelet, Editors; and for passages from "Police and Community-As Viewed by a Psychologist" by Milton Rokeach; "The Police Role in a Democratic Society" by Frederick Routh; "Police Working in the Neighborhood" by Allen B. Ballard; "Full Enforcement vs. Police Discretion Not to Invoke Criminal Process" by Herman Goldstein, reprinted by permission from *Public Administration Review*, Vol. 23, No. 3, September 1963, a quarterly journal of the American Society for Public Administration, 1225 Connecticut Ave., N.W., Washington, D.C.; and for passages from "Professionalization of the Police" by Albert J. Reiss, Copyright © 1968 by the Glencoe Publishing Co., Inc., a Division of Macmillan Publishing Co., Inc.

The MIT Press, for extracts from *Violence and the Police: A Sociological Study of Law, Custom and Morality* by William A. Westley, Copyright © 1970 by MIT Press, Cambridge, Massachusetts.

Palisades Publishers for excerpts from *The Police Community* by Jack Goldsmith and Sharon Goldsmith, Editors, Copyright © 1974 by Palisades Publishers.

Pantheon Books for excerpts from *Police Power* by Paul Chevigny, Copyright © 1969 by Paul Chevigny. Reprinted by permission of Pantheon Books, a Division of Random House, Inc.

Transaction, Inc., for the passage from "Comment: Community Control of the Police" by Arthur I. Waskow, *Society*, Vol. 7, No. 2., Copyright © 1969 by Transaction, Inc.

1

THE POLICE SYSTEM: AN ORGANIZATIONAL PERSPECTIVE

CHAPTER
ONE

INTRODUCTION:
THE SETTING

These tremendous changes are more than facts in themselves they are the condition for the creation of a new pattern of human relations in this country. We often find it difficult to perceive this new pattern, primarily because our relationships are traditionally structured and we are disposed to maintain the traditional structure. . . .

Joseph D. Lohman (1966)[1]

There is an obvious need for a comprehensive study dealing with police–community relations problems. This is a field of interest that has developed rapidly—essentially from the mid-1960s to the present time. The fact that this is a relatively new field of interest is itself ironic, for certainly there have been police–community relations problems for as long as there have been organized policing institutions.[2] Recent interest in the subject has been stimulated, of course, by the convulsive history of urban crises during the mid-1960s, and by the series of official and private studies of various aspects of urban policing problems.

In this study, we attempt to accomplish many objectives by systematically placing these in an understandable behavioral and systems framework. In other words, police–community relations must be studied in the context of other social systems. Essentially, this study attempts to treat the following aspects of police–community relations:

1. Develop an outline of the major dimensions of police–community relations problems.
2. Inventory existing police–community relations programs.
3. Examine some alternative methods of internally and externally evaluating the effectiveness of programs.
4. Review the professional literature on the subject.
5. Chart some possible patterns of future development in the police–community relations field.

A behavioral and systems perspective necessarily involves focusing at least a portion of our attention on an analysis of the appropriate role of the police. As many readers will appreciate, that is not a simple task, for there are clearly divergent and antithetical views of what constitutes the appropriate role of the police in an essentially democratic political setting.

Behavioral and system perspectives also impose the obligation to identify significant points of interaction between an organized policing system and its operational environment. Policing apparatuses do not, of course, operate within a social vacuum. Neither do they act upon essentially inanimate and passive subjects. Rather, the totality of police action takes place within a dynamic, pluralistic, social, and governmental setting. To ignore these terms and conditions when studying police–community relations would be the height of folly and intellectual irresponsibility.

> We are all interested in the law; we are all interested in maintaining the peace of the community—the Negro and the white, the young and the old, the rich and the poor. All of us subscribe to a common language that, at least on the surface, seems to suggest that we are as one. But we have the problem of what this language means and the perspectives in which we stand. Many of the problems which are confronting us today have a meaning and significance which are quite different from what we have traditionally ascribed to them or to the situations they represent.[3]

There is a universal need in this nation for a system of equitable, effective, and sensitive civil policing. We have been involved officially in numerous investigations of police–community relations problems throughout the nation. In no single case in this combined experience have we individually or collectively encountered persons who were advocating the destruction or abolition of policing. No matter how hostile or engaged people were in a particular situation, the persons and groups with whom we have had contact over the years have uniformly and consistently recognized the social imperative of having a policing apparatus. This is an important point, for it demonstrates graphically that persons from all walks of life, representing a variety of social and political views, recognize the necessity of policing.

Concerns in police–community relations therefore take the necessity of a formal, organized system of policing for granted—as given. That is a nondebatable point. Concern in police–community relations focuses, therefore, on a different set of issues: policing methods, the "inputs" into policy decisions, the matter of quality control, the issue of fairness, the concern for representatives, and so on. Each of these issues—and others—is treated systematically in this study.

There is, therefore, a social symbiotic relationship existing between the citizens of a community and its policing agency. Symbiosis can be defined as "the habitual living together of organisms of different species. The term is usually restricted to a dependent relationship that is beneficial to both participants."[4] Neither organized society nor its operating policing agency can exist effectively without the other. If police agencies were abolished, society would have to invent some other agency for formal social control purposes. The crucial point is the interdependency that ideally must exist and be fostered between society at large and its policing apparatus. Neither society nor its police agency should lose sight of this point.

A graphic illustration of this interdependency was pointed up in a study involving one of the authors. This was a robbery study in five major cities: Atlanta, Chicago, Oakland, Seattle, and Washington, D.C. During the course of that study, questions were asked of experienced, working detectives in robbery investigation units in each of these cities. (It is important to note that these questions were asked of working detectives, not of police–community relations officers.) More than five hundred detectives participated in this portion of the study. Among the questions asked was the following: "Of all the obstacles that can interfere with the completion of a successful robbery investigation, which would you rate as the three most important?" The responses by city and in aggregate are shown in Tables 1-1 and 1-2. When the responses are aggregated and arranged in descending order, the responses of the detectives were as shown in Table 1-2.

Interestingly, when the responses of all five cities are grouped together, as in Table 1-2, more than 40 percent of the detectives pointed to an "obstacle" which properly could be called a "police–community relations problem." (Obviously, "unwillingness of the public to become involved" encompasses more than police–community relations. One objective of community relations may be to increase the willingness of the public to "become involved.") In this example, working detectives, not police–community relations officers, pointed out the extent to which police–community relations issues were possibly interfering with their ability to perform effectively in their crime control roles. These data emphasize an important point—that effective police–community relations has a payoff value to working line officers. Administrators, politi-

TABLE **1-1**   Detective Perceptions of Common Obstacles to Successful Robbery Investigations (percent; *n* = 542)

Obstacles to Investigation	City A	City B	City C	City D	City E	Total
1. Unwillingness of public to get involved	25.9	10.3	33.0	33.3	19.0	26.0
2. Hostility of some people toward police	11.7	0.0	11.4	3.7	4.8	10.1
3. Victim or witness fear of retaliation	18.0	7.7	17.0	14.8	0.0	16.2
4. "Social pressure" not to cooperate with police	7.1	17.9	5.7	7.4	14.3	7.9
5. Lack of adequate eye-witness identification	4.1	10.3	2.3	18.5	28.6	5.9
6. Insufficient detective staff	17.4	12.8	4.5	7.4	14.3	14.4
7. Insufficient detective equipment	0.3	0.0	2.3	0.0	0.0	0.6
8. Inadequate local and/or regional information retrieval	0.3	12.8	1.1	0.0	0.0	1.3
9. Insufficient training sessions or seminars	1.1	0.0	8.0	0.0	0.0	2.0
10. Inadequate preliminary investigation	8.4	2.6	9.1	0.0	4.8	7.6
11. Lack of informers	2.7	2.6	3.4	3.7	0.0	2.8
12. Lack of physical evidence	2.5	23.1	2.3	11.1	14.3	4.8
13. Lax court	0.5	0.0	0.0	0.0	0.0	0.4
Total	100.0	100.1	100.1	99.9	100.1	100.0

Gordon E. Misner and William F. McDonald, *The Scope of the Crime Problem and Its Resolution*, Vol. 2, *Reduction of Robberies and Assaults of Bus Drivers* (Washington, D.C.: U.S. Department of Transportation, 1970), p. 285. To disguise their identities, the five cities are identified by letters.

cians, and police–community relations specialists are not the only ones who benefit from effective community relations. Even working police officers benefit, for their jobs can be made easier, their performance can be increased, and their job anxiety level can be diminished.

The concept of symbiosis has both a behavioral and a systems significance. Behaviorally, the concept suggests that the interaction of either an individual police officer, or of the police organization as a unit, has effects and consequences upon the larger society and its members, individually and collectively. It also suggests that occurrences and actions in the social setting evoke responses by the police organization. These interactions, therefore, are situational, and as such consist of series of events, actions, and reactions. Consequently, they have a dynamic, not a static character.

TABLE 1-2   Aggregate Responses of Detectives (percent, n = 542)

Obstacles to Investigation	Percent of Detectives
1. Unwillingness of public to get involved	26.0
3. Victim or witness fear of retaliation	16.2
6. Insufficient detective staff	14.4
2. Hostility of some people toward police	10.1
4. "Social pressure" not to cooperate with police	7.9
10. Inadequate preliminary investigation	7.6
5. Lack of adequate eye-witness identification	5.9
12. Lack of physical evidence	4.8
11. Lack of informers	2.8
9. Insufficient training sessions or seminars	2.0
8. Inadequate local and/or regional information retrieval	1.3
7. Insufficient detective equipment	0.6
13. Lax court	0.6

Gordon E. Misner and William F. McDonald, *The Scope of the Crime Problem and Its Resolution,* Vol. 2, *Reduction of Robberies and Assaults of Bus Drivers* (Washington, D.C.: U.S. Department of Transportation, 1970), p. 286.

THE BASIC SYSTEM DESIGN

Using the perspective of systems analysis, we can gain added dimensions in attempting to understand important factors in police–community relations. A useful starting point would be to examine the elements of a basic system design. Our examination will use a police system as our frame of reference, but the same design is just as appropriate a starting point for analyzing the operation of the Brown Shoe Company, Middle States University, or Hobart's Cafeteria. In other words, almost all operating systems possess common elements; consequently, there are certain universalities when one endeavors to examine any operating system.

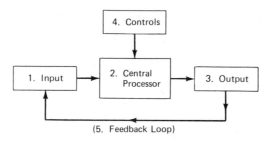

FIGURE 1-1 Outline of a Basic System

The outline of a basic system is shown in Figure 1-1. This basic system consists of at least five elements: (1) the input, (2) the central processor, (3) the output, (4) the controls, and (5) the feedback loop. The basic, rudimentary nature of the system outline should be emphasized, for the authors are aware that different systems perspectives approach the subject of explanation from a variety of points of view. We believe, however, that this particular illustration has usefulness for explanatory purposes.[5]

Each of the elements in the system is important in the overall functioning of the system. Concentration upon any one element, at the risk of ignoring the importance of another element, impairs one's ability to understand the functioning of the system as a whole. In other words, if one were attempting to analyze the operation and functioning of a payroll system in a large corporation, one would have to have an understanding of each of the elements in order to comprehend the functioning of the total system. To concentrate attention prematurely upon machine processing may cause the analyst to overlook human factors involved in data inputs. One failure of the system may involve the simple matter of incorrectly making payroll deductions for withholding tax, involving simple human error in keypunching program cards.

What is the relevance of system elements to a discussion of police–community relations matters? What do we mean when we use the term and concept of input in a police–community relations matter? How do you translate particular system elements into a police frame of reference?

Input

In the field of data processing, there is a nonsense slogan that nevertheless has great import. Many readers will be familiar, at least with the slogan itself: "garbage in, garbage out." The slogan is so well known that there is even an acronym for it: GIGO. The import of the slogan is the caution that if a system designer wants a particular bit of data out of the system (i.e., as an "output"), the designer must be certain that the required data are fed into the system. In other words, if the data fed into the system are information taken only from Internal Revenue Service Form 1040, there is no way that the computer can print out data about religious affiliation, spectator-sport preference, or the number of taxpayers who have felony criminal records. Translated into police operations terms, nothing can be retrieved from the police system that is not invested in the system in some form of "input" (i.e., in the form of money, human or material resources, leadership, etc.).

It would be difficult to prepare an exhaustive list of police system inputs. For explanatory purposes, however, it is useful to develop a suggestive list organized in a strictly random fashion. Each reader can certainly prepare his or her own list.

1. Annual budget of department
2. Judicial review
3. Departmental traditions
4. Quality of entry-level personnel
5. Local and state governmental traditions
6. Federal, state, and local statutes
7. Preservice social and political views of personnel
8. The political environment of the community and region
9. Community and subcommunity expectations of police
10. Administrative and command styles of leadership
11. Entry-level personnel requirements
12. Preservice socialization of applicants
13. Organizational structure of department
14. Styles of policing
15. Prevailing economic conditions
16. Public fear of crime
17. Police–press relations

It should be emphasized that the foregoing list is meant to be suggestive; the authors make no pretense that it is an exhaustive, all-inclusive list of inputs.

Obviously, the political and social traditions of the local jurisdiction, and of the region in which it is located, have an impact on police operations. If the community and political leadership always permitted or "winked at" corruption—as long as it was kept within acceptable bounds—this tradition will have significant impact on the totality of police operations. If the community has always insisted upon excellence and integrity in police performance, this insistence will be noticed even by new residents of the community.

The Central Processor

For our present purposes, the term "central processor" simply refers to the police organization itself, as a totality and as a set of suborganizations; it includes patrol, personnel, identification, planning and development, and so on. The term as used here also includes the command structure, the articulation and coordination between subunits, and the training standards.

Output

As with inputs, we will attempt to compile only a suggestive list of outputs. An exhaustive list would be limited only by the imaginativeness of the compiler.

1. 2,081 felony arrests
2. 163 lives saved
3. 17 "positive" newspaper editorials during the past 12 months
4. 103,781 patrol miles driven last year
5. 461 public letters of commendation
6. 167 resignations from the department last year
7. 23 false arrest suits during the past 12 months
8. 8.5 minutes average patrol response time
9. Physical evidence samples collected in 1.6% of felony cases
10. 4,567 arrestees processed
11. 31 percent felony conviction rate during the past 12 months
12. 4.7 percent personnel turnover last year
13. 264 police recruits trained
14. 1.1 percent Chicano applicants for recruit training class
15. 15 disciplinary actions taken last year
16. 105 recoveries of stolen automobiles during the past 12 months
17. 982 family disturbances handled
18. 3,542 warnings issued to motorists

Used in a systems context, it is obvious that the terms "input" and "output" are both broadly defined. Both terms take into account all the multiple factors that may be ingested into the police system and result in either conscious or unconscious products of the system. Using this model, we can see, for example, that public attitudes toward a particular police system may be influenced by such disparate factors as the perceived social attitude of patrolmen, the way they were trained and otherwise socialized into the system, or the specific management styles used in administering the department.

Controls

The concept of control includes not only internal controls emanating from and decided upon by factors internal to the organization, but also factors emanating from outside the organization (e.g., common and statutory laws governing the behavior of the organization). Broadly construed, therefore, "control" includes a wide range of functions, procedures, and processes, including but not limited to the following:

1. The annual budget of the department, especially its internal allocations
2. The policies and regulations of the department
3. The administrative attitudes and styles of command personnel
4. Internal inspection and supervision policies and standards
5. The number of personnel assigned to inspections and internal affairs
6. The characteristics and the capacity of radio communication systems
7. Appellate court decisions on search and seizure and other matters

Feedback

Technically, feedback consists of any portion of a system's output which is utilized as an input for the purposes of monitoring or controlling the system's performance. "It is generally agreed among system theorists that a basic principle underlying these purposive, or goal-seeking mechanisms is embodied in the concept of 'feedback.' "[6] A "governor" on a steam engine and the thermostat on a furnace system are two of the simplest examples of feedback. "Basically, an input to the system is received and operated on by a transformation block (i.e., The Central Processor). The results of the transformation are then monitored, and by suitable procedures the output is compared to the input standard."[7] Feedback "loops" exist in all systems and organizations, whether consciously designed into the system or not. One explanation for poor organization performance is the inadequacy of the feedback loop—that it was not deliberately designed into the operation, is too long and circuitous, or is rampant with blockages: "Control through feedback is a circular process; and this give-and-take of goal-setting, communication, and continuous correction is not only the essence of feedback but also comprises the heart of coordination in large scale organizations."[8] This point made by Pfiffner and Sherwood cannot be overemphasized, for efficiency within the feedback loop is absolutely crucial to effective system performance. "Feedback-controlled systems are referred to as goal-directed, and not merely goal-oriented, since it is the deviations from the goal state itself that directs the behavior of the system, rather than some predetermined internal mechanism that aims blindly."[9]

RELATIONSHIP OF THE BASIC SYSTEM
TO THE COMMUNITY

Throughout this discussion, we have constantly underscored our systems orientation toward police–community relations issues. This study is certainly not intended to replace a thorough analysis of systems theory. It is our point of view, however, that ignoring systems issues leads to an incomplete understanding of the police and their interactions and relationship to the community in which they operate. "A system of activities is that complex of activities which is required to complete the process of transforming an intake (or set of inputs) into an output."[10] A point made earlier must be reemphasized here: Systems, in general, and the police system, in particular, operate within a social setting—not within a social vacuum. In other words, the system or "black box" outlined in Figure 1-1 does not stand by itself. Rather, it stands in relation to other governmental systems and other social systems—indeed, it stands in relation to the total environment.

Consequently, a more appropriate illustration of the police system is that shown in Figure 1-2. Here the "black box" used to represent the police system in Figure 1-1 is now shown in relationship to its operational environment. It is shown in direct, proximate relationship to other black boxes representing separate systems of the criminal justice process. The police system is also shown in close relationship to other "official" governmental systems (e.g., the social welfare system, the emergency health care system, the traffic safety system).

It is appropriate to show the police system in close proximity to other systems, for much of police service involves active participation in these other social, governmental services. Police activities in the field of traffic safety—in the regulation of traffic flow, in the investigation of traffic accidents, in the citing of drivers for violation—are directly and intimately related to other operating systems. Traffic engineering, driver behavior, and judicial attitudes are directly influencing the performance of the police as well as their job satisfaction. The importance of the environment has been pointed out by Churchman: "The environment of the input–output system is the set of conditions that are relevant to but not under the control of the managers."[11] The phrase "conditions that are relevant to but not under the control of the managers" is crucial to proper understanding of the police–community relations issue.

An understanding of police–community relations therefore involves not only technical mastery of police skills, but also a somewhat global appreciation of the extent to which police action is related to, and conditioned by, factors outside the police system itself. This imposes a heavy—though not impossible task—upon the person desirous of understanding the issues and the dynamics involved in police–community relations. "Any theory of organization requires, therefore, not only a theory of systems of activities and their boundaries, but also a

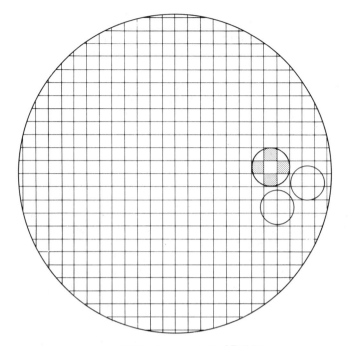

FIGURE 1-2 The Environment of Policing

theory of human behavior."[12] If police–community relations issues involved nothing more complex than the manufacture of shoes or the laying of tile in a subway tunnel, mastery would be infinitely simpler. The challenge of effective police–community relations is found in the fact that it is inextricably bound up with human behavior patterns and involves the delivery of vital social services. The extent to which these services are equitably and effectively delivered to the public influences the well-being of the society at large.

Summary

In Chapter 1 we have discussed police–community relations in terms of a behavioral and systems framework. The necessity for policing has been made evident. We have outlined the basic system involved and delved into its component parts and their effect upon each other. It was particularly noted that a symbiotic relationship exists between the police and the community it serves; the relationship is one of interdependency, with neither component able to exist effectively without the other. Obstacles encountered by police in the administration of their duties are pointed out, not the least of which is the "noninvolvement" of the public, a characteristic that has had unfortunate consequences in crime prevention. In brief, this chapter has defined the setting and problems with which the police and community must deal in the hopes of achieving an effective and harmonious working relationship.

Chapter 2 more clearly defines the role of the police in the context of the values and concepts of a democratic society and the structure of the criminal justice system.

End Notes

[1]Joseph D. Lohman, "Current Decline in Respect for Law and Order," paper prepared for the Section of Judicial Administration, American Bar Association, Montreal, August 8, 1966, p. 9.

[2]See, for example, almost any study of earliest civil policing endeavors in either the United Kingdom or the United States. AMS. Press, Inc., New York, probably publishes the most comprehensive list of important historical titles.

[3]Lohman, "Current Decline," pp. 6, 7.

[4]*The Columbia Encyclopedia,* 3rd ed. (New York: Columbia University Press, 1963), p. 2081, emphasis added. Caution is advisable in the use of most analogies, and this is certainly true in this case. Technically, symbiosis in a biological science sense involves different species of organisms. We are not making that point in this case. The analogy is useful, however, in pointing up interdependencies.

[5]Richard A. Johnson, Fremont E. Kast, and James E. Rosenzweig, *The Theory and Management of Systems* (New York: McGraw-Hill, 1963), p. 70.

[6]Walter Buckley, *Sociology and Modern Systems Theory* (Englewood Cliffs, N.J.: Prentice-Hall, p. 52.

[7]Van Court Hare, Jr., *Systems Analysis: A Diagnostic Approach* (New York: Harcourt Brace Jovanovich, 1967), p. 42. For a discussion of different "orders" of feedback, see ibid., pp. 111–30.

[8]John M. Pfiffner and Frank P. Sherwood, *Administrative Organization* (Englewood Cliffs, N.J.: Prentice-Hall, 1960), p. 106, emphasis added.

[9]Buckley, *Sociology,* p. 53.

[10]E. J. Miller and A. K. Rice, *Systems of Organization: The Control of Task and Sentient Boundaries* (London: Tavistock, 1957), p. 6.

[11]C. West Churchman, *The Systems Approach* (New York: Delta, 1968), p. 63.

[12]Miller and Rice, *Systems of Organization,* p. 14.

CHAPTER
TWO

POLICING
IN A DEMOCRATIC
SOCIETY

INTRODUCTION—THE DELIVERY OF HUMAN SERVICES

In 1964, Ben Whitaker's excellent and concise study of the police in the United Kingdom was published. Many of his observations about British policing also pertain to policing in the United States:

> We expect him [the policeman] to be human and yet inhuman. We employ him to administer the law, and yet ask him to waive it. We resent him when he enforces the law in our own case, yet demand his dismissal when he does not elsewhere. We offer him bribes, yet denounce his corruption. We expect him to be a member of society, yet not share its values. We admire violence, even against society itself, but condemn force by the police on our own behalf. We tell the police that they are entitled to information from the public, yet we ostracize informers. We ask for crime to be eradicated, but only by the use of "sporting" methods.
>
> What . . . do we want the police for? Only by resolving the conflict and values between liberty and law enforcement can we determine the paradox of the policeman's position in our future society.[1]

The fundamental concept underlying police–community relationships is the concept that the terms and conditions of the "police setting" in a democratic society are absolutely crucial. After all, it is these sometimes confusing sets of terms and conditions that define, modify, change, and articulate police–community relationships.

Police agencies and their personnel developed in response to at least perceived needs on the part of community leaders. Why else would the citizens consent to paying taxes to support the early Night Watches, which were the precursors of organized, municipal police agencies? Although their responsibilities have seldom been clearly defined, police agencies—then and now—have been presumed by the public to exist to provide sets of protective services to the community.

Having said this and agreed to it, however, does not address the issue of how to effect a comfortable and useful union between society and its hired, professional protectors. A former chief of police, James F. Ahern, attempted to put this matter into a proper framework for public understanding.

> Crime and the police are big issues in the United States today and properly so, since most Americans are increasingly afraid, often with good reason. Yet most Americans subscribe unthinkably to at least three important myths in this area.
>
> Myth number one is that the police devote the preponderance of their time and resources to combatting serious crime. The second myth is that there is a fairly fixed, definable and measurable thing called crime. The third is that police work can somehow lower crime rates regardless of what other institutions do.[2]

This statement is an important one, not only because it was written by a perceptive former chief of police and career police officer, but also because it is a concise statement of some serious dilemmas facing both the public and police personnel.

Although he would probably have had serious disagreements with Ahern on many contemporary issues, the late William H. Parker, chief of police in Los Angeles, spoke often about the complexities of modern policing.

> It would be difficult to devise a combination of factors more conducive to crime and disorder than is found in a typical great city of the United States. Rarely does history record so many people of varying beliefs and modes of conduct in so competitive and complex a social structure. The confusing variety of religious and political creeds, national origins, and diverse cultures is matched only by the extremes of ideals, emotions, and conduct found in the individual.[3]

The important point here is that we are talking about policing in a contemporary American urban setting, a setting different from any that preceded it. It is also a setting that differs from any other setting in today's world. We are not talking of policing in a homogeneous, totalitarian society. We are not talking about a rural, sparsely populated setting. What we are talking about is policing functions that must operate in the middle of all the diversity, all the conflict, all the social and economic competitiveness that characterizes contemporary America.

We are also talking about a governmental apparatus—the police—which of necessity is involved in the delivery of important human services. As much as we may wish to insulate this service from the vagaries and vulgarities of day-to-day politics, we can never separate policing from the political process. It is the political process, after all, which seeks to resolve major social conflicts, establishes governmental priorities, and allocates various governmental services.

POLICE RESPONSIBILITIES IN CONTEMPORARY SOCIETY

James Q. Wilson first pointed up the significant organizational distinctions between "order maintenance" on the one hand, and "law enforcement" on the other.[4] It was an important distinction, for citizens had generally ignored the police except in times of emergency or when they desired some offensive nuisance abated. Certainly, the body politic had not thought seriously about the proper function of the police—indeed about police functions, at all.

Actually, it was not until 1966, when President Johnson appointed the President's Commission, that we began as a society to think seriously about the police—or any other aspect of the criminal justice process. Stimulated by national-level interest and attention, and national funding, series after series of studies of policing began to appear.

Until that time, if the typical adult resident of urban America had been asked to describe the function of the police, he or she would probably have responded something like this: "The principle responsibility of the police is to combat crime." The typical citizen would therefore have accepted James F. Ahern's "myth number 1," and critically, so too, probably, would have the bulk of working police personnel. The relationship between crime and the operating police apparatus has become so ingrained into American folklore as to be widely accepted, even by many persons who staff police agencies. As Ahern implied, many citizens tend to believe that the police spend the preponderance of their time dealing in some fashion with "serious" or "major" crime.

Any number of studies have disproved this false assumption.[5] Uniformly, the data from many of our largest cities, and from small and medium-size cities, show that general-duty police officers spend from 70 to 85 percent of their time dealing with non-crime-related matters.[6] The point is, enough data have now been collected by a series of different researchers to say that there is little variance in this matter from department to department. We can safely generalize that crime, per se, consumes only a small portion of working police officers' time on duty. The bulk of their time is spent in dealing with other issues.

Certainly, the early purposes of the police were to keep watch over the community, particularly during its sleeping hours, to assure the safety and order of the community. As with the generic responsibilities of military personnel pulling "guard duty" or duty as "charge of quarters," the essence of the duty was vigilance while the rest of the troops—or community—were busy going about their normal routines or while they were sleeping. Ahern describes the duties of early police units, as follows:

> In a way... police departments were born in situations of stress which molded them according to the times. It is significant that police departments' first historical role was one of *order maintenance* rather than strict law enforcement, as serious crimes were handled not by the night watch but by private agents who were armed with warrants from magistrates and collected fees for arresting offenders. As time went on, however, rising crime forced the change in emphasis. The public conception of police roles shifted more from order maintenance to crime control and the police became regulated by a fixed set of societal ideals embodied in a code of laws.[7]

A study completed by the American Bar Association (ABA) has reaffirmed the unsystematic way in which the police role has changed as society itself has changed and as new demands were placed upon the police.[8]

The ABA study emphasizes the ad hoc basis upon which the changes occurred:

> ... to a great extent, without any coherent planning by state or local governments of what the overriding objectives or priorities of the police should be. Instead, what the police do is determined largely... by a number of factors which influence their involvement in responding to various government or community needs. These factors include
> 1. *Broad legislative mandates to the police*
> 2. *The authority of the police to use force lawfully*
> 3. *The investigative ability of the police*
> 4. *The 24-hour availability of the police*
> 5. *Community pressures on the police*[9]

We feel that this is an excellent statement about many of the factors that have given rise to the diverse set of current responsibilities of the police. After all, only selected correctional employees and military personnel share with the police the legal right to use deadly force. Firefighters share a 24-hour availability with the police, but it is the police who are decentralized in roving patrol units. The police, therefore, are more often than not more accessible to certain emergencies than are

	CRIMINAL	NONCRIMINAL
EMERGENCY	I A Emergency Criminal Matter	I B Emergency Noncriminal Matter
NONEMERGENCY	II A Nonemergency Criminal Matter	II B Nonemergency Noncriminal Matter

FIGURE 2-1 Police Field Services

firefighters. Logically, therefore, it makes complete sense from a service and cost point of view to assign many different tasks to the police. That is precisely what American society has tended to do. One consequence of this is that through the years, this has given rise to certain sets of expectations on the part of the general public. These become translated into service demands. If there is any doubt of this, the reader should prepare a list of 10 different types of public emergencies. For most of them, the reader would probably prefer the service or assistance of a police officer. So, too, would the general public.

A special typology for discussion of police services may be useful. The typology is based on the assumption that all police field dispatches, except routine administrative matter, can be arranged on a four-cell matrix, as shown in Figure 2-1. According to this typology, all emergency calls for service are category I events. In police parlance, they might be referred to as "Code Three" calls, often requiring siren, red light, and emergency driving conditions. All nonemergency calls would be considered to be category II events. Examples of how specific situations would fit onto this matrix are shown in Figure 2-2.

Of course, each situation has its own set of circumstances which could conceivably move it—for that particular case—from one cell to another. The "stale" burglary of a prominent citizen's home might, for public relations purposes, be moved from a category IIA to a category IA event. Lost animals straying onto an interstate highway could be reasonably classified as a category IB event.

It is interesting to note that according to the series of studies mentioned earlier, category IB and IIB events, noncriminal matters, usually comprise at least 70 percent of police patrol field services. This cluster of events may very well be "downgraded" euphemistically to "miscellaneous public services," but they still constitute an important series of activities for the police. Failure to perform them effectively can be very costly to the police in terms of public esteem. Failure of the police to perform these services effectively can be very damaging to the public.

Traditionally, textbooks on police administration solemnly pronounce the "functions" of the police. Depending upon the text used, one

IA EVENT	IB EVENT
Robbery in progress	Child fell into storm sewer
Hostage being held	Coronary case
Homicide	Man pinned under load
Kidnapping	Hospital fire
"Hot" burglary	Man jumping
Jail escape	Factory explosion
IIA EVENTS	IIB EVENTS
Bad checks	Lost animal
Larceny from newstand	Found property
Shop-lifting	Lock-out
"Stale" burglary	Escort, except VIP
Prostitution complaint	Overtime parking
Vandalism	Minor vehicular accident

FIGURE 2-2 Situations

will usually confront a list of six to eight functions. One such standard text lists police responsibilities as including the following:

1. Prevention of criminality
2. Repression of crime
3. Apprehension of offenders
4. Recovery of property
5. Regulation of noncriminal conduct
6. Performance of miscellaneous services[10]

The foregoing list of "functions" may lend itself nicely to memorization and grading for promotional examinations, but it is not very useful to either the police or the general public.

The principal problem with the list above is that it is so general as to be uninforming and misleading. There are ambiguities involved in each of the six responsibilities. What is meant, for example, by the responsibility for "prevention of criminality"? The police role in crime prevention is clouded with uncertainties, with differences of opinion even within police ranks. Most observers would admit that the police have some role in crime prevention activities, but there would be lengthy discussion about the precise character of that role, about the relationship of the police in this matter to other social institutions.

A much more helpful starting point for analyzing the role of the police is to consider the material prepared by the American Bar Association.

In assessing appropriate objectives and priorities for police service, local communities should initially recognize that most police agencies are currently given responsibility, by design or default:
1. *To identify criminal offenders and criminal activity and, where appropriate, to apprehend offenders and participate in subsequent court proceedings*
2. *To reduce the opportunities for the commission of some crimes through preventive patrol and other measures*

3. *To aid individuals who are in danger of physical harm*
4. *To protect constitutional guarantee*
5. *To facilitate the movement of people and vehicles*
6. *To assist those who cannot care for themselves*
7. *To resolve conflict*
8. *To identify problems that are potentially serious law enforcement or governmental problems*
9. *To create and maintain a feeling of security in the community*
10. *To promote and preserve civil order*
11. *To provide other services on an emergency basis*[11]

This seems to be an impressive and useful starting point from which to begin an analysis and understanding of the police function.

Certainly, there are ambiguities even in the ABA statement. For the first time, however, there has been a systematic endeavor not only to describe the police function, but also to place it in some environmental context. In other words, it is important to begin with the assumption that we are a nation of laws, that due process and constitutional safeguards are important to all citizens—to nonpolice and police, alike. It is also important to see that the "prevention of criminality" function, referred to earlier, has been placed in a more realistic context by the ABA.

In any genuine analysis of modern American policing, it also becomes patently obvious that a police officer has a much more complex task than serving simply as a "law enforcement" officer.

> The job of police officer is grossly underrated in its importance and its complexity.... The average police officer, providing the full range of routine police services, is performing a job of utmost importance and complexity and one in which citizens increasingly are demanding humane and fair handling.[12]
>
> Most police work takes place under isolated conditions, often involving only the police officer and the citizen to whom he is relating. The infinite variety of circumstances that might be present in any one contact are unpredictable. Guidance, even when provided in advance, is not alone enough. Speed in decision-making is often essential. Consultation with supervisors under such conditions is difficult.[13]

If police officers dealt only with crime-related matters, their task might be infinitely easier. Even the solution of the typical homicide is a relatively easy task when compared with the complexities involved in many police non-crime-related tasks. In terms of personal hazards or dangers, too many police officers are, of course, injured or killed by gunfire in a crime-related call. Data from any large police agency, however, will show that the bulk of injuries to the police arise in other situations. In terms of job difficulty and the strain placed upon the police, should there be any doubt about the stresses in the typical crime call when compared with responding to family disturbances, rescue attempts, or resuscitation calls?

Herman Goldstein, formerly an executive assistant to the late superintendent O. W. Wilson in Chicago, discusses the different "worlds" of the police.

The police function in two worlds. They play an integral part, along with the prosecutor, the courts, and correctional agencies, in the operation of the criminal justice system.... Thus as a highly structured world, defined by statutes and court decisions and subjected to strict controls.

The second world is less easily defined. It comprises all aspects of police functioning that are unrelated to the processing of an accused person through the criminal system. Within this world, a police department seeks to prevent crimes, abates nuisances, resolves disputes, controls traffic and crowds, furnishes information, and provides a wide range of other miscellaneous services to the citizenry. In carrying out these functions, officers frequently make use of the authority which is there by virtue of their role in the criminal process—the first of their two worlds. Thus, the ability of the police officer to resolve a dispute and to eliminate a nuisance stems, in large measure, from widespread recognition of the fact that he has the authority to initiate criminal prosecutions.[14]

To amplify the point made by Goldstein and others, it is probably useful to present a complete outline of the variety of categories of events to which police field officers must respond. Essentially, this is taken from the complete listing of the "Uniform Classification of Cases" developed by the International Association of Chiefs of Police in the late 1920s. Unfortunately, today, this exhaustive listing is known only as "Uniform Crime Reports," "Part I Crimes," or "Index Crimes." The listing, which shows the wide range of police field activities, is, as follows:

PART I CASES—CRIMES (CASES OR OFFENSES)

1. Criminal homicide
2. Rape
3. Robbery
4. Aggravated assault
5. Burglary
6. Larceny
7. Auto theft

PART II CASES—CRIMES

8. Other assaults
9. Forgery and counterfeiting
10. Embezzlement and fraud
11. Stolen property (buying, receiving, possessing)
12. Weapons (carrying, possessing, etc.)
13. Prostitution

14. Sex offenses (except 2 and 13)
15. Offenses against family and children
16. Narcotic drug laws
17. Liquor laws
18. Drunkenness
19. Disorderly conduct
20. Vagrancy
21. Gambling
22. Driving while intoxicated
23. Violations of road and driving laws
24. Parking violations
25. Other traffic violations
26. Other offenses (not classified above)
27. Suspicion

PART III CASES—LOST AND FOUND (PERSONS, ANIMALS, PROPERTY)

28. Lost
29. Found

PART IV CASES—CASUALTIES

30. Fatal motor vehicle accidents
31. Personal injury motor vehicle accidents
32. Property damage motor vehicle accidents
33. Other traffic accidents
34. Public accidents (except firearms and dog bites)
35. Home accidents (except firearms and dog bites)
36. Occupational accidents (except traffic, firearms, and dog bites)
37. Firearms accidents (not suicide)
38. Dog bites
39. Suicides
40. Suicide attempts
41. Sudden death and bodies found
42. Sick cared for
43. Mental cases

PART V CASES—MISCELLANEOUS PUBLIC SERVICES

50. Personal services (e.g., lockouts, death messages, ambulance runs)
51. Safety services and training
52. Nuisance abatement
53. Assist other agencies
54. Miscellaneous patrol "availability" services[15]

The intent of the foregoing listing is to put the police officer's field duties into a more realistic framework than is normally done. The implication is clear: The general-duty policeman is an individual who must respond effectively to a wide range of calls for service. Activities 1 through 27 are obviously important—and socially valued—but they typically account for only 15 percent of the policeman's on-duty time.

Individual readers may quarrel with this listing, challenging some of the "duties" on the list as not proper functions of the police. Individual challenges are certainly easier to make than broad-gauged social and governmental challenges. Which of the functions outlined above would the reader recommend eliminating from the list? If there is still social need for the function, what other governmental or private agency should provide the service? Is this substitution a more efficient and effective means for society to provide the service? Would substitution of some other entity really eliminate the necessity of the police from having to participate in some fashion in the call?

OVERRELIANCE ON THE CRIMINAL LAW

In speaking of social control—the police are, after all, one of but many social control agencies—Michael Banton speaks of informal and formal means of social control.

> The level of control, be it high or low, is determined by the kinds of social relationships that exist among the individuals who make up the society, and their effectiveness in getting people to follow prescribed patterns of behavior. The number of people who obey the law and follow such patterns without ever a thought for police efficiency is striking testimony to the power of social norms and humanity's methods of training children to observe them; most people grow up so well conditioned that they cannot feel happy if they infringe the more important norms. Thus, control is maintained by the rewards and punishments which are built into every relationship, and which are evident in the conferring and withholding of esteem, the sanctions of gossip, and the institutional, economic, and moral pressures that underlie behavioral patterns. Law and law-enforcement agencies, important though they are, appear puny compared with the extensiveness and the intricacy of these other models of regulating behavior.[16]

Banton and others have emphasized that maintenance of order and social control are generally easier to bring about in a small, homogeneous, nontechnological society. Furthermore, in such simple societies, informal means of social control are relied upon more than formal means.

> As the problem of maintaining order becomes more severe, society must increasingly adopt formal controls, summarized by an anthropologist as courts, code, constables, and central authority. In the early days the parish constable was simply "a citizen on duty."

Some years ago a Home Secretary observed: "The British Policeman is a civilian discharging civilian duties and merely put into uniform so that those who need his help know exactly where to look for assistance." Today, especially in connection with the traffic laws, this description is not accurate: the policeman is increasingly seen as an official exercising authority and power over citizens.[17]

Previously, we have mentioned terms and conditions as the central concept in effective police–community relations. The late Joseph D. Lohman is probably chiefly responsible for the development of this concept in relation to modern policing. What Lohman meant by this was that the criminal law process is drastically limited in its ability to maintain a stable and just social order. This is particularly true in today's complex, heterogeneous society.

American society today tends to be centrifugal in character; its elements are being forced outward, thus forming smaller groups, each with its own local pool of experience and culture. This is true of young people of the poverty-striken, and of members of racial minorities. Prior to the mid-twentieth century, American society was centripetal; it was directed to one standard, one norm, one set of values. The European immigrants of the nineteenth and early twentieth centuries searched for a way to participate in a society as a whole and to be one with it. They wanted to become acquainted with its customs, arts, skills, and technology. The concept of the "hyphenated" American on the whole de-emphasized origins and emphasized the melting-pot process—the transition from what they had been, to what they were to become in the new society. The reverse of this tendency is markedly in evidence at the present time.[18]

Lohman went on to say that one consequence of centrifugal character of contemporary society was the formation of a congery of subcultures. These are natural social groupings which are at one and the same time important and crucial to their members but threatening to the larger culture.

The human animal, of course, attempts to find answers to problems. The sub-cultures are, in short, the problem-solving answers to their situations of stress and trial; correspondingly, the sub-culture, which many of us see only as the evidence of a set of negative attributes and only to be deplored, is to many individuals a solution to their life's problems. It is their means of making life tolerable under the conditions of their deprivations.[19]

Lohman then went on to explain something of the relationship of large numbers of subcultures to formal means of social control. In other words, if law and the justice process were formal means of social control, what was the importance of large numbers of subcultures as an informal means of social control?

We are experiencing an eclipse of the formal controls of society because of the prior claims these sub-cultures have upon their members. There's a natural antagonism between the children of the slums, the racial groups, and the police as well as the general community. Today the "real controls" are in the area of the local, the primary, the face-to-face experience of these groups (the sub-cultures) which are often at odds with the general society.

The power of the sub-culture to effect reversal of values and norms is not fully appreciated. We are still asking ourselves why it is that formal ordering and forbidding techniques are not able to produce conformity. . . . We are continuing to subscribe to the notion that we can police the community without having it formally supported by the informal systems of control.[20]

Obviously, effective policing must be supported by the community.

Lohman was almost evangelical in his attempts to point out the potential of symbiotic relationships between criminal justice agencies and various informal, but important, social groupings. He had a high regard for the technical and social competences of the professionally trained police officer. His years of service as an elected official, public administrator, and police official had convinced him that properly trained and managed police agencies were absolutely essential. Such agencies could make important contributions to the overall quality of life—in a just society. In Lohman's opinion, it was the diversity of police tasks, and the scope of police discretion, which gave the police such a crucial role to play in effecting a stable and just social order.

In other words, police involvement in the noncriminal aspects of their task gives them an opportunity to meet citizens in essentially a nonadversary relationship. In such situations, the police are automatically cast into a helping role by all the participants and witnesses to the noncriminal situation. For example, in responding to the report of a possible drowning, or in rendering first aid to an injured person, the police have essentially no adversary. They have been called to the scene of an occurrence strictly to perform a helping function. In the course of an 8-hour tour of duty, the typical police officer has numerous opportunities to meet people "on their own turf," where police authority will not be challenged and where police assistance has been requested. The same thing is true when the police are going about their "appointed rounds."

This is not necessarily true, however, if either society, the agency, or the peer group has convinced police officers that their primary concern rests with the criminal law process. This has to do with the police role set, which is discussed in subsequent chapters. The point is that the police officer's set of job tasks is very broad, and if for any number of reasons, the individual officer or police agency tends to emphasize only the criminal law aspect of the job, the social consequence can be dysfunctional. That means that the total police task will be neglected, and the police officer's eventual ability to perform this whole set of tasks will be jeopardized while the officer maximizes concentration on the criminal apprehension process.

At this point, it is important to be reminded of a comment by Banton:

> The observer, who tried to predict, from a knowledge of the criminal law alone, what actions an ordinary policeman would take would not be very successful. To explain what the policeman actually does it is necessary to see his actions as being governed much more by popular morality than by the letter of the law; most often morality and the law coincide, but when they do not, it is usually morality that wins.[21]

We consider "popular morality" and the police in greater detail later. Here it is enough to say that popular morality probably wisely cushions most attempts at "total enforcement" of law and regulations. Often, the term "popular morality" is used synonymously with the term "common sense." As such, it is used to symbolize one of the most important attributes of experienced police officers.

Only the suicidal or the overzealous would attempt to enforce the "letter" of the speed law on a freeway during rush hour, or the drinking regulations at a professional football game. Other examples are too numerous to mention. "While 'full enforcement' has been the posture of many police agencies, there has always been a widespread awareness that many laws—especially those attempting to regulate public morals—have not been fully enforced."[22] Indeed, even when they were passed, it was often not the genuine intent of the legislature that every law be fully enforced.[23]

It is important to remember that the police are a product of their community; as such, they share both the virtues and the faults of that society. And they are also often under tremendous pressure—administratively and from the media—to be vigilant in the protection of life and property, in the maintenance of order, and especially in the apprehension of offenders. Popular morality, of course, may either aggravate or moderate police response to a given situation.

> Because the policeman is a member of the society, he perceives the behavior of his fellow members in moral terms as good and bad, and not as constituting a market in the way a manufacturer might see it. . . .[24]
>
> If the police organization encourages the development of in-group solidarity among its officers, it is likely to remove them more from the informal control of community expectations and to reduce their moral authority.[25]

The police, therefore, need both moral authority and legal authority if they are to act effectively in dealing with various problems. If they react illegally to a particular situation or series of situations simply because their own moral values have been outraged, they risk losing the support of the community. If, on the other hand, the community feeling develops that police action, although technically and legally correct, violates community norms and expectations, they suffer the same risk—loss of community support.

Community support, therefore, is a two-edged sword. It can definitely be supportive and encouraging to what it deems appropriate police behavior. It can also be controlling and confining if community feeling becomes widespread that police action is not in the best interest of the community. Effective police operations, in the long run, involve more than mere reliance upon the criminal law process; even more important is reliance upon intuitive and rational judgments of community expectations.

POLICE DISCRETION

The principal way in which "community expectations" temper the criminal law process is through the use of police discretion. The President's Commission was the first national body to recognize the importance of police discretion, despite the fact that discretion had been an important "tool" of policing since its inception. The President's Commission recognized a number of different factors as being instrumental in discretion. These were, as follows:

1. The sheer magnitude of the volume of technical violations
2. The limited police resources to handle this volume of activity
3. The overgeneralized nature of many legislative enactments
4. Various local pressures which reflect community values and attitudes[26]

They might have listed another factor—perhaps the most important—and that involves the personal values and popular morality of individual police.

As James Q. Wilson points out, discretion is found in all large public organizations.

> But the police department has the special property (shared with few other organizations) that within it discretion increases as one moves down the hierarchy. In many, if not most, large organizations, the lowest-ranking members perform the most routinized tasks and discretion over how those tasks are to be performed increases with rank.[27]

Wilson also points out, correctly, that discretion is an integral part of the order maintenance function of the police.

> The order maintenance function necessarily involves the exercising of substantial discretion over matters of the greatest importance (public and private morality, honor and dishonor, life and death) in a situation that is, by definition, one of conflict and in an environment that is apprehensive and perhaps hostile.[28]

Because their duties place them in a position to deal with the public, and because of the discretion this position gives them, patrol officers are more important in the organization than this rank would imply.[29] The American Bar Association recommended that the police be provided with effective means for accomplishing the variety of governmental responsibilities delegated to them. These "means" would include the following:

1. The development of a variety of skills in the individual police officer
2. The development of community arrangements by which police officers could make appropriate referrals to public and private agencies
3. A broad use of formal means of resolving conflict[30]

In its Commentary section, the ABA study explained, as follows:

If the police officer is to have a broad range of responsibilities, he ought to be provided with the methods by which his responsibilities can be effectively carried out. This requires replacing the present concept under which an officer, at least in formal terms, is viewed as being equipped primarily with the authority to arrest, with a newer concept with which a police officer is viewed as being equipped with numerous alternative forms of action from which he can, based upon carefully established guidelines, and training, select the response most appropriate to the situation at hand.

An effort should be made to develop the ability of police officers, through education and training, to relate more effectively to individuals in a wide range of circumstances and under varying conditions. Highly-developed skills in interpersonal relations would, in itself, constitute a new form of response on the part of many policemen to situations they commonly confront, thereby significantly increasing the ability of a police officer to handle such situations. An officer who is trained only to determine, in response to a call, whether or not an offense has been committed is extremely limited in his effectiveness as compared with an officer who, for example is equipped to recognize obvious symptoms of mental illness, is taught how to best relate to persons under the influence of alcohol or drugs, and is trained and encouraged to attempt to resolve conflict.

There are several indications that the police, by identifying conflict situations in their early stages and by responding to them in a helpful fashion, prevented an escalation of violence.[31]

There are countless situations involving the police which do not require any formal arrest authority and do not present any need to resort to the use of force.[32]

The American Bar Association noted that careful consideration be given to the authority of the police when dealing "with a variety of behavioral and social problems."[33] The ABA paid particular attention to the following four different categories of situations in which the police find themselves operating, generally without too much guidance for their organization or from legal authorities:

1. To deal with interferences with the democratic process....
2. To deal with self-destructive conduct such as that engaged in by persons who are helpless by reason of mental illness or persons who are incapacitated by alcohol or drugs.
3. To engage in the resolution of conflicts....
4. To take appropriate action to prevent disorders...[34]

It is obvious, therefore, that policing is much more complicated an endeavor than is generally recognized by the public, and unfortunately by many of the writers on the topic of police administration. Too little attention has been paid to the matter of how policing "fits" into the fabric of democratic government. Too little attention has been paid to the matter of police discretion and its relationship to the maintenance of order. As former Los Angeles deputy chief of police James Fisk has noted:

> The cryptic admonition, to "enforce the laws," is deceptively simple. It does not assign priorities to the various crimes for enforcement purposes, even though the police department does not have resources to enforce all of the laws all of the time. The courts have not resolved the dilemma of priorities. As a matter of fact, they have added to the confusion by decisions that range from imposing the responsibility to make an arrest in order to prevent the commission of a crime to an impossible mandate to arrest for every violation. Other, more realistic decisions concede that the police must overlook some arrests. However, the courts have offered very little in the way of guidelines, although constitutional provisions require uniform application of the law.[35]

It is obvious that discretion is involved in even the criminal law aspect of policing. Its social utility is even more prominent in the order maintenance and emergency service aspects of the occupation.

DEMOCRATIC POLICING

Effective police–community relations is inseparable from the fact that, in this nation, we are referring to policing in a democratic setting. That is the most important term and condition. Again, we reiterate that we are not talking of policing in a totalitarian society where the police are deliberately ordered to operate apart from the community. The late Joseph D. Lohman put the matter as precisely as anyone:

> Democratic societies, like all other societies, require order. Unlike other societies, they need a distinctive kind of order, namely, one that is not imposed by an uncontrollable force. The police, in a democracy, must not only

know the most effective techniques for maintaining order, but they must also know techniques which maintain order in a manner that serves to preserve and to extend the precious values of a democratic society.

Our discussion of the police and the public in a democracy is intended to provide a definite policy for the evaluation of police work. This policy applies particularly to the specific police practices for preserving law and order in human relations. The policy, in sum, is to maintain order in ways that preserve and advance democratic values.[36]

Fisk also approaches the matter from the perspective of the potential values of effective policing. According to Fisk, "the police exist for the purpose of producing a value—the value of freedom—freedom from disorder and those criminal acts that interfere with the freedom to pursue personally and socially fulfilling objectives."[37] This point of view—that of both Lohman and Fisk, and certainly of the authors—is an uncommonly pronounced perspective. Too often, the positive values of effective policing are entirely ignored. Rarely has discussion of policing been approached from the perspective of having a positive relationship to the pursuit of democratic goals.

There is an advantage to approaching the discussion of policing from that body of law known as the law of agency. Unfortunately, the phrase that the police in a democracy "act as the agents of the public" is often used, but the phrase has never been examined in detail. It is taken for granted as a "pat" phrase, something that sounds good in semiserious discussions. Although the full discussion of the matter is beyond the framework of this book, we should make a few points in passing.

Under the law of agency, the agent (i.e., the police) possesses only the authority of the principal (i.e., the employing society). Consequently, the authority of the agent may never exceed the authority of the principal. If the principal may deny liberty only under due-process provisions of the Constitution, the same limitation binds the actions of the agent. In addition, the principal may limit the authority he or she gives to the agent: for example, grants a power of attorney but only, for example, for the purpose of transferring title to a particular automobile owned by the principal. Finally, the principal has the authority to determine the term of the appointment of the agent, and the principal may rescind the authority of the agent.[38] In other words, it is the principal, not the agent, who possesses the greater authority. The implications of the phrase that the police serve as agents of the public, therefore, are obvious.

Jeffrey Reiman, a contemporary philosopher, recently reinforced the authority of the general society over its policing agents.

The authority of the police (i.e., their right to use force, to execute the law) lies in the fact that the members of society invest their private power to use coercion in a public agency. The justification for this "investment" lies in the presumed gain in security and thus in the liberty for all which results from removing the dangerous use of force from the judgment of private individuals. Hence the authority of the police can be viewed as a perpetual loan of the community's own power to the agents of law enforcement—a loan which pays a dividend of increased freedom.[39]

Perpetual Loan

The concept of perpetual loan is extremely important. When related to the concepts of agency and of the terms and conditions of contemporary American society, it emphasizes the potential moral authority of the police when they operate in concert with community goals. Reiman also adds explanation to the significant issue of public versus the private dangerous use of force.

The relationship between the concept of the police acting as agents for the broader society and Reiman's philosophical rationalization of police authority seems obvious. What is the logical consequence of illegal or excessive police action, or of police action that is violative of community standards? "The upshot of this is that whenever the power of the police stops being our public power and starts to be their private power, the right of the police to exercise that power is undermined, and the obligation of the citizen to recognize that right is eliminated."[40]

"The sovereignty of law is the public's protection against the unfettered power of officials. That is what we mean by 'the rule of law.' "[41] Robert Dahl approached the same important point from a slightly different more universal perspective.

> One of the most important political resources needed by elites everywhere, particularly in countries with established legal traditions, is legality. By this I mean conformity with the law, as the law is prescribed, interpreted, and enforced by governmental officials, including judges.
>
> In the United States, the tradition of legality is venerable, strong, and widely accepted—not so much perhaps as in some countries but more than in most.[42]
>
> Legality then is a political resource. Any group of people having special access to legality is potentially influential with respect to government decisions. The individuals who have the most direct access to legality are government officials. A noted chief justice of the Supreme Court, speaking with unusual candor and a little over-simplification, once said that "the Constitution is what the judges say it is"; he might have mentioned that what is legal at any given moment is what government officials enforce as legal with the sanctions officially available to them.[43]

Legality is not only a political resource, as Dahl points out, but is more than that; because of its stability, average citizens are free to go about their daily routines without giving much thought to the matter. If those citizens were to think reflectively on the matter, however, they would probably admit that legality is also an essential ingredient of our whole quality of life. Legality has a positive component that influences each of our lives. It may sound Pollyannish, but effective, democratic policing is an important social increment in that quality of life. The authors are aware of no better summation of this point than that of Lohman.

> When the law is the law of a democratic society the conduct of the police officer becomes the living expression of the values, meanings and potentialities of democracy. Democratic law is ethical law. It expresses and encourages equality and human dignity. It disciplines officials who otherwise lack definite standards to apply regularly and consistently. It provides for freedom of speech, press, and religion, for fair trial, and other democratic liberties. On the positive side, it provides for orderly, fair and reasonable methods of arriving at decisions, and of reviewing decisions, including decisions of government policy as well as judicial decisions, such as the decisions as to whether a man is innocent or guilty.
>
> If the police officer conforms to law, he becomes the most important official in the whole vast structure of government, able to facilitate the progressively greater realization of democratic values. How serious an obstacle, therefore, is the thoughtless attitude of much of the American public toward the police. Intelligent Americans and the police in particular, have a major job to do. First, they must understand the meanings of police service in a democratic society. Then by their joint efforts, they must maintain a police force that is capable of discharging its duties in a manner that strengthens the democratic way of life.[44]

Summary

Chapter 2 deals with those characteristics of society peculiar to a democracy and discusses police–community relations in view of these characteristics. Policing involves the delivery of human services under certain terms and conditions that are brought to light in this chapter. The duties and functions of the police are discussed in terms of roles that change as society changes. Also, police field services have been diagrammed—services that are wide-ranging and ever-changing.

If laws are identified as a formal means of social control, various subcultures of society can be seen as an informal means of social control. This chapter presented the concepts of police discretion in relation to community and subculture expectations and pointed out the factors that are instrumental in the use of this discretion.

A major point to be remembered is that the police are not separate and apart from the community. A "law of agency" is in effect; society, the principal, employs the police as agents, and it is the principal who possesses the greater authority. In sum, Chapter 2 points out that the police system exists to preserve and enhance democratic values.

End Notes

[1]Ben Whitaker, *The Police,* (Harmondsworth, Middlesex, England: Penguin Books, 1964), p. 171.

[2]James F. Ahern, *Police in Trouble: Our Frightening Crisis in Law Enforcement,* (New York: Hawthorne, 1972), p. 141.

[3]O. W. Wilson, ed., *Parker on Police,* (Springfield, Ill.: C C Thomas, 1957), p. 186.

[4]James Q. Wilson, *Varieties of Police Behavior,* (Cambridge, Mass.: Harvard University Press, 1968).

[5]See, for example, the following: President's Commission on Law Enforcement and Administration of Justice, *The Challenge of Crime in a Free Society,* and *Task Force Report: Police,* (Washington, D.C.: U.S. Government Printing Office, 1967); James Q. Wilson, *Police Behavior;* Herman Goldstein, "Police Response to the Urban Crisis, *Public Administration Review,* vol. 28 (1968); Elain Cumming, Ian Cumming, and Lourn Edell, "Policeman as Philosopher, Guide, and Friend," *Social Problems,* vol. 12 (1965): Raymond Parnos, "The Police Response to Domestic Disturbances," *Wisconsin Law Review* (1967); Gordon E. Misner, "The Urban Police Mission," *Issues in Criminology,* vol. 1 (1969); Gordon E. Misner, "Enforcement: Illusion of Security," *Nation,* vol. 208 (1969); and Thomas E. Bercal, "Calls for Police Assistance," *American Behavioral Scientist,* vol. 13 (1970).

[6]The term "general duty policeman" is important, here, for certainly some policemen, e.g. detectives, spend the bulk of their on-duty time on crime-related matters. Not so their uniformed colleagues in the Patrol Division, hopefully the largest unit in the Department. Not so their superiors and administrators.

[7]Ahern, *Police in Trouble,* p. 142, emphasis added.

[8]American Bar Association, *The Urban Police Function,* Project on Standards for Criminal Justice, Advisory Committee on the Police Function, (Chicago: American Bar Association, 1973), p. 8.

[9]*Ibid.,* pp. 8, 9.

[10]George D. Eastman and Esther M. Eastman, eds., *Municipal Police Administration,* 6th eds., International City Management Association, (Washington, D.C. 1969), p. 3.

[11]American Bar Association, *Urban Police Function,* p. 9.

[12]*Ibid.,* p. 193.

[13]*Ibid.,* p. 194.

[14]Herman Goldstein, "Police Response to Urban Crisis," *Public Administration Review,* 28:417–18 (1968). For a discussion of a variety of situations in which arrests or threats of arrest are used for purposes other than prosecution, see the following: Wayne R. La Fave, *Arrest: The Decision to Take a Suspect in Custody,* (Boston: Little, Brown, and Co., 1965), and Egon Bittner, *The Functions of the Police in Modern Society,* National Institute of Mental Health, Public Health Service Publication No. 2059 (1970).

[15]Adopted mainly from *Uniform Crime Reporting,* Committee on Uniform Crime Records, International Association of Chiefs of Police, New York (1929). This was essentially the first large-scale, national effort to effect uniformity in police recordkeeping and reporting. In order to write its report, the Committee found

it necessary to examine the codes of the then existing 48 states, and also to familiarize itself with the wide range of police field services rendered.

The listing included in this text is essentially *verbatim*. The Committee came up with a recommended uniform system of "case" reporting, consisting of five "Parts." Part V, "Administrative Cases," was never widely adopted. The other four parts were. The listing included in this text is virtually verbatim for the *Report* for Parts I, II, and III. For the "traffic" portion of Part IV, we have modified the list according to a more contemporary listing prepared by the National Safety Council. For Part V, we have eliminated the original list and substituted a listing prepared years ago by Professor Misner for various classes he has taught in administrative reporting. It must be remembered that this system of reporting was developed in 1929. Since that time, appeals courts have made numerous modifications, e.g., drunkenness, per se, is no longer a criminal offense, vagrancy has been ruled out as too vague a statute, and police may no longer arrest on "suspicion" alone.

[16]Michael Banton, *The Policeman in the Community*, (New York: Basic Books, 1964) p. 2, emphasis added. © 1964 by Basic Books, Inc.

[17]*Ibid.*, pp. 5, 6.

[18]Joseph D. Lohman, "Current Decline in Respect for Law and Order," prepared for the Section of Judicial Administration, American Bar Association, (Montreal), August 8, 1966, p. 11.

[19]*Ibid.*, pp. 15, 16.

[20]*Ibid.*, pp. 16, 17, italics added.

[21]Banton, *Policeman in Community*, p. 146.

[22]American Bar Association, *Urban Police Function*, p. 118.

[23]This reminds the authors of the so-called "Shirley Temple" ordinance which was passed several years ago by the Board of Supervisors (the legislature) of the City and County of San Francisco. The ordinance was directed at preventing "philanderers" from registering under fictitious names at San Francisco hotels and motels, obviously for immoral purposes. During the debate, one opponent of the bill brought up the point that many movie stars, corporate executives, sports personalities, and governmental officials use fictitious names at hotels, for the sole purpose of protecting their privacy. The opponent inquired what would happen if Shirley Temple Black registered at a San Francisco hotel using a fictitious name. The chief proponent of the bill retorted that the police would, of course, have to use "common sense" in enforcing the law. Certainly Mrs. Black would not be arrested.

The bill passed by a sizeable majority. As a consequence, the San Francisco Police Department was saddled with the responsibility of determining which use of a fictitious name should be grounds for arrest.

[24]Banton, *Policeman in Community*, p. 150.

[25]*Ibid.*, pp. 150–51.

[26]President's Commission, *Task Force Report: The Police*, (Washington, D.C.: U.S. Government Printing Office, 1967), p. 21.

[27]James Q. Wilson, *Police Behavior*, p. 7.

[28]*Ibid.*, p. 21.

[29]American Bar Association, *Urban Police Function*, p. 192.

[30]*Ibid.*, p. 186.

[31]*Ibid.*, p. 186–88.

[32]*Ibid.*

[33]*Ibid.*, p. 95.

[34]*Ibid.*

[35]James G. Fisk, "Some Dimensions of Police Discretion," in *The Police Community*, eds. Jack Goldsmith and Sharon S. Goldsmith, (Pacific Palisades, Calif.: Palisades Press, 1974), pp. 77–78.

[36]Joseph D. Lohman, "Human Relations and the Law" (unpublished paper, School of Criminology, University of California, Berkeley, 1968), p. 9.

[37]Fisk, "Some Dimensions of Police Discretion," *Police Community*, p. 79.

[38]Obviously, a full discussion of this matter of agency exceeds the scope of this chapter. The interested reader is referred to any general treatise on the subject and its relationship to democratic government.

[39]Jeffrey H. Reiman, "Police Autonomy v. Police Authority: A Philosophical Perspective," in *The Police Community*, eds. Goldsmith and Goldsmith, pp. 228–29.

[40]*Ibid.*, p. 230.

[41]Joseph D. Lohman, "Human Relations and the Law," p. 7.

[42]Robert A. Dahl, *Who Governs—Democracy and Power in an American City*, (New Haven, Conn.: Yale University Press, 1961), p. 246, emphasis added.

[43]*Ibid.*, p. 247.

[44]Joseph D. Lohman, "Human Relations and the Law," pp. 8, 9.

CHAPTER
THREE

THE POLICE
IN THEIR
CRIME CONTROL ROLE

Crime is a major concern to the American public. In fact, a poll released by George Gallup in early 1973 showed that the respondents viewed crime as the principal problem in their community. Given the responsibility to control crime by society, the efforts of the criminal justice system have historically focused upon the detection, apprehension, adjudication, and rehabilitation of offenders. It is, however, becoming increasingly clear that these efforts have failed; crime rates continue to be high, clearance rates are relatively low, and recidivism rates are soaring.

Our ability to control crime is hampered, in part, by the fact that we do not even know the exact extent of crime in this country. For example, as early as 1965, the President's Commission on Law Enforcement and Administration of Justice recognized that the crime statistics collected by the Federal Bureau of Investigation and reported in the *Uniform Crime Reports* (UCR) do not present a complete and accurate picture of either the extent or nature of crime in America. The Commission noted: "Crimes reported directly to the prosecutors usually do not show up in the police statistics. Citizens often do not report crimes to the police. Some crimes reported to the police never get into the statistical system."[1]

Because of the situation reported here, the Commission sponsored the nation's first survey of crime victimization, which was carried out by the National Opinion Research Center (NORC) of the University of Chicago. The results of that survey revealed that "the amount of personal injury crime reported to NORC is almost twice the UCR rate and the amount of property crime more than twice as much as the UCR rate for individuals."[2]

Following up on the work of the President's Crime Commission, the National Criminal Justice Information and Statistics Service of the Law Enforcement Assistance Administration (LEAA)—in conjunction with the Bureau of the Census—undertook the task of surveying victims of crimes to supplement the existing information available in police statistics. Created in July 1972, the National Crime Panel undertook a nationwide survey of crime victims. The results of the survey released in 1974 supported the findings of the President's Crime Commission. For example, the LEAA survey showed that unreported crime was twice as high as reported crime in the initial eight cities studied.[3]

The original victimization study completed for the President's Crime Commission and recent follow-up studies for LEAA by the Bureau of the Census show graphically the discrepancy between the *total* amount of crime and that reported or discovered by the police. Depending upon whether the crime is a violent assault, rape, robbery, or burglary, the discrepancy apparently ranges from a factor of 1.5 to a factor of 5. Much of this discrepancy is due to citizens not reporting to the police a large number of crimes perpetrated against them or their households. Among reasons given for failure to inform the police were the belief that nothing could be done (about 40 percent), a lack of conviction that the incident was "important enough" (about 30 percent), concern that the event was private or personal (about 5 percent), and the judgment that the police would not want to be bothered (about 5 percent).[4] The findings of both the President's Crime Commission and the LEAA victimization study clearly point to the need for the entire criminal justice operation to increase the level of the public's confidence in its operations. Public involvement and confidence must become an integral part of criminal justice if any real impact is to be made on the nation's crime problem.

Although this book is concerned primarily with the conceptual and programmatic aspects of police–community relations, it is also essential that the role of the police in controlling crime be examined. In making such an examination, it is important to recognize that the police are not soley responsible for controlling crime. Indeed, the other components of the criminal justice system, as well as the community at large and the social institutions that serve the community have an important role to play in crime control. This is true because the causes of crime are rooted in the community. In a real sense, the political and socioeconomic conditions of our society are responsible for a great deal of the crime that occurs. Its control, therefore, must rest with the community. The agencies of criminal justice (e.g., police, courts, and corrections), as well as governmental and private agencies, must share responsibility for the prevention and control of criminal behavior.

The extent to which the police are able to obtain the respect and cooperation of the public will determine, to a great degree, the extent they will be successful in performing their crime control role. Thus, efforts on the part of the police to improve their relationship with the community will have a direct bearing on their role in crime control. However, it must be constantly recognized that effective crime control depends largely on the effectiveness of both criminal and social justice agencies.

In the eyes of many citizens, the effectiveness of the police is directly related to the crime rate in their community. This is obviously an unfair measure of police effectiveness. Nevertheless, it is, in the minds of the general public, a gauge used to evaluate the efforts of police departments.

Unfortunately, the police themselves often equate this effectiveness with their ability to clear criminal offenses. Such an evaluation is reflective of the misunderstanding not only of the police role but also of the etiology of crime. A well-informed police department would do well to recognize that their role in crime control cannot be separated from the broader environment in which they must function. As indicated in Figure 3-1 there are numerous factors and forces that cause crime; therefore, the control of crime cannot be considered the sole responsibility of the police.

This is not to suggest, however, that the police do not have a responsibility for crime control, for they do. The point is that the successful control of crime must involve a concentrated effort on the part of all elements of the community, the police being only one component of one system—the criminal justice system.

If it is to control crime, the criminal justice system must reduce the number of individuals entering that system. This position is based upon empirical research and most recently advanced by the National Advisory Commission on Criminal Justice Standards and Goals. The Standards and Goals Commission was established in October 1971 by the Administrator of the Law Enforcement Assistance Administration to formulate, for the first time, national criminal justice standards and goals for crime reduction and prevention at the state and local levels. Similar to other national commissions concerned with the problem of crime, the Standards and Goals Commission also addressed the need for improving the police, courts, and corrections as a means of controlling crime. Unlike other commissions, however, the Standards and Goals Commission recognized the importance of the community in the cause of crime control and in fact had a task titled "Community Crime Prevention," charged with the specific responsibility of exploring methods by which the community can assist in controlling crime.

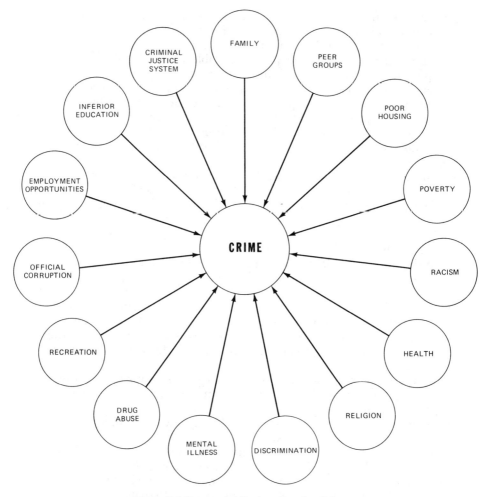

FIGURE 3-1 Forces and Factors Causing Crime

In establishing its priorities, the Standards and Goals Commission gave primary importance to:

1. Preventing juvenile delinquency
2. Improving delivery of social services
3. Securing more citizen participation in the criminal justice system[5]

The role of the police in controlling crime should be directly related to the priorities established by that Commission. Adherence to this position will, however, necessitate some basic changes in the assumptions under which the police currently operate. The first assumption that must be addressed is the dichotomy between the enforcement and the service aspects of the police role. This role conflict was succinctly summed up by Herman Goldstein when he wrote:

> The police function in two worlds. They play an integral part along with the prosecutor, the courts, and correctional agencies, in the operation of the criminal justice system. As the first agency in the system, their primary responsibility is to initiate a criminal action against those who violate the law. This is a highly structured role, defined by statutes and court decisions and subjected to strict controls.
>
> The second world is less easily defined. It comprises all aspects of police functioning that are unrelated to the processing of an accused person through the criminal system. Within this world, a police department seeks to prevent crimes, abates nuisances, resolves disputes, controls traffic and crowds, furnishes information, and provides a wide range of other miscellaneous services to the citizenry. . . . Police spend most of their time functioning in the second of these two worlds. . . . Despite this distribution of activity, police agencies are geared primarily to deal with crime.[6]

There exists a direct correlation between the effectiveness of the police in performing their service functions and their role in controlling crime. This position is presented in the context of the priorities established by the Standards and Goals Commission. For example, in establishing its first priority, the Commission stated: "The highest attention must be given to preventing juvenile delinquency, minimizing the involvement of young offenders in the juvenile and criminal justice system, and reintegrating them into the community."[7]

PREVENTION OF JUVENILE DELINQUENCY

In handling cases involving juveniles, the police have a great deal of discretion as to dispositions. This is illustrated by a departmental general order of one west coast police department.[8]

1. Arrest and confinement
2. Notice to appear
3. Juvenile citation
4. Official reprimand and release
5. Unofficial reprimand and release

The police use of their discretion in disposing of cases involving juveniles varies greatly. This variance tends to be directly related to the socioeconomic conditions of the juvenile involved. For example, Robert Carter found in his study at the University of California, Berkeley, that youthful offenders from middle-class families are handled out of the office of juvenile justice at a rate nearly twice that of the national average.[9] Data collected by the Department of Health and Human Services reveal that almost 40 percent of the cases coming before the juvenile courts involved cases such as running away, truancy, and other offenses that would not be crimes if committed by adults. Other evidence strongly suggests that the remaining 60 percent of cases handled by the juvenile courts for nonstatus crime involves individuals who have had previous contact with the criminal or juvenile justice system. This contention was supported by a recent study conducted in Philadelphia by Marvin Wolfgang. In his study of delinquency in all males born in 1945 and residing in Philadelphia from their tenth to eighteenth birthday, Wolfgang found that the more involvement a juvenile had had with both the police and the criminal justice system, the more likely he would be further involved. From his study, Wolfgang concluded that "the juvenile justice system, at its best, has no effect on the subsequent behavior of adolescent boys and, at its worst, has a deleterious effect on future behavior.[10]

What significance does the above have for the police role in controlling crime? First, it suggests that a dual standard exists in the manner by which the police dispose of cases involving juveniles. On the one hand, lower-class juveniles are referred to the official juvenile justice system in great disproportion to the number of middle- or upper-class juveniles. Second, it suggests that those handled by the juvenile justice system are more likely to persist in a pattern of delinquent behavior. This, in turn, suggests that incarceration is not an effective tool of rehabilitation. Hence, the current state of the art strongly suggests that the police would contribute more to the cause of controlling crime by developing policies which recognize that "a formal arrest is inappropriate if the person may be referred to the charge of a responsible parent, guardian, or agency."[11] Police agencies should therefore make greater use of pretrial diversion programs to break the vicious cycle of recidivism. As stated by the Commission, "the further an offender penetrates into the criminal justice process, the more difficult it becomes to divert him from a criminal career."[12] Thus, police practices relative to preventing juvenile delinquency, thereby controlling crime, should adhere to the notion that "formal adjudication may not be necessary if an offender can be safely diverted elsewhere, as to a youth service bureau for counseling or a drug abuse program for treatment."[13]

Numerous cities have youth service bureaus, a concept endorsed by the authors of this book.[14] Yet there are other pilot programs being operated throughout the nation that are worth examining. One is the Community Youth Responsibility Program (CYRP), which was initiated through Law Enforcement Assistance Administration funding in January 1971 in East Palo Alto, an unincorporated area in San Mateo County, California. Under this program, the East Palo Alto Municipal Council, a nongovernmental agency, persuaded the San Mateo Sheriff's

Department to decentralize its operation by assigning a lieutenant, selected by the Municipal Council, to serve as the East Palo Alto "chief of police." In addition, the San Mateo County Probation Department decentralized its juvenile probation operation and established a program in East Palo Alto, which utilizes the service of community workers and new careerists. These actions were based upon the theory that the community, if actively involved and responsible, can and will work toward the prevention of juvenile crime and on the concept that the local law enforcement agency and probation department are integral parts of the community.

Under this program, a community panel, composed of representatives of neighborhood people (including juveniles) was appointed by the board of directors of the CYRP and the Municipal Council. This panel has the responsibility of deciding matters concerning young people that are brought before them. Such matters come to their attention through referrals by the Sheriff's Department, the school, or parents. The Sheriff's Department referrals consist of those young people who are first offenders or those who have committed minor offenses.

Information concerning the alleged actions of young people is gathered and presented to the panel by the Panel Reporter, who also arranges to have people with relevant information (e.g., the juvenile and the Sheriff's deputies) available to tell the panel the circumstances surrounding the incident. If the panel determines that the young person is responsible for a significant violation of the law, he or she is required to carry out useful community work under the supervision of a work supervisor.

The legal basis of the decisions of the community panel is the voluntary participation of the young person and, where appropriate, the victims. In the event that the young person does not accept the conclusion or the work required by the Panel, he or she simply refuses to obey. In such cases, if the referral was made by the Sheriff's department, the youth is then referred to the juvenile probation department.

This particular program is cited because it represents a unique experimentation in community–criminal justice cooperation. It is a means of keeping juveniles out of the justice system, at the same time holding them accountable to the community for their actions. Although the program has not been evaluated to determine its effectiveness, its conceptual scheme is sound and merits consideration in other jurisdictions as a means of preventing juvenile delinquency and improving police–community relations.

In summary, the police could assist in the achievement of the Standards and Goals Commission's first priority by establishing formal criteria for diverting from the criminal and juvenile justice system all individuals coming to their attention for whom processing into the system would be inappropriate or for whom the use of resources outside the criminal and juvenile justice system would be more appropriate.[15]

DELIVERY OF SOCIAL SERVICES

The second priority for controlling crime, as developed by the Standards and Goals Commission, is only indirectly related to the role of police agencies. Nevertheless, the police, in developing their role, should be cognizant of the fact "that effective and responsible delivery of public services that promote individual well-being will contribute to a reduction in crime."[16] To that end, the Standards and Goals Commission set as its second priority: "Public agencies should improve the delivery of all social services to citizens, particularly to those groups that contribute higher than average proportions of their numbers to crime statistics."[17]

Although the foregoing priority is only indirectly related to police, such an indirect relationship is the result of traditional methods in which the police define their role. It is the contention of these authors that the police are themselves a service delivery agency. For example, John Webster, in his study of a west coast police department, found:

> Social service consumes much of the patrolman's time, much more in fact than most police administrators recognize. This is demonstrated by the little attention paid to social service in the areas of police training, management, and planning. For example, in Baywood, there were 255 more assignments for handling mental illness cases than for reports of robbery.
>
> Despite this, the operational emphasis is on robbery and the problem of mental illness is treated as though it does not exist. This is more significant when one learns that the policeman almost never arrives on the scene of a robbery in progress; while the mental illness case is always waiting for him. This also means that the officer is running greater personal risk with a mentally disturbed person than with a robbery call where the offender is not present and does not want to be found. Family fights are also more frequent and more hazardous to the officer than robbery, rape or murder cases. It is unfortunate for the policeman as well as for the public that he spends more training time learning to fire a pistol than handling a drunk, a person who is mentally ill, or a family fight.
>
> The amount of social service performed by the police is grossly underestimated and equally underrated. For example, in crimes against persons such as homicide, rape, robbery and assault, the police perform the very important tasks of reassuring the victim or his survivors and of reducing the trauma at the crime scene. This is social work of the highest order. Let us not confuse social service with the notion of filling out forms for the purpose of enabling a mother to qualify for aid for dependent children. It has been pointed out earlier that every policeman performs social service functions in his workday rounds. The tasks of referring the uniniated citizen to proper social agencies, assuaging the emotional trauma of one assaulted, and securing proper medical and psychiatric aid for the mentally ill are all proper social duties. And more often than not fall to the lot of the policeman.[18]

There are, however, some people who see the police role in the narrow context of "crook catching" and neglect the important service aspect of policing. Such a role identification (and acceptance of that role by the police) led David Bordua to conclude that the "police have come to be identified almost entirely with the coercive function of the state."

There are still others who advocate removing all nonenforcement functions from the police. Chief among those who advocate that position is Richard A. Myren, dean of the School of Criminal Justice, American University. In a paper prepared for the President's Crime Commission, Myren argues:

> Problems arising from current police role definition can be associated with the function out of which they arise. Performance of service activities leads to inflation of the police budget with consequent distortion of the apparent cost of crime control, to prevention of professionalism in the police career group, to dilution of attention to the primary task of combating traditional crimes, and to prevention of more efficient performance of the service function by a specialized agency. Goodwill that the police are alleged to earn from this service is offset by bad will attributable to a poorer job of crime control. Other more efficient mechanisms can be devised for obtaining the information useful in crime control that is alleged to be a by-product of service activities. Governmental economy alleged to flow from performance of service functions by the police is probably illusory.[19]

Myren's basic premise is that by removing the service functions from the police, they would be able to spend more time in their traditional role of enforcing the criminal law. If this position was ever adopted, we foresee the police becoming a military enterprise waging a calculated war against crime, thereby becoming as unscrupulously belligerent against "criminals," or perceived "criminals" as soldiers are against alien enemies. Beyond that point, but equally important, is the fact that crime control involves keeping the act from happening, not merely an after-the-fact reaction. Our position is not new. As early as 1829, commissioner Charles Rowan issued a general order to the new police of London, England, which read in part:

> It should be understood, at the outset, that the principal object to be attained is the prevention of crime. To this end, every effort of the police is to be directed. The security of person and property, the preservation of the public tranquility and all other objects of a police establishment would thus be better effected than by the detention and punishment of the offender after he has succeeded in committing the crime.

In relating the role of the police in controlling crime, we are in agreement with A. C. Germann, who in discussing the future role of the police, optimistically stated:

> I see increased commitments to those who lack social position, economic advantage, or political power—the police becoming the "ombudsman" for the weak and exploited. For example, I see new units formed to deal with white

collar crime, consumer frauds, and economic skullduggery. I see new units formed to deal with political graft and corruption. And I see new units being formed to see that all social groups and enclaves receive just and fair treatment from private and government institutions.[20]

If police agencies organized to perform the functions suggested by Germann, they would be consistent with the Standards and Goals Commission's priority—attack the causes of crime and move toward eliminating the gap that currently separates the police from the oppressed groups in our society. They would indeed constitute an effective effort of crime control.

INCREASING CITIZEN PARTICIPATION

The final priority developed by the Standards and Goals Commission to control crime states that "citizens should actively participate in activities to control crime in their community, and criminal justice agencies should actively encourage citizen participation."[21]

This priority has great significance for the police in their crime control role. The police and the entire criminal justice system will not be successful in controlling crime unless there is active citizen involvement. The Police Task Force of the Standards and Goals Commission specifically addressed this concern by developing a standard which reads in part:

> Every police agency should immediately establish programs that encourage members of the public to take an active role in preventing crime that provides information leading to the arrest and conviction of criminal offenders, that facilitates the identification and recovery of stolen property, and that increases liaison with private industry in security efforts.[22]

There is much the police can do to assist the public in not only understanding but also actively participating in controlling crime. First, the police should play an important role in educating the public on how they can protect themselves and thereby reduce crime. Such efforts should be directed toward elementary, secondary, and college-level schools, community organizations, businesses, industry, and the general public.

Many agencies have addressed this need by implementing crime prevention units. Such units are given the specific responsibility of developing and operating programs designed to inform the public how to assist in preventing crime. Such information includes crime trends in specific areas, the need to telephone the police regarding suspicious circumstances, and how to organize neighborhood security programs.

Second, the police should involve business and industry in programs designed to prevent commercial crime. This could be done by providing security inspections and recommending measures to avoid being victimized, advocating local ordinances relative to minimum security standards, and conducting training programs for business employees in appropriate situations.

What follows are some examples of programs designed to involve the public in crime control:

- The Michigan State Police developed a program whereby they rate residents and commercial establishments against a comprehensive checklist of security measures, and then encourage insurance agencies to give those who get a high rating, discounts on their burglary and robbery insurance premiums.

- A number of jurisdictions in California, through funds from the California Criminal Justice Council, have implemented comprehensive burglary prevention programs. The programs include the establishment of a special telephone number where residents can anonymously report crimes in progress or provide information on suspects, publicity campaigns on burglary prevention, volunteer inspection of residence and commercial establishments by police officers specially trained for that purpose, and assistance in establishing neighborhood security councils whereby the residents work with the police in reporting crimes of suspicious circumstances.

- The Monterey Park, California, Police Department initiated a program called "Operation Identification," which has been duplicated in many cities. Under this program, citizens are encouraged to watch the homes and businesses of their neighbors, report suspicious conditions and people, and take measures to protect their own premises. "Citizens Helping Eliminate Crime" (CHEC) in Lima, Ohio; "Chec-mate" in Kalamazoo, Michigan; "Silent Observer Program" in Battle Creek, Michigan; "Neighborhood Block Safety Program" in Philadelphia, Pennsylvania; and the "Vertical Policing Service" in Cleveland, Ohio, are all similar programs.

- "Turn in a Pusher" (TIP) is a program in Tampa, Florida, where citizens assist in combating the hard-drug problem.

- "Community Radio Watch" (CRW) in Buffalo, New York, utilizes the services of companies that operate vehicles with two-way radios to report crimes and/or suspicious circumstances to the police.

- The San Jose, California, Police Department established a crime prevention unit to develop crime prevention programs and material and train employees of businesses in crime prevention.

- Neighborhood consumer centers are operating in New York City in an attempt to reduce the incidence of consumer fraud.

- Shoplifters Take Everybody's Money (S.T.E.M.) is a multimedia company in Westmoreland County, Pennsylvania, designed to make people aware that shoplifting is a crime.

- "Safety Patrol" was organized in Laurelton, Queens, New York, to utilize volunteers to patrol neighborhoods. Utilizing a vehicle with a rotating blue light on top, the volunteers patrol the neighborhoods but do not get out of their cars. Instead, they report problems to the police department when they arise.

These programs and others reported elsewhere in the book are examples of what the police can and are doing to involve the community in their efforts to reduce crime. The extent of citizen involvement is limited only by the imagination and innovativeness of the police themselves.

A well-informed and involved citizen can do much in the cause of crime control. Such involvement does not necessarily have to be limited to interaction and cooperation with the criminal justice system. Rather, community involvement in the cause of crime control can take the form of attacking some of the socioeconomic conditions that are conducive to antisocial behavior. What follows are two examples of what some community groups are doing to attack the problem of crime:

- New Detroit, Inc., was established after the civil disorders in 1967 to address the problems of the poor and disadvantaged people of the city. With leadership from all levels of the community and staff on loan from other institutions, it acts primarily as a catalyst and advocate. Its activities are directed toward getting existing institutions to do their jobs properly, developing new institutions to get the job done where none exist and assuring that appropriate community-based organizations and efforts are properly considered, developed, and supported.

- The Greater St. Louis Alliance for Shaping a Safer Community has as its purpose the stimulation of dialogue and action among citizens and public officials for the purpose of improving the operations of the criminal justice system and to develop improved community-oriented prevention efforts and to assist ex-offenders and victims of crime. It is composed of citizen volunteers and has national, state, and local alignments.

Summary

In summary, crime will not be controlled by the criminal justice system alone. Indeed, without the support and assistance of the public, the nation's ability to control crime is severely hampered. Thus, the public role in crime control must be developed in concert with an overall strategy to reduce crime.

This chapter also explored the role of the police in controlling crime and set forth activities designed to meet specific crime-reducing goals. A discussion of priorities and a means of meeting these priorities was discussed.

End Notes

[1]President's Commission on Law Enforcement and Administration of Justice, *The Challenge of Crime in a Free Society* (New York: Avon Books, 1968), p. 96.
[2]Ibid., p. 97.

[3]Atlanta, Baltimore, Cleveland, Newark, Dallas, St. Louis, Denver, Portland, Ore.

[4]National Advisory Commission on Criminal Justice Standards and Goals, *Criminal Justice System* (Washington, D.C.: U.S. Government Printing Office, 1973), p. 199.

[5]National Advisory Commission on Criminal Justice Standards and Goals, *A National Strategy to Reduce Crime* (Washington, D.C.: U.S. Government Printing Office, 1973), p. 23, hereinafter referred to as Standards and Goals, *A National Strategy.*

[6]Herman Goldstein, "Police Response to Urban Crisis" 28, no. 5 (September 1968) 417–18.

[7]Standards and Goals, *A National Strategy,* p. 34.

[8]John A. Webster, *The Realities of Police Work* (Dubuque, Iowa: Kendall-Hunt Publishing Co., 1973), p. 83.

[9]Robert M. Carter, "The Middle Class Delinquency: An Experiment in Community Control," School of Criminology, University of California, Berkeley, Calif., April 1968, p. 82.

[10]Marvin E. Wolfgang, Robert M. Figlio, and Torsten Stellin, *Delinquency in a Birth Cohort* (Chicago: University of Chicago Press), 1972.

[11]Standards and Goals, *A National Strategy,* p. 35.

[12]Ibid., p. 34.

[13]Ibid., p. 35.

[14]For a Model Youth Service Bureau, see National Advisory Commission on Criminal Justice Standards and Goals, *Community Crime Prevention* (Washington, D.C.: U.S. Government Printing Office), 1973, pp. 51–83.

[15]Standards and Goals, *A National Strategy,* p. 116.

[16]Ibid., p. 36.

[17]Ibid.

[18]Webster, *Realities,* p. 103.

[19]Richard Myren, "The Role of the Police," paper prepared for the President's Commission on Law Enforcement and Administration of Justice, 1967 (unpublished).

[20]A. C. Germann, "The Police: A Mission and Role," *The Police Chief,* August 1968, p. 18.

[21]Standards and Goals, *A National Strategy,* p. 38.

[22]National Advisory Commission on Criminal Justice Standards and Goals, *Police* (Washington, D.C.: U.S. Government Printing Office, 1973), p. 66.

CHAPTER FOUR

THE ORGANIZATIONAL SETTING FOR POLICE SERVICES

INTRODUCTION: ORGANIZATIONAL IMPEDIMENTS

The majority of basic textbooks on police organization are written with a particular bias toward the subject matter. For the most part, these books view the subject matter from outdated perspectives.[1] They take a classical view of organizations. As John Angell points out

> The structures of modern American police organizations are rationalized, hierarchical arrangements that reflect the influence of classic organization theory as promulgated by Max Weber. . . . The most salient characteristics of these departments, as with all organizations that are based upon classic theory, are:
> 1. *Formal structures are defined by a centralized hierarchy of authority.*
> 2. *Labor is divided into functional specialties.*
> 3. *Activities are conducted according to standardized operating procedures.*
> 4. *Career routes are well established and have common entry points; promotions are based on impersonal evaluations by superiors.*
> 5. *Management proceeds through a monocratic system of routinized superior-subordinate relationships.*
> 6. *Status among employees is directly related to their positions (jobs) and ranks.*

The characteristics result in a firmly established, impersonal system in which most of the employees and clients are powerless to initiate changes or arrest the system's motions.[2]

The theory underlying police organization and the structuring of policing has important consequences for police–community relationships. In other words, the way in which a department is organized has an important influence on the work of the department and upon the way in which agency members perform their day-to-day duties.

The material cited above from Angell's seminal paper on "democratic policing" contains a number of important and relevant points. First is the matter of formal structures and clearly defined jurisdictional lines. Few people would quarrel with the notion that police agencies represent formal, legally constituted entities, exercising their authority over a legally defined jurisdiction. But Angell was talking about something quite different, about the intraorganizational definition of structure and jurisdiction: that is, "there will be a Patrol Division," "the Detective Division has primary jurisdiction over all felony investigations," and so on.

Angell was also talking about the monocratic system of authority of classic organizations. Monocratic means essentially "rule by a single person" and is the direct antithesis of the concept of "democratic." ("Rule" is perhaps an unfortunate choice of words here when we are talking implicitly of the authority of police executives. More and more police chief executives are witnessing the challenging of their formal authority from within the ranks, or at least they firmly believe their formal authority over departmental personnel has been seriously eroded.) In the old Weberian sense, the chief executive of a company or of a civil service bureaucracy had uncontested power within the organization. This theory or view not only flies in the face of what behavioral scientists now know about human behavior within organizations, but it also rejects—or fails to recognize—the increased concern of public employees about their working conditions. Fewer and fewer public bureaucracies are ruled by a single person, issuing edicts from some isolated office. Human perceptions have perhaps changed, for employees are apparently not as subservient as they formerly were.

Classic organization theory also overemphasized the importance of specialization to the matters of organization productivity and efficiency. For many years, it was thought that efficiency could be obtained only if there was an adequate level of specialization within the factory or within the agency. More current knowledge recognizes some of the limitations of occupational specialization; and actually blames it for much of the worker discontent and inefficiency within the organization. For a number of years, for example, it was felt that one of the important keys to effective police–community relations was the appointment of specialized police–community relations officers, assigned to a formally established police–community relations bureau. What happened in more cases than not was that the establishment of the P-CR bureau signaled the rest of the department that they did not have to worry about P-CR, "for that's the responsibility of the P-CR boys."

The same can often be said for the perils of having a specialized vice control unit, thereby signaling the rest of the department— unconsciously—that "non-vice" members of the department need no longer involve themselves in vice matters. A parallel development has occurred following the establishment of traffic units, juvenile affair units, rape units, and so on.

The point is that organization by the precepts of the classic theory of organization results in the development of bureaucracies which share certain common features. These features may actually hinder the development of effective police department relationships with the community it serves. Classically organized agencies are not usually terribly effective in problem anticipation or in problem solving. Employee morale is more often than not relatively low. These types of organizations seem to be peculiarly nonadaptive to change, for within the organizations there seem to be series and layers of blockages to the flow of timely information.

These deficiencies in classically organized agencies are all interrelated, stemming from the very nature of the organization itself. Unfortunately, very little literature about police organization and management exists which is not based upon the classic theory of organization.

All around us we see evidence of social and environmental change, and as citizens, we are implored in thousands of different messages to recognize the necessity of being capable of dealing with our changed environment. Our information base ranges from homey little fillers in the daily newspaper, articles in the *Reader's Digest* and the popular press, and Alvin Toffler's *Future Shock,* to essays written by professional "futurists." One thing seems certain: human beings seem to be infinitely more capable of adapting to change than do organizations staffed by human beings. This resistance to change on the part of many—if not most—large organizations is, again, the product of the organization itself.

At this point, it would be helpful to reflect upon the reasons why some organizations seem to be more capable of change than others, and why some other types of organizations seem to be particularly resistant to change. In this regard, some comments by a noted authority on large-scale organizations may be of assistance.

> Empirical studies of creativity suggest certain conditions conducive to creativity that are of special relevance to bureaucratic organizations. These conditions are: (1) psychological security and freedom (within the organization), (2) a great diversity of inputs, (3) an internal or personal commitment to the search for a solution, (4) a certain amount of structure or limits to the search situation, and (5) a moderate amount of benign competition.[3]

The points made by Thompson seem particularly important when reviewing the constraints of classically organized police agencies. Obviously, Thompson was talking generally about the creative process; in addition, he was talking about the creative process as it takes place within the research and development (R&D) units of large, nonpolice organizations. His comments are germane, however, to our discussion of organizational structure and its receptivity to change, as we talk about the implications of police organization on the matter of improved police-community relations.

We are reminded about the point made a number of years ago in an essay written by Los Angeles police chief Thomas Reddin. Essentially, Reddin asked the rhetorical question of his fellow chiefs of police: "What are we doing to keep them?" Specifically, Reddin was deploring the fact that the professional police service was losing large numbers of its most highly educated, young personnel. Reddin was questioning whether there wasn't something endemic to their organization which was not actually driving these young people out of the police service.[4]

Each of the authors has spent a number of years in university teaching, associating with large numbers of preservice and in-service police personnel. (We estimate that collectively we have had more than 4,000 students who were either already employed in the police service or were career-oriented toward the police service.) One thing that has uniformly impressed us is the large numbers of these persons who have felt a little disillusioned between the ideal of policing and its operational realities. The reasons for disillusionment are many and they are varied. Essentially, these reasons can be listed as follows:

1. The quasimilitary discipline of police organizations
2. The organizational restrictions on their personal freedoms of expression, association, and dress
3. The organizational attachments to outmoded methods of operation
4. The lack of real challenge, or the eventual routinization of the more challenging aspects of the job
5. The narrowness of the job descriptions of most lower-ranking jobs within policing

We certainly are not saying that these complaints are universally justified; we are relating some rather commonplace "gripes" about policing's organizational environment, attitudes held by seemingly large numbers of college-educated police personnel.[5]

DIFFERING EXPECTATIONS AND SKILLS

Certainly, a portion of the problem revolves around differing expectations of the police system—expectations of young, preservice persons and of older, seasoned personnel, and expectations of the general public. We have reported elsewhere about the differing role expectations of line patrol personnel, police supervisors, police commanders, and the general public.[6]

These differences in expectations are not surprising in view of the general controversy surrounding the police mission. Contradictions are inevitable when we presume to talk about the role of democratic policing, that is, *civil* policing in a democratic society. As Bittner points out, from the beginning of policing in the United Kingdom in 1829, the function of the police was cast in ambiguous terms; the function of the police was

> to advance and protect conditions favorable to industry and commerce and to urban civil government in general. . . .[7]
>
> the locus and mandate of the police in the modern polity were ill-defined at the outset. On the one hand, the new institution was to be a part of the executive branch of government. . . . On the other hand, the duties that were given to the police organization brought it under direct control of the judiciary in its day-to-day operation.
>
> The dual patronage of the police by the executive and the judiciary is characteristic for all democratically governed countries.[8]

James Q. Wilson, Skolnick, Lohman and Misner, Bittner, Banton,[9] and others have all pointed to the fact that the police are inevitably called upon to perform in more than one principal role. Bittner refers to these as two often opposed and "relatively independent domains of police activity."[10] These two independent domains are, of course, "order maintenance" and "law enforcement."

With no apologies to Shakespeare, Albert Reiss "set the stage" for policing.

> Patrol work usually begins when a patrolman moves onto a social stage with an unknown cast of characters. The setting, members of the cast, and the plot are never quite the same from one time to the next. Yet the patrolman must be prepared to act in all of them.[11]
>
> Police officers must deal not only with the actors on stage, but often with the audience as well. This audience may be comprised of members of a family, strangers in the street, or a mob. The officers must assess the audience as well as the actors, since the audience may have an important effect on police work. . . . The police must be concerned with the audience's acceptance of them as well as with their own judgment and control of that audience.
>
> This characterization of the social stages, the participants, and even the action for all police work in an area fails to capture the shifts that may occur for a policeman in his tour of duty. No tour of duty is typical except in the sense that *the model tour of duty does not involve an arrest* of any person. . . .[12]

General police work therefore requires an elaborate array of skills—some quite general and others quite specific. In sum, these skills are theoretically directed at deciding, in each specific circumstance, when to intervene, and in what ways to intervene. "Police patrol work calls for intervention in social situations, where the problem for an officer is to gain control of the situation. This generally means he must establish his legitimate right to intervene."[13] Shearing characterizes the police as "both the supplier and the applier of decisions crucial to the organization."[14]

The vast array of police field activities surprises nearly everyone except experienced police personnel. In many of these situations, the police are at the scene as "community helpers."[15] Situations in this category of police service range from dealing with sick and injured persons and assisting in the handling of mentally ill persons to the giving of information on a variety of matters, including community resources. Many so-called "peacekeeping" functions would also fall under this category of event.

In other patrol situations, patrol personnel are at the scene in a more neutral role, primarily gathering information on a past event or an anticipated event. Their mere presence may effect an order-reestablishing function for the overall community.

In still other events, patrol personnel at the scene stand in an adversary capacity, at least as a potential adversary to one or more parties at the scene. In each of these categories of events, police personnel are at the scene of what Bittner refers to simply as "police trouble."[16] Usually, they are there in response to some citizen complaint; often, they are at the scene on their own initiative, anticipating either that there is trouble or is likely to be.

If we were to draw a typology of all these events, with necessary subclassifications, we might very well develop a list of as many as 100 different major scenarios. In each of these, patrol personnel may need some rather generic skills, such as interviewing techniques, and some very specialized skills, such as the handling of mentally ill persons. Bittner refers to these as police "practical skills." James Q. Wilson has described them generally as the skills necessary "to handle the situation," and Bruce Smith and others have simply summarized them as part of the "policeman's art."[17]

A significant portion of field activities for police patrol personnel would fall into that category of event which Wilson describes as "order maintenance."[18] Previously, we have reported that as much as 75 percent of patrolmen's consumed time was spent in non-crime-related activities, much of it in emergency public service of a noncriminal nature.[19] Much of this could be classified as simple peace-keeping. Unfortunately, as Bittner points out: "No one can say with any clarity what it means to do a good job of keeping the peace. Peace keeping appears to be a solution to an unknown problem arrived at by unknown means."[20] In peace-keeping, the range of discretion exercised by the police is probably larger than the range in other sets of activities. This fact of discretion—central to policing—coupled with the vast amount of time allocated to peacekeeping makes it a particularly difficult matter for the police organization itself.

ORGANIZATIONAL POSTURE

As is the case in any medium-size or large bureaucracy, the administration feels a necessity to make wise, accountable use of its personnel's time. Many police field personnel, however, resist—directly or indirectly—these attempts by the administration. Bittner relates the absence of any realistic control in many police organizations.

> The virtual absence of disciplinary control and the demand for discretionary freedom are related to the idea that patrol work involves "playing by ear." For if it is true that peace keeping cannot be systematically generalized, then, of course, it cannot be organizationally constrained.[21]

This points out an interesting, almost universal dilemma for police administrators: the balance to be sought between recognizing the need for discretion in police work, and allowing for a large measure of it rather than attempting to control administratively through rules, regulations, and procedure manuals.

Ericson would seem to be arguing for virtually a "hands-off" policy for police administrators in regard to attempts at controlling behavior within their organizations.

> The police organization is constantly faced with a hostile environment. The reason for this is that the police are confronted with a multitude of community factions with divergent interests, so that attempts to appease one faction may create animosity and hostility in another. . . . The police are faced with the constant dilemma of *either employing improper procedures to attain community goals, or procedural regularity which prevents the attainment of community expectations.* . . .
>
> As a result of this situation the police must enter their environment with the idea of placating as many factions as possible while maintaining order in the community. This is a task which cannot be established through administrative directives and inflexible rules, but can only be effected by allowing low ranking officers wide discretion to deal with an apprehensive and hostile environment. . . . *The organization must be committed to a system of unarticulated improvisation, where emphasis is on whatever means will effect the ultimate need to cope with conflict situations and reduce threats.*[22]

We do not quarrel with the point Ericson made about a hostile environment, although he has overdrawn a point when he attempts to generalize about policing throughout the nation. However, Ericson has set up a perilous "either–or" situation in regard to the attainment of community goals. In essence, Ericson has said that the attainment of community goals is impossible if working police officers follow "regular" procedures (i.e., approriate, specified procedures). Surely, perhaps without meaning to do so, Ericson has said that "due-process" policing is improbable; if not impossible, then it is highly impractical. We reject this notion, and we have been joined by a number of police executives throughout the nation who believe that due-process policing is possible.

We accept Ericson's point about organizational posture, however. It is certainly difficult, if not impossible, for administrators to anticipate all the situations and subsituations that can take place out on the street. Consequently, "administration-happy" administrators and subadministrators should resist the temptations to cover these with rules, regulations, and procedure manuals. Therefore, the capable administrator would be one who attempted to set the tone of the organization to permit and encourage improvisation. But this must be done within sets of general guidelines.

Too often, administrators, command officers, and supervisors have limited their guidance to the trite and too frequently used phrase, "just use common sense." Such a phrase is little actual guidance at all. It leaves to operational-level personnel the perilous task of choosing between alternative methods of handling a situation, when some of these methods may either be illegal or be frowned upon by the administrator or the community at large. The use of firearms and other force is the classic example. Administrators who fail to give specific guidance to personnel in these matters are neglecting their official duties. They are imposing an incredible burden on each and every member in an agency.

The point is simply this: There must be some appropriate balance between not giving adequate administrative guidance and giving too much, attempting to be entirely too specific in the development of policy and procedural guidelines. Where do we draw the line representing appropriate balance? Certainly, there is no precise point on a scale which represents that balance. Certainly, also, this precise point will vary from agency to agency and from time to time. One of the errors or shortcomings of classical police organizational theory has been the fact that it was largely based upon an absolutist's unchanging view of the world. The world has changed, and so have the conditions of policing in the past 20 years, in the past 10 years, and even in the past 5 years. The social stakes are quite different today than they were even 10 years ago; consequently, so is the police environment. Police personnel on all levels are facing situations today they could not have conceived of even 10 years ago.

THE DEFINITIONAL ROLE OF ADMINISTRATORS

Fundamental to the responsibilities of a police administrator is the necessity to articulate a department's current definition of its problems and those of the community. We emphasize current, for too often some administrators have relied exclusively upon pronouncements about "doomsday" and other time-worn, hackneyed exhortations about the decline of social morality, the irresponsibility of parents, the threat of internal subversion, and so on. Police problems and community problems, of course, change over time, in both their description and characterization.

The audiences of these pronouncements are important, and they should include not only the community at large and significant parts of its infrastructures, but also elected community leaders and members of the department itself. Administration, after all, is supposedly synonymous with leadership; at least sound administration involves an essential ingredient of leadership.

If anything, departmental administrators are supposed to exhibit a more global approach to community policing than are rank-and-file members. A more global view of community problems includes, of course, some understanding of the interrelationship of problems. It also includes an understanding of the interrelationships between various departments of local government: the police and urban planning, the police and the fire department, the police and the schools, the police and public health, and so on. If an administrator possesses this greater global understanding of community problems, hopefully that same administrator can help rank-and-file members of the department understand their overall social importance—their importance to the resolution of community problems.

An important aspect of this definitional process on the part of administrators is an outline, broad in nature perhaps, of general departmental policy in dealing with many of these community problems. Simple exhortations of "full enforcement" may be pleasing to some in the department and the community, and they may even make for a stack of nice press clippings. On the other hand, these same exhortations may simply be recognized as phony by others, including many members of the department itself. If a particular jurisdiction has more than 15,000 different statutes and ordinances to enforce, talk of full enforcement is not very meaningful.

In communicating within the department, the administrator must structure not only the department's general operating posture, but also the use of discretion in many situations. (As we stated earlier, it is impossible to structure the use of discretion in all, or even in most situations.) However, giving members of the department free rein in the use of discretion is foolhardy, as well as dysfunctional, for a variety of reasons. The American Bar Association warns: "Since individual police officers may make important decisions affecting police operations without direction, with limited accountability, and without any uniformity within a department, police discretion should be structured and controlled."[23] In its Commentary section, the ABA study explains:

> In the absence of adequate guidance from his supervisors, the tendency of an individual police officer is to attempt to meet the varied demands made upon him through a very personal form of improvisation. Confronted each day by frequently recurring situations, the officer tends to develop his own informal criteria for disposing of matters coming to his attention—depending heavily upon his imagination and resourcefulness.

The individual officer succeeds, to an amazing degree, in muddling his way through: disputes are resolved; dangerous persons are disarmed; people not in control of their capacities are protected; and many individuals are spared what, under some circumstances, would appear to be the undue harshness of the criminal process. The results, however, are sometimes less satisfactory. . . .

The police, probably more than any other municipal agency, are intimately involved, on a regular basis, with resolving sensitive social problems. The ways in which these problems are resolved often have broad ramifications for municipal government. The ways in which police departments or individual officers, for example, respond to a diverse range of problems . . . ; the tactics or methods that are used to prevent or to investigate crime or maintain order . . . ; and the general attitudes or efforts towards recruitment and other personnel practices . . . have great impact on the perception of citizens toward the police and local governments.[24]

That last phrase is an important one. After all, what does democracy really mean to average citizens? Primarily, the content and meaning of democracy to average citizens is the level of professional and understanding services they and their families receive routinely from only two governmental agencies: the police and the schools. Average citizens have little other face-to-face contact with government. Therefore, the influence of the police and the schools is more pervasive and more lasting than contact with any other aspect of government.

The point made above should be emphasized over and over: individual members of the police patrol force occupy a key position in the community structure. The work of the rank-and-file member of the police department, because of the nature of the work itself, occupies a crucial position in the community. If the work is performed effectively, the overall community benefits; if the work is performed poorly, the results of an individual police officer's work can be absolutely disastrous for the community. In doing their jobs, rank-and-file members of the police department need the help and support of their administrators.

The ABA study quoted above talks about individual police officers "muddling through" their tasks; this was not meant to be disrespectful of these persons. No aspersions were cast toward the patrol ranks. Rather, this was indirect criticism of the bulk of the nation's police administrators, for leaving the patrol ranks to "fend for themselves" without much administrative direction.

This is a point made by countless other commentators on American policing. James Q. Wilson, for example, talks about the informal "cost/benefit analysis" systems devised almost intuitively by many patrolmen.[25] In other words, part of being able to "handle the situation" is calculated risk taking, determining intuitively and by experience what action should be taken to avoid further "police trouble." Part of the trouble is criticism from supervisors or administrators.

Again, it is useful to refer to something written by Egon Bittner, in criticism of the quasimilitary structure of policing.

> Another complex of mischievous consequences arising out of the military bureaucracy relates to the paradoxical fact that while this kind of discipline ordinarily strengthens command authority it has the opposite effect in police departments. This effect is insidious rather than apparent. Because police superiors do not direct the activity of officers in any important sense they are perceived as mere disciplinarians. Not only are they not actually available to give help, advice, and direction in the handling of difficult work problems, but such a role cannot even be projected for them. Contrary to the army officer who is expected to lead his men into battle—even though he may never have a chance to do it—the analogously ranked police official is someone who can only do a great deal to his subordinates and very little for them.[26]

Again, we emphasize the difficulty of determining the exact balance to be achieved between doing too little and attempting to do entirely too much in the control of discretion. This is a difficult area with which management must deal. Toch, Grant, and Galvin have addressed portions of the problem by focusing upon interesting aspects of administrative management of police discretion.[27]

THE TRAINING AND MONITORING ROLE OF ADMINISTRATORS

We have linked the administrative subfunctions of training and monitoring in this section primarily because we feel that they form a "loop" in an ongoing administrative operation. The design of training supposedly takes into account the inculcation of skills one wants operational level personnel to have, as well as familiarization with policies and procedures designed to handle typical police situations. At the same time, hopefully, there will be changes in that training as the result of information picked up in supervisory and other monitoring activities. For example, as we gain new insights into the conflict management tasks of patrol personnel, we may decide to embark on department-wide training in these matters. This may be followed by periodic refresher sessions, utilizing new scenarios developed as the result of increased experience in dealing with family disputes, landlord–tenant disputes, and so on.

Monitoring, therefore, is an administrative responsibility which has several functions. One of these is to assess the overall readiness of the department to handle certain situations. As weaknesses in the readiness state are uncovered, hopefully, new programs will be inserted not only in recruit training, but also in in-service training.

In the design of training programs, one of the most effective means of assessing the state of the art is to inventory the existing body of "practical skills" possessed in a department. "Those methods of doing certain things, and . . . the information that underlies the use of the methods, that practitioners themselves view as proper and efficient."[28] This, by the way, is related to the methodology which Toch, Grant, and Galvin used for the peer counseling and training of violence-prone policemen in Oakland.[29]

This implies, therefore, that administrators should make a practice of using members of their department as "informed observers" about the state of the art and as "commentators" about current street problems personnel are facing daily. This practice not only has the advantage of giving the administrator access to important and accurate information, but also assists in building a sense of participation by rank-and-file members of the department. Too often, employees of an organization spend their careers in a work environment that seems almost hostile. To many, it seems as if they work for "a system designed for geniuses, to be run by idiots."[30] We spoke above about the "accuracy" of information. This does not imply, necessarily, that we believe that all information coming from rank-and-file personnel is accurate. On the contrary, rank-and-file personnel are no different from the rest of us; they have their vested interests and selective vision. However, if administrators make a practice of dealing with groups of rank-and-file personnel as part of the routine of monitoring, the distillation of rank-and-file views can be extremely important.

The methodologies for the development of effective employee task forces, of building a tradition of employee participation, are too complex to be dealt with here. It is sufficient to say that there are dozens of sources of information about how to build effective employee task forces within organizations.[31] The point to be made here is that it is foolish for administrators to overlook this source of information within their organization. Care must be taken, of course, to protect the administrator from being co-opted by rank-and-file personnel. In the final analysis, administrators are responsible for the quality of the information gathered. They cannot use the excuse that employees have misled them. With precautionary safeguards, however, this is a vital source of information for administrators.

The authors have an abiding respect in the collective intelligence and integrity of working police personnel. By getting enough opinions and allowing for self-correction within the group, administrators can obtain accurate, timely, and useful information. This reminds us of a statement Egon Bittner made concerning police emergency apprehension of mentally incapacitated persons.

> Making emergency apprehensions is, among others, a matter of economy.... Though the police could readily multiply the number of arrests for some petty offenses, they somehow manage to produce just the right number to keep the courts busy and the jails full. With the same uncanny instinct they burden the hospital just to the limit of its capacity.[32]

There is something uncannily accurate about collective wisdom, provided that the correct techniques are used to obtain an accurate distillation.

THE CHANGE ROLE OF THE ADMINISTRATOR

Paul Whisenand and Fred Ferguson devote the final chapter of their book on police management to the topic of change—organizational change, in particular. Among other things, they make the following point: "Habitual thought patterns can have the effect of insulating parts of a system from desirable environmental challenges."[33] They discuss the "change process" and the role of the administrator in creating the environment in which change can take place. "In a society based on large scale organization, the saviors will mostly be public executives, for it is they who bring people together in organizations to make things happen in the public interest."[34] Frankly, we find that last quotation a little sanguine. A statement such as that would probably be more appropriate as part of the keynote address at an administrator's conference. We personally do not attach a messiah-like vestment to any public administrator. We think the point made by Whisenand and Ferguson is generally correct, however, in stressing the importance of the administrator in setting an organizational tone that is receptive to the very concept of change. Administrators, by the examples they set, may either foster or impede needed organizational change.

It is also the administrator's responsibility to select the general type of change needed and to be encouraged within the organization.

> The problem for the police manager . . . is not how he can take control of the changes he himself institutes—but how to avoid concentrating on change where it is easy (in science and technology) and neglecting change where it is hard (in the social institutions)—and to control and give ethical content to the new technologies.[35]

One could quickly survey the changes that have taken place within policing since the publication of the President's Crime Commission studies in 1967. The grand share of these changes have taken place precisely in the area of science and technologies (e.g., helicopters, portable radios, computer systems, etc.). Only a small portion of the changes have taken place within the fabric of policing itself.

If administrators are to be effective in effecting and being a party to change, they must recognize the existence of subcultural values within policing as an occupation. Administrators must recognize that all subcultures develop a value system which is different than that of the overall culture. This means that policing has developed, over the years, some unique value systems and shorthand notions of what the world looks like. Not only that, but administrators must recognize that large-scale policing organizations consist of series of occupational subcultures. We have previously depicted some of the unique attributes of the "patrolman sub-culture."[36] Depending upon the particular department we are discussing, there may be as much variance between the values of the patrol force members and the administration of the department as there is between the department and the community as a whole. This dissonance between the patrol rank and the department's administration may be the principal obstacle to organizational change. Detectives and other specialists may very well develop their own peculiar subcultural values, at variance with the rest of the department.[37]

Related to this is the necessity for administrators to recognize some of the more subtle effects of overspecialization and bureaucratization. Although specialization and bureaucratization are not identically synonymous terms, they are inextricably related. Reiss and countless others have made the point that bureaucratization is the very antithesis of professionalization.[38] The more an organization is subdivided into sets of specialized bureaus, each having its own submission within the larger organization, the greater may be the attempt by the administration to routinize the functions of the organization and to exercise control over its multifaceted functions. With this grows an increased tendency to attempt to limit the discretion of the individual workers in the organization.

Centralized control is at the heart of large-scale police operations, but administrative attempts at control are countered constantly—subtly and not so subtly—by the operational field forces. Among many of the biases the authors have found in their policing careers, one of the strongest seems to be an almost universal "antiadministration" bias by rank-and-file personnel in large police agencies. Surely this is compounded by the degree to which large departments have found it necessary or advisable to specialize—to bureaucratize. Where specialization and centralization have set in, operational field personnel often feel that they are viewed as simple automatons by their administrators.

Unlike large federal agencies or large private industries, the bulk of police personnel are deployed in a decentralized fashion. They do not work simply two desks removed from a watchful supervisor; rather, they are operating largely on their own, away from close supervision. (That may be one of the original attractions of policework!) Lacking this closeness of supervision and command, police administrators have developed alternative means of supervision: centralized radio systems, car locator systems, centralized on-line computer command and control systems, and others. Attempts to limit the discretion of individual patrol personnel and new efforts to increase their productivity have often also served to limit the command discretion of police supervisors and commanders.[39]

One effect of all of this has been to encourage, albeit unknowingly, the development of ingenious sets of techniques for circumventing the planned "central order." With their cousins in countless other bureaucracies, including the armed forces, rank-and-file police personnel have often developed their own techniques for "screwing up" the administration.

Specialization has other perils. Merton points to Veblen's concept of "trained incapacity" and Dewey's notion of "occupational psychosis."[40] The point that is being made has to do with the necessity for constant renewal of talents and skills in a department, and the extent to which structure (i.e., specialization) can interfere with the capacity of organizational members to perform their generalized duties. Ericson makes another interesting point about specialization:

> One unintended consequence of being committed to some specialized subunits is that members of the units may be forced into a role that is incompatible with the role usually ascribed to policemen. This is salient to juvenile officers, who are subject to the conflicting expectations of police law enforcement and a social welfare orientation. Indeed, this welfare orientation may unintentionally commit the organization to a policy not originally anticipated by its formal program.[41]

Skolnick relates ludicrous but believeable stories about the competition generated between burglary, narcotics, and vice investigation units in "Westville."[42] Too often, specialization designed to improve departmental effectiveness has the exact opposite effect; the competition that it engenders among members of the department actually diminishes overall departmental effectiveness.

Whisenand and Ferguson conclude that much of the competition within police departments is actually disabling to the department. "One of the major problems affecting organizational effectiveness is the amount of energy expended in inappropriate competition and fighting between groups that should be cooperating."[43] The effective administrator, therefore, is one who has the ability to set an appropriate tone within the department, one who can combine that with an ability to strike the balance necessary to ensure an "environment of change," without jeopardizing the psychological security of members of the department. We wish we could present readers with a blueprint and a set of prescriptions to assure that a particular plan would work in each and every situation. Obviously, that is not possible, for this is not in the nature of modern organizations.

The reader should reflect back on a statement by Victor Thompson, quoted earlier in this chapter, listing the conditions necessary for creativity within organizations.

> In sum, the empirical conditions for individual creativity suggest a sort of golden mean: some freedom, but not too much; high internal commitment to the task, but not too high a commitment; a high proportion of intrinsic rewards, but some extrinsic rewards as well; some competition, but not cutthroat, winner-take-all competition.[44]

The effective administrator is one who can set the tone, give leadership to the development and updating of organizational missions, and serve a "linking-pin" function in the coordination of various organizational endeavors.[45]

Raymond Galvin has suggested that there is a good deal of "Rube Goldberg" in the better, more creative organizations.[46] In other words, the litmus is *not* whether the organization chart looks "pretty" and symmetrical on paper; the real test is whether the organization functions, as planned; whether it provides a proper environment for change; whether the final product is improved service to the public. Since there are few absolutes, creative administrators are those who are willing to admit when something—even their own ideas—do not work; effective administrators are those who can make appropriate adjustments when one of their pet ideas falls short of expectation.

Effective change within an organization necessarily involves "the troops." As Toch, Grant, and Galvin point out, "passive change is terminal change."[47] In other words, if only administrators and their immediate staff are involved in a change, that fact alone may spell doom for that particular planned change. Change that is most effective involves the participation of rank-and-file personnel. Many writers on the subject of organizational change suggest the *deliberate* creation of temporary and open structures, permitting and encouraging the free flow of ideas and field validation experiments.[48] If Clarence Kelley had done nothing else while he was chief of police in Kansas City, he could rest on his laurels as an administrator who permitted and encouraged the participation of rank-and-file personnel in efforts at planned change. He created special task forces, with representatives of all ranks participating, and gave these task forces a role in departmental experiments. Without this tone of encouragement from "The Chief" himself, the department could not have succeeded in its famous patrol experiment or in the development of other new programs. Certainly, Kelley and his immediate staff could have initiated the experiments, but what sort of real cooperation would they have gotten from the troops? On that cooperation rested the ultimate success of the changes.

Summary

Much more will be said in subsequent chapters about the ways in which organizations and organizational structures affect police field behavior. The purpose of this chapter was simply to set the stage for much that follows in the book. In addition, it was our goal in this chapter to open up a vast subject for individual exploration. Much remains to be learned about the behavior of human beings within organizational settings; behavioral science has contributed a great deal of data on the subject, but much remains to be discovered. This is particularly important with regard to human behavior within police organizations, because of the crucial role that police agencies play in our democratic governments.

End Notes

[1]See, for example, George D. Eastman and Esther M. Eastman, *Municipal Police Administration,* 6th ed. (Washington, D.C.: International City Management Association, 1969), and O. W. Wilson and Roy C. McLaren, *Police Administration,* 3rd ed. (New York: McGraw-Hill, 1972). For criticism of this particular traditionalist approach, see, among others, Jim L. Munro, *Administrative Behavior and Police Organization* (Cincinnati, Ohio: W. H. Anderson, 1974), esp. pp. 47–66.

[2]John E. Angell, "Toward an Alternative to the Classic Police Organizational Arrangements: A Democratic Model," *Criminology,* August–November, 1971, p. 186.

[3]Victor A. Thompson, *Bureaucracy and Innovation* (Tuscaloosa, Ala.: University of Alabama Press, 1969), p. 10.

[4]Thomas Reddin, "Are you Oriented to Hold Them?" *Police Chief,* March 1966, pp. 12–19.

[5]For this and for other reasons, many college-educated persons seem to prefer the status offered to employees of state and federal investigative agencies. In our career counseling, we have been inclined to say that the real social and personal challenges in policing are on the local—city or county—levels, rather than in state or federal agencies. We have counseled our students, however, that many organizations—on all three levels—will severely tax their "frustration levels"!

[6]Thomas A. Johnson, "A Study of Police Resistance to Police Community Relations in a Municipal Police-Department," Ph.D. dissertation, University of California, Berkeley, 1970.

[7]Egon Bittner, "The Police on Skid Row: A Study of Peace-Keeping," *American Sociological Review,* 32, No. 5 (October 1967), 699–715.

[8]Ibid.

[9]James Q. Wilson, *Varieties of Police Behavior: The Management of Law and Order in Eight Communities* (Cambridge, Mass.: Harvard University Press, 1968), Jerome Skolnick, *Justice without Trial* (New York: Wiley, 1967); Joseph D. Lohman and Gordon E. Misner, *The Police and the Community,* President's Commission on Law Enforcement and Administration of Justice, Field Surveys IV, vols. 1, 2 (Washington, D.C.: U.S. Government Printing Office, 1967); Bittner, "The Police on Skid Row," and *The Functions of the Police in Modern Society* (Chevy Chase, Md.: National Institute of Mental Health, Center for Studies of Crime and Delinquency, 1970); and Michael Banton, *The Policeman in the Community* (New York: Basic Books, 1964).

[10]Bittner, "The Police on Skid Row," p. 700.

[11]Albert Reiss, Jr., *The Police and the Public* (New Haven, Conn.: Yale University Press, 1970), p. 3.

[12]Ibid., p. 19.

[13]Ibid., p. 46.

[14]Clifford D. Shearing, "Dial-a-Cop: A Study of Police Mobilization," in *Crime Prevention and Social Defense,* (New York: Praeger, 1974), p. 78.

[15]Elaine Cumming, Ian Cumming, and Laura Edell, "The Policeman as Philosopher, Guide, and Friend," *Social Problems,* 12 (Winter 1965), 276–86.

[16]Egon Bittner, "Police Discretion in Emergency Apprehension of Mentally Ill Persons," *Social Problems* 19 (Winter 1967), 278–92; from p. 291.

[17]Bittner, "The Police on Skid Row," p. 701; Wilson, *Varieties of Police Behavior,* p. 31; and Bruce Smith, *Police Systems in the United States,* rev. ed. (New York: Harper & Row, 1949), pp. 19–21.

[18]Wilson, *Varieties of Police Behavior.*

[19]Gordon E. Misner, "The Urban Police Mission," *Issues in Criminology,* 3 (Summer 1967), 35–46.

[20]Bittner, "The Police on Skid Row."

[21]Ibid., p. 715.

[22]Richard V. Ericson, "Police Bureaucracy and Decisionmaking: The Function of Discretion in Maintaining the Police System," *Police* 16 (June 1972), 59–65; from pp. 59, 60, emphasis added. Courtesy of Charles C Thomas, Publishers, Springfield, Ill.

[23]American Bar Association, Advisory Committee on the Police Function, *The Urban Police Function* (Tentative Draft) (New York: Institute of Judicial Administration, March 1972), p. 121.

[24]Ibid., pp. 123, 124.

[25]Wilson, *Varieties of Police Behavior*; see chap. 2.

[26]Egon Bittner, *The Functions of the Police in Modern Society* (Chevy Chase, Md.: National Institute of Mental Health, 1970), p. 59, emphasis added.

[27]Hans Toch, J. Douglas Grant, and Raymond T. Galvin, *Agents of Change: A Study in Police Reform* (New York: Schenkman/Wiley, 1975).

[28]Bittner, "The Police on Skid Row," p. 701.

[29]Toch, Grant, and Galvin, *Agents of Change.*

[30]Apologies to Herman Wouk, *The Caine Mutiny.*

[31]Toch, Grant, and Galvin, *Agents of Change,* contains an excellent survey of the literature in this field. See also Warren G. Bennis, Kenneth D. Benne, and Richard Chin, eds., *The Planning of Change* (New York: Holt, Rinehart and Winston, 1962), and Leslie R. Roos, Jr., and Noralow Roos, "Administrative Change in a Modernizing Society," *Administrative Science Quarterly,* 15 (March 1970), 72–83.

[32]Bittner, "Police Discretion," p. 280.

[33]Paul F. Whisenand and R. Fred Ferguson, *The Managing of Police Organizations* (Englewood Cliffs, N.J.: Prentice-Hall, 1973), p. 409.

[34]Ibid., p. 413.

[35]Ibid., p. 414.

[36]Johnson, *Study of Police Resistance.*

[37]Reiss, *The Police,* p. 150.

[38]Ibid., p. 123.

[39]Ibid.

[40]Robert K. Merton, *Social Theory and Social Structure,* rev. ed. (New York: Free Press, 1957), p. 198.

[41]Ericson, "Police Bureaucracy," p. 64.

[42]Skolnick, *Justice without Trial,* p. 150.

[43]Whisenand and Ferguson, *Managing of Police,* p. 417.

[44]Thompson, *Bureaucracy,* p. 11.

[45]Whisenand and Ferguson, *Managing of Police,* p. 422.

[46]The authors are indebted to Ray Galvin for this and other suggestions about the subject. We take full responsibility for the alterations of the ideas.

[47]Toch, Grant, and Galvin, *Agents of Change,* p. 2.

[48]Among these are Whisenand and Ferguson, *Managing of Police,* and Bennis, Benne, and Chin, *Planning of Change.* For an excellent discussion of the role of the chief in fostering change within the police department, see Herman Goldstein, *Policing a Free Society* (Cambridge, Mass.: Ballinger, 1977), pp. 307–33, esp. pp. 307–11.

CHAPTER FIVE

RESISTANCE TO POLICE-COMMUNITY RELATIONS PROGRAMS

In an analysis of the structural characteristics of an urban police organization, or for that matter any typical large organization, the following structural characteristics can be observed: large size, specialization, hierarchy, status anxiety, oligarchy, cooptation, efficiency, and rationality.[1] Out of these structural characteristics organization theory has for the most part directed itself toward two dominant organizational objectives, productive efficiency and management control.[2]

Further clarification of the focus of organizational theory can be found in Koontz and O'Donnell's definition of organization. "The task of organizing is to establish a system of activity groupings and authority relationships in which people can know what their tasks are, how their tasks relate to one another, and where authority for decisions needed to accomplish these tasks rests.[3]

The classical theorists placed heavy emphasis on such structural factors as command, discipline, and authority in their organizational design. Since the role of authority in organizations has been diminishing because of decentralization, professionalism, coordination, communication, and participative management philosophies, the structural approach in addressing many of our organizational problems has been largely ignored.[4] Or as Leavitt suggests:

> The great early emphasis of structural people on authority led us for a while toward rejecting the whole structural approach. We tended as we so often do, to want to throw out the baby with the bath water. Recently, however, we have begun to come back to structural questions from very different angles. We have come back to structure largely because we have been forced to—because it has become so patently obvious that structure is an organizational dimension (1) that we can manipulate, and (2) that has direct effects on problem solving. If we decentralize things happen. Maybe not all the things we wanted to have happen, but things happen. If we change the definitions of roles of members of our organization, things happen. If we change communication lines by removing telephones or separating people, or making some people more accessible to others, things happen . . . Yet there is an important limiting factor in the structured approach. The structure of an organization makes some things possible, but it does not guarantee that they will happen.[5]

Furthermore, the importance of organizational design is increasingly gaining attention because of the work on role conflict and the increasing use of computers, which has forced us to make room for new kinds of people and new kinds of relationships. "These two developments, rather than killing off the idea of organizational structure, are putting it back into the spotlight, making us ask ourselves again, what is the ideal structural design for an organization aimed at performing a particular task?"[6]

One of the main theses of this research has been not only that there are structural and organizational deficiencies that are conducive to police resistance to police–community relations programs, but that remedial action might well be accomplished by changing the structure of police organizations. Leavitt reinforces this thesis by suggesting the following:

> We are really just beginning to reattack the structural problem after leaving it alone for many years. It is an important issue to attack, both because it is clear that the structure we work in has a great deal to do with how we behave, and also because structure is susceptible to relatively easy manipulation and change. If we could learn more about what effects we would get from particular manipulations, we might be able to answer a key question in applied organizational theory: "What organizational designs are appropriate for what task?"[7]

Finally, organization is viewed by many as a vehicle for accomplishing goals and objectives. As useful as this approach is, it does tend to obscure the inner workings of the organization. It is these inner workings, particularly when they manifest resistance to change, that we should be most concerned with in this area of organizational theory. Therefore, the main thrust of the review of the organizational literature will be in the area of resistance to change, since it plays such an integral part in the problem of police organizations accepting the concept of police community relations programs.

ORGANIZATIONAL CHANGE

Any organization, police organizations particularly, should change. Frederick Mosher perhaps best identifies the reasons, as his study focuses on governmental reorganizations. Mosher lists the following reasons why change is necessary:

A number of different and identifiable factors may over the course of time make major structural change within an agency desirable or even mandatory. All are manifestations of organizational obsolescence. One of the most pervasive of these in a growing society is simply growth in size, consequent upon growth in clientele or population serviced, with or without change in nature of services or techniques. . . .

A second factor contributing to the need for reorganization is changes in problems and needs and therefore in organizational programs and responsibilities. . . .

A third factor . . . is a changing philosophy as to the proper responsibilities of government. . . .

A fourth factor is a consequence of new technology, new equipment, and advancing knowledge. . . .

A fifth factor is the changing—and usually rising qualifications of personnel in fields of specialization used in the agency's work. . . .

Finally organizations of lower levels may in effect become obsolescent because of actions taken above them in their department of government or higher levels of government.[8]

Perhaps the strongest reason for which organizational change is mandatory is simply to keep the police department or any organization more responsive to the needs of its clientele.[9]

A social agency cannot immunize itself from the social situation—the community—in which it operates. It can for a time be unresponsive to new situations and new needs. But eventually, it must react and respond to situational forces, or decline in influence and in time pass out of existence.[10]

An excellent thumbnail sketch of what is involved in the management of change is presented in Irwin and Langham's article "The Change Seekers," in which the authors list 10 crucial stages in an organizational change:

1. Recognizing the forces of change affecting you and your business.
2. Determining your ability to change.
3. Establishing a climate for change.

4. Involving people in change.
5. Organizing for change.
6. Generating action.
7. Planning change.
8. Implementing change.
9. Minimizing risks and conflicts.
10. Providing leadership.[11]

In a most perceptive method of analyzing organized change and at the same time presenting a very precise review of the literature to organizational change, Harold Leavitt suggests four potential strategies for analyzing organizational change as being included within the following four variables:

Task—refers, of course, to the industrial organization's raisons d'etre: the production of goods and services, including the large numbers of different but operationally meaningful subtasks that may exist in complex organizations.

Actors—refers chiefly to people, but with the qualifications that acts executed by people at some time or place need not remain exclusively in the human domain.

Technology—refers to direct problem solving inventions like work measurement techniques, or computers, or drill presses. Note that both machines and programs may be included in this category.

Structure—means systems of communication, systems of authority (or other roles), and systems of work flows.[12]

Leavitt maintains that each of these four variables represents a particular strategy for addressing the problem of organization change, and that each strategy in turn attracts specialists who develop expertise in employing the particular variable in their change strategy for improving the organization's performance.[13]

For example, the people approach attempts to change organizations by changing the behavior of the organizations' members. The more outstanding contributions to the literature on human aspects of organizational change are Lippitt, Watson, and Westley's *The Dynamics of Planned Change;* Lawrence's *The Changing of Organizational Behavior Patterns;* Guest's *Organizational Change;* Ginzberg and Reilly's *Effecting Change in Large Organizations;* and Bennis, Benne, and Chin's *The Planning of Change.*[14]

In contrast, technological and structural approaches focus on problem-solving mechanisms while overlooking the internal operations of the organization. However, there are variations, as some of the structural approaches are not aimed directly at the task, but at people, in the hope that by changing structure to change people one improves task performance (Chapple and Sayle's *The Measure of Management*). Similarly, some of the people approaches seek to change people to change structure and to change or improve the task performance. Authors representative of this approach are Chris Argyris and Renis Likert.[15]

Greiner reviewed the literature on organization change and identified and categorized the most commonly used approaches to organizational change as falling within seven basic categories as follows:

1. *The Decree Approach.* A one-way announcement originating with a person with high formal authority and passed on to those in lower positions (e.g., Taylor, 1911; Gouldner, 1954).

2. *The Replacement Approach.* Individuals in one or more key organizational positions are replaced by other individuals. The basic assumption is that organizational changes are a function of personnel changes (e.g., Gouldner, 1954; Guest, 1962).

3. *The Structural Approach.* Instead of decreeing or injecting new blood into work relationships, management changes the required relationships of subordinates working in the situation. By changing the structure or organizational relationships, organizational behavior is also presumably affected (e.g., Burns and Stother, 1962; Chapple and Sayles, 1961; Woodward, 1958; Doltar, Barnes, and Zalennik, 1966).

4. *The Group Decision Approach.* Participation by group members in implementing alternatives specified by others. This approach involves neither problem identification nor problem solving, but emphasizes the obtaining of group agreement on a predetermined course (e.g., Coch and French, 1948; Lewin, 1958).

5. *The Data Discussion Approach.* Presentation and feedback of relevant data to the client system by either a change catalyst or by change agents within the company. Organizational members are encouraged to develop their own analysis of the data which has been given to them in the form of case materials, survey findings or data reports (e.g., Main, 1957; Andrews, 1953).

6. *The Group Problem Solving Approach.* Problem identification and problem solving through group discussion with the help of an outsider. This would be one type of "planned change" (e.g., Sofer, 1961).

7. *The T-Group Approach.* Training in sensitivity to the processes of individual and group behavior. Changes in work patterns and relationships are assumed to follow from changes in interpersonal relationships. T-group approaches focus upon the interpersonal relationships first, then hope for, or work towards improvements in work performance (e.g., Argyres, 1962; Foundation for Research on Human Behavior, 1960).[16]

RESISTANCE TO CHANGE

A most appropriate method of introducing a discussion on police resistance to police–community relations, or on resistance to change itself, is to follow Lippitt, Watson, and Westley's example of classifying forces that are either conducive to resistance or conducive to change.[17]

In other words, it is not only important to identify both forces pushing for change or retarding change, but it is also important to identify at what levels, stages, or times these forces manifest themselves. Furthermore, it should be stressed that these forces will emerge irrespective of any formal change process occurring.

Although resistance to change may emerge at any point in the continuum of a change process—at the beginning, while it is under way, or later on in the program—there are specific points at which various types of resistance occur. If these types of resistance are anticipated, remedial action can be taken to reduce their impact on the particular change being fostered.[18] Although these types of resistance are in response to formal programs of organizational change, they nevertheless will be highly useful in explaining some of the rationale for police resistance to police–community relations, which more often than not occurs quite informally.

Awareness of Problem

The most logical area for resistance to emerge is when the need for help or the awareness that a problem exists is not realized.[19] In many cases this certainly is the situation regarding police resistance to police–community relations. A variation on this theme is, if we do have a problem, but are not entirely convinced we do, it is beyond our capabilities to resolve the problem.

However, even if the problem is recognized, specifically in the case of police–community relations, there still may be reasons for resistance emerging. For example, there may be a reluctance to admit a weakness, or fear of failure in trying to initiate a new practice; or a fatalistic expectation of failure instilled by previous unsuccessful attempts to improve the police–community relationship.

Opposition to Change

One form of resistance most likely to occur at the beginning of a change process is opposition to any type of change. There are many explanations for this initial type of resistance. It can be founded on fear or ignorance or a combination of both.[20] Insofar as police organizations are concerned, most resistance to police community relations emerges because accepting this role implies change or innovative thinking. As Bayley and Mendelsohn suggest, police are more aligned with the status quo, since that is what their job is essentially all about, and there would be few innovative-oriented people attracted to police work. Nevertheless, fear and ignorance could also initiate police resistance to police community relations. The police department may fear that it would be unable to shift successfully its orientation to police–community relations, or that if it did, this change would require things of the police department that its individual members would not be able to deliver.

Opposition to Change Objective

However, in all fairness to police organizations, it must not be assumed that resistance is always organized against change, for the resistance might be focused more accurately against a particular objective of change.[21] An excellent example of this occurs within the police-community relations area, where resistance might be manifested not because police are against maintaining a sound relationship with the community, but because police consider police-community relations as irrelevant to their perception of their basic mission, which is law enforcement.

Opposition Because of Tradition

Resistance to police-community relations can emerge because the police department may be reluctant to give up traditional types of satisfaction, which might include the traditional manner of getting reward, which is certainly not amenable to police-community relations programs, as James Q. Wilson's writings have indicated. Other traditional satisfactions that might cause resistance are the familiar ways of avoiding pain or anxiety, especially the ways in which individuals conceive of their roles. These conceptions, and our views of the external world, are especially crucial.[22]

Mistrust of Change Agent

Police resistance to police-community relations is also centered in the relationship that exists between the police department and that segment of the community that is acting as a change agent in its demands for increasing police sensitivity to police-community relations. Lippitt suggests that when resistance between the client system and change agent occurs, it might well be because of the unfamiliarity and suspiciousness each has of the other.[23] There can be no doubt about similar feelings of mistrust and incompatibility existing between the police department and the community. This certainly accounts for a portion of police resistance to police-community relations.

Dissatisfaction with Community

Additional points of resistance that might emerge out of this relationship between the police and the community could center around dissatisfaction one has with the other. For example, police resistance to police-community relations may well intensify after the police department has made a definite commitment to improving police–community relations, but the response of the community is still characterized by avoiding any responsibility to facilitate this change. To the police this might well be considered as a rational reason for not taking seriously the demands of the community that police–community relations be improved. Another variation of this same theme occurs when factors that were considered of small consequence in the initial change phase later become major obstacles to change, such as the community demand for improved police–community relations, but no attendant commitment for providing the police department with the budget, personnel, materials, and consultant help necessary to achieve this improved police–community relationship. In essence, the community is avoiding responsibility again by its failure to make any commitment toward involvement in the entire problem. Whenever the loss of support or help becomes imminent, especially in such a sensitive problem as police–community relations, resistance to change may dramatically increase.

Resistance can also be observed when there is a faulty internal distribution of power either being too diffused or too concentrated.[24] This is especially the case when one considers that the patrolmen are a subculture within a subculture. Subcultures naturally possess different values and mores; thus one source of power to the patrolmen subculture is its ability to resist change that the administration considers necessary.

Defective Communication

Resistance might well be manifested when pathologically defective communication arises both within the hierarchial structure of the police organization and between the organization and the community. Police organizations are particularly vulnerable to communication problems, because no formal structure exists for maintaining a dialogue with members of the community.

Perceived Expectations

Lippitt et al. suggest that "the client system learns that the change agent expects certain things of it and these expectations constitute a force of change. The influence of the desires and expectations of the change agent will increase in accordance with the esteem and liking for him felt by the client system."[25] The corollary of this is equally important especially in terms of police resistance to police–community relations. There can be little doubt that the police sense the expectations of the community toward improving police–community relations. However, these expectations cannot be considered as a force for change, because the police do not feel they are held in high esteem by the community, and segments of the community do not feel that the police regard them with any degree of respect or esteem. When one's worth is being questioned, there will be little movement toward making significant change; thus another rationale is developed for resisting change.

Community Hypocrisy

Another explanation of police resistance to police–community relations can be observed when a subsystem of society or the administration of justice is given a problem it will be unable to change because there is resistance originating outside the subsystem, or coming from the larger system in which the subsystem is embedded.[26] In other words, the police department has long ago acknowledged the hypocrisy of the total community. A community insists on improved police–community relations, tolerates inadequate housing, inferior education, wholesale unemployment, and worst of all, maintains the very ghettos and slums of the city. The police response, a very normal one, is: "How can we improve police community relations when the overriding attitude of the majority community indicates that their attitudes toward minority groups have not only remained constant, but show little sign of changing." In short, what is the utility of the police improving their relationship with the community when the community itself cannot live in harmony? Moreover, how can the police improve their relationship with the community when other parts of the administration of justice system and the community itself degrades this relationship by the very process of their interaction?

Impartiality Challenged

Resistance can also be expected when a proposed change offers more benefits to one part of the organization's clientele at the expense of other portions of the clientele.[27] The defensive reaction, especially in police organizations committed to impartiality of service is to oppose the change automatically. This certainly personifies the dilemma of the police organization in the area of police–community relations. Therefore, resistance may emerge because individual members of the department feel that their ideas on impartiality are being tampered with.

Dissipation of Authority

Another traditional value, in fact, almost a religious belief of police organizations, is the idea that productivity and organizational authority will dissipate somewhat if community relations programs are adopted. Again, the point is not so much police resistance to police–community relations as it is to the accompanying change that may reveal latent forms of conflict that might challenge the hierarchical authority structure. Furthermore, police organizations, like almost all organizations, are geared to productivity and any organizational change either formally or informally might well be viewed as lowering productivity.[28]

Anxieties from Nonspecific Programs

Another source of resistance to police–community relations might reside in the anxiety the police organization possesses regarding both whether the department feels it will be competent to effectively improve the police–community relationship, and where in the organization or system the appropriate unit can be located to effectively assume this sensitive responsibility.

Alvin Zander indicates that "resistance can be expected if the nature of the change is not made clear to the people who are going to be influenced by the change."[29] This is certainly applicable to police resistance to police–community relations. Police officers often express their frustration by asking: "What does the community expect from us; what do they want us to do?" Not knowing what is expected certainly can generate misgivings about accepting any program or making any change.

Status Quo versus Innovation

Resistance to police–community relations can also be expected when the police administration is caught between strong forces pushing for a change, and strong forces pushing to maintain the status quo, or not accepting responsibility for police–community relations programs.[30] This indicates that not only are there different types of resistance, and that various kinds of resistance manifest themselves at certain times, but that resistance can also emerge from any level of an organization. This dilemma is important, as the conflict must be considered by the particular group or change agent desirous of lowering the resistance to the change.

Implication of Perceived Failure

Resistance to police–community relations may be more pronounced from the line personnel if they perceive that the change is being made on personal grounds or implying that they have been unsuccessful in their job of maintaining a sound relationship between segments of the community and the police department. People working at what they consider to be important jobs usually come to see their job performance as being consistent with the types of people they consider themselves to be. Therefore, with the suggestion that police–community relations need improvement, the police are required to change their conceptions of their job and role, and more important, their conceptions of themselves.[31] Perhaps, we should be more surprised by an absence of resistance than by resistance that is manifested toward police–community relations.

Ignoring Police Institutions

Resistance can also be expected in the area of police–community relations if the change ignores the already established institutions in a group or organization.[32] The police have, of course, long maintained that the issue of police review, so intensely embedded in improving police–community relations, is an irrelevant grievance. Many police see the proper grievance procedures for handling complaints already in existence in their own police department or some structure closely associated with the administration of justice, such as a district attorney, Federal Bureau of Investigation, and so on. Therefore, there is resistance to many police–community relation proposals on this count alone.

Unawareness of Change Responsibilities

Perhaps one potential cause of resistance to police–community relations is simply that some police personnel are unaware that they are expected to make efforts to strengthen the police–community relationship. Mann and Neff suggest that in some cases the need for change must be made explicit in that people are confronted with the difference between their present behavior and the specific new behavior required of them.[33] Part of the resistance problem in the area of police–community relations is that police are asking: "What specific behavior do you expect of us?" The question is quite broad and can be answered only in generalities, whereas the police are expecting a specific reply. When the specific reply is not forthcoming, many police officers summarize the situation as: "You're expecting me to change, but you can't tell me what to change to . . . forget it."

Group Pressures

Again focusing on the police department as a subculture, perhaps one of the major causes of police resistance to change is related to the extreme group pressures on conformity to norms.[34] Pfiffner and Sherwood comment on the police as a subculture and the attendant management and organizational problems this creates, as follows:

> The nature of the work helps to erect an institutional subculture. This is especially true where the organization is relatively homogeneous and where there is relatively little opportunity for employment mobility. . . . Police have highly irregular hours, reducing the possibility of normal social intercourse; furthermore the demands of their work have caused many police officers to develop a perception of incompatibility with other segments of soci-

ety.... The kind of organization and management required for this institutional subculture must differ markedly from that required in a newspaper office where individual initiative and creativity remain important.[35]

There will be certain forces that structure a police organization and make it more susceptible to resistance to change simply because it is an institutional subculture.

Perhaps the leading study to document the impact of group cohesiveness to resistance to change was Coch and French's study of the Harwood Pajama Manufacturing Company.[36] Although the group norms in their study were high in terms of their correlation to cohesiveness, the cohesiveness did not approach that found in most police departments, because police departments are more or less, institutional subcultures.

Patrol Officer's Socialization Process

While considering the police as an institutional subculture, an analogy from an anthropologist's examination of resistance to change is appropriate. Edward Bruner suggests the following:

That which was traditionally learned and internalized in infancy and early childhood tends to be most resistant to change in contact situations. This suggests that we view a culture from the perspective of cultural transmission, the process by which the content of culture is learned by and communicated to members of the society.[37]

With Bruner's view, patrol officers' infancy begins when they are recruits. The cultural transmission occurs in their recruit training in the police academy. Part of the police culture is learned at the academy, and a far greater part is learned on the job. If Bruner is accurate in his hypothesis that what is traditionally learned and internalized in infancy tends to be most resistant to change, rookies' association with older officers should be examined.

Organizational Attractiveness

Another explanation for police resistance to police–community relations can be found in William Starbuck's observation that "members may be attracted by the organization's goals; they may be attracted by the activities which they perform in the organization's task structure or they may be attracted by the interactions experienced in the organization's social structure."[38] Consequently, any changes that would alter what attracted particular members to the organization will in all probability be resisted. The problem presented by police–community relations is that few people are motivated to join a police department to strengthen the police–community relationship. Police–community relations proposals would seem to alter some of the basic elements Starbuck suggests have attracted members to the organization.

Johns suggests that where organizational change seems to threaten an individual's goals, that change will be highly resisted.[39]

Priorities

Lippitt suggests that it is quite important to differentiate between resistance and interference, as it can make a considerable difference in how one would address organizational change. Essentially, resistance forces originate in regard to the objective of the organizational change, whereas interference forces are not directly related to the objectives of the change process.[40]

> Sometimes, however, the change process may run into difficulty not because of opposing forces but because of competing forces. Thus, for example, a proposal to build a new city hall might be defeated not because of opposition to such a building, but because it seemed that a new school building was ever more urgent.[41]

A great deal of what initially appears to be police resistance to police–community relations is really not resistance but interference. In other words, police might perceive more urgent needs than that of establishing police–community relations programs. Naturally, a great deal of this interference would depend on the role conception of police officers.

Functional Aspects of Resistance

It is also incumbent upon any analysis to look at the functional properties of resistance to change, for all resistance to change is not negative in nature. For example, Johns suggests that resistance can be a source of new ideas. Resistance can also force both representatives of the police and the community to more sharply clarify the purposes of change. Resistance also forces both sides to look at the unanticipated or dysfunctional consequences of too fast a change. Finally, resistance not only discloses inadequate communication channels, but also inadequate problem-solving processes. Perhaps in this manner it allows both the organization and the community to measure whether or not the relevant involvement of persons and groups has been secured.[42]

Neutralization of Resistance to Change

To briefly recapitulate, most consultants and communities have suggested that police improve the police–community relationship by focusing on the police department, while largely ignoring the environment within which the police department functions. Second, as Leavitt suggests, the "people approach" has been used, in which consultants attempt to sensitize the personnel, particularly line officers, to the need and importance of police–community relations. This approach has been most dysfunctional primarily because the attendant structural changes were not made along with the people approach.

In fact, there is every reason to believe that the sensitivity approach alone has intensified police resistance to police–community relations. The literature documents two reasons for this occurring. For example, to provide training to one group of personnel, in the case of a police organization's patrolmen, but not to provide the same training to their superiors means that the superiors still retain their same expectations for the patrolmen's behavior patterns and will supervise accordingly. Thus, all the training really accomplished was to frustrate the line officers by presenting them with incongruities and conflict situations. Second, as Leavitt points out, any attempt to give power equalizations rather than power differentiation via sensitivity training in a police organization represents a clear confrontation with the traditional hierarchical structure of the police organization.[43] One certain outcome of this incongruity is first frustration, then resistance.

We would be well advised to take note of Donald Cressey's observation that in correctional work, management is an end, not a means, and that the management hierarchies extend to the lowest-level employee. "The correctional worker in other words is both a manager and a worker. He is managed in a system of controls and regulations from above, but he also manages the inmates, probationers, or parolees in his charge. . . . Because he is a manager, he cannot be ordered to accept a proposed innovation, as a turret lathe operator can be ordered. He can only be persuaded to do so."[44]

Patrol officers are low-line managers, and therefore they, too, must be persuaded to change, not simply ordered to do so, even though this does appear incongruent to the authority hierarchy within a police organization. Patrolmen do manage situations and do rely on discretion to facilitate their management. They must be approached in a persuasive manner to minimize resistance to organizational change.

The significance of this observation does suggest what Leavitt has maintained for any organizational change: that to accomplish the change with least resistance it would be well to broaden our scope and use structural, humanistic, and technological approaches as opposed to relying on one approach at the expense of the others. Furthermore, if any one variable is manipulated, one must be aware of the concomitant effect it will have on the others as well as on the task.

It is imperative to approach police–community relation problems with more than a structural approach. The two (structure and function), however, might be a perfect marriage in any attempt to either improve police–community relations or to reduce police resistance to police–community relations.

IMPACT OF GOALS AND CLIENT
ON ADMINISTRATIVE STYLE

Two additional variables that have an impact on the nature of the administrative style of policing and upon the texture of police-community relations are the organization's goals and clientele. For as Jameson Doig suggests, the police policies and procedures can no longer be disregarded as long as they are "efficient" in meeting law enforcement goals, because what those goals are and how to measure efficiency and effectiveness materially affects the police-community relationship.[45]

Also, to appreciate fully the dimensions of the problem of police resistance to police-community relations, it becomes incumbent on any such analysis to examine the two variables the school of modern organization theory has stressed in its systems approach. These two variables are goals and client.

Organization theory seems to focus on three principal elements: organizational structure, organizational roles, and organizational goals. A fourth element of critical importance that has not had the comprehensive coverage of the other three elements is environment.[46] The goals of an organization will invariably emerge out of a variation of one or more of these four elements. However, too frequently, especially in police organization, the goals are established in spite of the other three elements.

Amitai Etzioni suggests that an organization's goals serve many important functions; among them are guidelines for organizational activity, a means of measuring the success of the organization, and also an orientation for a future state of affairs that it hopes to achieve. However, organizations acquire their own needs and through cooptation can conceivably subvert the initial organizational goals. Furthermore, the question must be raised as to whose goals are being pursued in an organization: the individuals' goals or the organization's goals. In fact, "the participants should be specifically asked what they see as the organizational goal, as distinct from their own or from those which they think the organization ought to pursue."[47]

Cyert and MacCrimmon suggest that one way of describing an organization is to analyze the participant's goals and roles:

Such a description by itself, however, does not indicate what the (common) motivations of the participants are, that is what goals their joint efforts are directed toward nor does it indicate the types of interactions that occur among the members. . . . The goal structure itself is not sufficient to describe the organization because it indicates neither the compatibility of the organizational goals with those of the individual participants nor the operating structure by which the organization tries to achieve its goals. A third element necessary to describe an organization is therefore the structure of roles through which the participants interact and through which the organization attempts to achieve its goals. Related to the goal structure is a structure of programs and constraints specifying the activities necessary at each part of the organization to achieve the goals. These programs and constraints are formed into roles which are occupied by the participants. There is a stability inherent in the role structure itself that allows the organization to survive continual turnover of participants; however the role structure alone does not necessarily indicate which goals are being pursued, nor the future directions in which the organization is likely to move.[48]

It is quite clear that no organization can be understood without examining its relationship to its environment, because both the organization and the environment are parts of a complex interactive system in which each affects the other. Included among the facets of the environment of an organization, particularly a police organization, are the social, cultural, political, legal, economic, and technological influences.[49]

A common mistake made in assessing an organization's goals is the assumption that these goals exist at one plane or level. Goals are not only pursued differently by different members of the organization, but they are pursued in an instrumental manner, which facilitates the achievement of higher goals.[50] In other words, goal hierarchies can be found in an organization. This is particularly significant to the study of police resistance to police–community relations because resistance to change could not be properly addressed or the goals of that particular level of personnel in the organization are not appreciated.

Not only are there different levels of goals within an organization, but there are also stated and unstated goals. Stated goals often justify the organization to its environment. In the case of prisons and mental hospitals, the stated goal may be rehabilitation. In police organizations the stated goals may be crime prevention. As is so often the case with stated goals of this type, they are so broad that they can be relied upon to provide much insight into the organizational behavior.[51] Therefore, the unstated goals of the organization at specific hierarchical levels become quite important. For example, in police organizations the unstated goal is often that of maintaining control or manageability over situations. This, as is quite evident, provides more insight into organizational behavior in general, and police–citizen strains, in particular.

Depending on the intensity and importance of the unstated goals, it is quite feasible for the unstated goals to achieve such importance that they actually displace the stated goals. Etzioni states that when an organization displaces its goal, it in effect substitutes for its legitimate goal or other goals for which it was not created or known to serve.[52] This should not imply that all unstated goals displace the stated goals; nevertheless, the threat or hazard certainly exists.

One short step from goal displacement is cooptation, for as organizational goals are concerned, cooptation would enable the organization to control those who are supposed to control it.[53] This, of course, is a central problem to police–community relations—the structuring of a police organization that is truly responsive to the needs of its clientele.

In studying organizations it becomes quite important to determine whether the organization has a goal, and to what degree this is measured; whether the organization has more than one goal, and if so, whether the goals are compatible or if conflict emerges from the multiple goals.[54]

As Anthony Downs indicates, greater goal consensus reduces the number and intensity of conflicts among organizational members; thus, goal consensus has a crucial impact on the way the organization performs its functions. In a brilliant observation, Downs notes that there does not always exist goal consensus between an organization and its bureaus. As an example, Downs suggests that one reason the U.S. State Department rotates its overseas personnel so frequently is to prevent their increasing attachment to a country's particular culture, with the result that goals are shifted toward those present in that nation.[55] In this case the organization deliberately attempts to impede goal consensus. This same analogy can be extended to police organizations, particularly police-community relation units. One of the more overriding reasons why the police-community relations unit of the San Francisco Police Department was neutralized was because the goals of the unit fully assimilated the culture of the minority community. In the process it alienated itself so completely from the rest of the San Francisco Police Department that the unit commander was eased out of the police department. This implies that a tremendous problem exists for a police department that creates a police-community relations unit. Conflict will be built into the organization simply because the nature of a police-community relations unit implies goal dissension to a majority of the police department's remaining members or bureaus. This, of course, depends upon the proviso that the police-community relations unit is actually meeting the needs of the minority community.

There is very little literature on who comprises the clientele of a police organization. However, the more notable contributions in the police field seem to center around James Q. Wilson, Jerome H. Skolnick, and Albert Reiss, all sociologists. Those within the police field per se have largely ignored the entire question, and this is most unfortunate, especially in view of the policy-making ramifications the client has upon the organization. Perhaps this is part of the police-community relations problem.

Reiss suggests that the police, in fact, usually encounter a dual set of clients in adversary situations. One set is usually willing to accept the police authority and may well have initiated the call for police assistance. The other set is hesitant to accept police authority. Yet this does not mean that they are not a legitimate portion of the organization's clientele.[56] In defense of the police position of ignoring any analyses of serving a clientele, it must be pointed out that the police serve the public collectively rather than distributively. To this degree Reiss and Bordua suggest that the police are a service without clients, and that "given the lack of guidelines either from the public as client or from a specific victim or complainant as client, the police can become in effect their own clients."[57] This affects not only the organization's goals, but also the manner of measuring the efficiency of these goals.

For example, the measure of success of many police departments is correlated to the degree in which it has enforced the law, or its aggregate success as determined by crime rate, arrests, crimes cleared by an arrest, convictions, and value of property recovered. One of the salient points is that the police are free to define their own criteria of success in that they alone determine satisfaction when a case has been cleared by an arrest, separating their criteria for determining success from that of the courts. Naturally, one of the reasons for this is that the police department's arrest figures reflect police success or inefficiency, while the court acquittals would define the police organization's failures. This clearly documents that there is, in fact, no system of administration of criminal justice. It has created many informal adaptations toward an increasing measure of success by the informal institution of bargain plea or negotiated plea justice. However, what is even more ironic from the view of an organization's clientele is that these measures of success create a set of attitudes that define the police as alone in the "war on crime," specifically against all who would transgress society's laws.[58]

Although this suggests that only certain clients are acceptable to the police definition of clientele, there is yet another problem associated with the police definition of its clientele. This problem centers around the organizational assumption that the client's goals and the organization's goals are synonymous. In other words, those clients acceptable to the police organization's definition of "acceptable legitimate clients" might have different goals than those of the organization. This would be another reason for the police taking the posture that they serve the entire public as opposed to specific clients. Furthermore, the idea of impartiality further convinces the police that they have no real clientele, but instead provide services for the benefit of an entire public. Skolnick and Woodworth very provocatively discuss the relations between individual goals and organizational goals and the implicit assumptions made by the police organization:

> Let us suggest the idea of a nonvoluntary or ambivalent client—someone who comes to an organization, who asks for its service, but who lets the organization know (verbally or through demeanor) that he was compelled to come and that he would rather not be served. How will the organization respond? Let us guess the quality of service (measured by whatever goals the organization espouses) will be lowered whenever the organization officials believe (1) that the client did not voluntarily ask for this service in the first place, or (2) that, despite his original intent, the client does not now desire the service.[59]

Another ramification of how the organization's perspective on clients and goals can affect its policies and consequently its police–community relations was pointed out by Egon Bittner, who suggests that patrolmen are more interested in managing situations than in managing people. When this is the case, the goal of maintaining operational control clearly reflects organizational ignorance to its client's needs, or as Bittner suggests:

> The patrolman's conception of this goal places him hierarchically above whomever he approaches and makes him the sole judge of the propriety of the occasion. As he alone is oriented to this goal, and as he seeks to attain it by means of individualized access to persons, those who frustrate him are seen as motivated at best by the desire to "give him a hard time" and at worst by some darkly devious purpose.[60] . . . Peace keeping procedure on skid row consists of these elements. Patrolmen seek to acquire a rich body of knowledge about people by cultivating personal acquaintances with as many residents as possible. They tend to proceed against persons mainly on the basis of culpability. And they are more interested in reducing the aggregate total of troubles in the area than in evaluating individual cases according to merit.[61]

Make no mistake about it, police–community relations will not simply be improved by conceiving of the police as an organization that has a clientele. The goals of the organization should be interpreted in terms of both the client and the organization's benefit. For as Reiss suggests: "What is lacking, it seems, is not only a 'human relations' approach toward Negro citizens, but an approach to both white and Negro citizens that is based on the rights and dignity of individuals and a recognition of them as persons rather than clients."[62]

However, part of the dialogue between minority groups and the police department seems to suggest something more than hoping the police will become more responsive to their needs. Perhaps part of the plea is to be considered as a client of the police organization, a relationship minorities perceive as existing between the majority community and the police department. If there is any validity to this observation, perhaps part of the resistance to police–community relations is, in fact, police resistance to having any clientele imposed upon their organization.

Peter Blau and W. Richard Scott present a most interesting classification of organizations, part of which is based on the question of whether an organization has or does not have a clientele. Their classification is based on the question of who benefits from the operations of the organization. They suggest that four types of organization emerge from the application of this sort of a criterion: (1) "mutual benefit associations," where the prime beneficiary is the membership; (2) "business concerns," where the owners are the beneficiary; (3) "service organizations," where the client group is the prime beneficiary; (4) "commonweal organizations," where the prime beneficiary is the public at large.[63]

Blau and Scott consider the term "service organization" misleading. In their view not all organizations dealing with people provide a service for these people. They cite the case of a prison organization in which they maintain it is hardly correct to describe the function of a prison as furnishing services to its prisoners.[64]

In contrast to service organizations, the authors suggest that commonweal organizations are not really expected to be oriented to the interests of their "clients"; for example, a police department is considered representative of a commonweal organization. Furthermore, in describing commonweal organizations, the authors suggest that "it is not always meaningful to speak of the clients of an organization, since this term refers to both the segment of the public in direct contact with the organization and the segment that benefits from its services."[65]

This analysis seems quite accurate, and it is this accuracy which reflects a portion of the police–community relations problem. For to conceive of the police department as serving the general public at the exclusion of a clientele omits two very important considerations. First, that police, while serving the general public, interact with individuals on a one-to-one basis. They do not have collective interactions with an entire general public. Second, and more important, the issue of the police being more responsive to the needs of citizens tends to become more diffused when the prime beneficiary of the police organization is referred to as the public at large. Therefore, it would be most disturbing for such an analysis to legitimatize that police organizations do not have a clientele, especially when there is emerging a body of literature within modern organization theory which suggests that organizations should define their clientele and orient the goals of the organization so as to benefit the "client" as well as the general public. Illustrative of this philosophy would be a systems approach in which the following types of questions might be focused on: "Who is the client—Who does the system serve, as perhaps one of the more critical issues the organizations will have to address. Secondly, how do we identify the 'client's' goals or values; and how does the organization assess their legitimacy? Thirdly, how does an organization design a measure of performance that would maximize the goals of its clientele."[66]

However, merely identifying a clientele for a police organization would not alone improve the relationship between the police and the community, for there are, unfortunately, bureaucratic mechanisms for neutralizing any such clientele. Blau suggests that there are, in fact, bureaucratic constraints that limit organizational service to its clients.[67]

For example, unless there is something more than a superficial attempt to relate client characteristics to the organizational structure of a police department, there will be little indication of the organization's fully accepting its clientele. Equally compelling will be the necessity to modify the bureaucratic expectations that the organization's clientele be dealt with impersonally. Such administrators require that clients be treated as cases, and that officials disregard all personal considerations and maintain complete emotional detachment.[68] This modification of impartiality, however, comes into conflict with the police ethic that police officers remain the impartial arbitrators of justice. However, involvement can be created to indicate that police officers are interested in the client as a person, not as a means for abusing or taking advantage of any set of circumstances. In short, police organizations do not necessarily have to address the issue of impartiality at the extreme ends of the continuum.

Another point that will have to be addressed is that of destroying or removing the anticlient norms existing within a police organization. Ridiculing clients within various work groups is practiced to legitimatize inconsiderate treatment of clients. This is, of course, a practice inherent in many organizations; it is not peculiar to the police system.[69] Blau and Scott suggest that the norm might manifest itself as follows:

> The laughter elicited by a story about a client constituted social evidence that his behavior was ludicrous or incongruous, thus placing the blame for the client's troubles on his own shoulders and relieving the official from having to mitigate these difficulties; it conveyed the message, 'Nobody could have helped such an impossible person.' This practice is analogous to that of teachers who tell one another jokes about the 'ridiculous' answers students give on examinations, thereby eliciting laughter that absolves them from feeling guilty for not having taught their students better. Joking about clients not only relieved tensions created by the work situation but also strengthened group cohesiveness by uniting its members in laughing together. Simultaneously, however, the practice of ridiculing clients established and perpetuated anticlient norms in the work group legitimating inconsiderate treatment of clients.[70]

To a certain degree this process is functional in terms of relieving tensions, especially within a police organization. However, the real danger is present in its establishment of anticlient norms.

Organizations can also neutralize their clientele by allowing organizational policy to become the prevailing criteria for decisions; thus, the organizational policy becomes the organizational goal, and the client's needs are made to fit the organizational policy.[71] This might well be another leverage point for which police personnel rationalize police resistance to police–community relations.

Organizations can also limit their service to their clientele by a process of cooptation. Etzioni suggests that this usually occurs in the communication flow of an organization to its clientele:

> Co-optation is often used in order to create a semblance of communication from clients to those in control, without actually providing for effective communication. . . . It not only fails to co-optate the consumer, but blocks the expression of his needs. Simulated co-optation suggests that the communication problem has been solved, whereas actually it only conceals the need for real communication and influence.[72]

The application of cooptation to a police–community relations unit is a very real threat, in that the creation of the unit appears to establish communication with various groups in the community. However, the quality of this communication and whether it will actually address the needs of the community group is of less importance. In interviewing police officers about the desirability of police–community relations units, occasionally a "real hard line policeman" favors the creation of such units. However, upon further discussion, the reason for such approval often results from the fact that the individual really is approving of cooptation and not the unit itself or the philosophy behind the unit. Fortunately, this is the exceptional case, because most police officers are honest and direct enough not to conceal their resistance. Therefore, resistance is again functional in terms of not creating larger, more disguised problems through cooptation.

Other factors that definitely limit an organization's service to its clientele, although not emerging from bureaucratic constraints, might be as simple as organizational members not being prepared to meet their clientele. For example, police training is more oriented to dealing with criminals than it is to the common interactions involved with citizen requests for noncriminal services. A form of reality shock for rookies is to encounter so many situations of a civil nature, where police enforcement of the law is both ambiguous and undesirable. Just as social workers experience reality shock in hoping to be of service to a clientele, only to find themselves resented by that clientele, the police experience the same phenomenon. However, the police dilemma results more from being taught how and when to enforce the law, and not being provided with situations in which it is advisable not to invoke the legal process. Thus, officers are really not prepared for coping with their own reactions to the sympathy-evoking plight of various "clients" or citizens they encounter.[73]

The untutored response to the tensions produced by these experiences is resolved differently by social workers and police personnel. The way the police resolve this frustration has a profound impact on police–community relations. First of all, social workers respond to this frustration by either becoming more emotionally involved with the client, leaving the agency, or losing concern for the welfare of the client.[74] Police officers' response is limited because the police ethic of impartiality requires no emotional involvement with clients. Therefore, the only remaining alternative is to have less welfare for their clients or simply to become more calloused or hardened to the citizen's state of affairs. Needless to say, this is not the sort of situation that improves police–community relations. Therefore, until substantial structural change is achieved within police organizations, specifically in terms of services provided to the community, police–community relation strains may be intensified by demanding that police become more responsive to the needs of their clientele. The police are aware of these needs. They are not, however, organizationally structured to fulfill these needs.

Another consequence arising out of not sufficiently being prepared to meet one's clientele is simply the fact that the police cannot appreciate fully or be sensitive to the role behaviors of various clientele.[75] Perhaps personnel in such jobs cannot really appreciate their own roles or fully understand them, until they can conceptualize and appreciate the roles of their clients.

Finally, one of the cold, hard facts about organizational limitations on clientele servicing is probably best described by Etzioni in the following passage:

> Contact with clients is usually relatively concentrated on the lower levels of the organization; those who are successful in their relations with clients may find it more difficult to attain promotion than those who prepare themselves for the next, less client-oriented stage by being more organization than client minded. To sum up: To be overly client oriented and to transmit client's demands upward is a relatively unrewarding experience in many organizations.[76]

In attempting to account for how and why any organization could divorce itself so completely from the concept of providing service to a clientele, C. West Churchman's comments are appropriate: "We have developed such elaborate ways of doing things and at the same time have developed no way of justifying any of the things we do."[77]

More specifically, until police organizations come to terms with the fact that they do have a clientele, they will be faced with the same problems that perplex the idealist and long-range planner.

> One cannot perfect the operations of one component of the system without looking at the way in which this effectiveness is accomplished and the way in which it reacts with other parts of the system. Thus many realists become very puzzled and annoyed by what they consider the irrationalities of their social world, crime, slums, discrimination, cheating in social welfare; they wish to clear up the mess wherever they find it. But in their attempts to "improve things" they create disturbances in other parts of the system, disturbances that come back on them and forestall their improvements.[78]

Until police organizations not only acknowledge that they have a clientele, but also entertain the goals and values of their clientele, police–community relations will have little chance of appreciably improving. As far as police–community relations programming is concerned, how can any organization measure "improvements" or "disturbances" unless it conceives of the organization as providing services to something a little more specific than the public at large.

Summary

Decisions with respect to professionalizing police organizations to improve police–community relations should not be taken without considering those public administration principles which suggest that "efficiency" or "management" can rarely be "improved" without some effect or relationship to the goals of the organization. Or as James Q. Wilson states: "It is not possible—as we should have known all along—simply to make a police force 'better.'" These questions must first be answered: 'Better for what?' and 'Better for whom?' "[79]

End Notes

[1] Robert Presthus, *The Organizational Society: An Analysis and a Theory* (New York: Random House, 1962), p. 27.

[2] William T. Greenwood, *Management and Organizational Behavior Theories: An Interdisciplinary Approach* (Chicago: South-Western, 1965), p. 437.

[3] Harold Koontz and Cyril O'Donnell, *Management: A Book of Readings,* 2nd ed. (New York: McGraw-Hill, 1964), p. 174. Used with permission of McGraw-Hill Book Co.

[4] Ibid., pp. 381–82.

[5] Ibid., pp. 382–83.

[6] Ibid., pp. 384–85.

[7] Ibid., p. 385.

[8] Frederick C. Mosher, ed., *Governmental Reorganizations: Cases and Commentary* (New York: Bobbs-Merrill, 1967), pp. 494–96.

[9] Ray Johns, *Confronting Organizational Change* (New York: Association Press, 1963), p. 20.

[10] Ibid., pp. 61–62.

[11] Patrick H. Irwin and Frank W. Langham, "The Change Seekers," *Harvard Business Review,* 44, no. 1 (1966), 81–82.

[12] Harold J. Leavitt, "Applied Organizational Change in Industry: Structural Technological and Humanistic Approaches," in *Handbook of Organizations,* ed. James G. March (Chicago: Rand McNally, 1965), p. 1144.

[13] Louis B. Barnes, "Approaches to Organizational Change," in *The Planning of Change,* 2nd ed., ed. Warren G. Bennis, Kenneth D. Benne, and Robert Chin (New York: Holt, Rinehart and Winston, 1969), p. 80.

[14] Leavitt, "Applied Organizational Change," p. 1151.

[15] Ibid., p. 1146.

[16] Barnes, "Approaches to Change," pp. 82–83.

[17] Ronald Lippitt, Jeanne Watson, and Bruce Westley, *The Dynamics of Planned Change* (New York: Harcourt Brace, Jovanovich, 1958), pp. 71–72.

[18]Ibid., p. 83.

[19]Ibid., p. 131.

[20]Ibid., pp. 83-84.

[21]Ibid.

[22]Ibid.

[23]Ibid., p. 85.

[24]Ibid., p. 23.

[25]Ibid., p. 76.

[26]Ibid., p. 77.

[27]Ibid., p. 82.

[28]Ibid., p. 181.

[29]Johns, *Organizational Change,* p. 117.

[30]Ibid.

[31]Floyd C. Mann and Franklin W. Neff, *Managing Major Change in Organizations* (Ann Arbor, Mich.: Foundation for Research of Human Behavior, 1961), p. 23.

[32]Johns, *Organizational Change,* p. 117.

[33]Mann and Neff, *Managing Change,* p. 170.

[34]Goodwin Watson, "Resistance to Change," in *The Planning of Change,* 2nd ed., eds. Warren G. Bennis, Kenneth D. Benne, and Robert Chin (New York: Holt, Rinehart and Winston, 1969), p. 493.

[35]John M. Pfiffner and Frank P. Sherwood, *Administrative Organization* (Englewood Cliffs, N.J.: Prentice Hall, 1960), p. 266.

[36]Lester Coch and John R. P. French, Jr., "Overcoming Resistance to Change," in *Group Dynamics: Research and Theory,* ed. Darwin Cartwright and Alvin Zander (Evanston, Ill.: Row, Peterson, 1953), p. 263.

[37]Edward M. Bruner, "Resistance to Change: Cultural Transmission and Cultural Change," in *Personality and Social Systems,* ed. Neil J. Smelser and William T. Smelser (New York: Wiley, 1963), p. 483.

[38]William H. Starbuck, "Organizational Growth and Development," in *Handbook of Organizations,* ed. James G. March (Chicago: Rand McNally, 1965), p. 493.

[39]Johns, *Organizational Change,* p. 83.

[40]Lippitt, Watson, and Westley, *Dynamics of Change,* p. 88.

[41]Ibid., p. 86.

[42]Johns, *Organizational Change,* p. 118.

[43]Leavitt, *Managerial Psychology: An Introduction to Individuals, Pairs and Groups in Organizations* (Chicago: The University of Chicago Press, Second Edition, Revised, 1965), p. 378.

[44]Donald R. Cressey, "Sources of Resistance to the Use of Offenders and Ex-offenders in the Correctional Process," in *Offenders as a Correctional Manpower Resource* (Washington, D.C.: Joint Commission on Correctional Manpower and Training, 1968), p. 35.

[45]Jameson W. Doig, "A Symposium: The Police in a Democratic Society," *Public Administration Review,* 28 (September-October 1968), 393-94.

[46]Richard M. Cyert and Kenneth R. MacCrimmon, "Organizations," in *The Handbook of Social Psychology,* 2nd ed., vol. 1, ed. Gardner Lindzey and Elliot Aronson

(Menlo Park, Calif.: Addison-Wesley, 1968), p. 569. © 1968 Addison-Wesley Publishing Co., Inc. Reprinted with permission.

[47]Amitai Etzioni, *Modern Organizations* (Englewood Cliffs, N.J.: Prentice-Hall, 1964), pp. 5-6.

[48]Cyert and MacCrimmon, "Organizations," p. 569.

[49]Ibid., p. 569.

[50]Ibid., p. 570.

[51]Ibid., pp. 570-71.

[52]Etzioni, *Modern Organizations,* p. 10.

[53]Amitai Etzioni, *Complex Organizations: A Sociological Reader* (New York: Holt, Rinehart and Winston, 1961), p. 144.

[54]Darwin Cartwright and Alvin Zander, eds., *Group Dynamics Research and Theory* (Evanston, Ill.: Row, Peterson, 1953), pp. 306-7.

[55]Anthony Downs, *Inside Bureaucracy* (Boston: Little, Brown, 1967), pp. 223-25.

[56]University of Michigan, *Studies in Crime and Law Enforcement in Major Metropolitan Areas,* vol. 2, report of a research study submitted to the President's Commission on Law Enforcement and the Administration of Justice (Washington, D.C.: U.S. Government Printing Office, 1967), p. 11.

[57]Albert J. Reiss and David J. Bordua, "Environment and Organization: A Perspective on the Police," in *The Police: Six Sociological Essays,* ed. David J. Bordua (New York: Wiley, 1967), p. 30.

[58]Ibid., pp. 34-36.

[59]Jerome K. Skolnick and J. Richard Woodworth, "Bureaucracy Information and Social Control," in Bordua, ed., *The Police,* p. 127.

[60]Egon Bittner, "The Police on Skid Row: A Study of Peace-Keeping," *American Sociological Review,* 32 (October 1967), 699-715; from p. 708.

[61]Ibid., p. 714.

[62]Albert J. Reiss, "Professionalization of the Police," in *Police and Community Relations: A Sourcebook,* ed. A. F. Brandstatter and Louis A. Radelet (Encino, Calif.: Glencoe Press, 1968), p. 220.

[63]Peter M. Blau and W. Richard Scott, *Formal Organizations: A Comparative Approach* (San Francisco: Chandler, 1962), pp. 43-43.

[64]Ibid., p. 41.

[65]Ibid., p. 54.

[66]C. West Churchman, *The Systems Approach* (New York: Delta, 1968), pp. 179-84.

[67]Peter M. Blau, "Orientation towards Clients in a Public Welfare Agency," *Administrative Science Quarterly,* 5 (December 1960), p. 342.

[68]Ibid., p. 33.

[69]An excellent account of anticlient norms and their functional value can be found in Blau, "Orientation towards Clients," pp. 341-61.

[70]Blau and Scott, *Formal Organizations,* pp. 84-85.

[71]Etzioni, *Modern Organizations,* p. 12.

[72]Ibid., p. 101.

[73]Blau, "Orientation towards Clients," p. 361.

[74]Ibid.

[75]Howard M. Vollmer and Donald L. Mills, eds., *Professionalization* (Englewood Cliffs, N.J.: Prentice-Hall, 1966), p. 199.

[76]Etzioni, *Modern Organizations,* p. 100.

[77]C. West Churchman, *Prediction and Optimal Decision: Philosophical Issues of a Science of Values* (Englewood Cliffs, N.J.: Prentice-Hall, 1961), p. 1.

[78]C. West Churchman, *Challenge to Reason* (New York: McGraw-Hill, 1968), p. 183.

[79]James Q. Wilson, "The Police and the Delinquent in Two Cities," in *Controlling Delinquents,* ed. Stanton Wheeler (New York: Wiley, Inc.), 1968.

2

THE POLICE
AND THEIR
COMMUNITY
RELATIONSHIP

CHAPTER
SIX

HISTORY OF POLICE-
COMMUNITY RELATIONS
PROGRAMS

INTRODUCTION: A LEGACY OF NEGLECT

Conflicts between the police and the public are not new to the American scene. Quite to the contrary, it is safe to say that the problems of police–community relationships began even before this country established its first full-time salaried police force. In 1815, for example, a prominent politician in Boston, writing on the subject of police forces, expressed a widespread sentiment when he stated: "If there ever comes a time when Americans have to have in their cities a paid professional police force, that will be the end of freedom and democracy as we know it."[1]

Police forces, as we know them today, were not established in America until around 1840. Until that time, law enforcement was considered to be a responsibility of the total community. This posture was a carryover from our European heritage, even though our country experienced much more violence than that in European countries. When police departments were established in America, they were objects of disrespect and held in low esteem. A prevailing attitude that accompanied the development of the American police system was that it was a foreign invention, imported from abroad. To some it was considered to be un-American, and to most it was given low social status.[2]

The first police forces established in the mid-1800s were plagued with many problems, many of which still confront the police of the twentieth century.[3] They were frequently the scapegoat for unrelated social problems. The salaries were low; consequently, the pioneering police forces were unable to attract a high caliber of officer. They were not respected, and often with good reason, since they were far from being successful. A respected historian viewed the emergence of American policing in retrospect and concluded that "the aim of the police departments was merely to keep a city superficially clean and to keep everything quiet. . . ."[4]

Many of the problems that confronted these earlier police forces have been attributed to political control. In that area of concern, Bruce Smith, after studying police systems in the United States, concluded that "political manipulation and law enforcement seem always to have been closely associated with the United States."[5] The political influence exercised by the colonial sheriff obviously carried over into the metropolitan areas. This resulted in the police becoming "identified with the corruption and degradation of the city politics and local government of that period."[6]

Several major reform movements occurred that were designed to resolve the problems associated with nineteenth-century policing. The first such attempt was the creation of police administrative boards. The objective of this move was to remove politics from policing. Thus, police administrative boards were given the responsibilities formerly held by mayors and/or city councils to appoint police administrators and manage the affairs of the police. Unfamiliar with police matters, these boards proved to be relatively unsuccessful in bringing about desired changes in American policing.[7]

At the end of the nineteenth century, state legislatures addressed their attention to the police. Not satisfied with the results of local control of the police, the state legislatures passed legislation that allowed the state to appoint police administrators. Under that arrangement, the cities continued to pay for police services and often the policies developed by the state public administrators were out of harmony with the local communities. As a result, the reform met with little success. Consequently, at the start of the twentieth century, local governments regained control over the police.

The emergence of the American industrial revolution further complicated the role of the police in society. Indeed, the transition of our nation from a rural agrarian society to a predominantly urban industrialized one brought along with it new, serious, and challenging problems for the police—many of which they were ill-equipped to handle. Poorly trained and suffering from the lack of a defined sense of mission and direction, the police entered the twentieth century still occupying a low status in the eyes of the general public.[8]

Suffering from the phenomenon of benign neglect, the development of the police in America was relatively uneventful during the first part of the 1900s. The problems continued to exist, and indeed were complicated by the rapid social change that was occurring. Consequently, not only did the public continue to hold the police in low esteem, but the police themselves maintained a low regard for their positions.

Probably the most noteworthy improvement in American policing was associated with the implementation of civil service. Civil service served the purpose of alleviating many of the problems associated with political interference. The second major improvement occurred in the 1950s and 1960s when police agencies greatly expanded their training programs.

RESISTANCE TO CHANGE

As seen in preceding chapters, policing in America has always been fraught with problems. Community acceptance, a most necessary ingredient to successful law enforcement, has been absent. Events of the 1900s, characterized by a rapid increase in the crime rate, civil disorder, and political campaigns based upon a "law and order" platform, focused unprecedented attention on the police.

During the 1960s, a number of studies were conducted which showed that a majority of the public had a relatively high opinion of the police.[9] The fact that the majority of the general public expressed a high opinion of the police even surprised many police officers. For example, in a national survey conducted for the President's Crime Commission (1966) by the National Opinion Research Center (NORC), only 8 percent indicated that they thought the police were doing a poor job of enforcing the law.[10]

Taken alone, the results of these studies would tend to give the impression that there was no real crisis in police–community relations. This obviously was not the case, and is evident by the response of nonwhites, young people, and the poor to questions posed about law enforcement. The NORC survey clearly pointed out that minorities, particularly blacks, harbored more negative attitudes toward the police than did whites. When responding to the question of whether the police provide protection to citizens, minorities gave a "very good" response only half as often as whites. Similarly, minorities gave a "not so good" rating twice as often as whites. The responses included both men and women, as well as all income levels, which indicated that the difference in attitudes was not just a reflection of lower socioeconomic levels for nonwhites.[11]

Former police commissioner George Edwards clearly described this situation when he pointed out: "The relationship between the police and minority groups in big city ghettos is one of the sorest spots in American life today."[12] Edwards cited two facts to support this statement. First, he felt that the civil rights movement had increased the level of political awareness among blacks, and they were no longer willing to tolerate the indignities inflicted upon them by the police. Second, he pointed out that every time illegal violence was employed against blacks, it had the latent effect of increasing animosity against police officers everywhere.[13]

Edwards' position was supported by the National Advisory Commission on Civil Disorders when it reported:

> The abrasive relationship between the police and minority communities has been a major—and explosive—source of grievance, tension, and disorder. The blame *must* be shared by the total society.... The police are faced with demands for increased protection and service in the ghetto. Yet the aggressive patrol practices, though necessary to meet these demands, themselves create tension and hostility.[14]

In addition to the increasing polarity between the police and the black community, friction also existed between the police and the youth.[15] For example, in a 1965 Gallup poll, 57 percent of the respondents in the 20–29 years age bracket said they had a great deal of respect for the police; 31 percent some respect; 8 percent hardly any; and 4 percent did not know.[16]

The third critical area in police–community relations centered around the relationship between the police and the poor. Two polls conducted in the mid-1960s showed that low-income people generally had less respect and less favorable attitudes toward the police than did more affluent citizens.[17]

The situation had developed whereby certain subcultural groups within the society had increasing disrespect for the police. This led James Q. Wilson to conclude: "The fact that the police can no longer take for granted that non-criminal citizens are also non-hostile citizens may be the most important problems which even the technically proficient department must face."[18]

There was a general tendency to say that the aforementioned groups (minority, youth, and the poor) were estranged or alienated from the social norms because they did not conform to the opinions held by the general community. At the same time, it was suggested that this estrangement, this alienation, should be regarded in a quite different way.[19]

> It will profit us ... to examine the agencies, institutions, and organizations to which we subscribe, and to apply the notion, which we are applying to individuals, to the institutions themselves. I think it might be properly suggested that even as we speak of persons as being estranged and alienated from the conventions and norms of society and from its institutions, we may be confronted in the current day by a crisis of these same institutions. For it can be seen that *the institutions are not necessarily as one with the changing social scene.* They do not reflect in themselves the trends, and so there are, indeed, stresses in education. There are stresses in welfare. There are stresses in law enforcement. It is these crises and the dilemma of our traditional services which need to be made explicit.[20]

In analyzing the increasing polarity between the police and the public, it is not sufficient for the student of criminal justice to merely focus upon the attitudes of the public toward the police. One of the first sociological studies done on the police describes a close-knit group set apart from and at odds with the public:

[The policeman] regards the public as his enemy, feels his occupation to be in conflict with the community, and regards himself as a pariah. This experience and these feelings give rise to a collective emphasis on secrecy, an attempt to coerce respect from the public, and a belief that almost any means are legitimate in completing an important arrest.[21]

This feeling of being a pariah (on the part of the police) was studied by Michael Banton in his observation of five police departments in Scotland and the United States.[22] He found, for example, that there was a relatively greater isolation of the British police than of the American police.[23]

Even so, the police in America do feel isolated from the larger society. Consequently, they develop a close group solidarity which is characterized by a strong "we versus they" attitude.[24] The police complaints against the public evolve around physical and verbal assaults on officers, interference and defiance with arrest procedures, many unwarranted charges of police brutality and other misconduct, lack of respect, public apathy, and noncooperation.[25]

The demands made in the 1950s and early 1960s for the establishment of civilian review boards to handle citizen complaints against the police added emphasis to the police feeling of alienation from the public.[26] The police reaction to such demands were both emotional and thoughtful. A statement made by chief of police Edward M. Davis of the Los Angeles Police Department, for example, captured the support of the authors of a leading law enforcement textbook.[27] Davis took the position that the right to discipline carries with it the power to control the conduct, actions, and attitudes of the employer of an organization. For that reason, he saw discipline as a management tool and to remove this tool from management strips it of an essential power needed to run the organization.[28]

In discussing the grievances of citizens toward the police, the President's Crime Commission did not recommend the "establishment of civilian review boards in jurisdictions where they do not exist, solely to review police conduct."[29] The Commission did, however, state the need for procedures to be established to handle individual grievances against any governmental official and recommended that "every jurisdiction should provide adequate procedures for full and fair processing of all citizen grievances and complaints about conduct of any public officer or employee."[30]

This recommendation paralleled the recent American interest in the ombudsman concept as a means of citizen redress for grievances against governmental abuses.[31] Stanley V. Anderson summarized the ombudsman concept as follows:

> The Ombudsman is a grievance commissioner appointed by Parliament to investigate citizens' complaints of administrative abuse. Anyone may complain, but the Ombudsman has complete discretion in deciding which cases to probe, including those which he initiates spontaneously. At the investigation, the Ombudsman may express an opinion, privately or publicly, as to the propriety of the governmental action. Following exposure, agents may change the challenged action against the erring official. The Ombudsman has no power, normally, to compel such a response. For the effectuation of his recommendations, he must rely on the persuasiveness of his views, the pressure of public opinion.[32]

The obvious advantage of the ombudsman concept is that it does not single out one agency (e.g., the police); rather, it covers all governmental agencies. Even so, police officials have opposed the idea with force equal to their opposition to the civilian review board. Thomas J. Cahill, ex-chief of the San Francisco Police Department, vocally opposed any form of outside review, including the ombudsman concept. He felt that although the ombudsman concept included other agencies, it did not change the picture. Therefore, as a member of the President's Crime Commission, Cahill strongly opposed any form of outside review of the police.[33]

The demands for outside review of the police may very well be defined as a case of "the chickens coming home to roost."[34] Numerous studies, surveys, and reports have revealed many deficiencies in the police establishment. This is shown by the 1931 Wickersham Report, the 1961 United States Commission on Civil Rights Report, the 1967 Report on the President's Commission on Law Enforcement and Administration of Justice, and the 1968 Report of the National Advisory Commission on Civil Disorders. According to A. C. Germann, a leading criminologist, these reports all "point to the crude deficiencies that continue within the American police service. Ongoing outrages of inefficient, ineffective, illegal, immoral, noncompassionate, and irrational policing continue to blight the American civil landscape."[35]

Even though the President's Crime Commission strongly pointed out the need for changes and experimentation in law enforcement, police administrators were slow to accept this need. As a matter of fact, there is strong evidence to indicate that many police administrators really do not want change. Thomas Reddin, former chief of the Los Angeles Police Department, writing in the *Police Chief,* accused law enforcement of "stifling creativity and encouraging conformity." He advocated the position that many police administrators attribute their success to their ability to maintain the status quo and concluded that to the extent conformity is the doctrine of an organization, stagnation and mediocrity prevail.[36]

Arthur Niederhoffer, policeman turned sociologist, also addressed what he termed the "conformity syndrome." According to Niederhoffer, many police administrators master the promotional system and upon doing so became a part of the bureaucracy by being conquered by it. In doing so, they adopt a conservative policy and a "don't rock the boat" posture.[37]

The current social revolution which is occurring in society is presenting new problems for the police. Joseph Lohman pointed out the importance of seeing the problems as they are posed in context:

> The contemporary American revolution involves three factors: the explosive rate of population increase; the doctrine of civil rights, an ideological force which has no precedent in recent history; the impact of technology which is producing a shape of things for which we have not bargained and which is profoundly affecting many individuals. These tremendous changes are more than facts in themselves—they are the condition for the creation of a new pattern of human relations in this country.[38]

Many of the established institutions, particularly the police, find it difficult to understand this new pattern. Generally, the police relationships are traditionally structured and are disposed to maintain the traditional structure. Consequently, as the problems of our urban society became even more complex, the traditional policing of the public became less capable of dealing with those problems. Ill equipped to relate positively to contemporary problems, the police have the tendency to react vindictively toward those elements of society they view as being responsible for this plight.[39]

The police cry of "disrespect for law and order" stems from their failure to understand the new dimension of community life. Their attempt to maintain the status quo by repressive measures will not stop the social and political changes from occurring.

> Just as police are not responsible for programs to change social mores, neither are they justified in taking steps to prevent such change. *Police authority derives only from the law and not from social mores.* Police are required to enforce the law but are not authorized to enforce social mores.[40]

James Q. Wilson, who has made some valuable contributions to the literature on the police, aptly summarizes the contemporary law enforcement crisis:

> The criticisms directed at the police are well-known and often sound, but conditions giving rise to these criticisms are frequently not well understood by the critic. For example, police departments are frequently charged with hiring unqualified personnel, suppressing or manipulating crime reports, con-

doning the use of improper or illegal procedures, using patrol techniques that create tensions and irritation among the citizens, and either over-reacting (using too much force too quickly) or under-reacting (ignoring dangerous situations until it is too late) in the face of incipient disorder. All of these criticisms are true to some extent, though the extent of the deficiencies is often exaggerated. But let us concede for the moment that they are all true. Why are they true?

Explanations vary, but commonly they are some variation on the "bad men" theme. Unqualified, unintelligent, rude, brutal, intolerant, or insensitive men, so this theory goes, find their way (or are selectively recruited into) police work where they express their prejudices and crudeness under color of the law. Though a few of the commanding officers of the department may try to improve matters, on the whole they are ineffective. At best they invent paper palliatives—empty departmental directives, superficial community relations programs, one-sided internal disciplinary units—which do little more than offer a chance for issuing favorable, but misleading, publicity statements about the "new look." And at worst, the theory continues, such administrators exacerbate tensions by encouraging, in the name of efficiency of anticrime strategies, various techniques, such as aggressive preventive patrol, that lead to the harassment of innocent citizens. The solution for these problems is clearly to hire "better men"—college students, Negroes, men who can pass tests that weed out "authoritarian" personalities, and the like. And those on the force should attend universities, go through sensitivity training, and apply for grants to develop "meaningful" community relations programs.

Some critics go even further. Not only do the police fail to do the right thing, they systematically do the wrong thing. Not only do the police fail to prevent crime, *the police actually cause crime.* Not only do the police fail to handle riots properly, *the police cause riots.* Presumably, things might improve if we had no police at all, but since even the strongest critics usually recognize the need for the police under some circumstances, they are willing to permit the police to function provided that they are under "community control"—controlled, that is, by the neighborhoods (especially Negro neighborhoods) where they operate. If police departments are at best a necessary evil, filled with inept or intolerant men exploiting the fact that they are necessary, then the solution to the problem of abuse is to put the police under the strictest and closest control of those whose activities they are supposed to regulate.[41]

The question of community control, which is discussed in Chapter 11, is similar to the question of civilian review boards, in that it has broader implications than the issues themselves tend to point out. Consequently, by polarizing on the symptoms of the illness, the underlying causes are neglected. The crisis of law enforcement is really no different from the crisis in other social institutions. In fact, it might very well be only a reflection of what occurs in the larger society. Since the police are produced by the same social machinery that produces everyone else in a society, it is logical to assume that the problems of the total society will be manifested in its policing function. The general "revolt of the clients," which is evident in education and welfare, is also evident in law enforcement. The problems of society, as reflected in the problems of police and community relations, were recognized by Alexis de Tocqueville in his implicit warning that repressive forces will not provide a viable solution to the problems.

> If ever the free institutions of America are destroyed, that event may be attributed to the omnipotence of the majority, which may at some future time urge the minorities to desperation and oblige them to have recourse to physical force. Anarchy will then be the result but it will have been brought about by despotism. James Madison, in the *Federalist,* states that it is of great importance in a republic, not only to guard the society against the oppression of its rules, but to guard one part of the society against the injustice of the other part.[42]

POLICE-COMMUNITY RELATIONS PROGRAMMING

The genesis of police–community relations as an organized and structured police function is of recent origin. Nevertheless, the broad philosophy of police–community relations has a long history, reverting back as far as our law enforcement precedent in England. Although it is impossible to pinpoint an exact date in history as the beginning of police–community relations in the United States, we can safely say that the police became increasingly interested in race relations during World War I. It was during that period of history that the massive black migration from the South to the North began.

In 1931, the National Commission on Law Observance and Enforcement released its report, which at that time was the most comprehensive study ever done on law enforcement. The Commissioner's *Report on Police* did not deal with the problem of police–community relations as we know it today, but it did refer to immigrants and the foreign-born as they affected the crime problem. The report did, however, stress the importance of recruiting minority-group police officers because of their familiarity with the language, habits, customs, and cultural background of the various ethnic groups.[43]

In its conclusion, the Commission recommended that "a crime prevention unit should be established if circumstances warrant this action and qualified women police should be engaged to handle juvenile delinquents and women's cases."[44] The Commission's concept of crime prevention did not envision the creation of police–community relations units as a method of preventing crime. Rather, it discussed the creation of crime prevention units for predelinquent youths or juvenile delinquents to prevent them from becoming adult criminals.

In 1940, Bruce Smith, in his study of American policing, recognized the importance of police–community relations. Although he did not label it as such, he pointed out a principle which is still prevalent today:

> It is not courtesy, but civility that our uniformed forces should cultivate, while the actual extent of civil rights violations and third degree practices is largely irrelevant so long as they do exist and are popularly believed to be both frequent and general. That belief will persist until the full, equal, and lawful enforcement of the law is freely accepted by police as their standard of performance and is consistently applied, year in and year out, as a matter of corps discipline and administrative routine.[45]

Structured programs in the broad context of police–community relations began during World War II. These programs, however, were mainly training programs in human relations. The special police training focused primarily on race relations, racial tension, and the police and minority groups. Such programs had as their objective the development of an understanding of the causes of interracial friction, a better understanding of the groups involved in the struggle for racial justice, and the professionalization of the police in handling racially motivated situations.[46]

Joseph Lohman, late dean of the School of Criminology, University of California at Berkeley, was a pioneer in this field. Lohman wrote one of the first books dealing with this subject, entitled *The Police and Minority Groups*.[47] This was a manual prepared for the Chicago Park District Police Department's Training School. This training manual (published in 1946) concerned itself with the police relationship with minority groups. The intent of the manual was to alert the police to their responsibility for maintaining equal service for all groups at all times.[48] This training program was the first of its type in the nation and concerned itself with:

1. Worldwide, national, state, city, and neighborhood aspects of human relations.
2. Background and condition of racial, nationality, and religious tension.
3. The facts about race.
4. The social situations in which tensions arise (e.g., discrimination in employment, substandard housing, segregation, and discrimination in recreation and social activities).
5. The role of the police officer in dealing with tensions (e.g., crowd and mob behavior, rumor, etc.).
6. The law and administrative controls as they affect human relations.

Two years previous to the publishing of Lohman's book (1944), the International Association of Chiefs of Police published a pamphlet entitled, "The Police and Minority Groups."[49] This pamphlet was prepared by J. E. Weckler of the American Council on Race Relations in Chicago, and Theo E. Hall, Chief of Police, Wilmette, Illinois. The pamphlet was designed as "a program to prevent disorder and to improve relations between different racial, religious and national groups." It included a discussion of the 1943 Detroit riots in which 35 people were killed, the Harlem riot, and the Pachuco riots in Los Angeles. The pamphlet concerned itself primarily with (1) the method of officer conduct to prevent riots, (2) police training in interracial relations, and (3) the police role in preventing riots.

In 1946, the California Department of Justice, under attorney general Robert Kenny, published a police training pamphlet entitled, "A Guide to Race Relations for Police Officers,"[50] which was prepared by David McEntire and Robert Powers of the American Council on Race Relations. The preface of this pamphlet indicated that it was designed to "offer peace officers, for the first time, a concrete practical guide for training in the vitally important field of race relations or, more accurately, the racial aspects of human relations." Also during the same year, a pamphlet was published by Joseph T. Kluchesky dealing with "Police Action on Minority Problems."[51]

In 1949, the first Citizen's Advisory Committee was established in San Jose, California, by J. R. Blackmore. That department's "Citizen's Advisory Committee was organized so the police department could have the advantage of the counsel of a distinguished group of citizens informally representing many elements of the community."[52]

During the summer of 1952, while associated with the University of Chicago, Lohman conducted a two-week seminar centered around the theme, "The Police and Racial Tension." This seminar was attended mainly by police training officers representing over 30 police departments.[53]

During the Korean conflict in the 1950s, attorney general of California Edmond G. Brown published a pamphlet entitled, "Guide to Race Relations for Peace Officers."[54] The primary concern of this pamphlet was attacks on minority-group members by the white community.

In 1953, G. D. Gourley did an extensive survey of the public attitude toward the police in Los Angeles. The results of his study were published in the book entitled *Police and the Public.*[55]

The 1954 Supreme Court decision on school desegregation and the events leading up to that decision "served as an additional impetus, for many a police agency to begin stirring in its peace-keeping responsibility."[56] For example, in April of that year, police chiefs from 27 major cities attended a conference in Philadelphia together with representatives from professional human relations agencies to consider "the potential for violence which could result from that decision."[57]

Most of the previously mentioned training programs had one thing in common: they were programs geared for the police only, often taught by the police, tactically oriented, and concerned exclusively with racial tension. None of the training programs involved the community and none attempted to work on socioeconomic problems confronting the community. The programs did not attempt, therefore, to establish communication between the police and the community.

The National Conference of Christians and Jews (NCCJ) has been involved in a program of police–community relations since 1947. NCCJ was established in 1928 by a group of religiously motivated laymen who were concerned with the bigotry and hatred exhibited during the 1928 campaign of Alfred E. Smith. This group formed a civic organization to work through educational channels to combat bigotry, ignorance, and misunderstanding. Their program was centered around five basic areas: (1) interreligious affairs, (2) education, (3) equal job opportunities, (4) parent–youth training programs, and (5) police–community relations.

In 1947, NCCJ established a nationwide program in police–community relations which involved specialized workshops and institutes, publication of papers on basic issues in law enforcement, consultative services for police departments, and human relations training for citizens and the police through their 75 regional offices.

In 1955, NCCJ was instrumental in establishing the National Institute on Police and Community Relations, which continues to meet annually at Michigan State University. This institute convenes for a one-week period, bringing together citizens and police to study the problems relating to police and community relations. The 3,000 graduates of the school have represented nearly every state in the nation.

In 1961, the School of Police Administration and Public Safety at Michigan State University, under a grant from the Field Foundation, completed a national survey which involved 168 police agencies. The results of that study vividly pointed out the need for a National Center on Police and Community Relations. In July 1965, through a $100,000 grant from the Field Foundation, the National Center on Police and Community Relations was established at Michigan State University as a part of the School of Police Administration and Public Safety in the College of Social Sciences. The functions of the center are listed as follows: (1) undertaking action-related research projects; and (2) preparing, publishing, and circulating reports, manuals, pamphlets, booklets, and other literature in the field of police and community relations.

In 1964, the International Association of Chiefs of Police and the United States Conference of Mayors jointly conducted a national survey on "Police–Community Policies and Practices." The most important aspect of this study was that it revealed the small number of police departments having formalized police–community relations programs. Less than one-third (46) of the responding primary study departments had developed police–community relations programs. Of that number, 37 had specialized police community relations units to administer their programs. An average of three persons were assigned to each of the 37 units.[58]

The survey also revealed that about 40 percent of the reporting departments (cities with 30,000 population and over) still did not offer a training program in human relations. In respect to those departments that were offering human relations training, the survey concluded: "There is wide diversity in the type and quality of training involved."

The passage of the Civil Rights Act of 1964 caused police officials to become concerned with the implications the act had for law enforcement. Consequently, under the auspices of the International Association of Chiefs of Police, over 130 police executives representing all areas of the United States, met in August 1964, at the University of Oklahoma, to discuss the Civil Rights Act of 1964 and its implications for the police.

In mid-1966, the National Center on Police and Community Relations, School of Police Administration and Public Safety, Michigan State University, conducted a multifaceted survey on the police relationship with the community for the President's Commission on Law Enforcement and Administration of Justice. The major recommendations resulting from the survey can be summarized as follows:

- It is recommended that the police place greater emphasis upon the concept of public service as a legitimate goal of their organizations.
- It is recommended that police agencies develop extensive formal, and comprehensive community relations programs.
- It is recommended that every police agency carefully and honestly review and evaluate the existing procedures through which citizens may register complaints. It is further urged that police and other governmental executives adopt all appropriate mechanisms, including external advisory review, to encourage all citizens to offer their criticism of public services.
- It is recommended that the personnel policies and practices of police agencies, and their training programs, be organized with scrupulous attention and sensitivity to community relations.
- It is recommended that police administrators review and assess their current field procedures in light of police and community relations; that they recognize the maintenance of positive community relations as an indispensible means to the accomplishment of their desired organizational goals; and that they employ or disregard such field procedures in full knowledge of the consequences of their action.
- It is recommended that present methods of data collection and presentation, insofar as crime statistics are concerned, be reevaluated and employed in the light of police and community relations considerations.[59]

In October 1966, the School of Criminology, University of California at Berkeley, completed its study for the President's Commission on Law Enforcement and Administration of Justice, which focused on two major cities, San Diego and Philadelphia. This project involved six different research methods and concluded with a number of recommendations designed to improve police–community relations. These recommendations were organized along the three levels of government: federal, state, and local.[60]

In February 1967, the President's Commission on Law Enforcement and Administration of Justice released its report, which contained some sweeping recommendations for the improvement of police–community relations. In this area, the Commission recommended:

- Police departments in all large communities should have community-relations machinery consisting of a headquarters unit that plans and supervises the department's community-relations program. It should also have precinct units, responsible to the precinct commander, that carry out the programs. Community relations must be both a staff and a line function. Such machinery is a matter of the greatest importance in any community that has a substantial minority population.
- In each precinct in a minority-group neighborhood there should be a citizen's advisory committee that meets regularly with police officials to work out solutions to problems of conflict between the police and the community. It is crucial that the committees be broadly representative of the community as a whole, including those elements who are critical or aggrieved.
- It should be a high priority objective of all departments in communities with a substantial minority population to recruit minority-group officers, and to deploy and promote them fairly. Every officer in such departments should receive thorough grounding in community relations subjects. His performance in the field of community relations should be periodically reviewed and evaluated.
- Every jurisdiction should provide adequate procedures for full and fair processing of all citizens grievances and complaints about the conduct of any public officer or employee.[61]

The reports, studies, surveys, and analyses done by the Crime Commission succeed the Wickersham Report as being the most monumental study ever done on the police. The Commission's final report, *The Challenge of Crime in a Free Society*,[62] together with the Commission's *Task Force Reports,* should occupy a valued position in every police officer's professional library.

On March 1, 1968, the National Advisory Commission on Civil Disorders released its report on a study of the causative factors behind the various civil disturbances that swept the nation during the mid-1960s. This report (commonly called the Kerner Report) identified five basic problem areas relating to the police and the community:

- The need for change in police operations in the ghetto, to insure proper conduct by individual officers and to eliminate abrasive practices.
- The need for more adequate police protection of ghetto residents, to eliminate the present high sense of insecurity to person and property.
- The need for effective mechanisms for resolving citizen grievances against the police.
- The need for policy guidelines to assist police in areas where police conduct can create tension.
- The need to develop community support for law enforcement.[63]

In 1973, the National Advisory Commission on Criminal Justice Standards and Goals completed its work and released its reports. Although Standards and Goals Commission had as its primary purpose the development of standards designed to reduce crime in America, it did address itself to the role of the public in that endeavor. It is interesting to note that this Commission had a task force that addressed itself exclusively to the role of the community in crime prevention. The Community Crime Prevention Task Force's report addressed itself to such issues as education, employment, drug abuse, integrity in government, and community participation in the cause of crime prevention.

The Police Task Force of the Standards and Goals Commission strongly advocated public involvement in the police function. The focus of the work of that task force can be summed up as follows:

- Every police agency should formally recognize the importance of communication with the public and constantly seek to improve its ability to determine the needs and expectations of the public, to act upon these needs and expectations, and to inform the people of the resulting policies developed to improve the delivery of police services.
- Every police agency with more than 400 employees should establish a specialized unit responsible for maintaining communication with the community. This unit should identify impediments to communications and devise methods to overcome these impediments. Units should establish lines of communication between the agency and community leaders and should elicit information directly from citizens at large. In smaller agencies, the police chief executive should assume direct responsibility for maintaining communication.
- Every police agency that has racial or minority groups of significant size in its jurisdiction should insure effective communication with these groups and establish specialized procedures to insure that the needs of minorities and the disadvantaged are actively considered in the establishment of policy and the delivery of police service.
- Recruit and inservice police training programs should provide explicit instruction in community culture.
- Every police agency should insure that recruit, hiring, assignment and promotion policies do not discriminate against minority groups.
- Every police agency should engage in positive efforts to employ ethnic or minority group members. When a substantial ethnic or minority population resides within the jurisdiction, the police agency should take affirmative action to achieve a ratio of minority group employees in approximate proportion to the makeup of the population.
- Every police agency should establish procedures to facilitate full and fair processing of complaints about general police services and about individual officer's conduct.[64]

Although there has been a decade of presidential and other national commissions advocating improvements in police-community relations and more activities on the part of the police in this area, the public's attitude toward the police has not changed. In fact, the relationship between the police and the public may be more strained today than ever before. This can be attributed in part to antagonistic activities on both sides. The police, for example, have been the objects of guerilla tactics, which included a period of isolated incidents of snipers shooting police officers. Although such shootings have not been linked to any organized effort, they have served to reinforce the "we versus they" attitude of police officers.

Far from being an open organization responsive to the concerns of the community they serve, contemporary police activities are still embedded in an aura of secrecy:

> Secrecy is a direct product of public distrust of the police on the one hand, of police corruption on the other. In turn, the two are related. Since policemen feel that they are despised by the public and since naturally they don't like being disliked, they do all they can to prevent the public from getting evidence against them. This is best done by sticking together and keeping mistakes within the department.[65]

The situation has evolved whereby the police and certain subculture groups (e.g., minorities, youth, the poor) are at odds with each other. Both groups have negative expectations when they meet, and unless drastic changes are forthcoming, these expectations are likely to be manifested.

The student of criminal justice should clearly understand, however, that the current crisis in police–community relations is directly related to the current conditions that exist in the broader society. The battle is, in reality, one involving the powerful versus the powerless. More people from different levels of the social structure are demanding a share in the decision-making powers of government. Since the police are the visual representatives of the authority of government, increasing efforts are being made to influence police policy. The traditional posture of the police of responding only to the prevailing power structure of their community is hardly adequate under existing circumstances. In the final analysis, the contemporary problems of police–community relations are precisely the same as the problems so evident in the broader community.

Summary

In this chapter we have tried to present an overall picture of the forces and conditions that brought about the development of police–community relations programs. The public's attitude toward the police has changed little over the centuries. Initially, although the necessity for a policing system was evident, the police were held in low esteem, paid very little, and were not respected, a fact that increased the difficulty of recruiting capable police personnel.

Many of the early problems in police-community relations were due to political control of the police, but this was partially alleviated by the advent of the civil service system and expanded training programs. Another major source of friction arose over the question of outside review of the police through such means as civilian review boards and the ombudsman. Most police agencies were strongly opposed to outside review of their activities.

In the mid-1900s, various presidential and national commissions were established to study problems arising from law enforcement, including the need for better police-community relations. Although the need for such programs was recognized, the development and implementation of specific units were slow in coming. The first broad programs appeared during World War II. Initially, police-community relations programs developed as a result of racial tension and civil rights movements, and the first manuals made available to aid police concerned the police relationship with minority groups. The National Conference of Christians and Jews was instrumental in extending police-community relations programs nationwide. In spite of the efforts to improve police-community relations, many of the problems still exist.

End Notes

[1] Oscar Handlin, "Community Organization as a Solution to Police-Community Problems," in *Police and the Changing Community: Selected Readings,* ed. Nelson A. Watson (Washington, D.C.: International Association of Chiefs of Police, 1965), p. 107.

[2] Ibid., p. 108.

[3] For a history of the development of police forces, see William G. Carleton, "Cultural Roots in American Law Enforcement," *Current History,* July 1967, pp. 1-7, 49.

[4] Arthur M. Schlesinger, Sr., *The Rise of the City, 1878-1898,* vol. 10 of *A History of American Life,* ed. Arthur M. Schlesinger, Jr., and Dixon Ryon Fox (New York: Macmillan, 1933), p. 115.

[5] Bruce Smith, *Police Systems in the United States* (New York: Harper & Brothers, 1949), p. 4.

[6] Ibid., pp. 105-6.

[7] The President's Commission on Law Enforcement and Administration of Justice, *Task Force Report: The Police* (Washington, D.C.: (U.S. Government Printing Office, 1967), p. 6.

[8] Ibid.

[9] See, for example, Joint Commission on Correctional Manpower and Training, *The Public Looks at Crime and Corrections* (Washington, D.C.: Joint Commission on

Manpower and Training, 1967); University of California at Berkeley, *The Police and the Community,* Field Survey IV, a report submitted to the President's Commission on Law Enforcement and Administration of Justice (Washington, D.C.: U.S. Government Printing Office, 1966); Michigan State University, *A National Survey of Police and Community Relations,* a report submitted to the President's Commission on Law Enforcement and Administration of Justice (Washington, D.C.: U.S. Government Printing Office, 1967); National Opinion Research Center, "A National Sample Survey Approach to the Study of the Victims of Crime and Attitudes toward Law Enforcement and Justice, unpublished, Chicago, 1966; Gallup Poll, *Tabulations Request Survey,* AIPO No. 709, prepared for the President's Commission on Law Enforcement and Administration of Justice, 1966; Bureau of Social Science Research, *Salient Findings on Crime and Attitudes toward Law Enforcement in the District of Columbia,* a preliminary technical report submitted to the U.S. Department of Justice, Office of Law Enforcement Assistance, 1966; Louis Harris, "Eye-for-An-Eye Rule Rejected," *The Washington Post,* July 3, 1966, Sec. E., p. E 3, col. 4.

[10]National Opinion Research Center, "National Sample Survey Approach," p. 1.

[11]President's Commission, *Task Force Report,* p. 146.

[12]George Edwards, *The Police on the Urban Frontier—A Guide to Community Understanding* (New York: Institute of Human Relations Press, 1968), p. 2.

[13]Ibid., p. 17.

[14]*Report of the National Advisory Committee on Civil Disorders* (Washington, D.C.: U.S. Government Printing Office, 1968), p. 8.

[15]There have been various publications which illustrate the conflict between the police and the black community. See, for example, Paul Jacobs, *Prelude to Riot: A View of Urban America from the Bottom* (New York: Vintage Books, 1966); Robert Conot, *Rivers of Blood, Years of Darkness* (New York: Bantam Books, 1967); John Hersey, *The Algiers Motel Incident* (New York: Bantam Books, 1968); J. E. Curry and Glen D. King, *Race Tensions and the Police* (Springfield, Ill.: Charles C Thomas, 1962); and Juby E. Towler, *The Police Role in Racial Conflicts* (Springfield, Ill.: Charles C Thomas, 1964).

[16]Gallup Poll, *"Tabulations Request Survey,* p. 13.

[17]Ibid., p. 15; and National Opinion Research Center, "National Sample Survey Approach," Table 8-1.

[18]James Q. Wilson, "Police Morale, Reform, and Citizen Respect: The Chicago Case," in *The Police: Six Sociological Essays,* ed. David J. Bordua (New York: Wiley, 1967), p. 158.

[19]Joseph D. Lohman, "Current Decline in Respect for Law and Order," speech delivered before the Section of Judicial Administration, American Bar Association, Montreal, August 8, 1966, p. 4, emphasis added.

[20]Ibid.

[21]William A. Westley, "Violence and the Police," *American Journal of Sociology* 59 (July 1953), 135. Also see Westley, "Secrecy and the Police," *Social Forces,* 34 (March 1956), 254–57, and "The Police: A Sociological Study of Law, Custom, and Morality," Ph.D. dissertation, University of Chicago, 1951.

[22]Michael Banton, *The Policeman in the Community* (New York: Basic Books, 1964).

[23]Ibid., p. 215.

[24]On this issue, see James Q. Wilson, "The Police and Their Problems: A Theory," *Public Policy*, 12 (1963), 189–216; and Jerome H. Skolnick, *Justice without Trial: Law Enforcement in a Democratic Society* (New York: Wiley, 1966).

[25]Nelson A. Watson, *Police Community Relations* (Washington, D.C.: International Association of Chiefs of Police, 1966), pp. 34–36. Also for a discussion on police attitudes toward the public, see Donald J. Black and Albert J. Reiss, Jr., *Studies in Crime and Law Enforcement in Major Metropolitan Areas*, Field Surveys III, vol. 2, report prepared for the President's Commission on Law Enforcement and Administration of Justice (Washington, D.C.: U.S. Government Printing Office, 1967).

[26]Many articles have been published discussing the pros and cons of police review boards. See, for example, Henry J. Abraham, "A People's Watchdog against the Abuse of Power," *Public Administration Review*, 20 (1960), 152–57; William P. Brown, "The Review Board Proposals Do Not Go Far Enough," paper presented at the 71st National Conference on Government, New York, November 17, 1965; William R. Hewitt, "An Open Letter on Police Review Boards," *Police*, 10, no. 5 (May–June 1966); "Administration of Civilian Complaints," *Harvard Law Review*, 77 (1964), 499; and "International Association of Chiefs of Police Position on Police Review Boards," *The Police Chief*, 32, no. 6 (1965).

[27]A. C. Germann, Frank D. Day, and Robert R. J. Gallati, *Introduction to Law Enforcement and Criminal Justice* (Springfield, Ill.: Charles C Thomas, 1968).

[28]Ibid., p. 215.

[29]The President's Commission on Law Enforcement and Administration of Justice, *The Challenge of Crime in a Free Society* (Washington, D.C.: U.S. Government Printing Office, 1967), p. 103.

[30]Ibid.

[31]A great deal of interest has been expressed in this country in the ombudsman concept. See, for example, Stanley V. Anderson, "Ombudsman Proposals: Stimulus to Inquiry," *Public Affairs Report*, 6, no. 2 (April 1965); Alfred Bexelius, a paper prepared for the *United Nations Human Rights Seminar on the Effective Realization of Civil and Political Rights at the National Level* (New York: United Nations, SO 216/c (13) AME, 1967); Eugene J. Bockman, "Ombudsman," *Municipal Reference Library*, 40, no. 10 (December 1966); Walter Gellhorn, "Ombudsman in America," *American Trial Lawyers*, April–May 1967; Donald C. Rowat, *The Ombudsman, Citizen's Defender* (London: Allen & Unwin, 1965); Walter Gellhorn, *Ombudsman and Others* (Cambridge, Mass.: Harvard University Press, 1966); "Ombudsman, The People's Champion," *American Bar Association Journal*, 53 (January 1967); and Kent W. Weeks, "A Comparative Analysis of the Civil Ombudsman Offices in Denmark, Finland, New Zealand, Norway and Sweden," reprinted by the Institute of Governmental Studies, University of California at Berkeley.

[32]Stanley V. Anderson, "The Ombudsman: Public Defender against Maladministration," *Public Affairs Report*, 6, no. 2 (April 1965).

[33]Letter from police chief Thomas Cahill, June 12, 1967.

[34]For examples of police misconduct and a discussion of the issues, see Ed Gray, *The Big Blue Line* (New York: Coward, McCann, 1967).

[35]A. C. Germann, "The Problem of Police–Community Relations," paper prepared for the National Commission on the Causes and Prevention of Violence, October 1968, p. 3.

[36]Thomas Reddin, "Are You Oriented to Hold Them?" *The Police Chief,* March 1966, p. 18.

[37]Arthur Niederhoffer, *Behind the Shield: The Police in Urban Society* (New York: Doubleday, 1967) p. 184.

[38]Lohman, "Current Decline," p. 9.

[39]William W. Turner, *The Police Establishment* (New York: Putnam, 1968), pp. 20–21.

[40]James Q. Wilson, *Varieties of Police Behavior: The Management of Law and Order in Eight Communities* (Cambridge, Mass.: Harvard University Press, 1968), p. 78, emphasis added; also see Jack J. Preiss and Howard Ehrlich, *An Examination of Role Theory: The Case of the State Police* (Lincoln, Nebr.: University of Nebraska Press, 1966).

[41]James Q. Wilson, "Dilemmas of Police Administration," *Public Administration Review,* 28, no. 5 (September–October, 1968), 409. © by the American Society for Public Administration. All rights reserved.

[42]Alexis de Tocqueville, *Democracy in America,* vol. 1 (New York: Vintage Books, 1945), p. 279.

[43]*National Commission on Law Observance and Enforcement* (Washington, D.C.: U.S. Government Printing Office, 1931).

[44]Ibid.

[45]Bruce Smith, *Police Systems in the United States* (New York: Harper & Brothers, 1949), p. 344.

[46]Michigan State University, A *National Survey of Police and Community Relations* (Washington, D.C.: U.S. Government Printing Office, 1967), p. 3.

[47]Joseph D. Lohman, *The Police and Minority Groups* (Chicago: Chicago Park Police, 1947).

[48]Ibid.

[49]J. E. Weckler and Theo E. Hall, "Police and Minority Groups" (Chicago: International Association of Chiefs of Police, 1944).

[50]David McEntire and Robert B. Powers, "Guide to Race Relations for Police Officers," State of California: Department of Justice, 1946.

[51]Joseph T. Kluchesky, "Police Action on Minority Problems" (New York: Freedom House, 1946).

[52]San Jose Police Department, *Annual Report,* San Jose, 1967, p. 4.

[53]Kluchesky, "Police Action," p. 4.

[54]Emmet Daly, "Guide to Race Relations for Peace Officers," Department of Justice, State of California, 1952.

[55]G. D. Gourley, *Police and the Public* (Springfield, Ill.: Charles C Thomas, 1963).

[56]Kluchesky, "Police Action," p. 4.

[57]Ibid.

[58]*Police-Community Relations Policies and Practices: A National Survey* (Washington, D.C.: International Association of Chiefs of Police and United States Conference of Mayors, n.d.).

[59]Louis A. Radelet and Raymond T. Galvin, *A National Survey of Police and Community Relations,* a report prepared for the President's Commission on Law Enforcement and Administration of Justice, Field Surveys IV (Washington, D.C.: Government Printing Office, 1967), pp. 377–82.

[60]Joseph D. Lohman and Gordon E. Misner, *The Police and the Community,* a report prepared for the President's Commission on Law Enforcement and Administration of Justice, Field Surveys IV, 2 vols. (Washington, D.C.: Government Printing Office, 1967).

[61]President's Commission, *The Challenge of Crime,* p. 103.

[62]Ibid.

[63]*Report of the National Advisory Commission on Civil Disorders,* p. 8.

[64]National Advisory Commission on Criminal Justice Standards and Goals, *Police* (Washington, D.C.: U.S. Government Printing Office, 1973), p. 477.

[65]William A. Westley, "The Police: A Sociological Study of Law, Custom and Morality," in *Urban Sociology,* p. 169, 174.

CHAPTER
SEVEN

ISSUES
IN POLICE–COMMUNITY
RELATIONS

The 1967 report of the President's Crime Commission accurately pointed out that "no lasting improvement in law enforcement is likely in this country unless police–community relations are substantially improved."[1] That statement is as valid today as before. The purpose of this chapter, therefore, is to explore what is needed and what must be done to improve the police relationship with the community.

Although we have previously suggested that police–community relations programs, as conceived and implemented during the 1960s, have not delivered what they promised, the concept of police–community relations is nonetheless still valid. In fact, the need for workable police–community relationships is as crucial to the successful accomplishment of the police mission today as ever. This fact was recognized by the National Advisory Commission on Criminal Justice Standards and Goals, the latest national commission established to examine the problems of crime and criminal justice, when it recommended that "police agencies in major metropolitan areas establish a specialized unit responsible for maintaining communication with the community.[2] In smaller agencies, the police chief executive should assume direct responsibility for maintaining communications."[3]

The philosophy alluded to by the Standards and Goals Commission is consistent with what we believe must be done to establish effective police-community relationships. Specifically, we feel that the most crucial element of any agency's approach to police-community relations programming must be citizen involvement.

Historically, police agencies have isolated themselves from the public. Secrecy and the development of a "we versus they" attitude has permeated the police establishment, thereby creating suspicion and distrust on the part of many segments of the community. Recognizing this condition as being a major problem, the Standards and Goals Commission stated:

> As an essential ingredient to cooperation, every police agency should formally recognize the importance of communication with the public and constantly seek to improve its ability to determine the needs and expectations of the public, to act upon these needs and expectations, and to inform the people of the resulting policies developed to improve the delivery of police services.[4]

An effective police-community relations program, however, must go beyond that. To be truly effective, the program must be designed to address both the problems *within the police department* and the problems of the community. Such programs must be designed to ensure that the police are, in fact, an integral part of the community and not an entity unto themselves. To accomplish this, the public must have a voice in defining the police role, establishing police policies, and evaluating the effectiveness of police service. It is essential that such public involvement not be restricted simply to the "power elements" of the community, but include all segments of the community structure, even those who might be openly critical of the police. Charles Gain, former chief of the San Francisco, California, Police Department, clearly recognized the need for total community involvement when he, as chief of the Oakland California, Police Department, wrote:

> Who to involve in police-community relations programs?
>
> In a word, everyone! Everyone possible within the community.
>
> As regards involvement of police personnel, every member of a department from the chief to the patrolman must be imbued with the concept and philosophy of community relations. It is of critical importance that the uniformed officer on the street be a *community relationist,* for it is on the street that police-community relations is developed or destroyed; if the man on the street is alienating and systematically enraging every minority and unpopular group in the community, and creating an entire generation of anti-police citizens, no one should be surprised at the resulting chaos. (There is an absolute need for a police administration that will not tolerate offensive con-

duct; if superiors from the top of the chain of command to the bottom are determined to correct subordinates, if they themselves are held accountable for inexcusable failures to detect and discipline offenders, much of the behavior which now brings police agencies into disrepute can be eliminated.)

Insofar as possible, uniformed and plainclothes policemen from line units should appear before community groups to present explanations of agency functions. Although community relations officers may necessarily have to attend community organization meetings on an ongoing basis to maintain liaison, it is most desirable to have line personnel appear as representatives of the agency whenever possible so as to involve them in community relations, present expert knowledge, have citizens relate with as many different agency representatives as possible, and preclude the situation where citizens come to look upon community relations unit officers as the police department. (Such situations have come to be in cities and have resulted in grave turmoil within and without the police agency.)

As regards involvement with the community, the community relations unit and the department as a whole (especially the Chief) must not only be willing to relate with *all* segments of the community, but must welcome and actively solicit such relations. There should be no group or organization with whom the police agency will not relate!

Comment may be in order with respect to what constitutes *the* community or *a* community. The community is too often defined in people's minds as composed of all persons, and they are thought of as feeling and thinking the same thing as regards the police and issues. As a matter of fact, there are, of course, many different communities within a city if we view a community as composed of people who are bound together by common interests. There are white, black, and brown communities; there are homeowners and tenants; there are sportsmen, etc. . . .

As *community relationists,* we must know each of our communities and what they are thinking. We might set forth these principles as a guide:

1. *Know your public.*
2. *Know what it thinks.*
3. *Know why it thinks so.*
4. *Know how it arrives at its conclusions.*

A comment is in order, also, regarding those who presume to speak for various segments of the community, even though they may be characterized as extremists or radicals; they may not in fact speak for many but they may certainly convey the sentiments of many and we should pay heed to them for this reason if no other.[5]

In an effort to visually depict the various interest groups that comprise any given community, Gain developed the classification shown in Table 7-1 as examples of common-interest groups.[6]

The degree to which citizens are involved with the police tends to vary from one community to another. Figure 7-1 shows a paradigm for developing a comparative perspective on the degrees of this involvement. Two of the implicit and explicit notions included in the conceptualiza-

TABLE **7-1**   Examples of Common-Interest Groups

Race and nationality	Sex	Residence
Negroes	Men	Urban
Chinese	Women	Suburban
Poles		Rural
Jews		
Italians		
Age	Income	Class
Children	High	Labor
Youth	Low	White-collar
21 to 40	Below $2,000	Management
Aged	Middle Income	Capitalist
Religion	Professional	Business and trade
Catholic	Lawyers	Stockholders
Protestant	Doctors	Employees
Jewish	Journalists	Customers
Presbyterian		
Methodist		
Occupational	Economic	Fraternal
Farmers	Consumers	Masons
Salesmen	Manufacturers	Elks
Transportation workers	Distributors	Rotarians
Government employees	Suppliers	Kiwanians
Political	Patriotic	Educational
Republicans	American Legion	Parent–teachers
Democrats	D.A.R.	College graduates
Farmer-Laborer		

Note: This classification by no means includes all publics there are. Every organization, every special-interest group, will constitute a public.

tion of police–community relations programs are cross-classified: (1) the degree to which the public is involved with the police department and (2) the degree to which the police are influenced by citizen participation.

Of the types generated in the classifications of Figure 7-1, "no formal programs" refers to a police department that does not operate any program designed to improve its relationship with the public. Such a classification, however, does not mean that the department is inefficient in its overall police operations; it refers only to departments that have not developed formal programs or activities designed to involve the citizenry in the police operation. The classification "public relations and/or crime prevention programs" refers to police departments that have developed formal programs, but ones in which the involvement of citizens is passive and acceptive. That is, citizens do not play an active role—they are only the *recipients* of whatever information is given to

	LOW	HIGH	
Citizen involvement is nonexistent	No Formal Programs	Operational Police-Community Relations Program	Responsive listening to community advice
Communication is one-way from police to public. Public's role is acceptive and passive	Public Relations and/or Crime Prevention Programs	*Total Community Involvement*	*All policies and procedures subject to review by the community*

FIGURE 7-1 Degree to Which Citizens are Involved with Police

them by the police. Such information is generally designed by the police to project a favorable image of the police or to provide information of a crime prevention nature (e.g., "lock your car," pamphlets, etc.).

The classification "operational police–community relations programs" refers to police departments that are trying to be responsive to the voice of the community. Most police departments that operated a formal police–community relations program during the 1960s would fall into this category, at least to some degree. The degree of response, however, varies greatly.

The classification "total community involvement" refers to police departments where all police policies and procedures are subject to review by the community. Implementation of the concept of community control over the police would usually be necessary to reach this degree of community involvement.

The four types of police agencies depicted in Figure 7-1 may also be divided according to their beliefs about the distribution of police powers. A monolithic department (no formal programs and public relations and/or crime prevention programs) has fixed notions about what information should be given to the public. A pluralistic department (operational police–community relations programs and total community involvement), on the other hand, is responsive to both the *ideal* of decentralization of police power—to varying degrees—and to the *need* to be sensitive to public opinion.

The essential point to remember in developing or evaluating a department's police–community relations posture is that unless the police involve the public in their operations, police–community relations programs become mere "police" programs. Unless the police establish meaningful communications with all segments of the public, they will not know of the legitimate grievances of the public; therefore, they will be programming in a vacuum. This is not to suggest that citizens do not have a responsibility for initiating and operating police–community relations activities. However, the police, being an organized public service agency, must provide the leadership in developing programs designed to make good police and community relations a reality.

To a large extent, the success of police–community relations efforts will depend upon how the concept is interpreted by the police department. As pointed out in Appendix I, many police agencies have misinterpreted police–community relations to mean simply public relations. For that reason, it is important to distinguish between the several terms that are frequently heard when discussing police and community relations.

Human relations is a relatively new field in the behavioral sciences that concerns itself with what people do and how they do it. Being new, it necessarily draws heavily upon the bodies of knowledge of the established social science disciplines which are concerned with human behavior (e.g., sociology and psychology). The aim of human relations is to improve human behavior through interpersonal and intergroup relationships.[7] From this broad and all-encompassing definition, human relations can be considered the umbrella under which intergroup relations, police–community relations, interpersonal relations, and conflict resolution all operate.

Intergroup and interpersonal relations falls under the umbrella of human relations and is concerned with conflicts and relationships between groups. "Understanding conflict, resolving it, and using it creatively are all the concern of intergroup relations."[8] There are some writers who treat the terms intergroup relations and interpersonal relations as though they were different. Practically, however, both involve the understanding of conflict, which, in turn, provides the foundation for developing meaningful programs in police–community relations. Intergroup relations addresses itself to group conflict, and interpersonal relations is concerned with conflict between individuals who belong to different groups.

Recently, the police have begun to articulate their role in the area of intergroup and interpersonal relations through an increased emphasis on conflict resolution. *Conflict resolution* refers to the police role in handling conflicts that occur between groups or individuals. For the police, the objective of conflict resolution is to resolve the conflict before it turns to violence and to do so in the least restricted manner possible.

PUBLIC RELATIONS

A review of the literature would reveal that public relations, in its broadest sense, is a way of making the public aware of what the agency is doing, why it is doing it, whom it serves, and how it contributes to the welfare of the community as a whole.

Public relations for the police involves planning and conducting activities in such a manner as to give the department a good image with the public. According to Richard L. Holcomb: "The fundamental principle of good public relations can be summed up very briefly. It amounts to doing a good, efficient job in a courteous manner and then letting the public know about the job."[9]

Public relations plays an important role for the police—to help them win recognition and status. Equally important, it is a vehicle for gaining support for the department. Police departments, like business and industry, have come to realize that in addition to doing a good job, they must also let the public know of their good performance. Public relations performs that function for the police.

POLICE-COMMUNITY RELATIONS

During the 1960s, many police departments established specialized police-community relations units specifically to deal with the pressing problems of the police relationships with the community. In defining police-community relations in context of a specialized police unit, the St. Louis Metropolitan Police Department, the first department to establish a police-community relations unit, listed the basic objectives of its program as reducing and preventing crime in its city through joint police-community cooperation and to improve intergroup relations in the community.

The San Francisco Police Department stated:

> The true meaning of the term police-community relations, as we interpret the term here in San Francisco, is embedded in a myriad of functions that we do not normally perceive as part of the customary police mission. . . . A police-community relations program in its finest sense concentrates its efforts and services in reaching the *unreachables.*[10]

According to former San Francisco police chief Thomas Cahill, "the real objective of a police-community relations program is to focus the community on the mobilization of its resources, and to call for the organization of services that can deal with the marginal conditions of subculture groups."[11]

The San Jose, California, Police Department defined its police-community relations program, as follows:

> Police-community relations is not a magic formula offering a solution for the ills of society. Rather, it is a means by which the police along with other public and private agencies and individuals in the community can recognize the needs and responsibilities to work together for the common good.[12]

More specifically, police-community relations in San Jose involved basically the following:

1. Working with the community in solving community problems.
2. A day-by-day relationship between the police and the public.

3. An ongoing dialogue between the police and the public. This involved meeting with groups, individuals, organizations, or committees and explaining the role of the police in the community.
4. Identifying the informal means of organization. This makes reference to groups such as gangs, who constitute an informal organization. These groups must be recognized and a relationship established with them.

The important element of police–community relations, as seen by the San Jose Police Department, was getting to know people and talking with them about one another's problems, and then working together to solve these problems. The aim of the San Jose program was to *reconcile communication with action,* and theory with practice, thereby making the police a part of and not apart from the community it serves.

The Winston-Salem, North Carolina, Police Department described its program as an "integrative function of police work." The community service unit of that department had a threefold purpose: (1) to find people in need, (2) to direct them to those agencies or community resources where the need can be met, and (3) to search out those things which are conducive to crime and see that they are rooted out of the community.[13]

The National Center on Police and Community Relations at Michigan State University, with over 15 years of experience in this field, developed the following *definition* of police–community relations:

> Police–community relations in its generic sense means the variety of ways in which it may be emphasized that the police are indeed an important *part of,* not *apart from* the communities they serve. Properly understood, police–community relations is a concept for total police organization, functionally speaking—a total *orientation,* not merely the preoccupation of a special unit or bureau within the department. It bears upon administrative policy, it bears upon planning and research, and perhaps more significantly, it bears upon line service through the uniformed patrol division. In short, police–community relations, ideally, is an emphasis, an attitude, a way of viewing police responsibilities that ought to permeate the entire organization. Every major issue in American law enforcement today is, in a substantial sense, a challenge and an opportunity in terms of police–community relations. For it is only in an effective partnership of police and community that there is any prospect of dealing constructively with these issues.[14]

The Michigan State definition provides an excellent conceptual scheme for understanding police–community relations. From a programmatic standpoint, however, we have defined police–community relations as the *process* by which the police work in conjunction with the community to identify the problems that cause friction between the two groups, and then working together to solve these problems. This entails a *meaningful* relationship between the police and the community. For example, a meaningful police–community relations effort would be a case where the police went into a neighborhood and *openly* met with the residents in an effort to determine what they saw as being the problems involving the police and that particular enclave. This does not mean that the police are going to tell the residents what the problems are; rather the police are going to *listen* to the residents tell them what the problems are. After identifying the problems, the police would then take steps to solve them, if possible. For purposes of illustration, let us say that this particular neighborhood was concerned about a specific police practice such as field interviews. The police would then reassess their field-interview procedures to determine if they are, in fact, a source of irritation to the residents. If so, the police would not make excuses to justify this source of irritation, but would change their practices to alleviate the problem.

The essence of this definition is there would be a *meaningful* and not a superficial relationship between the police and the public designed to identify problems and then find workable solutions. Inherent in this definition is the necessity for citizens to have an input into the policies and procedures of the police department. For a police–community relations program to be meaningful, citizen input into the policies of a police department is needed. This philosophy was postulated by Thomas Reddin while he was chief of the Los Angeles Police Department:

> Your community relations programming must provide an essential ingredient. That ingredient is the opportunity for the community to exert *constructive* influence on the aspirations of this Department. We need to examine our operations from the point of view of the resident of the community. We must make our policies and practices more understandable, and thus more acceptable. It must be a two-way process, though, because the members of our community need to know more about the nature of the police task—more about the reason for Departmental policies and practices—more about those things which daily confront our officers. Our experiences during the last year indicate that there are phases of our operations which have implications to the citizen that are not apparent to us. Some of these engender misunderstanding.[15]

Police–Community Relations versus Public Relations

From the foregoing definitions we can see that police–community relations and police–public relations are not analogous. The main difference relates to the objective of the two concepts and the degree and extent of community involvement. Public relations can be likened to a one-way street whereby the police department attempts to project a good image to the public. It carries with it the inherent hazard of becoming a "selling job" that may sometimes reflect to the public a false image.

Police–community relations, on the other hand, is like a telephone, not a broadcasting system, it is a means for two-way communication. Police–community relations is a sincere effort on the part of the police to develop mutual understanding. From this understanding will develop an atmosphere conducive to a good day-by-day relationship between the police and the community.

Although police–community relations and police–public relations differ in their involvement and approach to the community, they should not be considered opposing forces. The important thing to remember is that *there is a difference* and that police–public relations will not allow for problem solving or be acceptable to subcultural groups that possess the problems unless there exists an effective police–community relations program.[16]

PURPOSE OF POLICE-COMMUNITY RELATIONS

Fragmented programs in police–community relations date back over 30 years. Structured programs, however, have a history of about 20 years. The National Center on Police–Community Relations at Michigan State University listed the purpose of police–community relations as follows:

1. To encourage police–citizen partnership in the cause of crime prevention.
2. To foster and improve communication and mutual understanding in the relationship of the police with the total community.
3. To promote interprofessional or teamwork approaches to the solution of community problems, and to stress the principle that the administration of criminal justice is a total community responsibility.
4. To enhance cooperation in the relationship of the police with other members of "the family" in the administration of criminal justice, specifically the relationships among and between the police, prosecution, the courts and corrections.
5. To assist police and other community leaders in an understanding of the nature and causes of increasingly complex problems in people-to-people relationships, and especially to improve police–minority group relationships, and finally,
6. To strengthen in every possible way practical implementation of the principle of equal protection under the law for all persons.[17]

An effective police–community relations program, therefore, is one that deals with the prevailing problems confronting the community. We will readily admit that the police are not the cause of social problems. The police did not invent ghettos. The police did not institute a system of poverty, segregation, discrimination, racism, poor housing, or inadequate education. Yet these are the pressing problems of our cities. These are the problems that prompted the President's Commission on Civil Disorders to warn: "Our nation is moving toward two nations, one Black, one White—both separate and unequal."[18] These are, in effect, the real problems of our society. These are the problems which, when not corrected, evolve into police problems. Consequently, the purpose of an effective police–community relations program should be to mobilize the total community resources to solve these problems. Police–community relations alone will not solve the problems. At best, an effective police–community relations program can only give society time to correct the deplorable conditions which exist. A police–community relations program can be deemed successful only if it benefits the community. The latent effect of such a program will be benefits for the agency itself.

We believe, however, that the police and indeed the entire system for the administration of justice can no longer continue to operate under the philosophy that social problems are the concern of social agencies and not the criminal justice system and, thereby, continue to sweep society's debris under the rug, which makes resolution of the problems even more difficult. The police, as well as other components of the criminal justice system, have a role to play in respect to social problems that have yet to be recognized.

In addition to involvement in the community, a police–community program can do much *internally* to improve police and community relations. Many programs developed, implemented, and operated under the title of police–community relations have not made a significant change in the overall relationship between the police and the various enclaves that are at odds with the police.

Consequently, we feel that one of the greatest benefits from a police–community relations program will be derived from what it does internally. The purpose of a police–community relations program should be (in addition to its work in the community) to bring about changes in the existing policies and procedures that exhibit themselves in a dual standard of justice. As stated by William J. Osterloh: "A police–community relations unit should represent much more than an inconspicuous and unimportant appendage of a department, a modest unit which seemingly apologizes for its existence from the quietude of the administrative sidelines."[19]

As such, the police–community relations program should have as one of its major purposes to serve as the eyes and ears of the police department to identify police practices that create hostility, and then assist in alleviating these practices by being intimately involved in the departmental administrative and policymaking activities. We submit that if this was the main purpose of police–community relations, great gains would be made toward bettering the relationships between the police and the public.

In that regard, there are a number of issues that readily lend themselves to review with improvement of police and community relationships in mind.

Firearms Policy

One of the major issues that creates friction between the police and the community is the shooting of a member of the minority community by the police. That reason, superseded by a general concern for human life, should compel all police chief executives to carefully evaluate their firearms use policy to ensure that it allows police personnel to use firearms only when the life of a police officer or the life of someone else is in danger.

This is the most pressing issue in policy–minority group relations today. One of the best-thought-out positions on this subject was developed by Charles Royer after he was elected mayor of Seattle. His letter to the Public Safety Committee of the Seattle City Council dated January 31, 1978, is worth printing in its entirety:

> Police shooting policies have been the subject of a great deal of public debate in recent years. The use of deadly force has disrupted relations between the police and many communities, and has caused confusion among the law enforcement officers who receive mixed signals about their obligations and their limits.
>
> Because it so greatly affects public and police safety and respect for law enforcement, Seattle's shooting policy must be determined by accountable public officials. As the elected Mayor, and as the chief law enforcement officer in this city, I have the responsibility to put a new policy into effect, and to make certain it works. Therefore I have a great interest in an approach that is easy to understand and carry out, and one that has the best overall protections for citizens and police officers.
>
> There are many aspects to a deadly force policy, but the key issue before your committee at this time is when police can fire at human beings. I support the following rule: "An officer may discharge a firearm: To defend himself or herself, or another person, from what the officer reasonably believes is an immediate threat of death or serious injury, when there is no apparent alternative."
>
> **THE PROPOSED POLICY IS SIMPLE TO UNDERSTAND AND TO APPLY**
>
> The police officers with whom I have spoken are concerned, more than anything else, that we set out a policy that is clear and easy to implement. They believe, and I am confident, that our law enforcement people will effectively carry out a rule when they stop getting contradictory signals about what the rule is.
>
> The policy supported by the previous Mayor, and the one suggested earlier by the Office of Police Planning is confusing and will result in mistakes, criticism of the police, and legal disputes. It requires the officer, in a split second, to judge whether a fleeing person is armed, is armed with a deadly weapon, may inflict serious harm with that weapon, or has committed, or has attempted to commit, a crime that is a felony, and in particular, one of a particular class of felonies which "could result or could have resulted" in serious injury or death.
>
> That is a great deal to expect in a severe stress situation, from even the most experienced officer.
>
> It is much simpler for an officer to decide that someone is about to attack him or another person, and that deadly force is the only way to protect his life or the life of a victim.

THE PROPOSED POLICY WILL DECREASE CRITICISM OF POLICE AND LEGAL CHALLENGES

Because the policy I propose is more restrictive than the current one, officers will use their firearms less often. This will result in fewer situations where the police in general, and individual officers, are criticized for "overstepping" their bounds. This will result in fewer lawsuits against the City for improper use of force, both because of the lower gross number of police shooting incidents, and because officers will have a simpler standard to follow.

In a legal opinion dated January 24, 1978, the Law Department suggested that a more restrictive policy (in that instance the OPP-recommended approach) might increase the City's tort liability. The opinion says that a problem could arise where an officer follows the old regulations, shoots in a "wrong" situation, and the new guidelines are used in court as evidence against the police and the City. The problem with this argument is its assumption that officers will not follow the new policy. I have confidence in the intelligence and judgment of our police and believe they can apply the new rules whatever they are.

THE PROPOSED POLICY ENSURES PROTECTION FOR THE POLICE AND THE PUBLIC

There is no evidence that shooting policies affect the incidence of crime, escapes, or attacks on police. Policies similar to the one I propose are followed in Kennewick, Kelso, Longview and Des Moines, also by the Federal Bureau of Investigation. There is no consistent impact of their policies on crime rates. I can predict, however, that the suggested approach will improve police relations with the community, and thus will result in better law enforcement. I am ready to commit the training resources necessary to ensure that the policy works. When implemented, it will reduce confusion for officers, reduce injury, and will decrease the likelihood of legal challenges. It will best serve our citizens, the police, and the City, and I ask for your support.

Police administrators, in developing their firearms policy, should do so based upon a philosophy that reflects "the value placed on human life and should result in a policy that clearly states that the use of lethal force should not only be legally justified but should be socially and morally warranted as well."[20]

Complaint Procedure

During the 1960s, great efforts were made in many cities throughout the nation to establish civilian police review boards for the purpose of receiving and investigating citizens complaints against the police. Such efforts were initiated because large segments of the community did not trust the internal police complaint procedures. The National Commission on the Causes and Prevention of Violence addressed this issue and concluded:

A major criticism of internal review is that it seldom produces meaningful discipline of persons guilty of police misconduct. Even when an officer is disciplined, the punishment is often so light as to be a token that aggravates rather than satisfies the grievant. By contrast, many departments impose relatively severe penalties for violations of minor internal regulations. Thus, tardiness or insubordination may warrant an automatic suspension that is more onerous than the sanction for physical abuse of a citizen. . . . The inference is that internal review is more attuned to enforcing organization disciplines than redressing citizen grievances.[21]

John Swan makes this statement in the book entitled *Local Government Police Management:* "The police chief has the responsibility to run his department, and he cannot abdicate his authority and accountability."[22] Nevertheless, the police chief executive must develop a procedure whereby citizens' complaints are courteously received, objectively investigated, and appropriate disciplinary action taken when warranted. Unless that occurs, we are likely to see a return of the demands to remove the function of internal discipline from the control of the police department in favor of some form of external review.

Minority Recruitment

In 1973, the National Advisory Commission on Criminal Justice Standards and Goals adopted a standard that reads in part:

> Every police agency should engage in positive efforts to employ ethnic minority group members. When a substantial ethnic minority population resides within the jurisdiction, the police agency should take affirmative action to achieve a ratio of minority group employees in approximate proportion to the make-up of the population.[23]

To date, few if any police agencies have achieved that standard. Although some improvements have taken place, notably in cities with minority political leadership and/or minority chief police executives, such as Atlanta, Georgia; Washington, D.C.; Detroit, Michigan; and Newark, New Jersey, most police departments throughout the nation do not have anything like a minority representation that equals the minority composition of the city. The problem is even more acute for state police agencies and sheriffs' departments. On a national basis, it is estimated, for example, that blacks comprise about 12 percent of the nation's population. At best, blacks constitute no more than 6 percent of the nation's police employees. Even that percentage does not reflect the magnitude of the problem, because it includes those few departments, such as Washington D.C., Detroit, and Atlanta, that have a large black population and a large number of black police officers.

The problem inherent in such an underrepresentation of minorities is self-evident. It is extremely difficult for the minority community to view its police agency as being responsive to their needs and free of prejudice when they find themselves drastically underrepresented as members of the agency. This is an issue that must be addressed and corrected if positive relationships with the minority community are expected.

Training

Although the number of hours devoted to police training have increased considerably over the past years, the nature and content of police training is still problematic. Many police training programs are still not reflective of what the individual officer will face when assigned to work in the community. Of particular concern to the authors is the absence of a training program that provides officers with an understanding and appreciation of cultural differences. Rather than being one big "melting pot," America is a pluralistic society, one in which different racial, ethnic, and religious groups retain their particular cultural traits. It is extremely important that this fact be recognized and training programs developed accordingly. Police officers must be trained not to place a value judgment on cultural differences; rather, these differences must be understood and respected.

Equally important, police training programs should provide officers with better training in the area of conflict resolution. Although it is generally recognized that a police officer spends more time managing conflict than enforcing the law, many police training programs devote more time to the latter than to the former. As a result, a substantial number of police officers in this country leave the training academy ill-prepared for the realities of their work. This unfortunate situation must be changed if we are to see positive improvements in the manner in which the police carry out their responsibilities, which in turn determines their relationship with the community.

Police Mission

To a large degree, the manner in which the police define their mission will determine how individual officers view their roles. If, for example, the mission of the police continues to be defined in the narrow context of law enforcement, individual officers will probably place little importance on their roles as providers of services. For that reason, it is extremely important for police administrators to develop an operating philosophy that places police service in its broader context.

One police agency has attempted to address this issue by developing the following statements that reflect the mission of the department:

- Provide emergency actions and services, not readily available from other agencies, that may save human life.
- Provide programs and actions directed at the causes and conditions of delinquency and crime that will result in the prevention of juvenile delinquency, criminal deviancy and crime.

- Provide programs and actions to acquire information about criminal behavior and responsibility and expeditiously handle that information in a manner consistent with the best interest of involved persons, the community and society.
- Respond by direct involvement, advice, or referral to those situations which, if left unattended, would logically result in serious mental anguish, disorder, injury, property damage, or loss of individual rights for people within the jurisdiction.
- Provide actions and programs for coordination between support agencies that seem to facilitate social justice and justice processes.
- Provide order maintenance programs, and actions to reduce danger and facilitate normal community and social operations during periods of unusual disruptive occurrences such as civil protest, natural disaster, riot and war.[24]

Reward System

In general, the police tend to reward officers mainly for their law enforcement activities. This is directly related to how the police define their mission. In developing a realistic reward system, it is important for the police to recognize that the measure of police effectiveness is the absence of crime and peace tranquility in the community. That being the case, it is important that a police reward system recognize officers for their efforts in areas of community service, referrals, and for being humanistic, community-oriented persons. No longer should recognition be given to the police solely for their efforts in enforcing the law.

The preceding list represents only a few of the major issues that should be addressed by the police in their efforts to improve their relationship with the community. A later section of the chapter will present a more detailed guideline for assessing problems in the area of police and community relations.

ORGANIZATIONAL ISSUES

At least three major organizational changes have occurred in police service in recent years: (1) deemphasis on police–community relations programs in favor of crime prevention programs, (2) implementation of the team policing concept, and (3) questioning of the traditional beliefs about detectives and preventive patrol.

Recently, police–community relations programs as specialized units have come into disfavor within many police departments. As a result, a substantial number of police agencies have abandoned their police–community relations programs in favor of crime prevention programs. Presently, the major emphasis on community involvement by the police center around efforts to reduce crime through the implementation of crime prevention programs. Thus, we find that crime prevention units are to the 1970s what police–community relations programs were to the 1960s.

In addressing the issue of crime prevention, the Standards and Goals Commission developed a standard that read in part:

> Every police agency should immediately establish programs that encourage members of the public to take an active role in preventing crime, that provide information leading to arrests and conviction of criminal offenders, that facilitate the identification and recovery of stolen property, and increase liaison with private industry in security efforts.[25]

Police agencies have gone about implementing crime prevention programs in a variety of ways:

- *Neighborhood Watch.*   Under this program, the police involve the public in the effort of crime prevention by encouraging citizens to watch each others' homes and report suspicious situations to the police.
- *Identification Program.*   Under this program, the police purchase electric marking tools and make them available to the public for marking their personal property with an identifiable number, either their social security number or their state driver's license number.
- *Tenant Patrol.*   In some cities where there are large public housing projects, the police have organized the tenants to patrol or sit and observe and report suspicious circumstances to the police.
- *Alarms.*   Some police departments advise the public on the types of burglar alarms that are the most effective. A number of departments have developed local ordinances to regulate the use of alarms.
- *Premise Inspections.*   Under this program, the police conduct security surveys of residents and/or businesses and advise occupants what to do to reduce their vulnerability to crime.
- *Educational Campaign.*   Through the use of pamphlets, displays, radio, and television, the police operate a public information campaign designed to educate the public on what steps to take to reduce their chance of being victimized.

The National Crime Prevention Institute at the University of Louisville has been a leader in training police officials in the techniques of crime prevention.

As previously stated, crime prevention programs have virtually replaced police–community relations programs in police departments. This change in emphasis, however, should not be interpreted to mean that the problems of police and community relationships have been resolved. Our statement about the issue of police–community relations versus police public relations is also applicable to the issue of police–community relations and crime prevention. Both serve a useful purpose and should not be considered as competing forces. In fact, police involvement in crime prevention programs offer a unique opportunity for establishing contacts with the community in the interest of developing mutual understanding. What is important to remember is the fact that the problems that lead to the creation of police–community relations units during the 1960s still exist. Similarly, the need for special efforts on the part of the police to address those problems, both internally and externally, still exist.

Unlike in the 1960s when police efforts in the area of community relations were externally directed, the decade of the 1970s has seen some internal organizational changes in police departments. One major change has been the reorganization of police agencies under the concept of team policing, a program advanced by the Law Enforcement Assistance Administration through its technology transfer program.

How team policing has been implemented tends to differ from one department to another. It does, however, generally involve "an attempt to decentralize the police organization to make it more responsive to the localized needs and interests of neighborhood and community groups,"[26] with the following general characteristics:

- Geographic stability of patrol through permanent assignment of police teams to small areas or neighborhoods.
- Maximum communication, interaction, coordination, and cooperation among team members, fostered through the practice of working together to solve common problems.
- Better communication and interaction between team members and residents of the community or neighborhood in which they work.
- Different styles of management, supervision, and decision making, which emphasize the involvement and participation of individual team members in making decisions that affect the operations of the team.
- Deemphasis of specialists' skills in favor of a generalist approach in which team members are given wider latitude in dealing with day-to-day problems.[27]

The element of team policing that offers the greatest promise for improved police and community relations is the emphasis on community involvement. How a particular department or team goes about involving the community in its operations is only limited by the imagination of the police themselves.

Probably the greatest debate in modern law enforcement centers around research findings that questioned the merits of preventive patrol and the effectiveness of the detective unit.

The Kansas City, Missouri, Police Department's preventive patrol experiment precipitated the debate on the merits of traditional preventive patrol through a well-controlled research demonstration project funded by the Police Foundation. The Kansas City experiment, which involved three levels of preventive patrol (e.g., normal patrol, increased patrol, and reduced patrol) concluded that the level of random preventive patrol had no significant effect on (1) the crime rate, (2) traffic accidents (3) police response time, (4) citizens' perceptions about their security, or (5) citizens' attitudes about police service.[28]

A study conducted by the Rand Corporation similarly raised questions about the effectiveness of detectives in conducting follow-up investigations. The results of that research suggested that the practices of patrol officers, and citizens' response and cooperation, were probably more significant in criminal apprehension than refinements in the investigative process would be.[29]

The importance of the Rand report on the investigative process is indirectly related to the subject of this book. It confirms our position that citizen involvement is essential for the police if they are to successfully carry out their mission.

ESTABLISHING A POLICE–COMMUNITY RELATIONS PROGRAM

There are two basic methods of starting a police–community relations program. The first, and most generally used method, is that where a police department decides that it should initiate a community relations program, develops the program on paper, and then attempts to implement *their* program in the community. The second method is to involve members of the community in both the planning and implementation stages of the program.

Under the first method, the program generally begins with the recognition by city officials (e.g., mayor, city manager, or chief of police) that there is a need for a program designed to improve the relationship between the police and the community. This recognition generally results from criticism of the police, community disorder, or the threat of violence. (In some cases, police–community relations programs have been established because "it is the thing to do," whereas others have been established as a preventive measure.) The chief of police generally assigns one or more officers to develop a program. This generally entails contacting other cities (either by letter or personal visits) with ongoing police–community relations programs to determine what they are doing. The officers given the assignment then adopt some of the programs they have learned about, to be tried in their city. After writing up a proposed program, it is submitted to the chief of police for approval, and then the implementation process begins.

The most obvious drawback of this procedure is that the community does not contribute to the planning of the program. The police have developed their program, generally based on what other cities have done, without consultation with the residents of the community. One anonymous informant commented on this procedure as follows: "If they (the police) are going to start a community program, why doesn't the community have something to say about it? We are the ones that have the problems. We are the ones that know the problems. We should be the ones who develop the programs."

Under the latter method, police and/or city officials decide to implement a police–community relations program, but the first step is to make an assessment of the problems in both the police department and the community. Based upon that assessment, and with input from the community, programs are developed (both internal and external of the police department) to improve the relationship.

ASSESSING THE NEED FOR POLICE–COMMUNITY RELATIONS

The Environment of Law Enforcement

1. Has the city council frequently involved itself in controversies concerning the police department?
2. What is the interest level of the city council in the police department? Is it generally favorable, generally unfavorable, or largely indifferent to the department?

These questions indicate the support the department has from the political structure of the city. That political perceptions may be inaccurate cannot be cause for the police administrator to disregard them—especially since they so often reflect perceptions of the community. A knowledge of how the department fares in the minds of political opinion makers is important for corrective action.

If political perceptions are inaccurate, the department should consider special efforts to correct them, such as briefings, activity reports, or position papers on major problems. The department must recognize, however, that attitudes (both among the politicians and the public) are frequently based upon some controversial action the department has taken in the past.

3. Do citizens often bring complaints against the department before the city council?
4. What types of complaints are most often leveled against the department?
   a. Slow response time
   b. Unnecessary use of force
   c. Improper arrests
   d. Lack of courtesy
   e. Poor investigation
   f. Other
5. Do citizens bring their complaints to the city council:
   a. Because they get no satisfaction from the department?

    b.   Because they feel the department would not make a full investigation?

    c.   Or because they're unfamiliar with the proper channels for registering complaints?

These questions can indicate the department's level of support and whether the citizens are satisfied with police services. If citizens are unaware of the complaint procedure, or if they have little faith in the department's willingness to investigate, the department must make every effort to follow through on complaints and make the complaint-processing system highly visible. By reviewing the types of complaints leveled against the department, the administrator can pinpoint which areas of training and discipline need additional emphasis.

    6.   Have community groups in high-crime areas established "citizen patrol" teams because they feel that police protection is inadequate? If such groups exist, does the department work with them or does it resent the intrusion?

When citizens take policing into their own hands, they believe that something is radically wrong with existing services. However, if the functions of a "citizen patrol" are coordinated with regular police services (through a neighborhood police auxiliary or through active liaison), the patrols can prove to be an asset both to the police and to the community, for they offer the opportunity to utilize citizen concern constructively.

    7.   In the event of a community crisis, are there people or groups to whom you can go for aid in calming tensions or dispelling rumors?

The existence of community resources to assist police in time of crisis can prevent the escalation of tensions and contribute significantly to increased police and community understanding. Policing is *both* a police and a public responsibility. When large-scale disruptions occur, it is almost impossible for the police to restore order by themselves. If police–community relations are not good, the police will have to stand alone and run the risk of further alienating the community.

    8.   Does the police administration have access to local sources of private money (foundations, chambers of commerce, etc.) to finance an important community relations effort when city or federal funding is lacking?

    9.   Does your city have a private organization that provides benefits to the families of police officers killed in the line of duty?

A "yes" response to these questions would indicate an important type of support for the department. Such support can prove invaluable to the department in time of crisis. If the local "power structure" can be involved financially, the department may be able to avert further escalation of tensions by directing nonpolice resources to troubled areas of the city.

The News Media

10. Have the local news media recently taken editorial positions critical of the department's policies or operations, and what were the issues?
    a. Unnecessary use of force?
    b. Improper arrests?
    c. Lack of courtesy?
    d. Rising crime rates?
    e. Racial imbalance in personnel?
    f. Police corruption?
    g. Other?
11. Is your department frequently the object of calls to local radio or television "citizen talk shows?"

The answer to these questions can indicate how a police department is perceived and point to actions that are creating resentment within the community. If media criticism is based on disagreement with department policy, the department should be less concerned than if it is based on inaccurate perceptions. Should the latter be the case, the department should consider the need for a more open press relations policy.

The Changing Urban Environment

The job of policing becomes increasingly difficult in a time of rapid social change, because the public has changing expectations of police performances. Conflict between different cultural groups, especially in congested urban areas, makes it imperative that police be sensitive to different life-styles and that they make every effort to ensure that their practices are not misunderstood.

12. Are there areas of your city where, either because of population density or culturally biased behavior, people congregate on street corners and stoops during warm weather?
13. Are recreational facilities lacking in some sections of the city, thereby forcing youth to congregate on street corners?
14. Do certain areas of your city experience conflicts between roving gangs of youth?

These questions indicate an environment in which police officers operate with an above-normal chance for escalating conflict. Police must give special attention to these areas, be especially sensitive to prevailing attitudes, and establish regular communication with local opinion leaders.

15. What percentage of your city's population is from minority groups?
16. Are these groups concentrated in certain areas of the city?
17. Do these groups have representation in the local government (i.e., elected officials, municipal employees, etc.) in proportion to their numbers?

It is important that the cosmopolitan nature of a city be reflected in its public agencies. If minority or cultural groups feel alienated from the city government, they are likely to vent their hostilities on the most visible part of that government—the police department.

18. Are the spokespersons for minority groups in your city openly critical of the police department?
19. Have there been political power struggles among disenfranchised groups in your city?
20. Do normal city tensions, minority-group problems, and rumors about political struggles hold the threat of violence in sections of your city?

These questions can indicate the problems your department is likely to encounter when dealing with minority-group members. It is advisable for police administrators to maintain regular communications with spokespersons for those groups.

21. Has there been racial tension within the police department in recent years?
22. Have there been incidents at roll call or over the police radio in which racial slurs or political comments have been made by police officers?

Police agencies frequently reflect the composition of the community. However, the department cannot hope to deal effectively with racial tensions within its community when similar tensions pervade the department's ranks and affect its performance. If racial slurs, bias in assignments, or other racial practices persist (or are perceived as persisting), the internal conflict likely to erupt within the department will have a negative effect on police–community relations.

The Department Administration

23. Is there a formal procedure within the department for handling citizen complaints?
24. Are investigation results available to interested community residents?
25. Does your complaint procedure incorporate a means of appeal beyond the police department?

The existence of a formal complaint mechanism is necessary to establish accountability. In times of crisis, or any time when the police must act in controversial situations, the department's willingness to be open about the complaint-investigation process will have a direct bearing on citizen confidence in the actions. When an open complaint process is absent, there is increased potential for escalating controversy. Failure of the department to maintain an open system is also indicative of police defensiveness—the basis of many community relations problems.

26. Do most arrests for disorderly conduct and resisting arrest occur in certain areas of the city?

27. Do minority-group members account for the majority of those arrested on such charges?

Arrests for disorderly conduct and resisting arrest are good indicators of conflict between individuals, community groups, and the police. As indicators, these types of arrests are even more significant if most of them occur in highly congested areas of the city. In such cases, the potential for escalating violence is a factor with which the police must continually be concerned. Generally, departments having significant numbers of these types of arrests should consider special programs to reduce them.

Service Demands by Type and Area

28. Does the department's response time to calls for service vary with the type of call?

29. Does the department's response time vary significantly in different sectors of the city?

Response time is a frequent factor in citizen complaints against the police, because it is so influential in determining public attitudes toward the police. A department's response time should be reviewed frequently, to ensure that variations reflect publicly set priorities and not location. Although it is not necessary that all calls be answered with equal dispatch, the department can be open to severe criticism if variations occur according to neighborhood.

30. Are citizens usually willing to cooperate with the police when asked to testify in court?

31. Does the number of resisting-arrest complaints filed by your officers constitute more than 3 percent of total arrests for a year?

32. Do your police officers encounter hostile groups of onlookers when responding to disturbance calls in certain areas?

33. Has there been a rise in the number of assaults on police officers in recent years?

34. If so, have these assaults been concentrated in certain areas of the city?

35. Have some patrolmen, although working the same areas as others, been the object of more frequent assault?

These questions indicate the degree of recognition for police author-ity. Resisting-arrest incidents indicate problems between certain citizens and the police department or individual officers. To pinpoint the prob-lem further, a correlation should be made between resisting-arrest com-plaints and the individual officers involved, to determine whether those officers represent a disproportionate share of such actions.[30]

COMMUNITY INVOLVEMENT IN PLANNING

The advantage of involving the community in the planning stages of such a program is that *they* are in the best position to identify *their* problems. A latent effect of doing so is that *residents* are more apt to participate in a program if *they* feel it is "*their*" program—something they have assisted in developing.

The development of any new program is usually done to satisfy an expressed and obvious need of the agency itself. Pioneers in the field of police–community relations have been confronted with the problems of developing a program that will correspond with both the capabilities of the agency and the needs of the community. The challenge in develop-ing a police–community relations program is to make it consistent with the needs of the social structure and at the same time satisfy the needs of the agency. This is viewed in terms of Merton, who said: "Every item of culture has some distinctive place in the total culture...."[31] We can further understand the need for police agencies to develop police–community relations programs by borrowing from Radcliffe-Brown:

> The function of a particular social usage is the contributions it makes to the total social life as the functioning of the total social system. Such a view implies that a social system (the total social system of a society together with the totality of social usages, in which that structure appears and on which it depends for its continual existence) has a certain kind of unity which we may speak of as a functional unity. We may define it as a condition in which all parts of the social system work together with a sufficient degree of harmony or internal consistency, i.e., without producing persistent conflicts which can neither be resolved nor neglected.[32]

Our cities are composed of many social systems and subcultural groups (e.g., youth, minority groups, the poor, the affluent). At this period in history, these are producing persistent conflicts which cannot be neglected. An effective and meaningful police–community relations program must be geared toward solving the *real* social problems of the community.

Once the decision is made to establish a police–community relations program, it must have the total support of the chief of police. If the chief is not totally committed to the concept of police–community relations (and the community relations program) and is only creating one because "that's the thing to do"—the program is doomed to fail. This is illustrated by one police–community relations officer, who said:

> We have a program, but we are not doing anything. The Chief doesn't support the program. We are a kind of "don't rock the boat" unit. By that I mean we can't do anything. I have submitted several programs to the Chief for his consideration but nothing ever happens. As long as we don't rock the boat, the Chief is happy. He can go to his meeting and say "I have a community relations unit."[33]

We cannot overemphasize the need for a full commitment from the chief of police. Former chief inspector Harry Fox of the Philadelphia Police Department put in in these words: "The key to successful police–community relations is the chief of police letting his commanders know that he wants good community relations."[34]

Deputy chief Theresa Melchione, director of police–community relations, New York Police Department, expressed her belief that any success of police–community relations in New York can be attributed to the support given the program by the commissioner of police.[35] Illustrative of what she spoke of is a talk given by former commissioner Vincent L. Broderick before the command officers of his department:

> You are superior officers. You are the leaders of the department. You are responsible for implementing the policy of the department in your own commands. If you are not willing, or able to maintain discipline, you should not be here today.[36]

Illustrative of this problem is the testimony of Robert Harris, who resigned from the Portland, Oregon, Police Department after 16 months of duty with the community relations unit. He stated that he quit the department "largely because he believed the Police–Community Relations Unit was not getting the support it needed to be effective."[37] Harris termed the program as "tokenism" and a program which will fail unless an understanding of police–community relations can be spread throughout the department, not just among specialists."[38]

Attempting to develop a community relations program which is not supported by the chief of police can be even more detrimental than no program at all. We strongly recommend that no community relations program be established for purposes of "window dressing" or because "that's the thing to do." A total commitment by both the police and city administration is essential to the development of an effective community relations program.

Police–community relations should not be assigned on a part-time basis. The job is so important and the need is so great that it demands that each department have a central unit, staffed with full-time personnel, to *coordinate* the department's overall program. It is difficult, however, to accurately estimate the number of officers who should be assigned full-time to police-community relations. One source suggested that, at the minimum, 1 percent of the total police personnel should be assigned to full-time police-community relations duty.[39] We shall not attempt to designate a formula for the number of personnel who should be assigned to police-community relations other than to say that the number will depend upon the size of the department; the characteristics of the city, for example, population, social, economic, racial and ethnic characteristics; and the level of friction existing between the police and the community.

The police-community relations unit should be given high prestige within the department's organizational structure. Its status should be equal to the highest line division below the chief. This is extremely important because the unit must be vested with the authority to carry out its responsibilities. In larger departments the unit should be given divisional status and commanded by a deputy chief. In medium-size departments the unit should be commanded by an officer one rank below the chief. In either case, the commander should report directly to the chief of police. It is important that the commander report directly to the chief of police, because he is the only person responsible for the overall operation of the police department. In smaller departments the chief himself should assume the direct responsibility for directing the police-community relations program.

The community relations unit should be given the responsibility of planning, developing, supervising, and evaluating all aspects of the department's police-community relations. It should respect the department in city-wide citizen groups, establish and maintain liaison with individuals and organizations in the community, assist groups in their projects of community improvement, supervise precinct-level community efforts, review and recommend departmental policy designed to improve police-community relations, and seek out community problems and develop proposed solutions to these problems. To be more specific, a police-community relations unit should have the following responsibilities:

1. Centralization of information and knowledge relating to police and community relations and specific problems of the entire community.
2. Stimulating the concern and interest of the entire department, aimed at correcting social problems.
3. The police-community relations unit should have the authority to participate in the formulation of departmental policies as they relate to police-community relations. If the department has a planning staff, members of the community relations unit should be represented on that staff and allowed a formal role in the formulation of policies as they affect community relations. The unit should also evaluate department procedures as they affect community relations.

4. Planning and development of the department's overall police–community relations program.

5. The community relations unit should be intimately involved in all phases of the department's training programs. In addition to developing human relations training programs and participating as instructors, the unit should see that community relations is incorporated into all phases of police training (e.g., car stops, use of firearms, writing citations, criminal investigations, etc.).

6. The police–community relations unit should open and keep open lines of communication between the police department and all segments of the community. This will entail maintaining liaison with all groups, organizations, and agencies in the community.

7. The police–community relations unit should participate in the selection of police candidates by participating on the oral examination board.

8. The police–community relations unit should constantly evaluate community attitudes toward the police. This should be accomplished by periodic surveys in the community. Such surveys should also be designed to evaluate the unit's own programs and should be designed to determine if its programs are effective and what new programs should be developed.

9. The police–community relations unit should not be afraid to become involved in the correction of social injustices. It should serve as a discovery and referral agency—operating to mobilize the total community resources to work vigorously on solving social problems. The unit and the chief of police should speak out on social problems and lend the prestige of the department in focusing attention on social problems. The unit should promote cooperation between the police, citizens, and other community agencies (both public and private).

10. The police–community relations unit should maintain a good working relationship with the news media and use it to promote good community relations.

11. The key to a successful police–community relations program is involvement in the community. As such, the unit should pursue all avenues necessary to improve police–community relations.

Upon establishing a police–community relations unit, the responsibility for police–community relations *should not be considered the sole responsibility of that unit.* Police–community relations is the responsibility of every member of the police department. It should be the responsibility of every police chief to see that the efforts of such units have the support of all department members. They should develop clear-cut policies relative to police and community relations through the delegation of administrative responsibility and assure that the dictates of their policies are carried out. Too often, police chiefs say that police–community relations is the most important function of a police department, yet this is not reflected in the police budget. The police budget should reflect the department's support for such a program and monies should be made available for the unit to carry out its responsibilities.

In summary, to develop a successful police–community relations program, the officers assigned to that unit must be totally committed to change and given the tools to effect change. If the program is not sincere, it could create even more animosity against the police, because insincerity is difficult to hide. If the department wants a public relations program, it should be called such and not police–community relations.

In the words of Radcliffe-Brown: "The function of any recurrent activity . . . is the part it plays in the social life as a whole and therefore the contribution it makes to the maintenance of the structural continuity."[40] *The structural continuity of our nation is at stake* and any sincere police–community relations program should be geared to alleviating the underlying causes of this explosive condition. Again, as pointed out by the President's Crime Commission: "Indeed, no lasting improvement in law enforcement is likely in this country unless police–community relations are substantially improved."[41]

Louis Radelet has indicated that community relations is

a kind of three-legged stool, each leg as important as the other, and indeed interdependent, one upon the other. One leg is represented by "public relations," in the traditional sense, i.e., the totality of efforts to develop a favorable public attitude toward product and producer. The second leg is that of "community service." One purpose in this is identical to that of public relations, but there is the added factor of a service rendered—to do some good in the community—to help solve some problems, perhaps. A Police Athletic League would be an example. The third leg is that of "community participation." . . . This is a concept of community organization which is essential, of course, a social work concept featuring the police as part of, indeed, as something of a *pivot* on a community team to deal with problems of concern not only to the police department but to the *total* community.[42]

Summary

In this chapter we have taken issue with Radelet's conception of police–community relations by redefining the term and making an explicit distinction between public relations and community relations. Whereas Radelet speaks of police–community relations as being "a kind of three-legged stool" vis-à-vis public relations, community service, and community participation, we maintain that public relations is not part of police–community relations. We accept the idea that community service is a part of police–community relations but not in the same context as that described by Radelet ("one purpose in this is identical to that of public relations . . ."), because the implication is that community service is undertaken to project a good image. We do accept Radelet's concept that community service is police–community relations in light "of a service rendered—to do some good in the community—to help solve some problem. . . ." This we see as the purpose and function of police–community relations. Any successful police–community relations program *must* place its greatest efforts on community service (problem solving) and community participation.

End Notes

[1] President's Commission on Law Enforcement and Administration of Justice, *Task Force Report: The Police* (Washington, D.C.: U.S. Government Printing Office, 1967), p. 144.

[2] National Advisory Commission on Criminal Justice Standards and Goals, *A National Strategy to Reduce Crime,* advance printing (Washington, D.C.: U.S. Government Printing Office, 1973), p. 105.

[3] Ibid., p. 107.

[4] Ibid., p. 106.

[5] Charles R. Gain, "Working Paper on Developing Methods of Evaluating Police–Community Relations Programs," paper presented at a two-day seminar on Police–Community Relations in San Jose, Calif., July 18–19, 1969, emphasis added.

[6] Ibid.

[7] Charlotte Epstein, *Intergroup Relations for Police Officers* (Baltimore, Md.: Williams & Wilkins, 1962), p. 6.

[8] Ibid.

[9] Richard L. Holcomb, *The Police and the Public* (Springfield, Ill.: Charles C Thomas, 1954), p. 6.

[10] San Francisco Police Department, "Police–Community Relations—The San Francisco Program," unpublished report, January 1967, emphasis added.

[11] Thomas Cahill, "The Police and Community Tensions," unpublished report on police and community relations within the San Francisco Police Department, n.d.

[12] Lee P. Brown, "Dynamic Police–Community Relations at Work," *The Police Chief,* 35, no. 4 (April 1968), 48.

[13] Winston-Salem, North Carolina, Police Department, "Community Service Unit Newsletter," May 10, 1968, p. 1.

[14] A. F. Brandstatter and Louis A. Radelet, *Police and Community Relations: A Sourcebook* (Encino, Calif.: Glencoe Press, 1968), p. IV.

[15] Thomas Reddin, "1968—The Year of Total Community Involvement," mimeo, n.d., p. 8, emphasis added.

[16] Lee P. Brown, "Community Relations," in *Local Government Police Management,* ed. Bernard L. Garmire (Washington, D.C.: International City Management Association, 1977) p. 351.

[17] Brandstatter and Radelet, *Police and Community Relations,* p. 15.

[18] *Report of the National Advisory Commission on Civil Disorders* (Washington, D.C.: U.S. Government Printing Office, 1968), p. 1.

[19]William J. Osterloh, "San Francisco Police–Community Relations in 1968," mimeo, n.d., p. 2.

[20]Brown, "Community Relations," p. 359.

[21]National Commission on The Causes and Prevention of Violence, *Law and Order Reconsidered* (Washington, D.C.: U.S. Government Printing Office, 1969), p. 385.

[22]John K. Swan, "Internal Controls," *Local Government Police Management,* ed. Bernard L. Garmire (Washington, D.C.: International City Management Association, 1977), p. 343.

[23]National Advisory Commission on Criminal Justice Standards and Goals, *Police* (Washington, D.C.: U.S. Government Printing Office, 1973), p. 329.

[24]Multnomah County, Oregon, Division of Public Safety.

[25]National Advisory Commission on Criminal Justice Standards and Goals, *Police,* p. 66.

[26]Charles D. Hale and Bernard L. Garmier, "Patrol Administration," *Local Government Police Management,* ed. Bernard L. Garmier (Washington, D.C.: International City Management Association, 1977), p. 181.

[27]Ibid.

[28]George L. Kelling et al., *The Kansas City Preventive Patrol Experiment: A Summary Report* (Washington, D.C.: Police Foundation, 1974).

[29]Peter W. Greenwood et al., *The Criminal Investigation Process* (Lexington, Mass.: Heath, 1977).

[30]Robert Wasserman, Michael Gardner, and Alana S. Cohen, *Improving Police–Community Relations* (Washington, D.C.: U.S. Department of Justice, 1973), pp. 60–63.

[31]Robert K. Merton, *Social Theory and Social Structure* (New York: Free Press, 1965), p. 22.

[32]A. R. Radcliffe-Brown, "On the Concept of Function in Social Science," *American Anthropologist,* 37 (1935), 396–98, cited by Merton, ibid.

[33]Interview with a police–community relations officer.

[34]Interview with chief inspector Harry Fox, Philadelphia Police Department.

[35]Interview with deputy chief Theresa Melchione, New York City Police Department.

[36]Speech given by former police commissioner Vincent L. Broderick, as quoted in the New York *Herald Tribune,* July 3, 1965.

[37]"Report Cites Need for Improvement in Police–Community Relations," *The Oregonian,* October 30, 1969, p. 38.

[38]Ibid.

[39]Nelson A. Watson, *Police–Community Relations* (Washington, D.C.: International Association of Chiefs of Police, 1966).

[40]Radcliffe-Brown, "On the Concept of Function."

[41]President's Commission on Law Enforcement and Administration of Justice, *Task Force Report.*

[42]Louis A. Radelet, "Current Developments in Police–Community Relations Nationwide," in *Proceedings of Police Administrators Conference on Community Relations,* ed. Jeptha S. Rogers (Washington, D.C.: International Association of Chiefs of Police, 1966), p. 4.

CHAPTER
EIGHT

POLICE-COMMUNITY RELATIONS: SOCIAL SCIENCE PERSPECTIVES

In examining the literature on police–community relations, it becomes apparent that there are two conceptions of what are considered "appropriate" police–community relations. One conception held by law enforcement personnel is the view that police–community relations are synonymous with public relations. The other view, held by academicians and others, both within and outside minority-group membership, suggests that police–community relations are more accurately referred to as a methodology for the police to become more responsive to the needs of its clientele.

Perhaps the distinction between what each group considers as "appropriate" police–community relations was best described by Michigan State University's National Survey of Police and Community Relations, where it was noted:

Community relations is the *two way* communication process focusing community resources on problem solving. It involves a recognition of two viewpoints, that of the police and that of the community. Public relations, on the other hand, is basically a *one way* communication process aimed at gathering support for police procedures and informing the public of departmental activities. We have found that if distrust among segments of the public is prevalent, the public relations activity will do little to garner public support.[1]

To suggest that public relations activity does not make a contribution to the mutual understanding of the police and the community would not be accurate. However, law enforcement officials should be aware of the fact that public relations is only one means of addressing the police–community relationship and should not become an end in itself. "Where public relations activity becomes an end in itself, the department runs the risk of falling victim to 'image pre-occupation' wherein they emphasize 'looking good' rather than 'being good.' "[2]

In short, the Michigan State Survey suggests that there is confusion among police departments as to the salient distinction between public relations and community relations, this misunderstanding itself is part of the problem for some of the failures in police–community relationships.[3]

Another dysfunctionality of police department's overreliance on public relations activities is that "when a program is essentially public relations in orientation it often fails to engage sectors of the community, thus police officials often become frustrated and embittered at being repulsed in their efforts 'to sell' their department."[4] Consequently, those within the police organization become quite cynical as to the utility of not only reaching but addressing the public.

The University of California's survey, *The Police and the Community,* further documents the distinction between public relations and community relations in its very articulate conclusion, stating that:

> The strongest caution should be directed toward the police assumption that police–community relations is equated with or is a function of police public relations. The latter stresses one way communication; the former, two way. This study has shown that a constant request of those who are alienated from the general community is that they be "understood." Their assumption is that they are not heard and thus not understood. "Hearing" requires that the police listen to varying viewpoints as well as present their own.[5]

To document the law enforcement conception of what is entailed in appropriate police community relations, standard texts relied upon and usually authored by police officers will be reviewed in the following section.

POLICE CONCEPT OF COMMUNITY RELATIONS

In securing information pertaining to what might be an "appropriate" police–community relations concept, or how the police may construct this concept, the literature was reviewed in search of significant material that could be classified under four main topics or factors:

1. Definition of public relations or police–community relations
2. Responsibility for police–community relations
3. Functions of a police–community relations program
4. Goals of police–community relations

Definitions

To really appreciate a typical police department's conception of police–community relations, the attitudes that shape many of our police organizations must be examined. Perhaps a not-too-typical attitude was reflected by an ex-chief of police, William Parker, in his comments as to why he did not miss the "good old days" and why he refuted earlier attitudes on police public relations shared by many police administrators:

> In those days many excellent police administrators held that public relations activity was highly impractical—almost a criminal waste of government funds. They took the attitude that they were paid to be policemen, not salesmen, and that the public was going to get old fashioned police work pure and simple— no frills, no information, no explanation. . . .
>
> The police considered themselves and the public to be separate entities. It was a case of the police versus the public—the police department decided what was good for the community and delivered just that and nothing else.[6]

Unfortunately, this attitude has left deep scars on the relationship that exists between the police and the public. Furthermore, this attitude is not entirely unchanged in present administrators or patrolmen.

Another authority on police systems has stated: "The almost palpable fact remains that city police forces waste a part, and sometimes a considerable good part of that available manpower on performance of unnecessary or so-called 'public relations' assignments."[7]

There might well be legitimate and illegitimate choices of what are considered proper public relations assignments; however, the police are progressively having less and less to say about what activities are proper or improper. The point of friction occurs when the police are directed to provide these public relations assignments. The dilemma for police is that they dare not resist many public relations assignments the public confers on them, because the public has already withheld its esteem or any status for which the police are striving. Not to cooperate with the public's demands seems only to exacerbate further relationships with police officers. This dilemma has a profound effect on officers' conception of "appropriate" police–community relations, simply because there is little chance of conflict being resolved in a manner acceptable to the police.

The police officer's conception of what might be "appropriate" police–community relations encounters immediate difficulty by the various definitions of police–community relations and public relations. For example, a principle textbook in the police field speaks in terms of both police–community relations and public relations. However, it classifies both activities as public relations. In essence, O. W. Wilson suggests that the goal of public relations is to create a favorable public attitude, which can only be created through respect and confidence in the police. To achieve this goal, Wilson suggests that the following items are of prime importance: police appearance, police conversation, telephone manners, attitude, relationship with offenders, relationship with complainant, and the handling of offenders.[8] The last four categories are more in the area of what many people conceive of as police–community activities, whereas the first three categories are definitely of a public relations activity. The difficulty encountered when categorizing both groups together is to allow officers to ignore the more important area of police–community relations while concentrating on the more superficial area of public relations.

If the confusion over public relations and police–community relations was not enough, Wilson's next chapter provides the climax as he discusses methods of informing the public. This has the effect of reinforcing public relations activities at the expense of police–community relations. Wilson suggests that the duties of public information officers all revolve around their mission of gaining support of the public in police policies and police programs so as to facilitate the accomplishment of various police tasks.[9] The duties of the public information officer fall into four broad categories, as Wilson sees it:

1. To evaluate public opinion and attitudes with respect to policies, methods, and personnel of the department.
2. To advise the chief with regard to the public relations aspects of new or revised department programs, policies, procedures, and activities.
3. To plan and carry out programs aimed at keeping the public informed of police activities.
4. To furnish a staff supervision of all police activities that may influence public support.[10]

Wilson then proceeds to emphasize the value of police–press relationships, press policies, police publications for the public, advertisements, speakers' bureau, special demonstrations, and community organization efforts that are so narrowly conceived as to only address the utility of these programs in terms of the benefits accruing to the police department.[11]

Significantly, when there is some confusion as to the distinction between public relations and community relations in a leading textbook in the police field, it is understandable that many police officers would conceptualize "appropriate" police–community relations as nothing more than public relations. Furthermore, it is always easier to provide one-way communication than to participate in two-way communication.

Another leading textbook in the police field also contributes to the confusion between public relations and community relations, and in the process constructs "appropriate" police–community relations conceptions more in terms of public relations than anything else. "The term 'public relations' is often confused with 'publicity.' Public relations is the sum total of the relationships which exist between the police and public. Publicity is one way of creating these relationships. It is, however, not the best way."[12]

To suggest that this is just a problem in semantics grossly over-simplifies the matter, for we discover that not only are the leading textbooks in the police field providing confusion as to what police might consider "appropriate" police–community relations, but it indicates the conception of the few articulate police authorities as observed in their subtle statements describing appropriate police–community relations as being little more than public relations. This suggests what the remaining body of law enforcement officers must regard as being "appropriate" or acceptable.

In a very perceptive article, "The Trouble with Troubleshooting," Mary Ellen Leary examines the duties and functions of police–community relations officers in San Francisco and presents officers' observations, such as the following:

> One of the most heartbreaking problems in such sordid urban centers today is the number of runaway boys, some as young as ten, who loiter the streets as prostitutes to homosexuals.... They won't talk to you until they've been around a while, gotten ditched, disillusioned, hungry. Then they'd give anything to go home, but they're scared. I can tell when they hit that stage and I used to talk to 'em. Easy like. Take a few days at it. Then I'd say, "Let me get your old man on the phone." Sometimes I've driven kids to the airport and stayed with them until the non-stop flight took off, then phoned the folks.[13]

The definition of police–community relations is but one factor influencing officers' conceptions of what is appropriate or inappropriate police–community relations.

Responsibilities

A second factor is the conception of where the responsibility for police–community relations should be appropriately located. For example, *Municipal Police Administration* maintains that by its very nature, a public relations program cannot be an entity unto itself, in which responsibility is assigned to any one unit. Since all police officers are responsible for public relations, each must share in this responsibility. Nevertheless, from an organizational perspective, public relations is sometimes a staff function which would necessitate the focusing of responsibility to an appropriate unit.[14]

Other factors that create confusion in terms of responsibility associated with community relations occur in those departments that feel they do not have the finances or personnel to carry out a community relations program. Implicit within this is the fact that everyone shares the responsibility, or that the police chief alone has the final responsibility for police–community relations.[15] In any event, there are too few police decisions and too much confusion in this critical issue.

A former chief of police, William Parker, took a rather narrow view of police–community relations, as the following suggests:

> Public relations is not an organizational position, or subdivision, or something you consciously do. It is a state of affairs. It is the relationship between the public and some identifiable group. As such it is not something you can either accept or reject. It is in continual existence.[16]

To suggest that police–community relations is something that you can neither accept nor reject simply because of its existence is a theoretical simplification. Quite the contrary; it is something that must, and demands, to be accepted, for unless it is couched in those terms, one can be assured that police–community relations will be rejected because of the organizational structure of our police departments, if for no other reason.

Parker goes on to comment:

> Perhaps it is time we stopped referring to public relations or public relations activities as something we assign to a personality, or unit, or even to the administrator himself. Every look, every word, every motion made by every man in the organization every moment of the day, communicates impressions to the public—and as such is public relations activity, good or bad.[17]

To suggest further diffusion of responsibility for this important concern is ludicrous. To do so would be to move in the opposite direction of what the community is demanding of police departments. The community wants to focus more responsibility on police departments. To respond by further concealing areas of responsibility would not only intensify the existing strain between the police and the community, but would convince the public that there are abuses of both authority and power within the police agencies.

Parker's position on police–community relations is completely incongruent to the position he usually took regarding application of any organizational principles to police tasks. Indeed, he remolded the Los Angeles Police Department into a giant of organizational principles. Therefore, his conception of what is appropriate police–community relations is instructive when we observe this incongruency in terms of diffusing responsibility for police–community relations.

Functions

A third factor influencing police conceptions of appropriate police–community relations pertains to the functions of a police–community relations program.

Functions of police–community relations units of police departments have varied from speakers' bureaus to preparing press releases. Some functions entail acquainting minority groups with police policies and procedures, thus establishing some form of communication between the community and the police. Some police units report discriminatory practices that are observed in the community. Other units serve as an intelligence listening post because they are so well situated within the minority-group framework and can detect trends of activities that are likely to become police problems.[18]

It is quite ironic that the only function generally acceptable to the police as a community relations activity is the gathering of intelligence information. This is one point that the academic community and minority-group community have been able to communicate to the police—that intelligence gathering will not be considered a legitimate activity of a police–community relations program. If this advice is ignored, the resulting manifestations could be more serious than the original phenomenon that caused the police to seriously consider creation of community relations units.

Nevertheless, many within the police field resist this advice and continue to program dysfunctionalities into the very units that might offer the police some chance of obtaining a more meaningful relationship with community elements. A perfect example of this can be viewed in Thomas Adams's book, *Law Enforcement: An Introduction to the Police Role in the Community*, where the author offers a very questionable recommendation pertaining to police–community relations: "The officer is responsible for identifying and getting to know the leaders in each neighborhood. He should develop them as cooperative informants on the lawful and unlawful activities in the community."[19]

The Michigan State Survey revealed that by and large many police officers throughout the nation consider the tasks performed by police–community relations units as "nonpolice" work and, consequently, as a type of "baby-sitting" service.[20] In fact, the only reason these "nonpolice" tasks are even addressed in many police departments is that there has been an order issued to attend to them.[21]

Not only are patrol officers offended by such conceptions of police–community relations, but the very functions that are assigned as responsibilities in police–community relations activities strike many patrol officers as "do-gooder," "social work," or "softness"—all qualities completely antithetical to patrolmen's self-images or role conceptions.[22]

To intensify further the conflict between patrol officers' self-concepts and their image of their job, within police–community relations units we observe the trend that communication itself is rather sterile unless communication occurs with those members of the community who should be talking to the police. To suggest that police officers talk to militants is again completely antithetical to police conceptions of their job—in fact, to many officers this is tantamount to treason.[23]

In essence, the very functions of successful police–community relations programs are not at all conducive to being accepted as appropriate by the police. Therefore, public relations or one-way communication is not only more acceptable to patrol officers in terms of its being more in line with their conception of police work, but there is less role conflict encountered by the officers. It is practically impossible to accept any job when it is completely antithetical to one's conception of the job.

Goals

The fourth main factor influencing patrol officers' conceptions of appropriate or inappropriate police–community relations revolves around the goals of the police–community relations program. The goals of such programs in the minds of those in the police field are to achieve public support, public understanding, and public confidence.[24] Although there is great agreement as to the goals, there is little consensus on how to achieve these goals.

Perhaps part of the difficulty in achieving the three goals noted above can be seen in police departments preoccupation with impartiality when dealing with the public. There is no question of the necessity for police officers to remain impartial. However, there is a distinction between impartiality and uninvolvement. Any medicine taken in excess soon loses its medicinal value. The analogy can be extended to police use of impartiality. In excess, impartiality becomes intolerable.

Arthur Aubry's comments on the dilemma incurred by the use of impartiality in smaller police departments are applicable to the police–community relations problem.

> For good public relations the elements of impersonal relationships and impartial dealings with all members of the public alike are required, and this desired state of affairs will be very hard to secure where the officer knows practically everyone with whom he comes in contact.[25]

The significant point that emerges from Aubry's comments is the confusion police have on the point of impersonality and impartiality. Police can and properly should remain impartial, but not necessarily impersonal.

Perhaps the most serious problem for the police administrator regarding police–community relations goals is that the goals themselves should transcend the entire spectrum of government and community. Accompanying these community-wide goals should be the responsibility for implementing and achieving such programs and goals. More often than not, both the goals and the responsibility for achieving them are contained solely within police organizations.

The tragedy of police administrators is that they are held accountable for matters over which they have no control. They cannot hope to make community relations compensate for a do-nothing mayor who is essentially apathetic about the problems of the poor; a governor whose solution to social problems is to cut budgets; or a business community that has not yet become attuned to the idea of black capitalism.[26]

The police conceptualize police–community relations goals as being far too one-sided. Perhaps many police officers are reluctant to accept the high goals that police–community relations would impose on them. Thus, conceiving of public relations as more "appropriate," the police are able to accept a far more manageable task.

While the previously mentioned factors influence the conception of "appropriate" police–community relations, what the police have not yet acknowledged is that failure to have a police–community relations program does not mean that an organization is without police–community relations.[27]

According to Gourley and Bristow, what the public does not recognize is that police organizations, unlike other organizations, are more than likely to create strains within the community since their basic missions are to enforce the law, restrict citizen activities, and control citizen conduct.[28] Perhaps the point is that the public does not perceive the strain as *endemic to police organizations.*

ACADEMICIANS' CONCEPTS OF COMMUNITY RELATIONS

The preceding discussion has addressed and reviewed the literature pertaining to the police conception of "appropriate" police–community relations. The following material will review what academicians and significant others conceive of as "appropriate" police–community relations.

In assessing the importance of police–community relations, the President's Commission on Law Enforcement and the Administration of Justice suggests that police–community relations has an effect on the police department as an organization, especially as it pertains to recruiting future officers. Beyond this, the commission could see police–community relations as being of enough importance to have more than just a passing effect on police operations, individual police officers, and the general stability of the community.[29]

However, as important as police–community relations units are, many who have studied the police do not regard a community relations unit as a cure-all. In fact, there is a dysfunctional effect of others in the department regarding the police–community relations units as the sole repository for the responsibility of good community relations work. In fact, both the University of California and Michigan State University studies discovered that those cities having police–community relations units still lack the confidence of minority groups.[30]

Individual community relations officers have occasionally been able to gain the confidence of all segments of minority groups, but collectively the units and personnel comprising the units are usually known to a small proportion of the minority group, and even then only to those who need the contact the least, the middle class of the minorities.[31]

In the words of Victor Strecher, police–community relations has been "preaching to the converted."[32] However, as pointed out earlier, we can expect resistance to the suggestion of establishing communication with the more militant and hard-core members of the community, because to many police officers this is tantamount to treason.

It is interesting to note that one of the problems the University of California study encountered in researching this area of police–community relations was a belief held by many officers regarding police–community relations.

> The controversy which surrounds the central problems of police–community relations tends to promote and to generate a "we" versus "they" dichotomy. The "actors" who are involved in the controversy are often prone to ask the question: "Whose side are *you* on?" The assumption is made that the issues are clear and that a decision of "commitment" should be forthcoming. Persons who express a neutral position are often made immediately "suspect." . . . In fact, the "choosing up" of sides is one of the current perils of the problem.[33]

In examining police–community relations, the University of California survey took a novel approach by identifying "problem areas" that existed in the respective city's police–community relationship. Quite significantly, these "problem areas" were identified on the basis of belief and not on fact. The significance of this methodology allows one to accept quite readily another's conception of "appropriate" police–community relations. In other words, if a specific belief is consistently held by persons in the community, then this belief—rather than the fact—becomes operational for the parties involved.[34]

Problem areas in police–community relations identified in the Philadelphia study were divided into two main groups: those from the general community and those from ethnic minorities. The problem areas discovered were as follows:

GENERAL COMMUNITY

1. The general quality of the police department
2. Corruption
3. Police and the administration of justice
4. The "Negro problem"
5. Police relations with the minority community
6. Police brutality
7. Youth problem

1. Discrimination and police brutality
2. Illegal searches and seizures
3. The mass media
4. Potential explosiveness in continued conflicts
5. Police-community relations—negotiate with real Negro leaders[35]

It is quite evident that what these "problem areas" signify are various conceptions of what "appropriate" police relations would involve. Based on the literature reviewed previously, it is safe to suggest that many police officers would find some or all of these "problem areas" as "inappropriate" to their opinion of what constitutes legitimate police-community relations.

The national survey completed by Michigan State University suggests various program assumptions and basic goals underlying the development of police-community relations programs. These assumptions and goals clearly indicate what Michigan State University considers to be appropriate police-community relations.

The basic assumptions of good police-community relations programming are enumerated as follows:

1. The police commitment toward bettering the police and community relationship must be formalized by the department and promulgated throughout the community.
2. Communication channels that are available to all citizens must be established between the police and the community.
3. The program undertaken by the department to reduce conflict and tension in the community must utilize the resources of the entire community.
4. The program must utilize those means through normal channels, even if this should necessitate diverting the police role in new directions.[36]

Although these goals and assumptions might constitute an "appropriate" design for police-community relations to academicians and minority-group members, they are not considered appropriate by many police officers. These goals, if accepted, carry with them the responsibility for remedial action, and to many police officers this responsibility is unfairly thrust on them alone.

However, the police response to and conception of what are appropriate police-community relations does not acknowledge that "the police and community relationships cannot be realistically isolated from some of the most vexing issues of our time. It is at the heart of such questions as civil rights and crime, and at least tangentially related to the problems of urbanization and poverty."[37]

To what extent should the police become involved in community affairs? The Michigan State survey suggests that there are essentially two polar positions on this issue. The first is the "traditional" police view, in

which the police feel that they should confine themselves to "law enforcement" matters only. The second stresses police involvement in the
community to the degree necessary to maintain the peace of that
community—a crime prevention outlook.[38]

> The repression of crime, for years the traditional police goal, can no longer
> successfully maintain social control in an urban society where the police have
> become alienated from major segments of the community. Vigorous repres-
> sion, if carried out in a manner offensive to large portions of the population,
> will increase rather than reduce community tensions. . . . No matter how ef-
> fective a procedure or technique is in controlling a specific criminal act, if the
> community finds that action repulsive they will fail to support the police.
> Citizens will become tense at the approach of an officer, in effect saying: "If
> they treat others that way, how will they treat me?" The police on the other
> hand, operate in such a manner that meets their expectation of "client" re-
> sponse. These mutual expectations result in widening conflict and distrust on
> both sides.[39]

It is not proposed that the police act as social workers, but the police
must recognize the extent to which they are exposed daily to social
problems.[40] Perhaps William Turner states the problem even more
clearly when he suggests that "most police stubbornly cling to the old
concepts of their role. They disclaim any sociological role on the grounds
that their mission is solely to enforce existing laws, overlooking the fact
that they are de facto sociologists."[41]

To suggest that the police become more involved in community problems is an extremely appropriate suggestion, especially in considering
that whether the police like it or not, many segments of the community
hold the police responsible for community problems. To submit that
police should not become involved simply because they are not totally
responsible for community problems is to retreat from an opportunity to
point out various existing distortions and to rectify to some degree various social problems within the community framework.

The report of the National Advisory Commission on Civil Disorders
discovered that in many ways the police officer, a symbol of the governmental power structure, symbolizes the deeper problems to which
various segments of our society are exposed. The police officer is not
only a symbol for problems within the community, but also within the
entire system of criminal justice.[42]

> he (policeman) becomes the tangible target for grievances against shortcom-
> ings throughout that system: against assembly line justice in too many lower
> courts; against wide disparities in sentences; against antiquated corrections
> facilities; against the basic inequities imposed by the system on the poor—to
> whom, for example, the option of bail means only jail. . . . At the same time,
> police responsibilities in the ghetto have grown as other institutions of social
> control have lost much of their authority; the schools, because so many are
> segregated, old and inferior; religion, which has become so irrelevant to those
> who lost faith as they lost hope; career aspirations, which for many young

Negroes are totally lacking; the family, because its bonds are so often snapped. It is the policeman who must fill this institutional vacuum, and is then resented for the presence this effort demands.[43]

The community is not asking that police become involved with it. Rather, it is demanding that police departments become involved with community-wide problems. This pattern is structured in sufficient terms that until police accept this cry for help, there is little chance of the community and the police moving closer together.

Unfortunately, the police conception of what is entailed in appropriate police–community relations does not acknowledge or even address the community cry for help. Therefore, police–community relations as conceived by the community not only requires police involvement, but has the impact of significantly restructuring police conceptions of their role. Police resistance to police–community relations also entails resistance to the community's demands to have the police officer's role redefined.

Also, as William Kephart observes, perhaps the main "drawback" to the community relations approach is not that such activity lies outside the sphere of police work, nor that the police do not have time to involve themselves in "social problems," but that the personnel within police organizations have not been the type who could relate to, or gain the confidence of the community.[44]

Regarding police conception of appropriate police–community relations, both the University of California and Michigan State University studies discovered that most police departments believe the primary purpose of police–community relations to be to sell the police image to the public. Indeed, in two large cities, police administrators felt that their community relations problems would be resolved if they could hire professional public relations firms. The problem has much deeper ramifications than merely failing to project a correct police image to the public.[45] Until the police acknowledge this, there is perhaps little hope that what police create as police–community relations programs entails something more meaningful and relevant to the community than excursions into image preoccupation and projection.

STRUCTURAL AND ORGANIZATIONAL DEFICIENCIES CONDUCIVE TO POLICE RESISTANCE TO POLICE–COMMUNITY RELATIONS

Bayley and Mendelsohn observe that police officers individually understand the needs for human relations in their contacts with citizens, but as an organization, the police have allowed themselves to be confined in a relationship defined by the minorities.[46] This is an extremely important observation. The distinction between an individual officer's appreciation of the value of police–community relations and the organiza-

tions's attitude toward police–community relations suggests that there
are not only other areas in which police–community relations training
could be directed, but that there are also other reasons that might explain police resistance to police–community relations.

Poor police–community relations requires something more than mere
concern about police officers' attitudes, or what type of personnel are
being recruited as police officers, although these are not insignificant
areas. Any real understanding and comprehension of the magnitude of
police–community relations problems may require a structural analysis.
Whether any remedies exist for the problem might well depend as
much, if not more, on organizational remedies as on measures directed
toward an officer's awareness to sensitivity and attitude sets.

The following discussion will focus on structural and organizational
weaknesses within police departments and relate these deficiencies to
police–community relations. The following areas have been suggested as
structural and organizational deficiencies; each will be briefly discussed
in terms of its impact on the police–community relationship:

1. Channels of communication and responsiveness to citizen needs
2. Grievance machinery
3. Recruitment
4. Training
5. Reward structure
6. Policies regarding the use of discretion
7. Discipline structure
8. Group sanctions
9. Problem of authority
10. Patrol tactics
11. Fragmentation of police service
12. Specialization of units
13. Organizational placement of police–community relations units
14. Police function too narrowly conceived
15. Objectivity obscured by organizational goals
16. Deficient structural arrangements for referrals to other agencies

Channels of Communication and Responsiveness to Citizen Needs

This area is identified as a structural and organizational weakness of
the police system because the police are organized to receive only complaints of a social control nature. Many police would like to restrict the
services citizens request of them to those of a criminal nature. However,
many citizens call the police and will continue to call the police for
services that are important to them and are not only of a criminal nature.

Since there are no visible communication channels to the police organization for noncriminal problems, citizens do not regard the police as more than a criminal-control organization, as opposed to an organization designed to share responsibility for social control. When citizens call or contact the police bureaucracy, they are asked the nature of the problem. If the problem can be defined with or without the help of the clerk, it is referred to an already existing component part of the bureaucracy designed to handle these problems. However, police departments are organizationally limited to the component parts they can create to handle citizen problems. Nearly all the component parts are related to a structure for apprehending criminals. Therefore, when a citizen calls with a problem that cannot be neatly categorized, the organization might not be able to respond, with the resulting impact that the citizen quite often is irritated.

This is not meant as a criticism of the police organization for not being organized to handle more requests of a public service nature, nor as a criticism of citizens for expecting the police to respond to their requests. There are organizational limitations that have little to do with the human relations aspects of the organization. The fact that these limitations exist does not preclude the organization from reexamining its priorities of service so that various limitations could be minimized.

The structural defect may lie within an organizational assumption that when police agencies receive information or citizen requests for services, the police system must process or fulfill this request. If this is the case, it is unfortunate, because the police are limited not only in the service they can provide, but there are perhaps other agencies that could provide these called-for services in a much more acceptable way. Therefore, police organizations should not only continue making the occasional referrals they already make, but this referral process should become a structural asset of the organization.

In Joseph D. Lohman's *The Police and Minority Groups*, the author suggests not only the mobilization of constructive community elements to deal with tensions, but indicates clearly that the police department is in a unique position to both accept such information from citizens and to identify various tensions themselves, and to communicate these facts to responsible circles or appropriate agencies.[47]

Police administrators should not oversimplify the impact of this problem as the report of the National Advisory Commission on Civil Disorders suggested that a major reason for police–community hostility can be found in the general breakdown of communication between the police and the ghettos.[48]

Kurt and Gladys Lang's article, "Racial Disturbances as Collective Protest," suggests that this feeling of absence of responsiveness to citizen needs by our power structure further increases the remoteness and impersonality of our government. Since the organization and political skills of those people most in need of governmental services are the least prepared to negotiate with the various organizations, the apparent effectiveness of a disturbance compensates both for their inarticulation and low level of political power in that violence becomes a way of forcing official cognizance on conditions that are considered intolerable by these people.[49]

Police organizations have a "professional creed" which suggests that police should not respond to pressure brought to bear on their operational policies by "pressure groups."[50] Police organizations regard much of the pressure in the area of police–community relations as "political pressure." This perception appears to be quite accurate in many cases. However, without this outside pressure from community groups and higher governmental officials, police might well still dismiss the idea of police–community relations as being a viable part of their organizational role. Police resistance to police–community relations can be partially explained in terms of resistance of pressure brought on by "pressure groups."

The dilemma facing the police in this crucial organizational deficiency is that the police will continue to function as a lightning rod for minority and community discontent as long as they enforce laws and provide services with which segments of our public can only imperfectly identify.[51]

> A change in police behavior then, necessary though it is, cannot be expected to eliminate the corroding distrust and massive unrest evident today in the minority communities. Police reform is not a substitute for social reform. Moreover, changes in police behavior may not even be able to produce a great deal of improvement in police-minority relations unless it is coupled with a program of social renovation so penetrating and effective that it shatters the barriers which make majority and minority communities coherent social groups.[52]

The problem of police–minority relations goes much deeper than does simply sending officers to human relations institutes. It even goes much deeper than structural and organizational deficiencies in our police systems. It goes right to the heart of our entire community, its social structure, mores, and values. This is not to suggest that the first two methods of addressing police minority relations are without value; they are of considerable value. It is just another reason why police organizations should have more viable channels of communication, so that the entire community becomes aware that police–minority problems only reflect community-wide problems and the solutions will not be found in restructuring the police organization alone.

Grievance Machinery

A second structural and organizational weakness identified within our police system is that relating to grievance machinery. The subject of police review is quite controversial. It is beyond the scope of this chapter to enumerate the pros and cons of police review boards, but some salient points pertaining to the police–community relationship will be offered.

It is notable that the report of the National Advisory Commission on Civil Disorders considers the problem of grievance procedures to be of such importance that it was considered a primary source of hostility between the police and many citizens of the community.[53]

Although some citizens will never trust an agency against which they have a grievance, there will be others who irresponsibly provoke distrust of every agency.[54] It is for this reason, if none other, that police should establish some form of grievance procedure that is not only accessible to the citizens of a community but is equally acceptable to them.

The U.S. Riot Commission's report went on to state:

> We believe that an internal review board in which the police department itself receives and acts on complaints—regardless of its efficiency and fairness, can rarely generate the necessary community confidence, or protect the police against unfounded charges.[55]

The Walker Report in commenting upon the violence in Chicago suggested "that some policemen lost control of themselves under exceedingly provocative circumstances can perhaps be understood; but not condoned. If no action is taken against them, the effect can only be to discourage the majority of policemen who acted responsibly and further weaken the bond between police and community."[56]

The misconduct of one police officer often brings the entire department into suspicion, and the police, much to their dismay, often discover that the integrity of the force cannot be restored simply by punishing the erring officer, because many citizens regard this punishment as an effort to make the individual a scapegoat while preserving the organization's collective image.[57] Perhaps this explains why Paul Chevigny concluded that the people within the police system do not admit police abuse exists: "The problem itself is a strange one, because many of the people concerned with it—law enforcement officers and citizens alike—do not admit that it exists."[58] Chevigny goes on to make a very significant contribution in terms of relating police abuse to the institutionalized role of the police.

> Why did these men commit police abuses? Were they poorly trained? Were they unintelligent? Did they come to the department with some special streak of authoritarianism? Were their abuses somehow the result of the extreme pressures of life in New York? As we shall have occasion to observe in more detail, the answer to these questions for the most part is no. The truth is that police abuses are the product of the police role as an instrument of authority in society, the traditions of police work, and the attitude of society toward the police.[59]

To illustrate the dimensions of the organizational deficiency in not having an effective grievance procedure and at the same time illustrating a not too typical police view on the subject, we can discover quite a bit from the following comments:

> We of the police profession must harvest the bitter fruit, regardless of who planted the seed. Let us clean house . . . let us clean our own houses. We do not need citizens' committees, grand jurys, or boards of inquiry to sweep out the filth. We have eyes to see and we are strong enough to do the job. Let us move the rug into the back yard, turn on the bright lights, so we can see and sweep the entire house.[60]

Although one can appreciate police sensitivity to this subject, we must not forget that law enforcement deals with the public, and it must have the public's complete confidence and trust to be effective. This trust cannot be gained by "cleaning our own houses in the backyard." Instead, we should seize upon the opportunity of citizen's complaints, and use these complaints to discover police department weaknesses, as indicators of more pervasive problems, while assuring the public that we have complete confidence in our own organizations and that we welcome the responsible participation of citizens.[61]

Many police take the position that citizen review boards will not work because the public does not understand the nature of police work. However, what they are saying is that the police will ensure that the public will never understand the nature of police work, because the police feel there are not enough mature responsible citizens to participate in reviewing police abuses. This type of attitude can only further confuse an already suspicious public.

Not all police would object to police review boards; however, one reason not frequently heard is made by Niederhoffer, who suggests that the "net effect would not be great because the police bureaucracy would have routinized its procedures and absorbed its impact with procrustean sophistication."[62]

As Jerome Skolnick has stated: "All we know at present is that the police do not want to have their conduct reviewed by an outside agency and that they have the political 'clout' to maintain their organizational independence."[63]

Although Skolnick considers the principle of external review necessary, he feels that this should be directed at all public agencies, not only the police. He goes on to suggest: "We know enough about bureaucratic processes to predict that within bureaucracies people in the same organization will tend to be self protective."[64]

There can be no question that police conduct is a real and present problem. The Michigan State University study observed that whereas the police tend to minimize their misdeeds, there are certain segments of the public that exaggerate police abuses. The Michigan State University study concludes that there are essentially two responses open to the public in view of this situation:

1. They can refuse to initiate any changes and be prepared to tolerate decreasing public respect and increased violence; or
2. They can admit some fallibility, welcome criticism, compromise a little, and initiate objectively considered changes in an effort to enchance public support and avoid violence.[65]

However, good government requires good citizens, as the citizens themselves significantly shape the service they receive. Walter Gellhorn observes in his book, *Ombudsmen and Others,* that he would like to see pictures of citizens hung in the same gallery where we see pictures of our brutal, lazy, inefficient public officials.

> along with that picture a few others should perhaps be hung. Some would show citizens who have corrupted officials to advance their own selfish purposes. Some would show citizens who, in dealing with governmental agencies, have cut so many corners that the agencies have reacted by becoming suspicious and severe. Some would show citizens who constantly demand more and better service of every kind and then balk at paying the taxes the services necessitate.[66]

Although it is important to maintain a balanced perspective, realizing that the public has significant responsibilities as well as the police, we must not overlook the fact that unless we organizationally allow for entry of citizen complaints, there will always be more than just the "usual" amount of citizen mistrust and fear.

Recruitment

Another organizational deficiency identified pertains to the recruitment structure of our police system. Too often we see in police recruitment drives an emphasis on a "spirit of adventure" rather than the "spirit of service." The importance of the position is emphasized as opposed to the work. Whittaker concludes that a matter of prime importance is

> what type of young man is likely to respond to such appeals; whether he is more likely to be a dedicated public servant or an insecure young man seeking status through his uniform and, more dangerously, the exercise of a potentially autocratic power.[67]

The image portrayed by police drives to potential recruits creates a "set" of role expectations that will shape the individual's idea of a police officer's role.

Police recruiting should clearly portray the work the police are required to perform, so that "reality shock" can be minimized. Banton suggests that "reality shock" is manifested when recruits go to work and find out for the first time that their new position is not the "romantic" role they expected.

There is also another reality shock, which Banton and other scholars do not discuss. This is the shock that recruits will experience in the sense that they will see "life" as they have never seen it before in their middle-class world. Furthermore, their view of this new "life" will be more than just passing; it will be pervasive.

> Twenty-one years old, and they come into this job, a young rookie, and he comes up here, and this is another world. And up here you have junkies, you have your winos, and your queers, your pimps and whores, and whatnot, and he comes up here and looks around and this is another world. He's seeing things here that he's never seen before in his life.[68]

Gordon Misner's article, "Enforcement: Illusion of Security," suggests another structural defect of our police systems' personnel policies in their "closed" approach. As Misner suggests, our "personnel systems freeze out people with different experiences or perspectives."[69] Officers we recruit today are tomorrow's administrators. If this is the case, are we recruiting people who have the skills or potential for this future assignment? Do these people have the social awareness and sensitivity to direct agencies that have been criticized for being so socially out of step with society? If we are to obtain leadership in the areas of police–community relations, is our organizational structure facilitating these recruiting needs or impeding them?

Training

A fourth structural and organizational deficiency identified which might be conducive to police resistance to police–community relations is that pertaining to the general area of training in our police system. Niederhoffer suggests that it is at the recruit academy where the umbilical cord binding the rookie to the civilian world is clipped. Using Erving Goffman's theory of how institutions avail themselves of a "stripping" and "mortification" process, Niederhoffer very astutely portrays the re-socialization process that police organizations apply to their neophytes.[70]

> The typical police recruit starts his career without a trace of cynicism, but after a short time at the academy, the alert student begins to realize that the professional atmosphere that surrounds him is partly a sham. This intuition may arise from the innuendoes of his instructor; more often it is the result of the demeaning restrictions imposed upon his private life. In class he is taught that his exalted status as a policeman and peace officer endows him with tremendous power and responsibility. Outside of class the department indicates in many ways that it does not trust the young probationer. It sets curfews for him; it declares stores where liquor is sold "off limits."[71]

Perhaps the worst of all the incongruities rookies face is that, after they graduate from the training academy and feel some degree of achievement, their confidence is completely stripped away by the older officers, who make it known to the recruits that to become real police officers, they will have to forget the ivory tower approach of the academy.[72] This is especially disorienting to rookies because they began their careers with faith in the police system. Now that they are out in a precinct station, they perceive the irrelevancy themselves—that life does not follow neat little categorized rules, the do's and don'ts they were required to learn in the training academy.[73]

The dilemma in training police officers revolves around preparing future officers for "ideal" practices in police work or for what officers in the field consider to be the more customary and practical procedures that recruits will encounter on the job.[74] The effect of choosing the first approach will be to place the recruit under heavier group sanctions, and the resocializing process of senior patrol officers will intensify to meet this threat. To choose the latter approach is to program complete stultification into our police system, in which traditions are rewarded at the expense of innovation. Therefore, the only alternative is to use a more balanced approach. The problem is: Does the department have the capabilities to do so, and beyond that, does it see the need to do so?

There is an astounding relationship between the role ambiguities that police officers perceive and the training to which they are exposed in the academy, with its follow-up value challenged by older officers. In short, cynicism plays a material part in altering the role conceptions of individual officers. More important, cynicism, group sanctions, and the resocialization process play an even more significant role in altering the role conception of many officers.

Any police force—like any organization—socializes its recruits, that is, indoctrinates them with the norms of group life in that organization.[75] It is this socializing process that fully documents the structural and organizational deficiencies of our police system.

Burton Levy, in his excellent article, "Cops in the Ghetto: A Problem of the Police System," suggests that he is no longer content to think of police–black problems arising because of a "few bad eggs" in a police department of 1,000 or 10,000 men, but rather of a police system that recruits a significant number of bigots, reinforces the bigotry through the department's value system and socialization with older officers, and then takes the worst of the officers and puts them on duty in the ghetto, where the opportunity to act out the prejudice is always available.[76]

Levy builds upon Niederhoffer's work of describing the impact of socialization on the police system and the model portrayed as a devastating indictment of our police system.

First, the police departments recruit from a population (the working class) whose numbers are more likely than the average population to hold anti-Negro attitudes; second, the recruits are more likely than the average population to hold anti-Negro sentiments; third, the recruit goes out on the street as a patrolman and is more likely than not to have his anti-Negro attitudes reinforced and hardened by the older officer. Fourth, in the best departments, the most able officers are soon transferred to specialized administrative duties in training, recruitment, juvenile work, etc., or are promoted after three to five years to supervisory positions; fifth, after five years the patrolman on street duty significantly increases in levels of cynicism, authoritarianism, and generalized hostility to the non-police world. Finally, it is highly likely that the worst of the patrolmen will wind up patrolling the ghetto, because that tends to be the least wanted assignment.[77]

Whether or not the situation is as bad as Levy suggests, as long as the potential exists, of which there can be no doubt, it is quite apparent that this type of structural weakness can certainly lead to police resistance to police–community relations.

Moving from the philosophical limitations of our training programs into the areas of what is involved in the actual curriculum, additional difficulties are encountered that are intimately related to the patrol officer's role conception.

For example, Germann submits that whereas police spend only 10 percent of their time in "crook-catching" activities, they receive 90 percent of their training in this area. The corollary of this is also significant. Police, then, are left with only 10 percent of their academy training time to devote to noncriminal activities on which officers spend 90 percent of their time. Based on these facts, Germann then suggests that "it's no wonder that many police view the public they serve as the enemy."[78]

To aggravate the little training offered in facilitating police officers' relationships to the community, the police are so thoroughly trained to be suspicious, and it is in fact part of their job, that this orientation has a neutralizing effect on any police–community relations training. Another classification should be made pertaining to the amount of training given in the area of police–community relations. It is not so much the problem of the little training given in this area as the neutralizing effect that all the crook-catching training has on police–community relations. There are already existing role conceptions that can be more than effective in screening superfluous or irrelevant training, regardless of the amount of time devoted to training in police–community relations.

The impact that an officer's predisposition to suspicion plays upon the police–community relationship is amply demonstrated in the following comments:

> By nature, training, or experience, policemen are suspicious. Let us say or do nothing here to change that. Being suspicious helps to make one a good policeman. However, this highly desirable quality can be overdone and cause him to become suspicious of everything and everybody. This essential quality can make him unhappy and cynical. It is his suspicion that keeps him from trusting people. If he doesn't trust people, he can't very well like them. If he doesn't like people, his very contact with them is an unhappy one, not only for them, but for him.[79]

Although looking for incongruities in the environment might be a good way to train police officers and increase their awareness and observation powers, it does create intense suspicion. The dysfunctionality of this approach must be weighed in terms of what the social cost is to us in maintaining some semblance of a relationship between the police and the community. Training police to increase their observational capacity for perceiving incongruities within the environment is one way of training, but *not* the only way. We must develop other methods of training that are not so successful in disengaging the police from the clientele they serve.

Training given in the area of police–community relations does not fit into the conception police officers have of their jobs. Thus, many officers regard this form of training as a waste of time.

Perhaps this impasse can be somewhat bridged by making community relations training implicit in all general instruction and training given to police officers.[80] Consider training officers in the use of firearms. If the training were enlarged to contain more than the mechanical parts of the gun, or tactical situations in which it were to be employed, and there was also included the community relations ramifications of firearms, perhaps the training would be more digestible to the officer's role conception and be more meaningful. This same approach could be applied to training in arrest procedures, field interrogations, and a host of other subjects where police–community relations is an important segment.

When training in police–community relations is limited to special courses as opposed to being incorporated as general material within an entire spectrum of courses, it is not only easier for police officers to miss the point of this training and to regard it as irrelevant to their jobs, but it is easier for them to resist the community relations training as well as the entire police–community relations program.

However, there still very definitely exist needs for specialized training in police–community relations, especially in the area of cultural shock.

> If our police departments would augment their present training in police community relations by developing courses that would facilitate adaptations to cultural shock, this might reduce the impact of the cultural shock on police officers and correspondingly increase the potential success of their assignment within the ghetto.[81]

Police training, in general, has not provided police officers with sufficient understanding of the social setting within which the police work. "Neither he [the officer] nor the department has been introduced to the population or social data which explains current community organization development, or the social forces which are actively involved in 'negotiating' changes in patterns of social relationships."[82] Consequently, as the University of California study so ably stated: "The individual policeman and the police department, therefore, remain static in an environment which is dynamic. Neither recognizes that there is any meaningful relationship between social service and social change."[83]

Reward Structure

A fifth structural deficiency identified pertains to the limited scope of any organizational reward structure within our police system. One of the dilemmas facing patrol officers which significantly affects their morale centers around their conception of "police work." Police work entails investigations, serious felonies, or good apprehensions. Unfortunately for the patrol officers, their role is structured so that they rarely participate in these events, and consequently, they stand little chance of receiving what little recognition and reward the police organization is structured to bestow on its members. In those cases where patrol officers can participate in "police work," they are made to feel quite useless.

> In the exciting cases, such as homicides or serious felonies, the patrolman on post must notify the station house as soon as he discovers the incident. Within minutes, a superior officer from the Detective Division assumes command. From then on the patrolman is a supernumerary. Detectives swarm over the scene searching for clues, interviewing witnesses and suspects, handling specific parts of the investigation. The photo unit arrives to take pictures. The mobile laboratory rolls up and scientific instruments are trundled into the crime area. The patrolman, shunted to one side, is sometimes allowed to guard the scene, by which time he may be wondering just how necessary he really is.[84]

The second part of the dilemma is that patrol officers always seem to receive the inevitable "buck" when situations go wrong; also, their role constrains them to service activity calls, both of which are unacceptable to patrol officers' conception of police work.

To intensify the patrol officers' dilemma, they soon learn that they have little control over their futures within the police department. For example, their opportunities for advancement are distinctly limited. McNamara indicates that this is an organizational uncertainty which emerges from organizational factors particularly representative of our police system. There are essentially only two other alternatives for patrolmen if they are unsuccessful in obtaining a promotion. One is that the hope for an appointment to the detective division might materialize. However, this is another area over which patrol officers have little control. Finally, they must resign themselves to the fact that they will remain in the patrol division. This allows them only the hope of obtaining a particularly acceptable assignment such as to a task force, traffic division, or other special assignment. The salient fact emerging from these three alternatives is that many police officers "come to believe that regardless of what they do in the way of effective police work they are not likely to be rewarded for the work, but are foreordained to remain in assignments they find undesirable. This feeling of having one's goals in life blocked underlies much ineffective performance."[85]

James Q. Wilson's insight in his article, "Dilemmas of Police Administration," discusses the problem of a reward structure for municipal police departments. Wilson first distinguishes between the objectives of a municipal police department devising two separate categories: order maintenance and law enforcement. Wilson submits that the police should come to terms with the fact that their main function is that of order maintenance. Hunting criminals occupies less of the time of patrol officers than do the demands made on them for maintaining order.[86]

> A police department that places order maintenance uppermost in its priorities will judge patrolmen less by their arrest records and more by their ability to keep peace on their beat. This will require, in turn, that sergeants and other supervisory personnel concern themselves more with how the patrolman functions in family fights, teenage disturbances, street corner brawls, and civil disorders; and less with how well they take reports at the scene of burglary or how many traffic tickets they issue during a tour of duty. Order maintenance also requires that the police have a wider range of options for handling disorder than is afforded by the choice between making an arrest and doing nothing.[87]

Accompanying this change in organizational goals must be a concomitant change in rewarding personnel for fulfilling their duties. The present reward structure in operation in our police system not only would not be able to address this change in function, but if left completely alone would be quite dysfunctional in that all the "major rewards open to patrolmen—promotion, higher pay, specialized duty—all take him out of the patrol force and place him in supervisory posts, criminal investigation, or headquarter staff units. If the patrol function is the most important and difficult job in the department, the best men ought to be rewarded for doing it well in ways that leave them in the patrol force and on the street."[88]

Traditional methods for measuring and rewarding both individual officers and organizational units place little positive value on the quality of the police response in noncriminal situations.[89] This is an extremely unfortunate occurrence, because what the employee does on the job is largely determined by the reward structure of the job situation. In essence, these rewards and punishments spell out what is and what is not worthwhile for the employee to do. Furthermore, "if the reward structure that the employee finds waiting for him back on the job does not reinforce and support the new things that he has acquired in his training, the employees simply will not practice these new things."[90]

Mosel further stresses the importance of the relationship between reward structure and training in the following manner:

We take an employee out of a job situation: We place him in a rather insulated training situation where he learns. And we return him to the job situation. But our training has not changed the reward structure of the job, so the employee's behavior doesn't change. He continues to do what he's always done because he finds it rewarding to do so.[91]

Further attention will have to be directed at identifying the informal reward structure present in police organizations. Informal and unofficial rewards and punishments can obstruct any meaningful police–community relations training.

The University of California study revealed an astounding organizational abuse, which documents this statement: "As one person put it, if the community liaison officer were really effective, he could 'kiss promotion opportunities goodbye,' for senior officers sit on his promotion boards."[92]

Not only is this a clear abuse of the reward structure of an organization, but we can raise serious questions about training patrolmen in police–community relations when management takes such a narrow-minded approach and simply refuses to reinforce the training directed at line patrolmen.

Furthermore, it is for these reasons that it is absolutely necessary to determine the structural and organizational defects of our police system. To do otherwise would be to miss the salient fact that usually when there is patrol officer resistance to accepting police–community relations programs, there is concomitant resistance by supervisory and management personnel. Too many people would like to think the "problem" of police acceptance of police–community relations can be negotiated with line officers, simply because they participate in police–citizen encounters. This view is not only wrong, but it absolves top management of any responsibility in the entire problem.

Use of Discretion

The sixth structural and organizational deficiency identified that has a significant impact on the state of police–community relations deals with the absence of policies and guidelines for the use of discretion within our police system. Juby Towler explains the police role in civil rights demonstrations in a manner characteristic of many police administrators' conception of the use of discretion.

Under the influence of its oath of office, the police duty is as simple for the civil rights movement as for any other police problem. The policeman knows what the laws require. He prevents them from being violated if he can. He makes an arrest when they are violated. The police role in social conflicts is as simple as that.[93]

In reality, the matter is not as simple as Towler would have us believe. In fact, many problems emerge from an oversimplified approach to this sensitive area of concern. Towler completely disregards the fact that discretion is an important variable that can either facilitate the police response to problems of this sensitive nature or can intensify many of the attendant insecurities that are possessed by both the police and those segments of the community confronting the police.

To suggest that vigorous enforcement of the law is a solution to police problems is very superficial thinking. For example, Roger Lane, in describing the history of policing in Boston, suggests that within the first 15 years of Boston's incorporation as a city, it became abundantly clear that full enforcement of the law was not going to relieve any of the city's police problems. "The department needed strength in order to maintain the peace, protect property, and alleviate misery in a city still swelling with immigration. But it also needed discretion, in order to serve as a buffer between the literal demands of the law and the desires of the citizens."[94]

The U.S. Riot Commission report maintained that the use or abuse of discretion within police departments was so important that it was one of the critical areas that does have an impact on the police and community relationship.

> How a policeman handles day to day contacts with citizens will, to a large extent, shape the relationships between the police and the community. These contacts involve considerable discretion. Improper exercise of such discretion can needlessly create tension and contribute to community grievances.
>
> Formally the police officer has no discretion; his task is to enforce all laws at all times. Formally, the officer's only basic enforcement option is to make an arrest, or to do nothing. . . . Informally—and in reality—the officer faces an entirely different situation. He has and must have a great deal of discretion; there are not enough police or jails to permit the levels of surveillance that would be necessary to enforce all laws all the time—levels which the public would in any event regard as intolerable.[95]

While the use of discretion in law enforcement work might well be dictated by the exigencies of various situations, Wayne LaFave seriously questions whether or not the discretionary authority appropriately belongs within the realm of a police department. LaFave suggests that the very nature and function of the police officer's role makes the exercise of discretion improper by police, and even more appropriate to prosecutor's offices, because centralizing the use of discretion in the prosecutor's office assures more uniformity of the use of discretion, and increases the visibility of those discretionary decisions, allowing for better control and review of the use of discretion.[96]

Joseph Goldstein suggests that not only is the visibility of discretionary decisions made by police low but that the internal structure of the police department itself cannot fully review and control the use of discretionary authority by its personnel.[97]

To illustrate the low visibility of the use of discretion by patrol officers and the accompanying problems in reviewing or controlling this exercise of discretion, a perfect example is provided by Robert McCormack and James Moen's study of the San Francisco Police Department's Mission District. In these studies, McCormack and Moen discovered that a consistent method of adjudicating many police calls was to adjudicate these calls as either "unfounded" or "gone on arrival." In view of the fact that 11 percent of the sampled calls were disposed of in this manner, coupled with the fact that on the average each of these calls involved 29 minutes of an officer's time, perhaps these calls were not "unfounded" but that the "unfounded" reply merely circumscribed the department's policy and provided officers with the increased ability to exercise discretion.[98]

> In many instances an agency's attempt to prescribe procedures for every eventuality—in effect, to control the use of discretion—results in department procedures which are at odds with the practical solution of some police encounters. The officer-initiated "shortcuts" in these cases should not be viewed negatively, since in a number of situations they are the most reasonable solution to an extremely difficult problem. It is important, however, that the department know in what areas this discretion is being used and weigh the benefits to the agency against the risks inherent in sanctioning a wide use of such discretion.[99]

Herman Goldstein observes that perhaps one of the reasons police administrators not only do not acknowledge the use of discretion, but even try to restrict its use is that "the exercise of discretion belies the very image in which he takes such pride and which he strives so hard to achieve. This is the image of total objectivity—of impartiality—and of enforcement without fear nor favor."[100]

For the most part, scholars are in agreement on the point that by increasing the visibility of the police use of discretion, one is in effect improving or could improve the use of this discretion. However, Jerome Skolnick introduces the sociologist's perspective of "delegated" and "unauthorized" discretion. This serves the purpose of differentiating between the organizational, sanctioned use of discretion (which is incongruent to the administration's normal posture on the exercise of discretion) and the creation of opportunities in which discretion can be exercised by individual officers.[101]

According to James Q. Wilson, not only the citizen but also the nature of the call can have a profound effect upon a police officer's exercise of discretion. Wilson envisions four kinds of discretionary situations revolving around two sets of circumstances: the nature of the situation, whether it is oriented toward law enforcement or order maintenance;

and the basis for the police response, whether it was invoked by citizens or by the police.[102]

Before explaining the four types of discretionary decisions with which both individual patrol officers and the organization are faced, consider the questions that go through an officer's mind prior to making a decision regarding whether or not to exercise discretion. Wilson suggests that the following types of questions guide officers in their decision regarding discretion and how to use discretion.

> Has anyone been hurt or deprived? Will anyone be hurt or deprived if I do nothing? Will an arrest improve the situation or only make matters worse? Is a complaint more likely if there is no arrest or if there is an arrest? What does the sergeant expect of me? Am I getting near the end of my tour of duty? Will I have to go to court on my day off? If I do appear in court, will the charge stand up or will it be withdrawn or dismissed by the prosecutor? Will my partner think that an arrest shows I can handle things or that I can't handle things? What will the guy do if I let him go?[103]

The impact these questions have on the four types of discretionary decisions in general, and police–community relations in particular, is as follows. Wilson describes police-invoked law enforcement, in which frequently the officer encounters situations in which there are "crimes without victims," or enforcement of laws dealing with vice, gambling, or traffic offenses. The citizen has not originated the complaint. In these situations the amount of police intervention is very sharply controlled by the police administrator. Furthermore, the administrator's performance measure is goal-oriented; however, the goal is that of enforcement of laws.[104]

Citizen-invoked law enforcement entails situations where the citizen is a victim of a crime, usually that of a property nature, such as larceny, auto theft, or burglary. In these situations, patrol officers usually function more as traveling secretaries, filing reports for detectives to follow up.[105]

Police-invoked order maintenance entails situations where patrol officers act on their own authority and initiative in the general area of maintaining the order and tranquility of the community. Since these situations are generally disorderly conduct or breach of the peace and so frequently are on-view-type occurrences, the administrator does not have a degree of control over patrol officers' use of discretion. Furthermore, administrators cannot devise "production" controls to increase their control over patrol officers, in fact, the administrator's only method of addressing the broad latitude of patrol officers is to issue general policies aimed at more vigorous patrol or less vigorous patrol.[106]

Citizen-invoked order maintenance involves situations, such as public or private disorder, in which a citizen requests assistance from the police department. Officers handle these problems in a manner they feel will be most acceptable and beneficial to the citizen. The only real guidelines imposed by the administration are that a police response, or report in some cases, must follow up the citizen's call for assistance. In other words, the manner in which patrol officers address these types of situations will depend more on both their own and the citizens' personal characteristics and less on departmental policies.[107]

> In sum, in Cases I and IV the patrolman has great discretion, but in the former instance it can be brought under departmental control and in the latter it cannot. In Case II the patrolman has the least discretion except when the suspects are juvenile and then the discretion is substantial and can be affected by general departmental policies and organization. Case III is intermediate in both degree of discretion and the possibility of departmental control.[108]

The significance of Wilson's conceptual framework to the area of police–community relations is such that one can immediately detect the importance of the exercise of discretion and its relationship to police–community relations. Every point at which police–citizen interaction most frequently occurs is a point at which police patrol officers exercise the most discretion accorded to and structured into their role. Furthermore, these are the instances where patrol officers need guidelines to facilitate their use of discretion.

As Wilson so astutely describes it, policies that summarily list things not to do rather than things to do have the effect of maintaining the low visibility of discretionary decisions. Also, they are perceived by officers as irrelevant restrictions which not only do not help patrol officers but structure the situation so that they "give the brass plenty of rope with which to hang us."[109] The entire problem is intensified by the fact that a police department is one of the few organizations in which discretion increases as one moves down the hierarchy.[110]

Finally, the University of California studies indicated the importance of the use of discretion by recommending that police training and supervision be exposed to instruction in case situations directed toward teaching patrolmen to use discretion to benefit the citizen, community, and the police organization.[111]

Discipline

The seventh structural and organizational deficiency within our police system can be observed within the discipline structure of many police departments. The dilemma facing police administrators today is how to maintain the discipline necessary to a police organization and at the same time facilitate the patrol officer's use of discretion in providing a more responsive service to citizens.

We have great evidence of what occurs when discipline is seriously impaired in a police organization that is confronted with demands for the entire government to be more responsive to citizen needs, and we can look to the violence that occurred during the 1968 Democratic National Convention in Chicago for the requisite documentation.

The Walker Report to the National Commission on the Causes and Prevention of Violence quotes a police inspector from the Los Angeles Police Department who was present as an official observer in the following manner:

> There is no question but that many officers acted without restraint and exerted force beyond that necessary under the circumstances. The leadership at the point of conflict did little to prevent such conduct and the direct control of officers by first line supervisors was virtually nonexistent.[112]

Although the Walker Report characterized the police response as a police riot, the more meaningful question that emerges is: Just who does control the streets?[113] Perhaps we are observing just how tenuously police administrators do control their departments.

For a police organization to possess any semblance of a discipline structure, it requires, above all, excellent supervision. Police supervisors are responsible not only for the conduct of others in the achievement of particular tasks, but also for the services that are to be rendered by personnel under their control.[114]

If this is the case, what accounts for so many suspensions and so much disciplinary action taken against patrol officers and not supervisors? In fact, if police administrators were to start taking disciplinary action against sergeants, lieutenants, and captains, the morale of patrolmen might well be increased, because they would know that the administrators were serious about having their policies carried out, and carried out by all members of the department at all levels.

J. L. LeGrande points out that a police department may have outstanding procedural statements regarding police–community relations, but unless they are adequately enforced, they are useless.

> The field sergeants must accept responsibility for properly executing and giving life to the administrator's policies. . . . The sergeants must give "teeth" to the procedures, and assure that the patrolmen adhere to them. With weak sergeants who display a lukewarm attitude toward these regulations, a weak community relations program will exist.[115]

Out of the police administrator's dilemma of maintaining discipline and supervision emerges a second dilemma: How can personnel be disciplined but still be useful members of the organization?

In addition to these dilemmas, a pattern of rationalization, projection, or scapegoating seems to develop in which all disciplinary action is blamed on placating minority-group members or on existing police–community relations activities.

Group Sanctions

Another deficiency within police organization can be identified as the structural problems surrounding the area of group sanctions from within an organization. Group sanctions amount to nothing more than "built-in resistance" to whatever the group wishes to resist. In this case the application should be extended to police–community relations.

Whittaker suggests that one of the unfortunate aspects of training recruits is that they will be exposed to police lore and mythology in such a way that the senior officers are actually communicating to the recruits what opinions and behaviors are considered acceptable to the group of senior officers.[116] This has the effect of reaffirming the old values acceptable to senior officers and programming out any new values brought in by new officers that may challenge the established norms. This process is referred to as the informal socialization of recruits. It is different from the formal socialization process enforced by the organization.

James Q. Wilson describes the formal socialization of police recruits as an indoctrination process with the norms of the entire police organization.[117] The distinction is that in the informal process of socialization the norms being presented to recruits are explicitly not those of the entire police organization, but are only those of the police organization's patrolmen. In essence we are suggesting that patrol officers are a subculture within a subculture. The implications this has on police–community relations are profound and will be described in greater detail after some initial observations are made.

Initially, it is necessary to identify where the subculture of patrol officers applies its group sanctions, and then to try to ascertain for what reasons. For the most part, group sanctions are projected by the patrol officer subculture in three primary areas: toward recruits seeking rites of passage into the subculture; toward the organization to preserve the identity of the patrol officer subculture; and toward the role conception of various organizational roles or positions to further purify the "proper" and "acceptable" role conception of those members of the subculture of patrol officers.

The first of the three areas to which group sanctions are applied by the patrol officer subculture center around the recruits' rites of passage into the subculture. At this stage the idealism of the academy is stripped from recruits and the problem goes beyond the bounds of leaving recruits frustrated because they have nothing with which to replace this idealism. The problem is so intense because it strikes recruits where they are most vulnerable—winning the approval, respect, and friendship of senior patrol officers.

The small amount of literature in the area discusses the problem more in terms of corruption, overlooking the primary problems occurring over much simpler matters, such as not patrolling the precinct, brusque handling of citizens who sometimes get offensive, accepting a reduced rate on lunches from merchants, the "practical" and more "expeditious" ways of processing suspects, and so on.

This is not to suggest that in commentary such as Richard Blum's "the conflict of loyalty" a recruit experiences when a senior officer throws him a fifth of whiskey from the shelf of a burglarized store is less intense than the simpler incongruities of a more frequent nature.[118] However, it is these less serious violations of administrative policy that are more difficult for recruits to resist, and it is only after this idealism of the training academy is stripped away that the officer becomes more vulnerable to the more serious group pressures. A graphic portrayal of this process can be seen in the article, "What Makes a Policeman Go Wrong."[119]

The literature in the area of group sanctions has confined itself to police criminality, especially to the problems of "reality shock" faced by recruits when practices taught in the academy are not sanctioned in the field.

The second area of sanctions directed by the patrol officer subculture are aimed at the organization specifically to protect the identity of the patrol officer subculture. Along these lines are supervisors who are reluctant to supervise because of the deep-rooted fear that their friendship with patrol officers will be sacrificed. Also, we can see that the informal group sanctions become "institutionalized" within the subculture of patrol officers in the form of Patrolmen's Benevolent Associations, which can gather a surprisingly large amount of power that must be reckoned with by the administration.[120]

The third area at which group sanctions are projected is the role conceptions of various organizational positions. An excellent discussion of this appears in Stanton Wheeler's *Controlling Delinquents,* in which James Q. Wilson discussed the frustrations of a juvenile officer:

> Almost every juvenile officer in Eastern City complained that patrolmen and detectives did not "understand" his work, that they regarded him as a man who "chased kids," that they "kissed off" juvenile cases onto him and did not take them seriously, and that they did not think arresting a "kid" constituted a "good pinch."[121]

Since this is representative of the role conception many patrol officers have of juvenile officers or the organization's position of juvenile officer, this role conception is communicated to other officers by group sanctions.

The application of the preceding example to police–community relations is important because it clearly documents the process by which the patrol officer subculture can collectively demean a position or goal and communicate the entire norm to other patrol officers or recruits seeking the rites of passage into the patrol officer subculture.

Jerome Skolnick provides another illustration of group sanctions affecting the role conception of a police officer. In Skolnick's example it is suggested that "holding a prostitute for a quarantine check is not considered as a 'credit' to the policeman's record. Neither the police officer nor the prosecution is primarily interested in anything but the central 'product' of law enforcement: felony convictions."[122]

As Skolnick observes: "There are systemic pressures upon the police to break certain kinds of rules in the interest of conforming to other standards."[123] It is imperative to identify these structural and organizational weaknesses, as much of the resistance to police–community relations has its genesis within these deficiencies.

The patrol officer subculture is distinctly different from the entire police subculture. Within the patrol officer subculture we can observe members interacting among themselves and producing their own values and norms, norms that frequently are in direct conflict with the administration. This is important to the ramifications of police–community relations because it suggests that there is resistance to police–community relations from the patrol officer subculture. Until the patrol officer subculture is either neutralized or effectively assimilated into the entire police subculture, the present approaches and appeals to enhance police–community relations activities will have little chance of success.

Problem of Authority

The ninth structural and organizational deficiency that is conducive to poor police–community relations centers around the concept of authority within our police departments and patrolmen's conception of authority. Chevigny suggests that policemen see themselves as personifying authority and a challenge to any one of them is a challenge to not only all of them but to our very system of law.[124] The important question to ask is: What does "challenge" mean, and how do police officers perceive this challenge? Chevigny again throws light on this by suggesting that anything as small as one criticizing the manner in which patrol officers handle situations can be, and is, interpreted not only as a challenge to the officers themselves but also to their authority.[125] In many cases a patrol officer's perception is probably quite accurate. However, the danger lies in the fact that this might also be a convenient rationalization for not accepting responsible constructive criticism.

Perhaps it should be made abundantly clear before progressing further in this area that if police officers' perception of authority is a bit confused, the public shares in this burden. More often than not the public is constantly feeding the fires of confusion. The following is a perfect example of this process:

> The policeman is called upon to direct ordinary citizens, and therefore to restrain their freedom of action. Resenting this restraint, the average citizen in such a situation typically thinks something along the lines of, "He is supposed to catch crooks; why is he bothering me?" Thus the citizen stresses the "dangerous" portion of the policeman's role while belittling his authority.[126]

Another interesting problem that develops within this area of authority is when police officers are confronted with hostility or extreme insult and degradation, they frequently rely on their authority to take action against arrogant citizens. The frustrating factor to police is that there are few lawful grounds on which to base arrests. Therefore, they are in a quandary as to how to maintain the respect of the population when they cannot sanction these arrogant assaults upon their authority.[127]

The police are open to greater frustration because when they face potential danger they are more likely to rely on their authority to reduce the perception of danger.[128] Whether or not they actually have the authority is an irrelevant question for patrol officers see their job as maintaining law and order and view any impediments to their mission as superfluous legal niceties that aid criminals and penalize law-abiding citizens.

Another curious aspect of police officers' idea of authority is manifested when the police actually catch someone in the act of breaking the law. Often the police will treat such a person quite deferentially, one of the reasons being that the officer and the citizen acknowledge the legitimacy of the arrest.[129] Many observers become confused as to how and why police can become rather personal and friendly with a clear-cut violator, yet may be quite menacing to a suspect, suggesting that when officers do not feel their authority is being challenged, their interaction with citizens is more amicable.

Authority is quite important to patrol officers, as it enhances their ability to gain respect. Werthman and Piliavin further point out that "a patrolman's capacity to gain respect is his greatest source of pride as well as his greatest area of vulnerability."[130] "If he is forced to make too many 'weak' arrests, he stands to lose prestige among his peers and superiors on the police force and to suffer humiliation at the hands of his permanent audience of tormentors on the beat."[131]

Confrontations by detectives or juvenile officers rarely culminate in violence, because the ability to command respect is not as crucial as it is to patrolmen. Detectives are not judged so much by their capacity to command authority as for their skills in interrogation. Therefore, what in effect has occurred with patrol officers is that they have structurally been placed into situations and circumstances where they are predisposed to "coerce respect."[132]

It is again important to emphasize that the structural nature of the patrol officer's conception and abuse of authority cannot be meaningfully corrected simply by appealing to the better nature of the officers or by increasing disciplinary actions against these officers. What is needed are structural modifications directed at both the police officers' and citizens' perception of authority.

Chevigny insisted that the most vicious aspect of the unlawful use of force was often not the brutality, but the arrest that followed. It was the abuse of authority and the impact of covering up the assault that Chevigny found so reprehensible.[133]

In essence, Chevigny has identified a structural defect of police organizations. To improve the police–community relationship, it will be necessary to identify these abuses so that proper structural remedies can be applied.

Patrol Tactics

The tenth police structural and organizational deficiency occurs in some of the patrol and police tactics used in many police agencies. The U.S. Riot Commission report observed that police conduct and patrol practices were one of the five major reasons for hostility between the police and the community. The Commission stated:

> Although police administrators may take steps to attempt to eliminate misconduct by individual police officers, many have adopted patrol practices which in the words of one commentator have "replaced harassment by individual patrolmen with harassment by entire departments."[134]

In other words, police administrators must analyze the various effects of task force patrolling, stop and frisk, and field interrogation reports to identify the latent or unanticipated consequences of such practices on the community. The President's Commission on Law Enforcement and Administration of Justice suggested that while aggressive programs of preventive patrol probably do reduce the amount of street crime, "it is also apparent that aggressive patrol contributes to the antagonism of minority groups whose members are subjected to it."[135] The commission goes on to state: "A basic issue, never dealt with explicitly by police, is whether, even solely from a law enforcement point of view, the gain in enforcement outweighs the cost of community alienation."[136]

What is the social cost of some of our police policies, particularly patrol procedures? Unless we begin to think in terms of the dysfunctionality of these tactics, the basic organizational design and mission could well be creating more problems than the police–community relations unit could address. Furthermore, significant gains in other departmental programs and policies in the area of police–community relations will be negated if the area of patrol procedures is unaddressed.

Fragmentation of Police Service

The eleventh structural and organizational weakness that plagues police–community relations efforts is implicit within the fragmentation of police service. The University of California studies suggest that each police department has its own concept of what constitutes police–community relations problems, and consequently has its own approaches to these problems. "Viewed as an area-wide problem therefore, the existence of a multitude of local police agencies dissipates the ability of any one agency to deal effectively with community relations problems."[137]

In essence, the absence of a single uniform and consistent law enforcement policy within any of our metropolitan areas then represents one of the more complex and recurring police–community relations problems.[138]

Furthermore, those interested in improving police–community relations must also recognize that there are also federal law enforcement agencies that affect the nature of police–community relations. The University of California report stated: "The point of the matter is that the term 'police' is often generic in the public mind and the actual or imagined misdeeds or inappropriate procedures of one policing agency will 'spill over' and cause problems for the police in general."[139]

The problem of fragmentation extends beyond the boundary of police agencies alone; it also incorporates the entire administration of justice system. Policies and procedures of our prosecuting attorneys, courts, correctional institutions, and probation and parole agencies affect the nature of police–community relations. Jameson Doig summarizes this point quite effectively: "The police are also the immediate representative of the broader system of law enforcement and criminal justice, and they inevitably are associated with all the weaknesses in that system."[140]

The University of California report recommended that regional associations of police–community relation officers be developed and that they share the relevant information of their respective metropolitan areas.[141] However, one of the main contributions by the University of California study was its conclusion that "one of the structural features of police organization which dissipates the effectiveness of police–community relations is the fragmented character of local police authority."[142]

Specialization of Units

The twelfth structural and organizational deficiency of the police system, especially in the area of police–community relations, occurs in the specialization of units or bureaus within our police departments. One danger in creating specialized units within police organizations is that it can narrow a police officer's perspective. It creates an impression in various personnel that they no longer need concern themselves with a particular portion of the police mission when they are not assigned to the unit that would normally handle calls representative of that unit's function.[143] This phenomenon can be observed when a police department creates a special traffic unit. Frequently, those members in the patrol division "kiss off" traffic violations or accidents to the traffic unit. The corollary is also true where a traffic unit car will be on patrol, see a fight in progress, and instead of taking action will call the dispatcher to notify a patrol division car to handle an incident that it could have easily resolved.

The danger with creating a specialized police–community relations unit is very similar in that there is always the threat that those officers not in this unit could well rationalize that police–community relations are not their concern. As the University of California report stated: "It must be emphasized here that police–community relations is central to the function of the uniformed forces. If that fact is not recognized as such, then this itself becomes a part of the police–community relations problem."[144]

The dilemma of police administrators is that if they create a special police–community relations unit, members of the department not assigned to this unit may rationalize that police–community relations are not their job. Also, if administrators do not create a special police–community relations unit, both they and the police department are vulnerable to charges by minority groups that the police department is not concerned with police–community relations when they might well be.

Perhaps the most appropriate way of resolving this dilemma is to create a special police–community relations unit while holding various command officers and their respective precincts responsible for police–community relations. As the U.S. Riot Commission Report states: Improving community relations is a full time assignment for every command and every officer—an assignment that must include the development of an attitude, a tone throughout the force that conforms with the ultimate responsibility of every policeman: public service."[145]

The creation of a special police–community relations unit itself will not resolve the hostility between the police and the community. Furthermore, resistance to police–community relations by some personnel can be anticipated, not simply because they may object to this area as a police function, although this might well be, but by creating special units, fragmentation of the policing task is intensified and certain areas or domains of responsibilities are created at the expense of larger responsibilities.

Organizational Placement of Units

A structural and organizational weakness that emerges out of the creation of specialized police–community relations units is the organizational placement of police–community relations units.

Exactly where police–community relations units are placed in a police department could well imply that police–community relations are less important than are other police functions. Also, from an organizational point of view, we must be aware that in whichever division the police–community relations unit is placed, the organizational importance of police–community relations can either be enhanced or downgraded.[146]

As the Michigan State University study pointed out, the organizational placement of the police–community relations unit has an effect upon the unit's ability to develop support among members of the entire police department.[147]

Narrowly Conceived Police Function

The fourteenth structural and organizational deficiency within the police system which has a profound effect upon police–community relations is the narrowly conceived manner in which the police function is visualized by police organizations. "One way of stating the central problem of police and community relations is to state it in terms of the role and function of the police in today's democratic society."[148] The problems of role perception, role conception, role conflict, and role enactment are intimately interwoven into the police–community relationship.

Howard Earle remarks that frequently the police complain that the public does not understand their role. Yet the police were so adamant on activities that were *not* their job and *not* part of their role that what in effect occurred was the elimination by police of many activities that constituted a positive public contact, and, in addition, left many members of the community in a quandary as to what the police role, in fact, was.[149]

However, this is more than just an elementary question, for its answer will significantly shape the organizational structure of our police agencies. Skolnick considers the question important enough that he rhetorically asks it as the first statement in his book, *Justice without Trial:* "For what social purpose do police exist?"[150]

This simple question has received little attention by both the public and the police and, as a result, various assumptions have been made as to what the police role is. Characteristic of such assumptions is the public response in Cleveland. When the Cleveland Civil Service Commission expanded its reading list to cover books that included topics on sociology, race relations, and national crime problems, the police response was the classic: "What are you trying to do—make us social workers?"[151] In other words, the police had already formulated a conception of the police function and did not wish to extend it.

Frustrating as it is to the police, authorities within their own field have not agreed on the role conception of the police. To cite one example, as far back as 1931 August Vollmer suggested that "the policeman is no longer the suppressor of crime, but the social worker of the community as well."[152]

John Webster brings a unique point of view into the debate over the police function. Webster asks: "What does the policeman do forty hours a week except solve sociological problems? What is the primary responsibility of the police? It is certainly not arresting felons." Webster then proceeds to offer arithmetic documentation to dispel the myth as follows:

In 1966 there were 29,737 sworn police personnel in California. There was a total of 114,283 adult felony arrests. The number of felony arrests divided by the number of sworn personnel reveals the startling figure of exactly 3.8; the average number of adult felony arrests per sworn individual officer per year.[153]

In discussing the urban police mission, Misner distinguishes between the police function and the police mission in that the former refers to the means, whereas the latter refers to the ends. In describing the social purpose of the police mission, Misner views only two functions as properly fitting these qualifications: provisions of public service, and the maintenance of peace and security; all other functions, he believes, can be subsumed under these two categories.[154] Misner offers a challenge to both the police and to future researchers in his following comments:

> the contemporary urban policeman's job is much broader than the investigation of crime and the apprehension of offenders. In fact, he probably could not effectively accomplish these two functions except for the fact that he is heavily involved and supported in other public duties. Often it is these "essentially secondary" duties which give to the policeman the public acceptance and cooperation which assists him in accomplishing what he considers to be his primary duties.[155]

What Misner is suggesting is that if the police do "purify" their role to the point that they become involved only in criminal matters, the response of the community might be such that the community could not tolerate the police, thus further aggravating police–community relationships. If it is these public service activities that are the only basis or means for which the community does tolerate a police department, this suggests a great challenge to researchers in this area, and perhaps an even greater challenge to the police to come to terms with this in their own role conception.

Joseph D. Lohman, former dean of the School of Criminology at the University of California, discussed the police function in terms of the entire community responsibility and made the following observation:

> It becomes apparent that the police function may be so structured and so organized that the enforcement of the law upon the marginal few may be seriously impaired and even stymied. It follows that the immediate concern of the police in apprehending and suppressing law violators is contingent upon a deeper and more pervasive mission, namely the activation of the whole public in the maintenance and securing of the peace of the community. It is, in my judgment, precisely because of this failure to define the basic and larger mission of law enforcement that so many law enforcement officials and other citizens of the society are bemused by the spectacle of so many of their fellow citizens in general and of poor Negroes in particular, who have come to believe that law and authority are not *their* law and *their* authority.[156]

Along these same lines, Lohman has more bluntly stated: "The police function is to support and enforce the interests of the dominant political, social, and economic interests of the town and only incidentally to enforce the law."[157]

Not only is it imperative to inquire what is meant by the police function, but the latitude of its conception becomes extremely important, as Misner and Lohman both indicated. Furthermore, to select the police leadership to guide our police organizations, it becomes incumbent to seek their concept of the police function. The President's Commission on Law Enforcement and Administration of Justice analyzed the problem of leadership and police function in the following terms:

> The need today is for a police administrator who is much more of a generalist rather than a person possessing narrow technical skills. He must have a sound grasp of the unique function of the police in a democratic society. He must support values which often are in conflict with the most immediate goals of arrest and successful prosecution. He must have the ability to relate police functioning to the functioning of other agencies in the criminal justice system; to analyze and resolve complex issues relating to the exercise of police authority . . . to be especially sensitive to legitimate community demands and interests.[158]

To stress the importance of relating police leadership and reexamining police officers' conception of their function in society, Lohman suggests that when the police are being called upon to put down student demonstrations or civil rights demonstrations, there is at the same time some gesture in the following direction for redressing of these grievances.[159] Furthermore, Lohman stresses the importance of police leadership conceptualizing the police function in society, even to the degree that there are occurrences where police leadership might well have to transcend the political leadership of the community.

> [The police] are not simply puppets to be utilized as a kind of exercise of force at the instigation of whomever is disposed to direct them. They must themselves enter into the picture and say that there are limiting conditions under which they are willing to exercise force. They must enter into defining these limiting conditions too in making it clear that there are certain things that cannot be done.[160]

Objectivity Obscured by Organizational Goals

The fifteenth suggested structural deficiency within the police organization is that, for the most part, police departments are organized in such a way as to find only what they are after. Naturally, this deficiency emerges out of the previously mentioned weakness of too narrow a conception of the police function. Again, the ramifications of this structural deficiency on police–community relations are profound.

The organizational structure of police agencies is not something external. It is the very embodiment of the problem. This organizational structure facilitates the police addressing the problem they encounter. Thus, the organizational structure of police agencies is, in fact, nothing more than our view of the problem.[161]

The textbook *Municipal Police Administration* states that "because the police have an inescapable responsibility when trouble does occur, they have a responsibility to be continually alert to symptoms of trouble."[162]

Both views taken together suggest that police not only have a responsibility to be alert to the symptoms of troubles, but that the organizational structure of police agencies is such that this might well be the only perception identified. Unfortunately, this is an overly restrictive view that has profound consequences on police–community relations. To begin with, police must understand that social institutions have built-in injustices inherent in them, and as Milton Rokeach suggests, we must "not automatically assume that everything which is lawful is necessarily good and everything which is unlawful is necessarily bad."[163]

Although lack of respect for law is very often assumed to be evident of a willful disregard for legitimate authority and an outright challenge to authority, Lohman's perceptive advice should be heeded. "It may well be that what we observe as 'disrespect for law' is a normal reaction of normal people to an abnormal condition."[164] Many of the problems facing police organizations today may well have a meaning and significance that differ from what police organizations normally have ascribed to them.[165]

For example, examine the social significance and functionality of a riot. To the police officer, riots may well be seen as pure and simple problems of law enforcement.[166] However, a riot does signify something more than a breakdown of law and order. Allan Silver provides us with this account of what riots may mean:

> The imagery of the "dangerous classes" is being reborn in contemporary America. The nascent demand for a pervasively benign environment arises as the urban poor, disorganized, and unemployed—especially Negroes—bear more heavily upon the awareness and daily life of an urban society in which proportionately more people are "respectable" than ever before. Violence, criminality, and riot become defined not only as undesirable but as threatening the very fabric of social life. Police forces come to be seen as they were in the time of their creation—as a sophisticated and convenient form of garrison force against an internal enemy. Lacking a strong tradition of urban violence as a form of articulate protest, it is all the easier to define such events as merely criminal. Such definitions work not only on the respectable but also on the riotous poor.[167]

Silver is suggesting that riots may be more than just criminal acts of violence and may well be an inarticulate form of expressing grievances and needs—of saying that something is wrong and that help is needed. In these terms riots are certainly more than "pointless," "irrational," or "criminal," but are more of a commentary on society itself that such conditions are allowed to remain on the American scene.

This is not to suggest that riots are a legitimate form of redress. It is to suggest that not only the police, but the entire community, have organized to look upon riots as a matter that can be addressed by more police, larger night sticks, and more guns, completely missing the "cry for help" coming from city ghettos. Police are organized to such a degree that they see only what they want to see, and any chance for providing constructive remedial help can be forever lost simply because the perspective on a given problem was too narrow.

Riots, like most other police problems, are only symptoms of a more pervasive malady, and the ultimate answer to the way police organizations are structured to address crime "is to see crime not alone as a problem in law enforcement, but as a problem in education, family organization, employment opportunity, and housing. . . . These are the structures inside of which deviance and hence crime and delinquency incubate."[168]

Deficient Referral Arrangements

The final structural and organizational deficiency identified pertains to the deficient structural arrangements for police agencies making referrals to other agencies.

One of the leading textbooks in the police field suggests that "due to their constant contacts with all neighborhoods of a city, the police are in an ideal position to maintain constant vigilance over troubled areas and to assume the responsibility for making basic causes of unrest known to agencies or groups that can eliminate or reduce them."[169] Unfortunately, in reality, this is not the case, although that is certainly not the fault of the police alone. However, this is an area in which police–community relations programming has been deficient. Therefore, future police–community relations proposals would be well advised to keep this area in mind. From the police point of view, this also happens to offer the distinct advantage of being able to transfer some of the responsibility for law and order back to society.

As Lohman has pointed out, the unfortunate truth about most police work is that not only are the referrals not being made, but much of this police work is itself part of the crime-initiating process. "Far too many police cases are not police problems at all. Much of the police officer's contact with the public should begin and end with referrals to education and welfare agencies which we must strengthen so that they can handle minor offenses, especially first offenders."[170]

Summary

In this chapter we have identified two conceptions of what might be termed "appropriate" police–community relations. One view, subscribed to by law enforcement personnel, suggests that police–community relations are synonymous with public relations. The corollary conception, subscribed to by social scientists and members of minority groups, suggests that police–community relations are more accurately referred to as a methodology for police organizations to become more responsive to the needs of the communities they serve.

Finally, sixteen organizational and structural deficiencies were identifed and described in terms of the implicit vulnerabilities that police organizations must address in the development of sound police–community relations programs. In essence, poor police–community relations programming is not simply a function of insensitivity which can be remedied by psychological strategies of sensitivity training, as this chapter has pointed out. There actually are structural and organizational factors that create latent and completely unanticipated tendencies for the personnel of police organizations to function or manifest their behavior in a manner not congruent with sound police–community relations programming. Therefore, one must examine the organizational principles of a police organization as well as the personnel when attempting to enhance sound police–community relations programs.

End Notes

[1]Michigan State University, *A National Survey of Police and Community Relations,* report to the President's Commission on Law Enforcement and Administration of Justice, Field Survey V (Washington, D.C.: U.S. Government Printing Office, 1967), pp. 86–87.

[2]Ibid., p. 87.

[3]Ibid., p. 86.

[4]Joseph D. Lohman and Gordon E. Misner, *The Police and the Community,* report submitted by School of Criminology, University of California, Berkeley, to the President's Commission on Law Enforcement and Administration of Justice, Field Survey IV, vol. 2 (Washington, D.C.: U.S. Government Printing Office, 1966), p. 304.

[5]Ibid., vol. 1, p. 178.

[6]O. W. Wilson, ed., *Parker on Police* (Springfield, Ill.: Charles C Thomas, 1957), p. 135.

[7]Bruce Smith, *Police Systems in the United States,* 2d rev. ed. (New York: Harper & Brothers, 1960), p. 120.

[8]O. W. Wilson, *Police Administration,* 2d ed. (New York: McGraw-Hill, 1963), pp. 182–93.

[9]Ibid., p. 202.

[10]Ibid.

[11]Ibid., pp. 203–19.

[12]G. Douglas Gourley and Allen P. Bristow, *Patrol Administration* (Springfield, Ill.: Charles C Thomas, 1961), p. 271.

[13]Mary Ellen Leary, "The Trouble With Troubleshooting," *Atlantic Monthly,* March 1969, p. 95.

[14]The International City Manager's Association, *Municipal Police Administration,* 5th ed. (Chicago: The International City Managers Association, 1961), p. 477.

[15]Paul H. Ashenhurst, *Police and the People* (Springfield, Ill.: Charles C Thomas, 1956), p. 7.

[16]Wilson, *Parker on Police,* p. 136.

[17]Ibid., p. 137.

[18]Raymond M. Momboisse, *Community Relations and Riot Prevention* (Springfield, Ill.: Charles C Thomas, 1967), p. 62.

[19]Thomas F. Adams, *Law Enforcement: An Introduction to the Police Role in the Community* (Englewood Cliffs, N.J.: Prentice-Hall, 1968), p. 145.

[20]Michigan State University, *National Survey,* p. 68.

[21]Ibid., p. 73.

[22]Linda McVeigh Mathews, "Chief Reddin: New Style at the Top," *Atlantic Monthly,* March 1969, p. 92.

[23]Ibid.

[24]International City Managers Association, *Municipal Police Administration,* p. 476.

[25]Arthur W. Aubry, *The Officer in the Small Department* (Springfield, Ill.: Charles C Thomas, 1961), p. 359.

[26]Mathews, "Chief Reddin," p. 93.

[27]International City Managers Association, *Municipal Police Administration,* p. 472.

[28]Gourley and Bristow, *Patrol Administration,* p. 270.

[29]The President's Commission on Law Enforcement and Administration of Justice, *Task Force Report: The Police* (Washington, D.C.: U.S. Government Printing Office, 1967), pp. 144–45.

[30]Ibid., p. 151.

[31]Ibid.

[32]Victor G. Strecher, "When Subcultures Meet: Police–Negro Relations," in *Law Enforcement Science and Technology,* ed. S. A. Yefsky (Washington, D.C.: Thompson, 1967), p. 701.

[33]Lohman and Misner, *Police and Community,* vol. 1, p. x.

[34]Ibid., vol 2, p. 87.

[35]Ibid., pp. 87–135.

[36]Michigan State University, *National Survey,* pp. 98–101.

[37]Ibid., p. 9.

[38]Ibid., pp. 92–93.

[39]Ibid., pp. 94–95.

[40]Ibid., p. 97.

[41]William W. Turner, *The Police Establishment* (New York: Putnam, 1968), p. 12.

[42]United States Riot Commission, *Civil Disorders,* p. 299. United States Riot Commission, *Report of the National Advisory Commission on Civil Disorders* (New York: Bantam Books, Inc., 1968), p. 299.

[43]Ibid., pp. 299–300.

[44]William M. Kephart, *Racial Factors and Urban Law Enforcement* (Philadelphia: University of Pennsylvania Press, 1957), p. 169.

[45]President's Commission, *Task Force Report*, pp. 152–53.

[46]David H. Bayley and Harold Mendelsohn, *Minorities and the Police: Confrontation in America* (New York: Free Press, 1969), p. 171.

[47]Joseph D. Lohman, *The Police and Minority Groups* (Chicago: Chicago Park District, 1947), p. 104.

[48]U.S. Riot Commission, Civil Disorders, p. 315.

[49]Kurt Lang and Gladys Engel Lang, "Racial Disturbances as Collective Protest," *American Behavioral Scientist*, 2, no. 4 (1968), 13.

[50]Lohman and Misner, *Police and Community*, vol. 1, p. 130.

[51]Bayley and Mendelsohn, *Minorities and Police*, p. 142.

[52]Ibid.

[53]U.S. Riot Commission, *Civil Disorders*, pp. 310–11.

[54]Ibid.

[55]Ibid.

[56]National Commission on the Causes and Prevention of Violence, *Rights in Conflict*, pp. 10–11. National Commission on the Causes and Prevention of Violence, Report of the Commission, *Rights in Conflict: The Violent Confrontation of Demonstrators and Police in the Parks and Streets of Chicago During the Week of the Democratic National Convention of 1968* (New York: Bantam Books, Inc., 1968), pp. 10–11.

[57]James Q. Wilson, "The Police and Their Problems," *Public Policy*, 12 (1963), p. 205.

[58]Paul Chevigny, *Police Power: Police Abuses in New York City* (New York: Pantheon Books, 1969), pp. xix–xx.

[59]Ibid., p. 29.

[60]Ashenhurst, *Police and People*, p. 35.

[61]President's Commission, *Task Force Report*, p. 194.

[62]Arthur Niederhoffer, *Behind the Shield: The Police in Urban Society* (New York: Doubleday, 1967), p. 178. Copyright © 1967 by Arthur Niederhoffer. Reprinted by permission of Doubleday & Company, Inc.

[63]Jerome H. Skolnick, *The Police and the Urban Ghetto*, Research Contribution of the American Bar Foundation, No. 3 (Chicago: American Bar Foundation, 1968), pp. 25–26.

[64]Ibid.

[65]Michigan State University, *Natinal Survey*, p. 256.

[66]Walter Gellhorn, *Ombudsmen and Others* (Cambridge, Mass.: Harvard University Press, 1966), p. 439.

[67]Ben Whittaker, *The Police* (Harmondsworth, Middlesex, England: Penguin Books, 1969), pp. 95–98.

[68]L. H. Whittemore, *Cop: A Closeup of Violence and Tragedy* (New York: Holt, Rinehart and Winston, 1969), pp. 5–6.

[69]Gordon E. Misner, "Enforcement: Illusion of Security," *Nation*, April 21, 1969, p. 490.

[70]Niederhoffer, *Behind the Shield*, pp. 40–41.

[71]Ibid., pp. 43–44.

[72]Ibid.

[73]Ibid., p. 50.

[74]John H. McNamara, "Uncertainties in Police Work: The Relevance of Police Recruits' Backgrounds and Training," in *The Police: Six Sociological Essays,* ed. David J. Bordua (New York: Wiley, 1967), p. 251.

[75]Wilson, "Police and Problems," p. 201.

[76]Burton Levy, "Cops in the Ghetto: A Problem of the Police System," *American Behavioral Scientist,* 2, no. 4 (1968), 31.

[77]Ibid., p. 33.

[78]A. C. Germann, "Community Policing: An Assessment," *The Journal of Criminal Law, Criminology and Police Science,* 60, no. 1 (1969), 94.

[79]Momboisse, *Community Relations,* p. 145.

[80]President's Commission, *Task Force Report,* p. 175.

[81]Thomas A. Johnson, "Police Community Relations: Attitudes and Defense Mechanisms," *Issues in Criminology,* 4, no. 1 (1968), 71–72.

[82]Lohman and Misner, *Police and Community,* vol. 1, p. 131.

[83]Ibid.

[84]Niederhoffer, *Behind the Shield,* pp. 58–59.

[85]McNamara, "Uncertainties in Police Work," pp. 186–87.

[86]James Q. Wilson, "Dilemmas of Police Administration, *Public Administration Review,* 28, no. 5 (1968), 407–12.

[87]Ibid., pp. 412–13.

[88]Ibid.

[89]Herman Goldstein, "Police Response to Urban Crises," *Public Administration Review,* 28, no. 5 (1968), 421.

[90]James M. Mosel, "Related Training to on the Job Effectiveness," *Bulletin on Hospital Education and Training,* June 1969, p. i.

[91]Ibid.

[92]Lohman and Misner, *Police and Community,* vol. 1, p. 56.

[93]Juby E. Towler, *The Police Role in Racial Conflicts* (Springfield, Ill.: Charles C Thomas, 1964), p. vi.

[94]Roger Lane, *Policing the City: Boston 1822–1885* (Cambridge, Mass.: Harvard University Press, 1967), p. 84.

[95]U.S. Riot Commission, *Civil Disorders,* p. 312.

[96]Wayne R. LaFave, "The Police and Non-enforcement of the Law, Part I," *Wisconsin Law Review,* January 1962, pp. 116–18.

[97]Joseph Goldstein, "Police Discretion Not to Invoke the Criminal Process: Law-Visibility Decisions in the Adminstration of Justice," *The Yale Law Journal,* 69, no. 4 (1960), 552.

[98]Robert J. McCormack, Jr., and James L. Moen, "San Francisco's Mission Police District: A Study of Resource Allocation," Center for Planning and Development Research, Institute of Urban and Regional Development, University of California, Berkeley, 1968, p. 51.

[99]Ibid.

[100]Herman Goldstein, "Full Enforcement vs. Police Discretion Not to Invoke

Criminal Process," in *Police and Community Relations: A Sourcebook,* ed. A. F. Brandstatter and Louis A. Radelet (Beverly Hills, Calif.: Glencoe Press, 1968), p. 386.

[101]Jerome H. Skolnick, *Justice without Trial: Law Enforcement in a Democratic Society* (New York: Wiley, 1966), pp. 71–73.

[102]James Q. Wilson, *Varieties of Police Behavior: The Management of Law and Order in Eight Communities* (Cambridge, Mass.: Harvard University Press, 1968), p. 85.

[103]Ibid., p. 84.

[104]Ibid., p. 85–86.

[105]Ibid.

[106]Ibid., p. 88.

[107]Ibid, pp. 88–89.

[108]Ibid.

[109]Ibid., p. 279.

[110]Ibid., p. 7.

[111]Lohman and Misner, *Police and Community,* vol. 2, p. 313.

[112]National Commission on the Causes and Prevention of Violence, *Rights in Conflict,* pp. 1–2.

[113]William Serrin, "God Help Our City," *The Atlantic Monthly,* March 1969, p. 115.

[114]William B. Melnicoe and Jan Mennig, *Elements of Police Supervision* (Beverly Hills, Calif.: Glencoe Press, 1969), p. 18.

[115]J. L. LeGrande, "The Patrol Division: Proving Ground for Police Community Relations," *The Police Chief,* January 1965, pp. 41–42.

[116]Whittaker, *The Police,* p. 109.

[117]Wilson, "Police and Problems," p. 201.

[118]Richard H. Blum, "The Problems of Being a Police Officer," in *Police Patrol Readings,* ed. Samuel Chapman (Springfield, Ill.: Charles C Thomas, 1964), p. 38.

[119]Mort Stern, "What Makes a Policeman Go Wrong," in *Police Patrol Readings,* ed. Samuel Chapman (Springfield, Ill.: Charles C Thomas, 1964), pp. 54–58; also see Chevigny, *Police Power;* and William Westley, "Secrecy and the Police," *Social Forces,* 34 (March 1956).

[120]Wilson, "Police and Problems," p. 206. Also see Turner, *The Police Establishment,* particularly his chapter on the New York City Police Review Board fight.

[121]James Q. Wilson, "The Police and the Delinquent in Two Cities," in *Controlling Delinquents,* ed. Stanton Wheeler (New York: Wiley, 1968), p. 23.

[122]Skolnick, *Justice without Trial,* p. 108.

[123]Ibid., p. 109.

[124]Chevigny, *Police Power,* p. 139.

[125]Ibid., p. 99.

[126]Skolnick, *Justice without Trial,* p. 56.

[127]Ibid., p. 90.

[128]Ibid.

[129]Carl Werthman and Irving Piliavin, "Gang Members and the Police," in *The Police: Six Sociological Essays,* ed. David J. Bordua (New York: Wiley, 1967), p. 86.

[130]Ibid., p. 92.

[131]Ibid.

[132]Ibid., pp. 93–94.

[133]Chevigny, *Police Power*, p. 98.

[134]U.S. Riot Commission, *Civil Disorders*, p. 304.

[135]President's Commission, *Task Force Report*, p. 23.

[136]Ibid.

[137]Lohman and Misner, *Police and Community*, vol. 1, p. 24.

[138]Ibid.

[139]Ibid.

[140]Jameson W. Doig, "A Symposium: The Police in a Democratic Society," *Public Administration Review*, 28 (September–October 1968), 394.

[141]Lohman and Misner, *Police and Community*, vol. 2, p. 309.

[142]Ibid.

[143]Ibid., p. 32.

[144]Ibid.

[145]U.S. Riot Commission, *Civil Disorders*, p. 320.

[146]Lohman and Misner, *Police and Community*, vol. 1, p. 22.

[147]Michigan State University, *National Survey*, p. 67.

[148]Ibid., p. 385.

[149]Howard H. Earle, "Police Community Relations: The Role of the First Line Peace Officer," *Police*, 14, no. 1 (1969), 24.

[150]Skolnick, *Justice without Trial*, p. 1.

[151]Louis H. Masotti and Jerome R. Corsi, *Shoot Out in Cleveland: Black Militants and the Police*, A Staff Report to the National Commission on the Causes and Prevention of Violence (Washington, D.C.: U.S. Government Printing Office, 1969), p. 85.

[152]Germann, "Community Policing," p. 92.

[153]John A. Webster, review of *Community Relations and Riot Prevention*, by Raymond M. Momboisse, in *Issues in Criminology*, 4, no. 1 (1968).

[154]Gordon E. Misner, "The Urban Police Mission," *Issues in Criminology*, 3, no. 1 (1967), 37.

[155]Ibid., p. 38.

[156]Joseph D. Lohman, "On Law Enforcement and the Police: A Commentary," paper presented at American Association for the Advancement of Science, New York, December 1967, p. 26.

[157]Niederhoffer, *Behind the Shield*, p. 12.

[158]President's Commission, *Task Force Report*, p. 35.

[159]Joseph D. Lohman, "Protest Groups: Objectives, Methods, Individual and Group Behavior," address to the Seminar in Police Responsibility in Civil Disturbances, Protest Demonstrations and Civil Disobedience, Southern Police Institute, University of Louisville, Louisville, Ky., November 29, 1965 to December 10, 1965, p. 44.

[160]*Ibid.*

[161]Lohman, "Protest Groups," p. 11.

[162]International City Managers' Association, *Municipal Police Administration,* p. 438.

[163]Milton Rokeach, "Police and Community—As Viewed by a Psychologist," in *Police and Community Relations: A Sourcebook,* ed. A. F. Brandstatter and Louis A. Radelet (Encino, Calif.: Glencoe Press, 1968), p. 52.

[164]Joseph D. Lohman, "Current Decline in Respect for Law and Order," speech delivered before the Section of Judicial Administration, American Bar Association, Montreal, August 8, 1966, p. 5.

[165]Ibid.

[166]Allen D. Grimshaw, "Three Views of Urban Violence: Civil Disturbance, Racial Revolt, Class Assault," *American Behavioral Scientist,* 2, no. 4 (1968), 5.

[167]Allan Silver, "The Demand for Order in Civil Society: A Review of Some Themes in the History of Urban Crime, Police and Riot," in *The Police: Six Sociological Essays,* ed. David J. Bordua (New York: Wiley, 1967), pp. 22-23.

[168]Lohman, "On Law Enforcement," p. 15.

[169]International City Managers' Association, *Municipal Police Administration,* p. 434.

[170]Lohman, "On Law Enforcement," p. 13.

3

ROLE THEORY
AND THE POLICE
ORGANIZATION

CHAPTER
NINE

THE EMERGENCE
OF THE PATROL
OFFICER'S ROLE

INTRODUCTION

In preceding chapters it is obvious that we believe that the matter of *role* is crucial in developing an understanding of police–community relations. The subject of role in social settings has intrigued behavioral scientists for generations.

Role-set theory begins with the concept that each social status involves not a single associated role, but an array of roles. . . . Thus, a person in the status of medical student plays not only the role of a student vis-à-vis the correlative status of his teachers, but also an array of other roles relating him diversely to others in the system: other students, physicians, nurses, social workers, medical technicians, and the like.

The notion of the role-set at once leads to the inference that social structures confront men with the task of articulating the components of countless role-sets—that is, the functional task of managing somehow to organize these so that an appreciable degree of social regularity remains, sufficient to enable most people most of the time to go about their business without becoming paralyzed by extreme conflicts in their role-sets.[1]

Perhaps the most useful way in which to examine the interactions between police organizations and the citizens they serve is from the perspective of the social–psychological concept of *role,* or *role set.*

This chapter is designed to speak definitively about roles, the way in which these roles are seemingly prescribed for police, the expectations of police and citizens as they each look at a particular problem, and the role conflicts that often result. To do this, we begin with a definition of various terms that will be used in this chapter and the following one. We then approach the problem of role, especially police role, from the perspective of behavioral scientists attempting to understand the dynamics of role theory in a police–community setting.

Unfortunately, certain terms often have both a commonsense or common-usage definition, and a more precise behavioral science definition. The term *role* is an excellent example. Even in this book, we have used both a common-usage definition or meaning of the term "role" and the more scientific definition. When, for example, the term "role" is used in the term the "police role," it is being used in the sense of the *proper or customary function.* However, when the term "role" is used in conjunction with attempting to understand what policemen perceive as the uses of their authority or how they attempt to resolve certain occupational dilemmas, the term is used in a more precise way. First, the definition of the terms:

Role:	A set of standards, descriptions, names, or concepts held for the behavior of a person or a position.[2]
Role set:	The people or roles of others that one interacts with. . . . A role set for a physician is other physicians, nurses, patients, and hospital administrators.[3]
Role location:	In the social structure . . . a role appropriate to the situation.[4]
Role enactment:	The actual overt social conduct of the actor, and when the object of observation is a person enacting a social role, the researcher makes inferences as to the appropriateness, propriety, and convincingness of the enactment.[5]
Role skills:	Characteristics possessed by the individual which result in effective and convincing role enactments: aptitude, appropriate experiences, and specific training. . . .[6]
Role expectations:	Specifications for adherence to group norms.[7]
Role acquisition:	Elements of role expectations . . . consist not only of specifications of the individual's own role but also of complementary roles, as well as the entire role set.[8]

Role strain:	The results of attempts to meet expectations that cannot be fully met either by a person or a social system.[9]
Role conflict:	Created in a formal organization whenever two conditions are met: (1) two or more inconsistent patterns of role expectations (2) in which both patterns of expectations are defined by the organization as being legitimate.[10]
Role ambiguity:	A direct function of the discrepancy between information available to the person and that which is required for adequate performance of the job.[11]

THE EMERGENCE OF A ROLE

Over the years, police officers have been quite successful in conveying to the public "that law enforcement per se is the primary and highest goal of American police officers."[12] The result of this has been the "cops and robbers" conception of the police. This has not only greatly simplified the role of the police in dealing with criminals, but, more important, has resulted in neglecting the more complex concepts of viewing modern police functions.[13]

The University of California report for the President's Commission on Law Enforcement and Administration of Justice surveyed the literature in police administration to ascertain what police conceive as the "proper" police functions. Out of a list of thirteen functions, the two most important to American police systems were the protection of the security of persons and property and the enforcement of laws. The report went on to state the following:

> It seems clear, then, that civilian police practice in the United States tends to emphasize the law enforcement function more than the peace keeping function. This distinction is more than a semantic distinction or play on words. If, in fact, these functions have a practical significance as far as structuring the role and orientation of personnel who perform these functions, there is a concomitant effect upon how the police mission is carried out.[14]

The policies and procedures of police departments play a significant part in creating a role concept for the position of patrol officer. This role concept has important consequences on the relationship between patrol officers and the police department's clientele. It is also very important to individual police officers in terms of their own career development "because the policeman is rewarded for performing 'properly' within this role concept and he is career-penalized if he does not perform adequately within this role."[15]

The typical patrol officer in our urban areas spends relatively little time on serious crimes or in responding to criminal calls serious enough to require an arrest, prosecution, and conviction. For the most part, the majority of the patrol officers' time is consumed in activities that settle disputes or keep order, functions that are of a complex nature and frequently involve difficult social, behavioral, and political problems.[16]

James Q. Wilson also suggests that the role of the patrol officer is defined more by responsibility for maintaining order than responsibility for enforcing the law.[17] Herman Goldstein refers to the distinction in the patrol officer's role as that of officers operating in one of two worlds. According to Goldstein, the first world is that of the criminal justice system, which provides the police with a highly structured role defined by various legal statutes. The second world entails all aspects of police functioning that are unrelated to the processing of people through the criminal justice system and consequently result in a very ambiguously defined role.[18]

Wilson maintains that the role of the police is complicated because they serve two essential objectives: order maintenance and law enforcement.[19] Wilson suggests that the difference between these two objectives is not simply the difference between "little stuff" and "real crime," but that the distinction is fundamental to the police role, since both functions involve dissimilar police actions and judgments.[20]

For example, the objective of law enforcement or crime deterrence is facilitated by the following:

1. Specialization
2. Strong hierarchical authority
3. Improved mobility
4. Clarity of legal codes and arrest procedures
5. Close surveillance of the community
6. High integrity
7. Avoidance of entangling alliances with politicians[21]

On the other hand, the maintenance of order objective is aided by departmental procedures that include:

1. Decentralization
2. Neighborhood involvement
3. Foot patrol
4. Wide discretion
5. The provision of services
6. An absence of arrest quotas
7. Some tolerance for minor forms of favoritism[22]

In effect, what this analysis indicates is that municipal police departments are often really two organizations in one, serving two related, but not identical functions. The relevance this has for role theory is quite substantial, because the first objective, order maintenance, actually creates conflict. The second objective, law enforcement, places police in an embarrassing position, because if they do characterize themselves as crime fighters, they are being judged by a goal they cannot obtain.[23]

Elaine Cumming and colleagues' article, "Policeman as Philosopher, Guide and Friend," definitely supports Wilson's contention that the order-maintenance function of a police department should cause conflict.

> Some modern advocates of "professionalization" of police work recognize that the policeman on the beat spends about half of his time as an amateur social worker and they hope, instead of improving the referral process, to equip him with the skills of a professional. The policeman will then have a role containing both overtly supportive and overtly controlling elements. If our assumption that these are incompatible activities is correct, this development would lead to a division of labor within police work that would tend once more to segregate these elements.[24]

Wilson comments further on the order-maintenance objective and suggests that in few other occupations will a role emerge that allows subprofessionals to work alone and exercise wide discretion in matters such as life and death, honor and dishonor, especially in an environment that is apprehensive and even hostile.[25]

> This role places the patrolman in a special relationship that is obscurred by describing what he does as "enforcing the law." To the patrolman, the law is one resource among many that he may use to deal with disorder, but it is not the only one, or even the most important; beyond that, the law is a constraint that tells him what he must not do but that is peculiarly unhelpful in telling him what he should do. Thus he approaches incidents that threaten order not in terms of enforcing the law but in terms of "handling the situation." The officer is expected by colleagues as well as superiors, to "handle his beat."[26]

Egon Bittner suggests that not only is the role of patrol officers unstructured and ill-defined regarding their peacekeeping mission, but that, more important, there is absolutely no structural form of control or review of actions taken under the "peacekeeping function."[27] Bittner illustrates this point by suggesting the following:

> Patrolmen have a particular conception of the social order of skid row life that determines the procedures of control they employ. The most conspicuous features of the peace keeping methods used are an aggressively personalized approach to residents; an attenuated regard for questions of culpability; and the use of coercion, mainly in the interest of managing situations rather than persons.[28]

This observation has profound consequences on police–community relations because if patrol officers are more interested in managing situations than in managing persons, there can be little doubt as to the strains developed within the context of police–citizen interactions.

In summing up the police officer's peacekeeping role, Bittner draws a distinction between the individual officer and the organization's conception of the role. To police officers, the use of common sense, altruism, and discretion is essential to their role enactment. However, the organization has, for the most part, not considered these variables and certainly has not facilitated the patrolman's increasing and improved use of them.[29] Therefore, to this degree, the police organization has shown little overt concern for the role enactment of its patrolmen in noncriminal situations, simply because there has been little concern for both the control or review of this role and the legitimization or improvement of this role.

The organization's, as well as the patrol officer's conception of the police role is, to say the least, not that of "maintaining order" or "keeping the peace." In fact, to both the patrol officers and the organization, real police work consists of acting out the important symbolic rites of search, chase, and capture.[30]

> Where the police perceive the menace of the criminal as great, morale among policemen tends to be high. In the absence of menacing attributes on the part of the pursued, the policeman feels cheated. He cannot properly play the police role because the criminal and the victim do not play the proper supporting and complementary roles. There is no suspense, no chase, no investigation, no danger.[31]

James Q. Wilson suggests that to patrol officers "real police work" is catching "real" criminals or felons, preferably while the crime is in progress. Also, a part of this real police work consists of keeping stores under surveillance which are high robbery hazards, interrogating various people in an area where a known criminal is believed to be hiding, or keeping an eye on suspicious people in general. One of the more frustrating dilemmas to patrol officers lies in their desire to do this real "police work," yet not having the time to do it because they must respond to "service" or "information" calls, which consume so much of their time.[32]

Perhaps one of the major contributions to understanding the patrol officer's role was made by Jerome Skolnick when he observed that the patrol officer's role contains two principal variables, *danger* and *authority*. However, to fully appreciate the impact of these two variables in the patrol officer's role, one must be aware of the constant pressure that patrol officers are under to appear efficient or "produce." With this awareness, the variables can be interpreted in terms of the impact they have on patrol officers. In short, the element of danger has the effect of isolating patrol officers, in effect creating not only solidarity but an actual subculture.[33] Perhaps the constant pressure to produce only speeds up the entire process of creating isolation and solidarity.

The combination of danger and authority found in the task of the policeman unavoidably combines to frustrate procedural regularity. If it were possible to structure social roles with specific qualities, it would be wise to propose that these two should never, for the sake of the rule of law, be permitted to co-exist. Danger typically yields self-defensive conduct, conduct that must strain to be impulsive because danger arouses fear and anxiety so easily. Authority under such conditions becomes a resource to reduce perceived threats rather than a series of reflective judgments arrived at calmly.[34]

Michael Banton suggests still another reason for solidarity among police officers, drawing attention to the problem of role segregation. In other words, "the more the incumbents of a role differ as individuals from the normal range in that stratum of society (by being better, worse, or just different from the majority), the more the role itself is apt to be set apart."[35]

It should be pointed out that the police system itself is not always forced into a subculture by outside pressures. There are reasons for which the police system feels it benefits from solidarity, in terms of the loyalty and unswerving allegiance that is often a part of police solidarity. Police management can and does encourage this solidarity through its semimilitary hierarchical authority structure. Another method of maintaining internal cohesion is through the use of a pension system in which officers reach a point where they have contributed so much money that they are forced to stay with the department or else risk the loss of money they have invested in the pension fund. However, for this to be operationally effective, there must be attached the proviso that officers lose their contribution if they quit before their twenty years are up, a standard feature of many retirement plans.[36]

Solidarity is an important aspect, or variable, of the police role. Whether it is encouraged from within or from outside the department, or from a management or line level, it is a force that materially affects role acquisition and role performance. Furthermore, it has more than a passing effect on police–community relations, since solidarity actually permeates the same role conception, while offering a formidable amount of resistance to any new role conceptualization. Unfortunately, many authorities on police–community relations feel that before we improve our police–community relationships, a radical change in the conception of the police role will first be necessary.[37] Role reconceptualization is frequently difficult enough without having problems of solidarity and tradition too heavily involved. However, add the variables of danger, authority, pariah feeling, and organizational subcultures, and one really gets some idea of from where the resistance to role reconceptualization will emerge. This is, to say the least, predicting a dismal future for any improvements that are to be made in the area of police–community relations. Yet we see little hope for meaningful improvements in police–community relations unless there is a pervasive, systematic, and responsive role reconceptualization of our nation's police service.

Citizen demands for or expectations of police service are not confined to services of a criminal nature. In fact, the police perform the functions of family counselors, obstetricians, and agents of socialization for potential delinquents. As McNamara suggests, it is this mixture of enforcement and service functions that creates conflicts and uncertainties that are only partly resolved by attempting to segregate the two functions.[38] Much of the uncertainty and conflict facing patrolmen pertaining to their role stems from the fact that citizens demand that police perform functions other than those associated solely with and of a criminal nature.

Perhaps, as Lohman suggested, it may be time for us to reduce this polarity and "give our police a role and the condition of implementing that role which can help bring about a unity of purpose . . . rather than accentuate the meaningless, purposelessness and self defeating polarity which evidently prevail."[39]

In addition to this, Skolnick indicates that we might well have to work out ways of changing the conception of the police role because police are performing social agency activities whether they want to admit it or not.[40] As Gunnar Myrdal stated in his classic work, *An American Dilemma: The Negro Problem and Modern Democracy,* "Ideally, the police officer should be something of an educator and a social worker at the same time that he is the arm of the law."[41] The fact that the police are not, plus the narrow conception of the police role pertaining only to matters of a criminal nature, results in the police not being liked or trusted as much as they rightly ought to be.[42]

The significant point pertaining to citizen demands or expectations for police services which police departments have not acknowledged is simply that when the public needs the services of the police department, it not only needs them unconditionally, but demands the service. These services are being challenged by a rapidly changing society. Therefore, the police must adapt themselves and their role to meet not only the traditional, but also the more innovative requests for police service.[43]

Before one expects too much of an innovative response from police departments, it must be acknowledged that police officers themselves are products of the same social experience to which all of us are exposed.[44] Just putting uniforms on people does not ensure that they should be able, or would be able, to respond to citizen needs any more effectively than the majority of the population. This becomes more evident in terms of police–community relations, especially considering that most police officers have "absorbed some of the prejudices and antipathies toward minority groups that are so tragically widespread in our society."[45] As a population we would be well advised to quit expecting our governments in general, and police in particular, to perform services and accept responsibilities that we, as a people, have been unable to collectively shoulder and resolve.

RECRUITMENT, SELECTION, AND SOCIALIZATION OF POLICE

There are few more important phases of police personnel management than that of recruitment and selection of police officers. Historically, public personnel management as well as police organizations have been preoccupied with attempting to bar the unfit from the particular police agency in which they are seeking to enlist. It is only recently that there has been any real concern toward a policy of positive selection for enlisting the better applicants to join the organizations.[46]

American police service has historically felt a shortage of police personnel throughout the country. Perhaps this is due in part to decades of political neglect, public apathy, or professional parochialism. To indicate the complexity of the historical shortages of suitable applicants for police agencies, in 1967, the President's Commission on Law Enforcement estimated that it would take 50,000 additional police simply to fill positions that were authorized throughout various municipal police organizations in the United States. Thereafter, to maintain the nation's police force at a strength that has been authorized, it was estimated that it would require, at the least, the recruitment of 30,000 persons annually. Perhaps this estimate is even a bit conservative in view of the continuing growth of urban populations and spiraling crime rates which our communities are presently enduring.[47]

Part of the selection problem of the American police service is that it is *selection by rejection.* Figures indicate that nationally, 77.7 percent of all candidates to municipal police departments are rejected. Although there can be no question of the fact that physical requirements are often unrealistically high and most assuredly contribute to high rejection rates, even so, other standards for screening tend to be quite low. Therefore, the future indicates that if our municipal police departments strengthen some of the screening procedures, rejection rates may tend to increase at the same time that the need for more police applicants also increases.[48]

To indicate more forcefully that we do select applicants to our municipal police departments via a rejection standard, we need only the reminder that in 1965, only 2.8 percent of the candidates for the Los Angeles Police Department were eventually accepted into the force. Also, in 1966, only 29 of 3,033 applicants were hired by the Dallas Police Department.[49]

A portion of the problem for selecting qualified applicants for employment with municipal police agencies centers around the following requirements. Age requirements in various municipalities may vary from 18 years of age, as a minimum, to a maximum of 35. Some organizations, such as the Colorado State Highway Patrol, have a minimum age requirement of 25 years. The point is that age requirements sometimes can act as an impediment to the selection and recruitment of young people who desire to enter the service. Another requirement that some-times acts as a distinct barrier is the height requirement. Again, in many municipal departments, height standards for men have been established at a minimum of 5 feet 8 inches to a maximum of 6 feet 6 inches. Unfortunately, a considerable portion of young men do not quite qualify for the 5 foot 8 inch standard and are automatically excluded. This is one of our continuing problems in the selection of potential police offi-cers. As long as there is no documented research to establish why a man under 5 feet 7 or 8 inches is not acceptable, municipal police service will suffer appreciably. Fortunately, there is a reversible trend in the applica-tion of height standards; however, this trend has not yet filtered down to all departments.

Another selection requirement that has a significant role to play in rejection of applicants pertains to sight requirements. Some depart-ments require 20/20 vision or correctable 20/20 vision. Unfortunately, some departments have taken the position that eyesight must be better than that required for some commercial airline pilots. Although the sight requirement is definitely an important consideration, we must also bear in mind its relationship to some of the high rejection rates on this factor alone.

Another requirement that sometimes plays a great role in applicant rejection is the weight requirement. Again, weight requirements are set at minimums and maximums—often from 150 to 250 pounds. Unfortu-nately, if we are going to have weight requirements, one would think that after a person has joined an agency, that the agency will continue its vigilance in enforcing the same weight requirement as was required when the person was initially recruited. Otherwise, it tends to suggest a bit of hypocrisy on the organization's part.

Part of the selection and entrance problems that potential applicants to police organizations have experienced has received some of the best attention by William Westley's 1951 doctoral dissertation, recently pub-lished as a book entitled *Violence and the Police*. Obviously, the recruit school of any municipal police department plays a very strategic and important role in the recruitment, selection, and socialization of patrol officers into its organization. As Westley indicates, it is quite difficult to make an objective assessment of the function of the recruit school in the initiation of the recruit. However, we can be sure that the recruit school does do two particular things: (1) it detaches recruits from their old experiences and prepares them for new experiences; and (2) the recruits learn the rough outlines of their job, at least as it appears on the books, and they do get some idea of what they will anticipate when they get into the field.[50] Westley provides a summarization of the initiation process recruits go through in their socialization into the new organization. He has identified three experimental stages and classifies them as the recruit school, contact with colleagues, and experiences with the public.

In school the recruit obtains a temporary definition of the situation, which will permit him to operate until he becomes oriented. In addition, he is brought into contact with the atmosphere of police work, with the themes of group solidarity, with the concept of being tough, with the need for maintaining and raising prestige of the group. Leaving school with this set of temporary definitions, the recruit begins his work in the company of an older and more experienced man. In this relationship he is expected to play the role of rookie—the quiet one, the listener. From this older partner he receives technical information and the rules of the game, explicit and wrapped in stories and homely wisdom. The older man enjoys his paternalistic expert role, provided that the younger man plays the role of recruit, a role he learns from interaction with the older man. From the older man he learns the importance of the police "sticking together," and the need for making the public respect the police, the need for being tough, the difference between the police and the public, the public condemnation of the police. He receives these ideas verbally, and he sees them demonstrated in action.[51]

Westley indicates that the initiate role is an essential part of integration into the group. In other words, recruits must play a role, a specific role, in the drama of experience versus inexperience; they are to be good listeners if they expect senior patrol officers to function as teachers and to indicate to them the particular ropes of the game. If recruits break out of this particular role and attempt to exhibit any abilities of their own, they may threaten the knowledge of the older officers and deprive them of the opportunity to derive some ego satisfaction from breaking in new recruits. At this point, recruits are confined to the status of being "too smart for their own good" and may be deprived of a great deal of information, both *informal* rules of the organization, and how to function effectively as patrol officers. Unfortunately for recruits, without knowledge of the informal rules, they are also vulnerable to violation of these informal rules and, of course, this will be met with disapproval by the other officers.[52]

One of the more pleasant surprises facing most recruits as they leave recruit training academies is that upon assignment to particular district stations and various offices, they find that they are genuinely and warmly received by the officers. Most recruits discussing this feel some relief from the anxieties they may have anticipated. This part of the socialization process between the younger recruits and the senior patrolmen is described by Westley as follows:

> Long hours between action have to be filled and the older men hungry for an audience use them to advantage. Here the experienced man finds an opportunity to talk about himself as a policeman, and about his hardships and happinesses. Here he is expected to talk. His talk makes him feel good—more important. Here is someone to whom he is an expert; here he finds none of the boredom of his wife, or the derision of the public, but an eager subservient listener. Thus amidst an incessant barrage of warnings as to silence, the

recruit is initiated into the experience of the man, the history of the department, the miseries of police work, the advantages of police work, and the
gripes and boasting of a long series of men. The older man who has been
long bottled up, who is insecure about himself and the worth of his job, who
faces from day to day an unfriendly world, exploits the situation to the full.[53]

One of the more formidable problems recruits suffer is insecurity
about their job: about handling domestic disturbances, about dealing
with irate merchants, about interacting with teenagers who seem to taunt
the officers' authority, about dealing with drunks—all of which pose
situations for the recruits for which recruit school offered little assistance. Therefore, recruits learn to follow the actions of senior patrol
officers in handling these particular situations. Recruits begin to emulate
senior officers until they gain enough confidence to make various adaptations that fit their particular police style.[54]

It is in the recruits' first experiences with the public that the officers
become emotionally involved with identifying themselves with the rest of
the police organization and find that they begin upholding its values.
They do this because they find the public to be uncooperative, unpleas-
ant, and quite antagonistic. Therefore, recruits find that the maintenance of their own integrity and self-esteem is linked with the maintenance of respect for police, generally; they therefore begin to defend
and follow the rules that senior patrol officers have conveyed to them
with all the conviction they can muster, and, as Westley says, "he has
become a policeman."[55]

Not only do the experiences with the public cause new recruits to
become emotionally involved with colleagues in the police organization,
but the role definition that the officers are allowed to play and the
involvement they have separate them from the rest of society. Westley
has described this in the following manner:

> The policeman's involvement in his role is very great. The pension ties him to
> the job for 20 years. It is a shackle that few are willing to throw off. The job
> dominates his time. He works 8 hours a day, 6 days a week. He puts in a lot of
> extra time in the courts. The job disrupts his life. He works on shifts, and
> working in this fashion sleeps when other people work and works when they
> sleep. He is thus cut off from establishing social contact with other people. He
> is emotionally involved in the job. Feeling that the good pinch is a high value,
> and many are willing to spend some of their off hours planning how to
> present a case in court or attempting to break a big case on their own. The job
> isolates the man and his family. The disrupting shifts make social participa-
> tion difficult. The rule of secrecy keeps his family and himself from talking
> about that in which he is most well versed and most interested. The isolation,
> the time allocated, the emotional involvement make the job a major, if not the
> most, important influence in the policeman's life. Accordingly, it constitutes
> an important part of himself. Furthermore, as he is a social stereotype and a
> public servant, the community obligates him to continue in the role even in his
> off duty hours. They come to him with their troubles and their complaints. In

the bar and in the tavern he is beset by those who want to tell him what an unfair deal they got from the police and by people who want him to do them a favor. The neighbors hold him responsible for maintenance of law in his territory. If the neighbor's child's bicycle is stolen, the policeman is held responsible, and he is expected to do something about it. The only refuge is isolation, to make certain that one does not become too friendly with the neighbors.[56]

Westley has noted that role involvement separates the police from the rest of society. In their interaction with the public, pressures from the public have an important consequence on the activities and actions that the recruit officers will then take, and it is a major problem for the police to deal with these pressures and expectations of the public. When the public is hostile, the police will react with hostility and secrecy. When their activities are likely to lead to criticism from the public, they will hide or eliminate these activities. Westley also discovered that in those areas that are likely to lead to public criticism, such as the use of force, the police became particularly secretive. Westley goes on to indicate that if there were no pressures for the police to use force, they probably would have abandoned it, but they felt that certain pressures were present: to protect themselves from violent people, to solve important crimes they felt could not be solved in any other way, and to control certain types of crimes for which the court made it difficult to convict or refused to hand out strong penalties. The police are in conflict about the use of force, according to Westley, because they know that they will be criticized, and yet they feel they have to use it. Like other people, the police were sensitive to the demands of their occupational audience. Their work tended to make this audience hostile, so they tried to hide what they were doing, to counter the hostility of the public, and at the same time, wherever possible, to seek ways of getting public approval. In essence, Westley concludes that where the police have respect from the public, there will be less need for use of violence and secrecy; where the public hostility grows, so will their utilization of violence and secrecy.[57]

Westley is suggesting that the particular pressures of police–citizen interactions, the hostility the police sense from the public, and the stereotyped attitudes in which the public regards the police cause the police generally to react to this by becoming a close social group in which collective action is organized for self-protection and as an attack on the outside world. This, then, becomes expressed to new recruit officers by senior patrol officers in the form of a major rule promoting silence and secrecy, because this will be the vehicle for self-protection of the group and its members. Secrecy among the police stands as a shield against the attacks of the outside world; against bad newspaper publicity that would make the police lose respect; against public criticism from which they feel they suffer too much; against the criminal, who is eager to know the moves of the police; and against the law, which they too frequently abrogate. Secrecy is loyalty, for it represents sticking with the group, and its maintenance carries with it a profound sense of participation. Secrecy is solidarity, for it represents a common front against the outside world and consensus in at least one goal.[58]

Even though Westley's observations were made three decades ago, we find ourselves in the unique position of not yet managing to minimize the devastating impact on our recruits of the community's multiple and conflicting expectations of police officers. Moreover, recruit schools have not been able, or have not tried, to prepare young recruits to locate their role or adapt to more than one particular role in their interactions with the public. Perhaps John McNamara described it best when he observed that police academies face two major dilemmas in preparing recruits for their duties in the field. The first involves the question of whether to emphasize training strategies aimed at the development of self-directed and autonomous personnel; the second, whether to emphasize strategies aimed at developing personnel over whom the organization can easily exercise control.[59] Not only does it appear that most municipal police departments are pursuing the second strategy, but it also is abundantly clear that we have yet to come to terms with some of Westley's initial observations as to how recruit officers are socialized into a police organization, and how this can be detrimental to their later experiences and interactions with the public.

This should indicate how futile our attempts have been and what little success we have experienced in our efforts to modify the socialization process of young recruits. In fact, some would suggest that we have not even attempted to cope with or understand the complexity of our recruitment, selection, or socialization problem. For as Burten Levy has suggested, in spite of all the money spent on police–community relations, on additional training, or on raising salaries to attract college graduates, we have still experienced massive unrest in our urban communities, and the resentment between the minority community and the police has not diminished greatly.[60] In Levy's view, the problem is one of values and practices within the police system, for no longer can we be content to see the problem as caused by a few bad eggs; instead, we should view the problem as existing within a police system, the department's value system, and socialization with older officers. Levy notes that sometimes this is compounded by taking the worst of the officers and putting them on duty in the ghetto, where the opportunity to act out their prejudices is always present.[61]

In the final analysis, it is quite easy to see how important the process of recruitment, selection, and socialization of police is to municipal police service in America today.[62] Not only have we been faced, historically, with shortages of personnel in our municipal police departments, but the future looks quite dismal in terms of attempting to recruit the caliber of personnel necessary to be able to blend into an organization without being socialized to such a degree that they are not able to interact with the public along lines that earlier recruits were not able to accomplish. Until our recruit schools attempt to counter the socialization process in which they are unknowingly involved, continued interactions between the police and the public will be as tenuous as they have been in the past; more important, we will have continued to obscure a role that police officers and the public could attempt to continue to define in better ways than have been done in the past.

THE POLICE ROLE FROM A RESEARCH PERSPECTIVE

It seems appropriate to place the matter of a patrol officer's role into a research perspective. To the authors this appears to have certain advantages in analyzing not only the patrol officer's role, but also some of the *dynamics* of that role. Consequently, in the remainder of this chapter and in the succeeding chapter we will be discussing various factors in terms of *dependent* and *independent* variables, attempting to shed some light on various interdependencies that become involved in a discussion of role and role set.

What is meant when one talks in terms of dependent and independent variables?

> The prototype of scientific experimentation, and in many ways its most fool-proof form, is the classical experiment. The general question it answers is whether, and to what extent, one variable (called the experimental or independent variable) affects another variable (the dependent variable).[63]

> The analyst is really thinking in terms of cause and effect. That is, he has in mind one or more variables, variation in which can be used to *explain* variation in another variable. These "causal" dimensions are termed *independent variables* and the values to be explained are called *dependent variables*.[64]

With this brief introduction, let us examine the patrol officer's role in its various facets.

By selecting as the dependent variable of this study the *enactment* of the patrol officer's role, we can select the following as independent variables and systematically observe their effect on the emergence of the patrol officer's role, especially as this emerging role is related to police–community relations.

1. Role acquisition
   a. Role set
   b. Role location
   c. Role skills
2. Organizational goals
   a. Perceived organizational services as legitimate–illegitimate
   b. Reward structure
   c. Sanctions

3. Role expectations
   a. Patrol officer
   b. Organization
   c. Client
4. Multiple role phenomena
   a. Role conflict
   b. Role ambiguity
   c. Role strain
5. Method of resolving multiple role phenomena conflicts
   a. The expectations of the police organization
   b. The expectations of the client
   c. A compromise resulting between the police organization and clients' expectations
   d. Avoiding either expectation

By designating role enactment as the dependent variable, this should facilitate systematic observation and appraisal as to how structural and organizational deficiencies intensify policy resistance to police-community relations. In addition to this, it should also serve as an appropriate forum for a systematic inquiry into what defensive tactics patrol officers adopt to protect themselves from the expectations of their clients.

Finally, the patrol officer's role enactment as the dependent variable also aids in systematically observing ways in which police resistance to police–community relations becomes manifested in an everyday or informal basis.

In their classic chapter on role theory, Sarbin and Allen treat role enactment as a dependent variable and proceed to discuss role enactment in terms of the following dimensions: number of roles, organismic involvement, and preemptiveness—are particularly useful in analyzing the enactment of the patrolmen's roles. The authors then specify the following as the independent variables: role expectations, role location, role demands, role skills, self-role congruence, and audience effects. In the remaining portion of their essay, they discuss problems associated with multiple roles, role conflict, and role acquisition.[65]

Sarbin and Allen suggest that in judging the effectiveness of a role enactment, an assessment of role enactment will not always be free of errors. However, to guide the potential role analyst's observations of this social behavior, the authors suggest that inferences can be made from three categories:

1. Is the conduct appropriate to the social position attained by the actor. . . . In short, has he selected the correct role?
2. Is the enactment proper? That is, does the overt behavior meet the normative standards which serve as valuational criteria for the observer?
3. Is the enactment convincing?[66]

The three dimensions around which role enactment has been described—number of roles, organismic involvement, and preemptiveness—are particularly useful in analyzing the enactment of the patrolmen's role. In fact, it would appear, at least as far as the police are concerned, that each of these dimensions has a reinforcing effect on the other. For example, the organismic involvement dimension for patrol officers in our large urban cities probably occurs at the high end of a continuum, in which one finds "enactments which involve great degrees of effort, that is, muscular exertion or participation of the viscera through autonomic nervous system activation, or both."[67] This is not to suggest that all police experience this high degree of organismic involvement, nor is it to emphasize the muscular exertion, as much as it is the activation of the nervous system. "In everyday affairs, roles tend to be enacted with a minimum degree of organismic involvement. Efficiency of conduct would be reduced if all roles were enacted with maximum effort."[68]

Part of the police–community relations problem is that we have too many interactions in which one or both of the actor's organismic involvement have exceeded a personally tolerable level. Associated with the organismic involvement aspect of the patrol officer's role enactment is the dimension entitled "preemptiveness," or roles that essentially entail "the amount of time a person spends in one role relative to the amount of time he spends in other roles."[69]

Since many patrol officers are technically on duty 24 hours a day, and their friends seldom let them forget that they are police officers, the preemptiveness of the patrol officer's role as a police officer must be quite pervasive, to say the least. Furthermore, the role conception most patrol officers have of themselves structures their role to be highly preemptive. For example, numerous authorities have suggested that police work really entails more social work than it does law enforcement work. Nevertheless, a great majority of patrol officers do not accept that portion of their role; instead, they prefer the "Marlboro image" of catching criminals and enforcing laws. In other words, through the use of what Goffman terms *role distance*, police do not actually deny other portions or roles available to them; but by disaffecting the virtual self that is implied in the other roles, they are, in effect, resisting the role.[70] This is significant in terms of structuring a highly preemptive role, which, associated with a high degree of organismic involvement, is quite explosive to any interactions patrol officers will have with members of the community, particularly minority members.

Perhaps even more significant, we have identified another source of police resistance to police–community relations. If patrol officers do invoke a process of role distance, and there is every reason to believe they do, it is quite convenient for patrol officers to refrain from involving themselves in the role that police–community relations demands of them, while not denying the role that police–community relations implies for police officers. The best rationale for this fact is to suggest that as officers of the law, the police feel that they are required to remain completely impartial and not to become personally involved in the duties of the job. If this occurs, the preemptiveness of the "law enforcement" orientation of the patrol officer's role can be manipulated to such a degree that practically no other conception or role could enter the police officer's repertoire of roles. Thus, not only does there appear to be a relationship between the dimensions or organismic involvement and the preemptiveness of the roles, but there is also a definite relationship between the ability of patrol officers to manipulate the preemptiveness of their role and thus limit the number of roles they can cultivate.

Along this dimension of number of roles, Sarbin and Allen state: "It is obvious that the more roles in an actor's repertoire, the better prepared he is to meet the exigencies of social life."[71] Thus, in various police–citizen encounters, the essential question is: Can the police react in more than one role? If the answer is no, there should be little confusion as to why a strain exists between the police and the community.

As far as the enactment of the patrol officer's role is concerned, the relationship between these three dimensions and the role enactment is more than crucial, especially if one dimension has a reinforcing effect on another dimension. To review the process of role enactment, a brief description of the appropriate independent variables will be presented. This, of course, is not to suggest that these are the only independent variables that could be associated with the dependent variable of role enactment. There can be others!

Role Expectations

Sarbin and Allen, as do most other role authorities, consider role expectations to be a central construct to the entire body of role theory. In fact, Sarbin and Allen suggest that it is the conceptual bridge between social structure and role behavior.[72]

> Role expectations are comprised of the rights and privileges, the duties and obligations, of any occupant of a social position in relation to persons occupying other positions in the social structure. . . . Thus, a person's conduct takes into account the role behaviors of occupants of other positions, the specific nature of the conduct varying with the position held by the other interactant.[73]

When people behave differently in interaction with various complementary roles in a system in which their position is but a unit, a role set is created, according to Robert Merton. The *role set* for patrolmen contains judges, prosecuting attorneys, defense attorneys, fellow patrolmen, supervisory and common police personnel, defendants, victims, and clients.

Sarbin and Allen state that "not only is the occupant of a position expected to perform certain acts and not others; he is also expected to perform actions in specified ways—that is a qualitative component and included. . . . These imperatives, by specifying 'how,' 'should,' and 'is,' ensure that the role enactment will be appropriate."[74] In applying this qualitative component to patrol officer's role enactment, what emerges so saliently is the patrol officer's orientation to substantive and procedural law. In fact, the Supreme Court is demanding that the police acknowledge this qualitative component in terms of developing more of an appreciation and awareness of procedural law. Until the police come to terms with this qualitative component, the courts will continue to indicate the inappropriateness of various role enactments by police officers.

Other dimensions along which role expectations differ are in their consensus and in clarity, both of which are measured in degrees.[75] For example, Gross, Mason, and McEachern correlate role expectations and consensus as follows:

> Although expectations are always held for position incumbents in situations for research purposes, it may be convenient to focus on a particular expectation (in a situation) or to focus on a situation and ask what expectations are held for the position incumbent in that situation. Whether or not there is consensus may be questioned with either focus.[76]

Abraham Zaleznik addresses the relationship that exists between clarity and role expectations, and in the process, distinguishes quite concisely between role conflict and role ambiguity: "In contrast to a role conflict where quite clear prescriptions point toward seemingly contradictory behavior, an ambiguity exists where the role expectations have not crystallized or are otherwise vague."[77]

Sarbin and Allen maintain that the effect of role expectations on the role enactment is of such importance that they have further differentiated this independent variable, and in so doing, they have analyzed two essential areas: *clarity of role expectations* and *conformity to role expectations*. In terms of application to the *enactment* of a patrol officer's role, both are of essential importance; however, conformity to role expectations is critical to an examination of the patrol officer's role and will be analyzed in great detail.

In dealing with clarity of role expectations, to "the extent that role expectations are unclear and ambiguous, behavior will be less readily predictable, resulting in ineffective and dissatisfying social interaction. In short, if role expectations are unclear, the person (i.e., the patrol officer) does not know what role enactments are appropriate and cannot forecast the complementary conduct of other interactants."[78]

One important source of unclarity in role expectations results from lack of agreement or consensus among occupants of complementary roles. This is usually referred to as *role dissensus*.[79] Another source of unclarity in role expectations "results from *incongruity* between the role performer's own expectations for his role, and the role expectations held by those comprising his audience."[80]

In their text, *Organizational Stress: Studies in Role Conflict and Ambiguity,* Kahn et al. observe that:

> In an absolute sense role ambiguity exists when the information available to a person is less than required for adequate performance of his role. Two types of ambiguity may be distinguished in terms of the focus of the individual's feelings of uncertainty. The first results from lack of information concerning the proper definition of the job, its goals and the permissible means for implementing them. This type of ambiguity concerns the tasks the individual is expected to perform, in contrast to a second set of concerns relating to the socio emotional aspects of his role performance.[81]

One of the most important variables affecting the role enactment of patrol officers centers upon the conformity of role expectations that exist for the ways in which they are expected to behave. In essence, the role expectations are specifications for adherence to group norms.[82]

Group norms also carry the concomitant power of sanctions, and perhaps norms and sanctions are more "natural" to the enactment of the role of patrol officer than many other role variables. A brief overview of norms and sanctions will be discussed in relationship to role expectations.

Norms and Sanctions

For the most part, Theodore Caplow suggests that organizational norms are statements supported by the organization which describe the behavior that is expected from incumbents of a given position. To make these norms meaningful, they must be supported by sanctions, or some means of punishing nonconformity.[83] The problem of *norm enforcement* on conformity was probably best described by Robert K. Merton in the article, "Conformity, Deviation and Opportunity Structure." Merton's contribution was to describe three major types of conformity, thus enlarging the scope of inquiry into norms and sanctions at three critical levels: attitudinal, doctrinal, and behavioral conformity.[84] "In other words, persons subject to norms may conform behaviorally, by following the norm in their overt behavior; or attitudinally, by communicating their acceptance of norms and their associated values; or doctrinally, by stating the norms to others and repeating their ideological justification."[85]

Newcomb, Turner, and Converse discuss group norms in terms of *processes* that make the sharing of these norms possible. Essentially, they are suggesting that three conditions must be present for a norm to exist: recognizing the existence of rules, accepting rules, and recognition by others that an individual has accepted the rule that others also accept.[86]

Jackson suggests that for a group or society to be really effective in socialization of its members, it must create an environment which perpetuates and reinforces the particular culture. In this way, the norms of the particular subculture are internalized by its individual members.[87] William J. Goode amplifies this point by suggesting that not only does an individual acquire commitments to norms through the various socialization processes, "but that he accepts the rightness of applying a particular norm or norms to a specified situation."[88] Thus, sanctioning is necessary to enforce role conformity, and acts of sanctioning then become the obligation and the role of others.[89] This has application to police organizations because police organizations certainly have an effective socialization process and comprise a subculture. Both of these conditions are necessary to the creation of an environment that perpetuates and reinforces the police culture.

Furthermore, Edward Walker and Roger Heyns have established that the more intimately the individual is associated with the group, the greater is the influence of the norm on the behavior of the individual.[90] As indicated previously, since the public regard the police as a pariah, and the police reaction is that of becoming a closer knit group, it is apparent not only why norms emerge in police organizations, but why they emerge with the intensity that is evident throughout our entire police system.

James L. Price's book, *Organizational Effectiveness: An Inventory of Propositions,* contains two propositions which deserve comment:

> Organizations whose ideologies have high degrees of congruence, priority, and conformity, are more likely to have a high degree of effectiveness than organizations whose ideologies have low degrees of congruence, priority and conformity.... Organizations which have a high degree of sanctions are more likely to have a high degree of effectiveness than organizations which have a low degree of sanctions.[91]

Price is writing essentially from the organization point of view. Perhaps these same two propositions could be applied to what we have identified as the patrolmen subculture. If this is possible, it certainly portrays how a subculture can use norms and sanctions to neutralize its parent culture. More specifically, in police organizations the question of norms and sanctions becomes so important that it can actually be legitimately asked: "Who does run the police department?" In other words, the potential sanctioning power accumulated by the Patrolman's Benevolent Associations and the patrol officer subculture itself can be intense enough to cause police administrators to weigh carefully decisions they ordinarily would not have considered so closely. In some cases administrators may actually formulate policies they might not have formulated at another time. When these situations occur, there is a question as to who is really making the policies and decisions, the patrol officer subculture or the administration. In many cases, it appears as though the policies and decisions are being made at the line level, and administrators merely ratify decisions or policies already established. However, if administrators choose not to ratify decisions but actually retain that domain as their own, they are then vulnerable to incurring the wrath of the patrolmen subculture, something that could very easily cost them their jobs. In essence, the police organization is a victim of its own socialization processes, its own norms and sanctions. To this degree, it is no moot question who really runs the police organization. This, of course, reinforces the view that perhaps police administrators do not really have control of their personnel.

Another manner in which the police organization falls victim to the same norms and sanctions it creates can be seen when group norms retard change because of the abundant stability these norms provide the police organization.[92]

In the final analysis, the effect of norms and sanctions upon role expectations are of such importance that any analysis of the enactment of the patrolmen role would be seriously impaired unless sufficient attention is allocated to the effect of role expectations on role enactment.

The importance of how role expectations are taught and learned must be emphasized to indicate the crucial importance of role expectations to the general process of role learning. "This view follows from sociological theory and research, which sees the learning of appropriate role expectations as a prerequisite to the orderly interaction of individuals in different status positions."[93]

Role Learning

Ironically, as important a concept as role learning is, most authorities generally agree that little research has been devoted to understanding the process of role acquisition.[94] Therefore, role location, role demands, and role skills will be related to the general area of role learning.

Sarbin and Allen offer one of the most concise statements on role learning, in which they clearly depict both its scope and its importance:

> For role learning, the implication of this point is that elements of role expectations to be learned consist not only of specifications of the individual's own role, but also of the other complementary roles. What must be learned are the expectations for a specific role and its complementary roles, that is, the interlocking system of rights and obligations of a role and complementary roles. Learning a role adequately requires the learning of the entire role set. Observation of complementary roles thus aids in the learning of one's own.[95]

Role location is an extremely important aspect of role learning, because the actors must select a role from their repertory that is appropriate to the situation or interaction. This implies that actors must be able to locate their position, and also the positions of other interactants. "If placement of the other, and coordinately, of self is incorrect, then the choice of role and resulting role enactment is likely to be inappropriate, improper, or unconvincing."[96]

Because the police are trained to observe the unusual, look for the incongruent, and generally be a suspicious lot, their training may well be quite dysfunctional in terms of a majority of police–citizen interactions they experience, and because their training is not broad enough to fully address the officer role location.

Role demands are another significant variable, as the conduct of "significant others" may place constraints on the actor's role enactment in terms of demanding a specific type of enactment.[97] The problem for patrol officers with this variable is that it appears to transgress the expressed value of police service as being completely impartial. It also challenges the patrol officer's authority by either requesting or demanding various services. Most important, though, is that the narrow conception of the patrol officer's role causes many patrol officers to resist citizen demands for a particular role enactment because of the deficiencies in role learning which have helped to permeate these narrow conceptions of role.

Role skills, also an important variable, refer to those characteristics possessed by an individual which result in effective and convincing role enactments. Sarbin and Allen suggest that one important component of role skills is the cognitive skills that facilitate role enactment:

> These include the ability to infer validity from available cues, the social position of the other, and of the self, and to infer appropriate role expectations for the position. Ability to analyze a social situation and accurately infer the role of the other is a necessary prerequisite for accurate role enactment.[98]

One aspect of role skills that has been dealt with in considerable depth by role analysis has been the *role-taking ability* or empathy of the actor. Although it can certainly be stated that police organizations are often lax in providing for development and cultivation of these skills by their officers, one must also bear in mind that a police organization might well be intensifying incongruities and dissonance if they did facilitate the officers' cultivation of role taking or empathy. To support this supposition, the following analogy is in order. "If a soldier, for example, were to put himself empathetically in the role of the enemy during wartime, it would hardly be conducive to his valid enactment of the role of soldier."[99] This is not to suggest that the police are at war with an enemy, although many would have you believe this; it is directed more at indicating that the role enactment of police officers takes them into situations of despair, hopelessness, complete depravity, confusion, ignorance, violence, and many other such repressible commodities. Perhaps if officers were to fully empathize or take the role of the other in many of these situations and interactions, they would experience so great an amount of dissonance that they would have to leave their jobs or accommodate in some other manner.

Therefore, what is quite salient to the area of resistance to police–community relations is that police–community relations training requires empathy and sensitivity, areas where most officers would not deny a need for improvement, if it were not for the fact that these are the same factors that would tend to eliminate their adaptations and defense mechanisms to all the other frustrations they encounter in their role enactment. In short, the police might resist police–community relations not because they would deny improving another citizen's lot or improving the police–community relationship, but because the sensitivity and empathy that is required in improving police–community relations tends to leave police officers vulnerable to the genuine frustrations and anxieties of their role. Therefore, until we somehow can address the frustrations police officers encounter, and facilitate their minimization of these frustrations, these far too reliable, but ineffective accommodations will continue to be made. Theefore, when police organizations come to terms with the important area of role skills, they might not only improve the emotional stability of their officers, but at the same time create an atmosphere in which police officers might be able to chance the risk of being empathetic, and in the process, improve police–community relationships.

Role Conflict

Perhaps one of the most significant and fruitful studies on the subject of role conflict was Gross, Mason, and McEachern's *Explorations in Role Analysis,* for it was this study of *consensus* on role definition, *conformity* to expectations, and role-conflict *resolution* that led many role analysts to reconceptualize their approach to the study of role theory.[100]

In short, the authors challenged the untested assumption of consensus of expectations for incumbents of the same position. Previous to this investigation, the authors maintained that Linton's formulation of the role concept blocked such inquiries because built into Linton's description of the role concept was a postulate that there was, in fact, role consensus.[101]

> This conceptualization of role does not allow for the investigation of the impact of variant and dominant orientations on role definition. . . . If individuals hold variant orientations this should be expressed in variant definitions of a role as well as in different behavior. This implies that one of the factors accounting for different role behavior may be variant role definitions, a possibility completely ignored by the postulate of role consensus.[102]

Furthermore, the assumption of consensus precluded its use as a variable, in terms of the degree of consensus that exists on role definitions.

This becomes especially significant to the study of role learning, socialization processes, and the application of sanctions, all relevant to a theory of social control.[103]

One outstanding study of role conflict that has tremendous application to the entire problem of police resistance to police–community relations is Merton's "Occupational Roles: Bureaucratic Structure and Personality." Essentially, Merton examines the structural source of conflict that exists in the relations of officials and their clientele, and suggests that while the client expects individualized and personal treatment, the officials are pressured to deliver formal and impersonal treatment[104] "the group is oriented toward secondary norms of impersonality, and failure to conform to these norms will arouse antagonism from those who have identified themselves with the legitimacy of these rules."[105] In other words, since patrol officers are definitely oriented to impartial police service, and that value is shared by other police officers, any deviation from this norm will be met by a sanction. Police-community relations programming may make police vulnerable to this position, because police–community relations programming often emphasizes the need to decrease the impersonality that exists between the police and the community. Unfortunately, it often does not offer any suggestions for bridging the impartiality–norm–sanction gap. Until police–community relations programming addresses *both* these problems, we can expect continued police resistance to police–community relations.

Sarbin and Allen indicate that role behavior is seldom enacted one role at a time; rather, "individuals are thrust into situations where they are required to choose among alternative roles, and where multiple role obligations impinge upon the role performer."[106] Therefore, in addition to role conflict, it is also necessary to examine the area of *role strain* and to illustrate its relationship to the enactment of an individual's particular role. The central argument implicit in Goode's "A Theory of Role Strain" is essentially:

> that social order or stability is to be explained, not by either the "normative consensual commitment" of the individuals of the group or by integration of the norms themselves, but as a result of a cumulative process characterized by dissensus, role strain stemming from the normal felt difficulty of fulfilling role demands, and the consequent role bargaining that serves to organize actors' total role systems and their performance.[107]

Turner also views *role playing* or *role taking* as a process which is based on more than an extension of normative and cultural deterministic theory. In Turner's view, the role transactions that occur generate compromises between role prescriptions that are demanded by others. In other words, role relations are "fully interactive" rather than merely conforming.[108]

Buckley suggests that empirical support for Turner's conception is illustrated by Anselm Strauss's study of a hospital as a formal organization. Strauss rejected an overly structural view and assumed that social order is not simply normatively specified, but that social order must be "worked at" and continually reconstituted. "On the basis of such considerations, Strauss and his colleagues developed their conception of organizational order as a negotiated order."[109] In other words, the morphogenic process of negotiation acknowledges that in role relationships and interactions, there are certain role performances that occur even though this role performance may not be called for by any of the organizational role prescriptions.[110]

The process by which this *negotiated order* is transacted between the patrol officer and citizens is through the use of discretion as to when the patrol officer will either choose to invoke or not to invoke the criminal process. According to Goode's theory of role strain, the role relations or transactions between patrol officers and citizens amount to nothing more than a sequence of "role bargainings," and any alternative role behaviors, in which each interaction seeks to reduce this role strain.[111]

The significance this has for police–community relations is that it places patrol officers into a situation of severe interrole conflict. Patrol officers are often being pressed hard by the police administration to improve police–community relationships, yet the administration often offers no effective approaches acceptable to patrol officers. Patrol officers accommodate to this situation by "negotiating" with citizens, all the time bearing in mind that they must "keep the lid on the situation." To negotiate or bargain implies and, in fact, demands, that patrol officers rely on the use of discretion. However, the police administration often will not condone or authorize use of the discretion necessary to facilitate the bargaining process. Therefore, the patrol officers's dilemma or conflict is that the police administration expects them to improve police–community relations while refraining from employing necessary discretionary decisions.

Systems Theory

The subject of role interaction and role relation introduces the role analyst to a rather new and uncharted area, that of role theory and its relationship to systems theory. The future will undoubtedly see systems analysis offering a significantly new approach in which, hopefully, both fields of specialization will mutually profit.

Gross, Mason, and McEachern indicate the utility of using a systems approach in role analysis by the following comment:

> A position can be completely described only by describing the total system of positions and relationships of which it is a part. In other words, in a system of independent parts, a change in any relationship will have an effect on all

other relationships, and the position can be described only by the relationship.[112]

Perhaps one of the most useful constructs to facilitate role theorists in becoming more involved in the systems approach resides in what are termed *linkage* roles. Positions that simultaneously involve individuals in two different systems constitute linkage roles.[113]

To appreciate fully the enactment of the patrol officer's role, one must be aware of the system consequences on the role perceptions and the degree to which the linkage role can influence the role conception. For example, patrol officers are simultaneously members of the community system and members of the administration of criminal justice system, of which the police subsystem is but a component part.

In the first case, the patrol officer's position, and subsequent role conception, can best be described by the relationship that exists between the community system and the police system. As described earlier, there appears to be a systematic and pervasive community consensus that the police are nothing but pariahs. While the community has exceedingly high expectations of the police, it refuses to accord the police the concomitant status and prestige that accompany its earlier expectations. The community has actually participated in creating a subculture of our police system. The impact this has on the role conception of patrol officers is devastating; one of the only defenses open to patrol officers for protecting their psychological selves from the community they serve is to manipulate the preemptiveness of their role and limit their role definition to that of being "law enforcement-oriented" police officers. In this way, by defining their role in the most universally accepted terms, patrol officers hope to gain the support of a community which has withheld the status police have so patiently sought.

In the second case, in which patrol officers hold simultaneous membership in both the police system and the administration of justice system, the impact of this dual membership on the patrol officer's role conception can best be described by viewing the officers in court. The linkage of patrol officer to the court system also has a devastating effect on the patrol officer's role conception, simply because a role reversal has occurred by their membership in the second system, and patrol officers are often not prepared to meet this. Indeed, few patrol officers can conceptualize this role reversal in anything more than "the courts are handcuffing us" attitude. This defense mechanism is very similar to the accommodation made by patrol officers in the first case; both instances center on the "law enforcement" orientation of their role. In short, patrol officers are not used to having their authority challenged, while membership in the second system ensures that the court will indeed question officers' judgment or propriety. Officers often internalize this role reversal in an interesting manner. Many officers regard the court as "trying" the police instead of criminals, when, in actuality, the court is often just invoking the rightful role of a check and balance on *another branch of our government.* Reiss and Bordua discuss this role reversal in the following terms:

> The formal linkage of the police to the prosecutor's office and the court has other implications for their adaptation. Interpersonal contact between police and court personnel involve both an inequality relationship and a reversal of roles. Normally, police are in a position of authority vis-à-vis the citizen; in a substantial number of situations they are in a superior status position as well. When they are not, police use tactics to assert authority in the situation. Furthermore, police work generally places an officer in the role of interrogator, a role requiring that little information be given to suspects. Now in contacts with the courts, role situations are reversed. Police are generally below the status of officials they deal with in the courts, particularly with men of the bar and bench, and they are interrogated. Under certain circumstances, they are subject to cross-examination. This kind of contact brings with it all the suspicion and hostility generated between status unequals where roles are reversed and authority is displaced. The ambivalence of the police toward the administration of justice and its role incumbents is further exacerbated under these conditions. This status reversal plus the generalized lower prestige of police when taken together with the institutionalized distrust of police built into the trial process creates a situation where the police not only feel themselves balked by the courts but perhaps, even more fundamentally, feel themselves dishonored.[114]

Summary

This chapter has discussed the emergence of the patrol officer's role in terms of peacekeeping and law enforcement. The fact that those entering police organizations are all products of the same social experiences we are all exposed to throughout our lives suggests the inherent role problems that patrol officers will eventually confront in the enactment of their role.

The recruitment, selection, and socialization of patrol officers was also discussed with particular reference to historical selection by rejection strategies, as well as the implications of norms of secrecy. The continuing impact of senior officers on the socialization of new recruits was also discussed within the parameters of role acquisition, role location, role enactment and the methods of resolving multiple role phenomena conflicts.

Finally, the role enactment process should facilitate systematic observation as to how the structural and organizational deficiencies identified in Chapter 8 do indeed intensify police resistance to police–community relations programming.

End Notes

[1]Robert K. Merton, *On Theoretical Sociology: Five Essays, Old and New* (New York: Free Press, 1967), p. 42.

[2]Bruce J. Biddle and Edwin J. Thomas, *Role Theory: Concepts and Research* (New York: Wiley, 1966), pp. 10–12.

[3]Erving Goffman, *Asylums: Essays on the Social Situation of Mental Patients and Other Inmates* (Garden City, N.Y.: Doubleday, 1961), pp. 86–87.

[4]Theodore Sarbin and Vernon Allen, "Role Theory," in *The Handbook of Social Psychology*, 2nd ed., eds. Gardner Lindzey and Elliot Aronson (Menlo Park, Calif.: Addison-Wesley, © 1968), pp. 506–507. Reprinted with permission.

[5]Ibid., p. 490.

[6]Ibid., p. 514.

[7]Ibid., p. 501.

[8]Ibid., p. 546.

[9]William Mitchell, "Occupational Role Strains: The American Elective Official," *Administrative Science Quarterly*, 3, no. 2 (1958), 211.

[10]Oscar Grusby, "Role Conflict in Organization: A Study of Prison Camp Officials," *Administrative Science Quarterly*, 3, no. 4 (1959), 469.

[11]Robert L. Kahn et al., *Organizational Stress: Studies in Role Conflict and Ambiguity* (New York: Wiley, 1964), p. 73.

[12]Gordon E. Misner, "Enforcement: Illusion of Security," *Nation*, April 21, 1969, p. 488.

[13]Joseph D. Lohman, "New Dimensions in Race Tension and Conflict," *The Police Chief*, July 1963, p. 24.

[14]Joseph D. Lohman and Gordon E. Misner, *The Police and the Community*, report submitted by School of Criminology, University of California, Berkeley, to the President's Commission on Law Enforcement and Administration of Justice, Field Survey IV, vol. 1 (Washington, D.C.: U.S. Government Printing Office, 1966), p. 25.

[15]Ibid.

[16]The President's Commission on Law Enforcement and Administration of Justice, *Task Force Report: The Police* (Washington, D.C.: U.S. Government Printing Office, 1967), p. 13.

[17]James Q. Wilson, *Varieties of Police Behavior: The Management of Law and Order in Eight Communities* (Cambridge, Mass.: Harvard University Press, 1968), p. 16.

[18]Herman Goldstein, "Police Response to Urban Crisis" *Public Administration Review*, vol. 28, no. 5 (1968), pp. 417–418.

[19]James Q. Wilson, "Dilemmas of Police Administration," *Public Administration Review*, 28, no. 5 (1968), 407.

[20]James Q. Wilson, "What Makes a Better Policeman," *Atlantic Monthly*, March 1969, p. 130.

[21]Ibid., p. 135.

[22]Ibid.

[23]Ibid., p. 130.

[24]Elaine Cumming, Ian Cumming, and Laura Edell, "Policeman as Philosopher, Guide and Friend," *Social Problems,* 12, no. 3 (1965), 286.

[25]Wilson, *Varieties of Police Behavior,* p. 30.

[26]Ibid., p. 31.

[27]Egon Bittner, "The Police on Skid Row: A Study of Peace-Keeping," *American Sociological Review,* 32, no. 5 (1967), 700.

[28]Ibid., p. 699.

[29]Ibid., p. 700.

[30]Jerome H. Skolnick and J. Richard Woodworth, "Bureaucracy, Information and Social Control," in *The Police: Six Sociological Essays,* ed. David J. Bordua (New York: Wiley, 1967), p. 129.

[31]Ibid., p. 130.

[32]Wilson, *Varieties of Police Behavior,* p. 68.

[33]Jerome Skolnick, *Justice without Trial: Law Enforcement in a Democratic Society* (New York: Wiley, 1966), p. 44.

[34]Ibid., p. 67.

[35]Michael Banton, *The Policeman in the Community* (New York: Basic Books, 1964), pp. 217–18.

[36]Paul Jacobs, *Prelude to Riot: A View of Urban America from the Bottom* (New York: Random House, 1967), p. 20.

[37]Bruce J. Terris, "The Role of the Police," *The Annals of the American Academy of Political and Social Science,* 374 (November 1967), 67.

[38]John H. McNamara, "Uncertainties in Police Work: The Relevance of Police Recruits' Backgrounds and Training," in *The Police: Six Sociological Essays,* ed. David T. Bordua (New York: Wiley, Inc., 1967), p. 164.

[39]Joseph D. Lohman, "Are Judges Today Aiding Criminals?" paper presented to the Commonwealth Club of San Francisco, Calif., November 19, 1969, pp. 12–13.

[40]Jerome H. Skolnick, *The Police and the Urban Ghetto,* Research Contribution of the American Bar Foundation, No. 3 (Chicago: American Bar Foundation, 1968), p. 12.

[41]Gunnar Myrdal, *An American Dilemma: The Negro Problem and Modern Democracy* (New York: Harper & Row, 1962), p. 545.

[42]Ibid.

[43]President's Commission on Law Enforcement and Administration of Justice, *The Challenge of Crime in a Free Society* (Washington, D.C.: U.S. Government Printing Office, 1967), p. 100.

[44]Joseph D. Lohman, *The Police and Minority Groups* (Chicago: Chicago Park District, 1947), p. 5.

[45]Ibid.

[46]A. C. Germann, *Police Personnel Management* (Springfield, Ill.: Charles C Thomas, 1958), p. 13.

[47]Charles B. Saunders, Jr., *Upgrading the American Police: Education and Training for Better Law Enforcement* (Washington, D.C.: Brookings Institution, 1970), pp. 35, 57–58.

[48]Ibid., p. 46.

[49]President's Commission on Law Enforcement and Administration of Justice, *Task Force Report: The Police* (Washington, D.C.: U.S. Government Printing Office), p. 134.

[50]William A. Westley, *Violence and the Police: A Sociological Study of Law, Custom, and Morality* (Cambridge, Mass.: MIT Press, 1970), p. 156. Reprinted from *Violence and The Police: A Sociological Study of Law, Custom, and Morality* by William A. Westley by permission of the MIT Press, Cambridge, Massachusetts.

[51]Ibid., p. 181.

[52]Ibid., p. 182.

[53]Ibid., pp. 157–58.

[54]Ibid.

[55]Ibid., p. 182.

[56]Ibid., p. 144.

[57]Ibid., pp. xiv–xv.

[58]Ibid., p. 111.

[59]McNamara, "Uncertainties in Police Work," p. 251.

[60]Burten Levy, "Cops in the Ghetto: A Problem of the Police System," *American Behavioral Scientist,* March 1968, p. 31.

[61]Ibid.

[62]Ibid., pp. 33–34.

[63]Bernard Berelson and Gary A. Steiner, *Human Behavior: An Inventory of Scientific Findings* (New York: Harcourt Brace & World, 1964), p. 19.

[64]William J. Goode and Paul K. Hatt, *Methods in Social Research* (New York: McGraw-Hill, 1952), pp. 353, 354.

[65]Theodore R. Sarbin and Vernon Allen, "Role Theory," in *The Handbook of Social Psychology,* 2nd ed., ed. Gardner Lindzey and Elliot Aronson (Menlo Park, Calif.: Addison-Wesley, © 1968), p. 497. Reprinted with permission.

[66]Ibid.

[67]Ibid., p. 492.

[68]Ibid.

[69]Ibid., p. 496.

[70]Erving Goffman, *Two Studies in the Sociology of Interaction* (New York: Bobbs-Merrill, 1961), p. 108.

[71]Sarbin and Allen, "Role Theory," p. 491.

[72]Ibid., p. 497.

[73]Ibid., pp. 497–98.

[74]Ibid.

[75]Ibid., p. 499.

[76]Neal Gross, Ward S. Mason, and Alexander McEachern, *Explorations in Role Analysis: Studies of the School Superintendency Role* (New York: Wiley, 1966), p. 72.

[77]Abraham Zaleznik, "Interpersonal Relations in Organizations," in *Handbook of Organizations,* ed. James G. March (Chicago: Rand McNally, 1965), p. 590.

[78]Sarbin and Allen, "Role Theory," p. 503.

[79]Ibid., p. 502.

[80]Ibid., p. 503.

[81]Kahn et al., *Organizational Stress,* p. 94.

[82]Sarbin and Allen, "Role Theory," p. 501.

[83]Theodore Caplow, *Principles of Organization* (New York: Harcourt Brace Jovanovich, 1964), p. 81.

[84]Robert K. Merton, "Conformity, Deviation and Opportunity Structure," American Sociological Review, 24, no. 1 (1961), p. 178.

[85]Caplow, *Principles of Organization,* p. 84.

[86]Theodore M. Newcomb, Ralph H. Turner, and Philip E. Converse, *Social Psychology: The Study of Human Interaction* (New York: Holt, Rinehart and Winston, 1965), pp. 241–244.

[87]Jay M. Jackson, "Structural Characteristics of Norms," in *Role Theory: Concepts and Research,* ed. Bruce Biddle and Edwin Thomas (New York: Wiley, 1966), p. 124.

[88]William J. Goode, "Norm Commitment and Conformity to Role Status Obligations," *The American Journal of Sociology,* 66, no. 3 (1960), p. 252.

[89]Biddle and Thomas, *Role Theory,* p. 311.

[90]Edward D. Walker and Roger W. Heyns, *An Anatomy for Conformity* (Belmont, Calif.: Brooks-Cole, 1967), p. 46.

[91]James L. Price, Organizational Effectiveness: *An Inventory of Propositions* (Homewood, Ill.: Richard D. Irwin, 1968), pp. 104–38.

[92]Newcomb, Turner, and Converse, *Social Psychology,* p. 254.

[93]Henry L. Lennard and Arnold Bernstein, *Patterns in Human Interaction: An Introduction to Clinical Sociology* (San Francisco: Jossey-Bass, 1969), p. 146.

[94]Sarbin and Allen, "Role Theory," p. 544.

[95]Ibid., p. 546.

[96]Ibid., pp. 506–7.

[97]Ibid., p. 510.

[98]Ibid., pp. 514–15.

[99]Ibid.

[100]Gross, Mason, and McEachern, *Explorations,* p. xi.

[101]Ibid., p. 30.

[102]Ibid.

[103]Ibid.

[104]Robert K. Merton, "Occupational Roles: Bureaucratic Structure and Personality," in *Personality and Social Systems,* ed. Neil J. Smelser and William T. Smelser (New York: Wiley, 1963), p. 262.

[105]Ibid.

[106]Sarbin and Allen, "Role Theory," p. 535.

[107]William J. Goode, "A Theory of Role Strain," *American Sociological Review,* 25, no. 4 (1960), p. 483.

[108]Walter Buckley, *Sociology and Modern Systems Theory* (Englewood Cliffs, N.J.: Prentice-Hall, 1967), pp. 151–52.

[109]Ibid., pp. 146–49.

[110]Ibid., p. 151.

[111]Goode, "A Theory of Role Strain," p. 483.

[112]Gross, Mason, and McEachern, *Explorations,* p. 53.

[113]Roland L. Warren, *The Community in America* (Chicago: Rand McNally, 1963), p. 253.

[114]Albert J. Reiss and David J. Bordua, "Environment and Organization: A Perspective on the Police," in *The Police: Six Sociological Essays,* ed. David J. Bordua (New York: Wiley, © 1967), pp. 38–39. Reprinted by permission of John Wiley & Sons, Inc.

CHAPTER
TEN

THE PATROL OFFICER'S ROLE IN THE ORGANIZATIONAL SETTING

INTRODUCTION

In Chapter 9, we focused our attention on the phenomenon known as role enactment. We attempted to show, in specific and graphic terms, the extent to which the police—as members of society, as members of an organization, and as members of a small work group—are subjected to a series of pressures. In this chapter we continue the discussion.

One of the points being made in this discussion is that the subject of the patrol officer's role is a researchable question. Certainly, not all questions in the behavioral sciences are capable—at least in terms of today's knowledge and methodological tools—of being researched. Careful research procedures have, however, yielded a rich body of knowledge not only about role theory, but also about its application to police–community relations.

Unfortunately, the application of research findings to the solving of particular problems is not always as easy in the behavioral sciences as it is in other fields. It is often easier to find *engineering* solutions to problems than *behavioral* solutions. Police–community relations, issues, and problems take place in a *social setting*—with all that that implies. The *actors* are human beings, working and living in a pluralistic mass society. All the actors have their own organizational, personal, social, religious, political, and economic allegiances. The action often takes place on a public stage, in a representative democratic political setting. It is in this social–political–organizational setting in which we must continue our examination of the police role.

ROLE ACQUISITION

In considering the independent variable of role acquisition, the following observations best illustrate the relationship between *role learning* and *role enactment*. The following case represents a classic, both in terms of illustrating police frustration and also how the probationary period of police recruits influences their subsequent role enactment. In this particular situation, one patrolman was in his fifth month of service with the police department while the other officer was a well-seasoned veteran of six years.

As soon as the call was received by the patrol unit—"see a lady about a lost man"—the older officer immediately exclaimed: "Oh no, the calls start right off the bat." This was the start of this unit's tour of duty. Upon arriving at the address of the citizen requesting help for the lost man, a deteriorating hotel in a lower-class area of midcity, the senior officer again muttered discontentedly about having to help these old drunks find their way home when we should be out doing "real police work."

After talking to the lost man, who was in his late sixties and had shown evidence of drinking, the senior officer reluctantly agreed to try to assist the man in finding his hotel. Since the man was new to the city and was not familiar with the streets or the hotels, the situation was exasperating.

The senior patrol officer showed his frustration by stating: "What's an old fool like you doing in a strange city without your hotel key or some identification or a receipt for the room rent?" The man's reply was: "I left the hotel room just to go for a walk and checked my key in at the desk, and when I tried to return I couldn't find my way and I have stopped in ten or fifteen hotels since. That's when I stopped at this lady's hotel and she tried calling other hotels for about an hour and then she called you gentlemen."

At this point, it was quite evident that the rookie patrol officer was very embarrassed by the brusque line of questioning by which his senior officer was addressing the citizen. The rookie tried to calm the lost man and talk to him rationally, but as the lost man continued to talk, the senior officer's anger intensified, probably because the lost man's statements were becoming more irrational, and possibly because the rookie's attitude was much different than what the senior officer would regard as proper and acceptable in this situation.

The following portion of this interaction is presented approximately as it occurred to illustrate the expectations of the citizen and the officer's response:

Lost Man:	Well, why don't you fellows drive me around town, maybe I can recognize my hotel.
Senior Officer:	Is that an order?
Lost Man:	No, I just thought it might help.
Senior Officer:	I will tell you what will help—if you will up and remember your hotel. Do you think all we have to do is drive old drunks like you around looking for hotels they think they checked into; hell, we can't even be sure you have enough money to rent a room.
Lost Man:	Oh, I have a room alright.
Senior Officer:	Well, then, where is it?
Lost Man:	I don't know.
Senior Officer:	Well, what in the hell are we supposed to do for you?
Lost Man:	Do your job, find my hotel room.
Senior Officer:	For Christ's sake, how in the hell can we find your room when you don't even know the name of the hotel?
Lost Man:	If you drive me around like I told you maybe I could recognize the hotel.
Senior Officer:	Yeah, and maybe you couldn't for christ sake; we have better things to do than drive old fools like you around all night.
Lost Man:	Well, I don't know what we are going to do then.
Senior Officer:	Son-of-a-bitch.
Lost Man:	Well, dammit, if you would do your job and drive me around maybe I could recognize the hotel.
Senior Officer:	Yeah, and maybe you couldn't but I will tell you one thing—we aren't going to play this little game of yours too long.
Lost Man:	It's not a game; how would you like to be lost?
Senior Officer:	I wouldn't be so god-damn dumb to get lost, and to sit around drinking.
Lost Man:	I admit I have had a few drinks.

The officers then proceeded to drive the lost man around town trying to help him recognize his hotel. The conversation continued with the lost man getting progressively anxious:

| Senior Officer: | Listen, you old fool, can you tell me what the inside of the hotel looked like? |

Lost Man:	Well, what do you suppose it looked like . . . it looked like the inside of every hotel.
Senior Officer:	Listen, don't you wise off to me or I will throw you out of this car. The question isn't as dumb as you think because if you can tell me where the elevator is, or what side of the room the stairs come down, or what the desk looked like, it will eliminate some of the hotels.
Lost Man:	Well I don't know how you would expect me to know that.
Senior Officer:	Yeah, maybe it is too much to expect of a dummy who doesn't even remember the name of his hotel.
Rookie Officer:	Can you describe the outside of the hotel?
Lost Man:	No, . . . well, it looks like any of them.
Rookie Officer:	Listen, we are going to stop in front of these hotels and you tell us if you think your room is in one of them.
Lost Man:	Now we are getting some place, that's what I told you a long time ago.
Senior Officer: (turning to observer)	Do you see what sort of bullshit we have to put up with; put this in your report about police–community relations.

As the officers continued to drive the man around the area, the observer noted that the lost man wouldn't even turn his head to look out the squad window when the officers pulled in front of the hotels.

Senior Officer:	God-dammit, the old fool isn't even looking at the hotels; oh christ.
Rookie Officer:	Sir, does this look like your hotel?
Lost Man:	Well maybe . . . they all look the same you know.
Senior Officer:	How in the hell are we going to get you back to your hotel unless you help us?
Lost Man:	I don't know but that is your job.
Senior Officer:	Oh christ, what a case.

Eventually, the officers located the man's hotel. It took two hours to satisfy the citizen's expectation. However, what is salient about this interaction is both the frustration it presented to the officers and the impact this had upon the rookie's role acquisition. The rookie officer, fresh out of the academy with all the idealism of good police–community relations, discovers his partner treating a citizen in a manner the academy has definitely portrayed as unprofessional. Thus, the rookie is faced with one of the first of many inconsistencies he will observe between how the job is done and how it was taught that it should be done. Of significance to the role acquisition process is that the recruit spends

12 weeks initially learning his role and 52 weeks being cajoled into what senior officers consider the correct methods of handling police calls. The rookie spends the most time in acquiring his role under the distinct fear of not being accepted by the senior patrol officer. Thus, he is faced with a role conflict of pursuing calls in the idealistic professional manner the training academy teaches, or of acceding to the demands of the senior patrolman. If he follows the former course, he may alienate himself from the rest of the patrol officers and, in effect, become an "odd ball." His alternative is to comply with the demands of the senior patrol officers and be accepted as a member of the patrolman culture. This response indicates severe frustration as he is, in effect, disregarding the initial instruction given to him by the training academy.

This documents the nature of the patrol officers group as being a subculture within the larger police subculture. The patrol officer subculture has its distinct norms, and unless rookies conform to these norms, they will be sanctioned to the degree of being excluded as accepted members of this subculture. Thus, the role-acquisition process has tremendous relevance to the ultimate role enactment patrol officers will choose to pursue.

The repertoire of roles available to patrol officers to meet the police–citizen interactions is generally limited to one role, that of the law enforcement specialist. However, this one role can be measured in degrees, as the following illustration will indicate.

In this example, the patrol car again contains a senior officer, with eight years' experience, and a rookie officer of 14 months' experience. It was observed that the senior officer conceived of his role not only as a law enforcement specialist, but as a law enforcement specialist primarily interested in the apprehension of wanted felons. This was visibly documented by the officer's possession of a "mug shot" file that was so awesome and impressive that other officers in the same district went to him before they would to the Identification Bureau whenever they wanted information or a picture of a suspect. There are other reasons to account for this phenomenon: (1) this officer worked in the highest-crime district in the city, an area in which one would expect to observe many suspects with warrants outstanding, or where many wanted felons might attempt to blend into the area; and (2) since the workload of the officers in this district was so heavy, other officers perhaps went to this man in the interest of saving time and being available for an assist calls, as opposed to taking themselves out of the area and district or going to police headquarters for "mug shots."

However, it is interesting to note the degree to which patrolmen can define their law enforcement role. In this case the officer spent all his free patrol time observing citizens in the street or in bars, looking for a potential "match" (i.e., a person in his file of wanted felons). Parenthetically, there were other officers working the same district, and the same detail or shift, who would spend their free patrol time checking the area for stolen cars. This required many hours of exceptionally slow patrolling and frequent identification checks on license plates which would indicate that the car was, in fact, "hot" or stolen. The point is: here are two different orientations to the role conception of a law enforcement specialist; each, however, requires two exceptionally distinct methods of patrol. More important, both influence the role-acquisition process of the recruit officer assigned to each squad. For example, the officer possessing the "mug shot" file did not, as he characterized it, "bother with traffic violations or checking for stolen cars." Consequently, the rookie assigned to this patrol car developed the same orientation. This influenced the rookie's role-acquisition process so significantly that the rookie has adopted a similar role conception. Perhaps even more significantly, when we observe the enactment of the rookie patrol officer's role, there is a high degree of correlation with his role-acquisition process, specifically as it was affected by the particular senior patrol officer. It would be rather interesting to discover if this same recruit would have adopted a different orientation or conception of his role if he was assigned to another patrol unit.

To further illustrate the patented effect that the role-acquisition process can have on the role with which the rookie eventually identifies and enacts, the following situation is presented. Both officers received a family disturbance call that was quite frustrating. The call involved a marriage situation in which four children were victims of the following living arrangement. The situation can probably best be portrayed by illustrating the more significant aspects of the officer–citizen dialogue.

Senior Officer:	Did you call the police, lady?
Wife:	Yes, I did; I want you to protect me from my husband.
Senior Officer:	What's the problem, lady?
Wife:	I am afraid he is going to beat me up again and I already have two bruised ribs from the last time.
Senior Officer:	Is your husband home?
Wife:	Yes he is, officer.
Rookie Officer:	Let's go in and talk to him. Are you the husband of this woman?
Husband:	Yes I am, officer.
Rookie Officer:	What's this all about, you beating up women?
Husband:	I don't beat women up.
Wife:	You do too, you liar, you beat me up.
Husband:	Oh shut up, you whore.

To quiet the two people, the senior officer suggested that they both shut up at once, and each tells his side of the story.

Senior Officer:	OK, lady, what's the problem here?
Wife:	My husband won't give me any money for milk for my babies.
Senior Officer: (turning to husband)	Is that true, sir?
Husband:	No, it is not, officer.
Wife:	It is too, you liar; anyway, go look in the refrigerator and see all the beer he has.
Senior Officer:	(*Returning from the kitchen and addressing the husband*) Sir, how come you have so much beer and you aren't buying food for your kids?
Husband:	You see officer, it is like this; everytime I give her money to buy food for the kids, she spends it on herself and on her boyfriends.
Wife:	I do not, you liar.
Husband:	You do too, you whore.

The dialogue continued in the same vein. Finally, the senior officer turned to the wife and suggested the following:

Senior Officer:	Look, lady, we can't tell who is telling the truth; all we want to know is that those kids will get fed.
Wife:	Well they won't, not with that drunk.
Senior Officer:	Lady, if you are so unhappy here, why don't you go and get a divorce and the court will order support of your kids?
Wife:	I can't get no divorce cause we ain't married—we are what you call common law.

At this point, the senior officer became so frustrated that he did not participate any longer in the interaction, and after about 10 more minutes of verbal sparring with the husband and wife by the recruit, the senior officer got up without saying a word and walked out of the house. This frustrated the rookie officer because he did not expect this action. He attempted to gracefully exit the house and then confronted the senior officer in the car as follows:

Rookie Officer:	Why did you leave; did I say something wrong?
Senior Officer:	Hell no, the whole call bothered me. There's nothing we can do for people like that.
Rookie Officer:	Yeah, but we can't walk out just like that; suppose they call up and file a complaint.
Senior Officer:	They are not going to file any complaint.
Rookie Officer:	Look, we will probably get another call back here in about 10 minutes, so why don't we go back and

	settle this. Anyway, if we don't, another one of the cars will get the call and I don't want them to think we can't handle our calls.
Senior Officer:	So what; this isn't even our beat.
Rookie Officer:	Yeah, but. . . .
Senior Officer:	Look, if you want to stay, go ahead, but I am going out and doing "police work," not this bullshit. Go on back if you want, I will be back and pick you up in 30 minutes.
Rookie Officer:	No, I guess you're right; let's get the hell out of here.

The rookie officer was confronted with the conflict of how the senior officer handled the call by leaving in the middle without an explanation to anyone, a situation clearly inconsistent with the professional orientation of the training academy; also, he was equally concerned with sanctions that might be imposed by the organization if a complaint was filed. However, both these concerns were abruptly repressed when the senior officer gently reminded the rookie that he was still a rookie and that the sanctions of the patrol officer subculture would prevail if the rookie wanted to stay there alone and handle the call. The sanction of the patrol officer subculture is implicit within the symbolic statement: "Look, if you want to stay, go ahead, but I am going out and doing police work, not this bullshit. Go on back if you want, I will be back and pick you up in 30 minutes." In other words, if you, as a rookie, feel this is your idea of patrol officer's role,you will not only handle all these calls alone, but you will, in fact, be alone in that the patrol officer subculture will not accept you. The patrol officer's subculture values acknowledge the law enforcement orientation as the acceptable police role, not this other orientation.

The example presented documents the two distinct stages of role learning for patrol officers. The first stage occurs in the training academy, and the second, more influential stage, occurs not just in the probationary period, but also in the time the officer is considered as a recruit or novice. Just when the "rites of passage" occur depend on each individual; however, some definitions extend far beyond the organization probationary definition of one year. This is further support for the proposition that patrol officers are, in fact, a subculture within a larger subculture.

One final observation can be made as to why the senior patrol officer received so many requests from other officers in the district for one of his "mug shots." It could be that the other officers were attempting to seek his approval because this patrol officer was definitely one of the most influential in the district. In this manner, their "rites of passage" would be improved, if not ensured, by their tacit acknowledgment that this law enforcement orientation was also their conception of the patrol officer's role. There is little doubt that either the acquiescence or rejection by this one officer would be sufficient to either bar or gain entry into the patrol officer subculture.

The second example, to illustrate the manner in which the one role, law enforcement orientation, can be measured in degrees, is illustrated by the following situation.

Again, this was a two-man squad, the senior patrol officer having 10 years on the job and the rookie seven months of experience. The officers received a call that there were prowlers in the area. Much to the amazement of the observer, the officers were exceptionally slow to respond to the call, stopping first to give street directions to a pair of young ladies who appeared lost. This behavior seemed quite incongruent to both officers' law enforcement orientation and aggressiveness. When queried about this incongruity, the senior officer replied: "I have been up before disciplinary charges three times and personally talked to the chief twice, and not on a social call; therefore, I am going to be particularly careful about taking any action that's going to get me back there again."

This officer suggested that every time a guy does good aggressive police work, "some idiot worried about police–community relations second-guesses you and you wind up with a complaint and a few days off." The few days off to which the officer referred are in reference to disciplinary action.

The officer went on to state: "These people interested in police–community relations don't seem to understand that we can either do police work or we can close our eyes and ride around for eight hours." This is exactly the attitude this officer took to the number of complaints he has received. In other words, to avoid further complaints, he did very little aggressive patrol.

Although this explained the officer's reluctance to be too aggressive on patrol, it does not explain how he came to accept or rationalize this accommodation. The rationalization was explained by the rookie in such terms that one can see that the rookie has internalized much more than rationalization, and that he, in effect, has had his role-learning process materially affected by this senior officer. "Why should we go out and pick up complaints for good police work if these guys are afraid to let us be aggressive. We will be damn sure to only pick times when we know the internal affairs unit won't harrass us."

The rookie went on to berate police–community relations, specifically the internal affairs unit, for the poor law enforcement in this country to date. In fact, he suggested that were he chief, he would abolish the unit the next day. Remember, this is a rookie with only seven months' experience and not once appearing before a disciplinary hearing!

This not only suggests the impact that the role-acquisition process has on the enactment of the patrolmen's role, but it also suggests how the role of law enforcement orientation can be measurably affected in terms of degrees and in either direction.

One final observation as to how the independent variable of role acquisition affects the dependent variable of role enactment can best be explained by illustrating the structural nature of placing rookies with senior officers. In this particular police department, rookies are assigned to a patrol car, which is, in effect, assigning them to two senior officers. The rookie fills in for the one "steady man" during his days off, court time, and so on. Both senior officers, therefore, work with the rookie patrolman a portion of each week.

Under these situations, both experienced officers can compare notes on the rookie's progress, where he has strengths or weaknesses, and on what they should specifically concentrate their attention. In short, the situation is structured in such a manner that the administration is actually facilitating the patrolmen subculture in terms of a patrolman's application of sanctions to induce conformity, not only to organizational norms, but also to patrolmen norms.

One positive outgrowth of this situation was observed one evening when two senior officers were discussing the rookie assigned to their unit. Both officers indicated that their primary problem with the rookie was his aggressiveness, and when they attempted to offer constructive criticism, he frequently reacted in a manner analogous to "pouting." One of the officers conceptualized the situation as follows:

> Hell, this kid comes on like gangbusters. We have a helluva time slowing him down and you have seen us work tonight. We can be damn aggressive when the situation calls for it. I try to tell this kid, act more calmly and talk very quietly, this way people listen to you.

The point is that the second stage of the rookie's role-learning process is not necessarily dysfunctional to the eventual impact it will have on the dependent variable, the role enactment of the patrol officer's role.

It is also significant to note that it appears that the role set for patrol officers does not extend much beyond the squad cars they inhabit eight hours a day and the people with whom they interact in those eight hours. In theory, their role set does extend much beyond the narrow confines of this definition. However, to patrolmen, the role set that conveys the most serious attention and importance is operationally internalized only at the point where they transact their most important business—and that originates within the confines of their squad cars and where those squad cars take them.

Equally significant is the fact that most of the role skills patrol officers learn are attributable to working with older, more experienced officers. This reinforces rookies' commitment to the patrol officer subculture. It also allows the patrol officer subculture the opportunity to develop its own value structure as to which role skills should receive what priority rating, in accordance with subculture values.

ORGANIZATIONAL GOALS

The independent variable organizational goals includes such areas as role conception, norms and sanctions, and reward structure. The impact of this independent variable on the dependent variable of role enactment can best be described by patrol officers's perception of what is, in fact, a legitimate service of the police organization. To this degree, role conceptions certainly emerge and this can probably be seen most easily by the following situation.

The tour of duty ended without any real criminal action taking place, although the officer did respond to assist in a heart attack case, a family disturbance call, and in investigating a hit-and-run auto accident with no injuries. In short, according to the officer, it was a "dead night," and accordingly, he apologized for it. As the next detail was coming on, the officer inquired: "Well, how was your night?" The reply was curt, short, and to the point: "Lousy."

Both the apology for lack of action and the response to the officer beginning the next detail clearly indicate that this officer, like so many others, regards his role as that of being a "crime fighter" as opposed to a "peace maintainer." This is significant from the standpoint of role conception because it provides the general framework from which organization goals and citizen demands for services can be considered and evaluated as being legitimate or irrelevant.

Frequently, police officers make reference to the term "real police work." The common assumption by many is that the police refer to "real police work" as responding to calls of a criminal nature. This assumption is somewhat erroneous, as the following situation indicates.

It was a Saturday evening and the detail worked was 7:00 P.M. to 3:00 A.M., a very active period. True to form, this Saturday evening proved to be quite active, especially in terms of the criminal calls that were received by the unit. In the first two hours of duty, the officers responded to three calls, all founded or legitimate: "See lady about threats of assault"; "See complainant about threatened assault by motorcycle gang"; and "an on-view gang fight." As the evening unfolded, there were two silent alarms, motorcycle drag racing, another woman threatened over the phone, a juvenile taken into custody for possession of narcotics, an on-view case in which a man was found lying unconscious in the middle of a four-lane highway, and finally, the squad car was shot at from ambush by a sniper. This is not even detailing the assists this car offered as backup service to other patrol cars. Near the completion of this tour of duty, one officer stated: "Well, it's a shame you can't work the next detail (referring to 3:00 A.M. to 11:00 A.M.) because there is where you can do 'real police work.'"

This statement came as a total surprise because it certainly appeared as though there were enough law enforcement types of situations to satisfy the role conception of any police officer. Not knowing whether the officer was serious or kidding, the officer was asked to clarify his statement. His response was as follows:

> You see, when you work the graveyard shift you have more time per call to handle each call. You can do a better job with it. Hell, this other way, like what we did tonight, all you can do is take down the report and clear out to handle another call. Don't get me wrong, these are good calls, but hell, this ain't police work.

In other words, there is a distinction between "real police work" and "real police calls." The conception of real police "work," then, involves not only a call of a criminal nature, but also the time to pursue this call by being able to follow up on it, even if it means spending three or four hours on it. This, of course, accounts for why the officer suggested that real police work could be done on the "graveyard" shift, a shift that is usually very inactive, and a shift during which when you get a call, it is frequently a "big call" and you can spend sufficient time pursuing it.

This officer's role perception was such that he enjoyed working the 3:00 A.M. to 11:00 A.M. shift because he could do real police work that involved such factors as getting to know what belonged where and to whom. By working this shift, the officers can tell immediately what cars are strange to an area, what business establishments should have such and such light on, what businesses never leave their night lights on, and so on. Thus, the time to pursue the above-mentioned situations is what this officer regarded as real police work. However, the officer was quick to point out that not everyone feels this way about it; in fact, he wished that the graveyard shift had more action, but not so much that one could not follow up on the calls.

The officer then proceeded to relate a situation that has relevance to role theory. It also illustrates the fact that many officers do not share this officer's role perception of being able to do real police work on the graveyard shift. For example, one rather slow morning, a close friend of this officer called in a "chase" from a parked squad in a remote alley. A "chase" is a particularly important call to police officers because it means that a suspect is trying to evade apprehension. In many respects this type of call complements the role conception of many police officers. In the particular case being described, the individual supplied such realism that he floored the gas pedal while the car transmission was in a neutral position, thus simulating the sound of a racing motor; he turned the siren on, and true to the fashion of most "chases," screamed directions into the radio as to which way the supposed vehicle was traveling.

The officer describing the story was working that shift, and in his words, described his actions until he discovered it was a fake call.

> Christ, we heard _____ start the chase so we thought if we could get the direction they were moving in, we could assist or at least get to an intersection and set up a road block. So we finally got their direction and we go down

below this viaduct knowing they can't possibly turn around or get by us. There we are standing there with our shotguns and the dispatcher is yelling that the chase is going right through our intersection. Hell, I start looking around thinking my eyes are going bad cause I can't see either one of these guys—then it occurs to me that this guy is just running a phony chase.

Not exactly knowing whether this officer was attempting to be funny or whether this did, in fact, occur, he was asked if he was serious. He insisted that this actually occurred. Still, having some reservations about this story, one of the authors approached a close friend who works in a nearby community as a narcotics detective. Not only did this friend attest to the feasibility of this sort of situation occurring, he also related a very similar situation that happened to him.

I am going home one night in the unmarked squad car I drive; my radio is on, but I'm not really paying any attention until I hear this "chase" being broadcast. So I try to get the path of travel the chase is pursuing; the chase car is naming off streets that are clear on the other side of town so I figure there is little chance of me helping out so I will just listen to the chase to see if they get the guy. Christ, all of a sudden I look up in front of me, and here the squad that is calling in the chase that supposedly is on the other side of town is doing 30 m.p.h. right in front of me. I couldn't believe my eyes. Especially in this case, because this guy is a good officer. So the next day I told the captain about this, figuring we should keep a close watch on this guy. We watched him like a hawk for the next two months, and nothing—this guy did as good police work as ever and he hasn't repeated anything like that since. I can't figure it out, here's an excellent officer, we are not talking about some flake, I mean like this cop is good. How do you explain something like this?

Indeed, how is something like this explained? It appears as though there are tremendous manifestations as to role conception and role playing. These two situations were not relayed in a manner that would demean police officers or impune their psychological adjustment, but to allow sophisticated role theorists the opportunity to examine the ramifications of such occurrences.

While role conception undoubtedly plays a crucial part in the enactment of the patrolman's role, another significant area defined under this independent variable is that of norms and sanctions and their relationship to any ensuing role enactment.

A unique attribute of the department under study was that the patrol officers would actually begin patrolling while they were still down on a call as far as the dispatcher's time card was concerned. This means that the officers would receive a call, complete the necessary police action in that call, and go right back to patrol; then within 5, 10, or 15 minutes, depending upon the situation, they would notify the dispatcher that their car was in service again. Normally, the procedure is to notify the dispatcher before patrolling again.

One of the primary reasons that the officers pursued this policy was because of an unstated organizational norm which suggested that the time spent on *X* calls better equal *Y* minutes. As an example of the pervasiveness of this norm, many officers in different police districts suggested that the amount of time expected on the following type calls was as follows:

Family disturbances	20 minutes
Traffic citation	15 minutes
Accident	40 minutes
Accident with injury	minimum of 1 hour; could be more

The uniqueness of this attribute is the eagerness of the officers to get back to work again. In similar-size communities, the authors have observed the reverse of this situation—where officers stay on calls longer than necessary, purposely not notifying the dispatcher they were back in service to allow for a few extra minutes to grab a cup of coffee. This, however, was not the case in this particular department; in fact, the entire genesis for the organization norm seemed to be that of the police administration's concern that the officers might not spend enough time on a particular call and, therefore, not provide proper service to citizens. In short, the administrative focus was not on checking to see if their officers were loafing, although they would follow this up; it was more in terms of ensuring that the officers spent enough time on each call to ensure proper police service. The adaptation made by patrol officers to this norm was admirable in terms of illustrating their desire to remain in service for calls and in terms of not abusing the norm by using it for coffee break time.

This norm is significant to the dependent variable of role enactment. It suggests there are certain acceptable time measurements for patrol officers to enact their role. Naturally, the administration would take into consideration that every call is unique and that arbitrary standards would be hard to defend. Nevertheless, this documents why this is, in fact, a norm and not a more formalized policy.

Organizational norms are not as effective as patrol officers norms because in the first case, adaptations can be made, whereas in the second case, the sanctions that accompany the norms are so severe that very few adaptations can effectively be made. One of the best illustrations of group sanctions taken against a patrol officer by other patrol officers occurred in the following situation:

Officer:	When I came on this job, I was the super cop, do you know what I mean? I wanted to be the best cop the department ever had, so I said to myself I am going to do everything better than any other officer in the district.
Observer:	What do you mean?

Officer: Well, like traffic tickets; I said to myself, man when some cat breaks the law I am going to nail him. Hell, I gave out 120 tickets a month, that's more than traffic cars write. In fact, I wrote as many tickets as the rest of the guys on my detail. Boy, the sergeant really loved me, but I couldn't get along with the other guys on my detail. I guess it's because I made them look pretty bad.

Observer: How did the other patrolmen react to you?

Officer: They must have really been upset because they wouldn't talk to me. I would walk into roll call as friendly as can be, asking them about their families and everything. Everyone just turned their back on me. Pretty soon it really started bothering me, so I asked this "old head" what I might have done wrong. He told me; boy, I stopped writing tickets so fast you wouldn't believe it.

Two significant facts emerge. The patrol sergeant was happy with the productivity of this officer while the other patrol officers resented the same productivity. This documents the different values held by administration, supervisors, and the line officers, again, clear documentation of a patrol officer subculture with its own values and norms. The second point is that the officer's desire to exhibit outstanding role performance was the genesis of the norm violation and accompanying sanction by the other patrol officers.

Curious as to what impact the use of sanctions might have had on this officer, and whether he would in turn sanction other rookies for norm violations, one of the authors engaged the officer in the following conversation:

Observer: Have you ever had occasion to use sanctions against other officers?

Officer: Boy, you better believe it. They were breaking in this one rookie with me, and the first thing this guy did was pick up the car keys and say to me, "I will drive the first half, you can drive the second." I took the keys from him and told him, you will drive when I tell you and not until then. This guy learned in a hurry.

Observer: Did you run into any other situations where you sanctioned an officer?

Officer: Once I was breaking in this other rookie, and if I told that kid to slow down in his driving so we could observe what was happening, it must have rolled right off his fat head. Hell, everyone was complaining about this guy's fast driving. So one day we are going through Washington Park about 40 m.p.h. in a 10- or 15-m.p.h. zone, I just reached over and pulled the keys from the ignition and threw them out his open window. By the time he stopped the car, we were two blocks from the keys. Boy, was he mad;

he asked me why I did a dumb trick like that. I told him he was just going to have to learn to drive slower. He said that he certainly wasn't going to get the keys that I had thrown out. I told him we are going to be here a long time then, because I sure in hell wasn't going to get them either. We sat in that car for two hours before he went back to look for the keys.

Curious as to in what manner the patrolmen subculture might sanction higher officials, the conversation continued:

Officer: There really isn't too much you can do to sanction command officers; however, this one captain issued an order for all officers to remain in their car at the end of their tour of *duty* until the next replaced them. This upset the men so much that they practically stopped writing tickets for three months. Pretty soon the order was rescinded. Officers can make superiors look bad by not writing tickets.

Observer: Other than not writing tickets, what could the patrolmen do to sanction command officers?

Officer: Really not a great deal, although when our new chief took office a lot of men resented him because he replaced the "policeman's chief." This new guy is too police–community relations oriented anyway."

Observer: What did the men do?

Officer: To register their disgust with the situation, they tried to make the new chief look bad by making crime appear to go up. You know, we would write up what are normally theft reports into burglaries; and we would write up simple assaults like a couple drunks fighting into aggravated assaults.

Observer: Do you think your strategy worked?

Officer: No, and I suppose it really doesn't matter, but at least we got our bitch in.

The salient point is that unlike most occupations, police officers can apply sanctions against other police officers by variations in their role enactment. This point is made even more forcefully by patrol officers's use of role enactment as a sanctioning agent against police radio dispatchers.

Before presenting the next example, the following background is necessary. In the police department under study, as in many police departments, an order from the radio dispatcher is equivalent to an order from the chief of police. Therefore, patrolmen have no choice but to obey the order.

However, to appreciate the radio dispatcher's position, one must be aware of the fact that once dispatchers get a citizen's call for help, they have to have it assigned over the air within 10 minutes or write a letter explaining why it was not dispatched efficiently. Therefore, if dispatchers feel that officers are taking too much time at lunch, or on calls in general, thereby causing calls to back up in the radio room, dispatchers will save calls that they know irritate officers and this way attempt to bargain for officers' cooperation. In other situations dispatchers can hold off rather involved calls until the shift is almost over, and then cause the officers to work overtime. In other words, dispatchers cannot only enact their role as a sanctioning agent but can also aim their sanctions at the vulnerable areas of the role enactment of patrolmen.

In this particular case, the confrontation began over the officer's request for a 10-7, permission to have dinner. The dispatcher replied negative and assigned a private parking complaint to the officer. This infuriated the officer and he replied sarcastically, "Thank you, Sir." Evidently, the reply aggravated the dispatcher because when the officer came back on the air to request dinner again, the dispatcher again refused and assigned another private parking complaint.

The officer acknowledged there were two ways to address the problem. The first was to call in again and request dinner; if allowed, he could forget the situation. However, if he was assigned another parking complaint, he could write the ticket and grab a bite to eat before going back in service. The second manner in which the problem could be handled was by applying sanctions against the dispatcher. The choice was resolved in favor of application of sanctions. This must be a classic case of applying one role enactment against another role enactment solely for the purpose of sanctioning a person.

For example, the patrol officer enacted his role in the manner of asking the dispatcher for a clearance on car license plates, which is a normal procedure in checking for "hot" cars or auto thefts. The enactment of this role structures a complementary role enactment by the radio dispatcher. The radio dispatcher will have to call the auto theft bureau or check with NCIC, the National Crime Information Center, and then call back the patrol car and report on the status of the license being queried.

In this instance, the officer proceeded to call in approximately 25 individual license checks, knowing quite well that one of the licenses was from a "hot" car on his beat that he had been watching for the past two days. Conveniently, he waited until the end to call that plate in so that the pattern of frustration had clearly been established for the dispatcher. After about the fifteenth call, it was apparent that the dispatcher was summarily clearing the license plates without checking auto theft or NCIC. Then the officer asked for a clearance on the car he knew was stolen. The dispatcher again summarily responded and cleared what was, in fact, a stolen car. The patrolman then called the auto theft bureau and asked if the dispatcher had checked that plate with them; auto theft responded "no." The officer then called the dispatcher and told the dispatcher that he had checked with auto theft and the car was stolen; he in turn asked the dispatcher if he (dispatcher) had called auto theft to check for the clearance. The dispatcher was then in the position of having to admit over the air and on a tape that he did not, in fact, check with auto theft. The officer then asked for permission to go to the radio room. This was acknowledged and the officer then confronted the dispatcher, asked for a truce, and received it.

Many patrol officers regard the dispatcher as their "lifeline." However, as shown in the preceding example, there are circumstances under which the dispatcher's attitude can influence patrol officers to such a degree that patrol officers are once again reminded that they are on the street all alone with only other patrol officers to share their frustrations. In short, the patrol officer subculture can collectively invoke sanctions against dispatchers. This came very close to occurring in the following situation.

It had been a very busy night for a group of officers, going from one end of the district to the other. Finally, the officers received a call, and their response was to give their location first and ask if the dispatcher still wanted them to respond. The dispatcher very curtly replied: "Well, I am at 11th and Champa" (referring to police headquarters, where the radio room is located). To put it mildly, this infuriated the officers to the degree that they suggested to another squad "that we all get together and ask this pompous ass to repeat the assignments every time he calls us." Evidently, this sanction works quite well, as the dispatcher is pressured by time considerations and repeating instructions only adds considerable confusion to his job. In the mind of one patrol officer, it drives the dispatcher "dizzy" and forces a truce.

In all fairness to dispatchers, one must realize that many officers abuse the principle that lies behind advising of location, hoping to "kiss off" particularly annoying calls or get these calls reassigned to another unit. The reason for advising a dispatcher of a car's location is to call attention to the fact that if this is a serious call, another car might be able to respond much sooner.

Perhaps the strongest empirical evidence of the existence of a patrol officer subculture that can be offered occurred one evening while speaking to two patrol officers who between them had less than three years' experience. In discussing the idea of a reward structure for patrol officers, their response was: "We don't need any reward—we give it to ourselves." For the most part, patrolmen consistently held that there was no meaningful reward structure in a police organization. One officer who suggested that no meaningful reward structure existed qualified his statement: "Well, it depends upon what car you are permanently assigned to, because if you are working with an officer you can respect, there is an informal sense of prestige or reward between both officers." This, of course, suggests two factors, one being the use of car assignments as a sanctioning and reward mechanism of the administration. The second point lends additional support to the idea of a patrol officers subculture in which the privilege to work with certain officers would not only be rewarding but also mutually supportive of patrol officer subculture values.

Perhaps what is commonly regarded as police criticism of the courts is not solely directed at the decisions of the courts, but is the unarticulated awareness that the courts are implicitly tied into the question of a police reward structure. For example, one officer suggested that when he came out of recruit school, he was not at all resentful of the courts' decisions and that he would do his job as he was instructed. However, the same officer emphasized how quickly this attitude dissipated.

This unarticulated awareness to court involvement in a police reward structure is undoubtedly tied into the role conception of patrol officers. The law enforcement orientation as to correct police role requires evidence of successful role performance, which is another way of stating "arrests and convictions." The court impedes officers' appraisals of their role performance when it grants acquittals, retrials, appeals or probation. When the court acquits suspects, officers can receive no acknowledgment from the public that their role performance was worthy. Furthermore, officers find it difficult to legitimately reward themselves, and when they do reward themselves, they become more deeply enmeshed in the patrol subculture.

The third independent variable of this study revolved around the area of role expectations. The empirical observations and methodology for inquiring of citizens why they called the police or what they expected the police to do indicates great confusion on the citizens' part. Perhaps this partly explains some of the police confusion over what the public expects of them.

Frequently, citizens replying to the question of what they expect the police to do by such statements as, "I guess I don't really know, but who else is there to call?" In many family disturbance calls, the citizen expectation is too frequently "I called them for protection." However, when officers ask them to sign a complaint, the situation becomes progressively involved. It appears that many citizens just do not want to accept the responsibility for their actions by signing complaints, but would prefer to pass this responsibility on to the police department.

Police officers often encounter citizens who have expectations for a particular police service which is later discovered to be an abuse. Whenever anyone is taking advantage of someone, it puts a strain on that relationship; this also applies to police officers, for they, too, are human.

A classic case of such abuse was observed in another city, where a woman called the police to arrest her husband for being drunk and beating her up. The woman stated she would gladly sign a complaint. The husband protested his innocence, claiming that all she wanted to do was to get him out of the house for the weekend so she could "turn a few tricks" (commit an act of prostitution) or go out with her boyfriend.

Situations such as the preceding one aggravate the police–community relationship by intensifying the citizen's suspicion of police officers. This causes the officer to be more apart from the community than a part of the community.

Many calls have been observed where citizens expected the police to perform an illegal act. In one case a woman's neighbors and relatives were visiting her house; she suddenly discovered that she was missing her welfare check. When asked what she expected of the police, she replied: "Get my money back, of course." The officers quizzed those in the house and all protested their innocence. When the officer stated that he could not do any more, the lady got furious and demanded that everyone be searched. The officers informed her that they did not have this right and told her to look around the house in case she had misplaced the check. In this situation, everyone was angry with everyone else: the woman at the police for not doing their job; the police at the woman for putting them in such a position and demanding that they break the law; and finally, the relatives at the woman for making such an accusation.

Countless situations have been observed in which the only citizen expectation was a police report for insurance purposes. This irritated many of the officers because they did not regard their role to be that of roving secretaries for insurance companies, much less to subsidize the companies, which could easily get noninjury accident reports in another manner.

There is one particularly significant case in which the expectations a citizen had regarding police officers' role behavior were actually instrumental in the citizen structuring the police officers into a linkage role.

This case involved a man who was stabbed in the arm. Officers inquired as to the identity of the assailant and the victim refused to help. Instead, he stated "that he would settle his own fights; he didn't need the help of the cops." The following conversation then took place.

Observer:	Sir, if you don't mind my asking you, why did you call the police if you won't disclose the identity of your assailant? What do you expect them to do?
Citizen:	No, I don't mind your question; you see, I know who the guy is and I will get him myself.
Observer:	I still don't understand why you won't let the police help you. You know you could become vulnerable to arrest yourself if you take the law into your own hands.
Citizen:	Hell, these guys ain't going to catch me because I am going to kill that _____ and he ain't going to tell no one at all.
Observer:	What do you expect the police to do since you won't cooperate with them?
Citizen:	Like man, can't you see, look at that cut. That is deep.

Observer:	In other words, you called the police just to get taken to the hospital.
Citizen:	Now you got the picture, man.
Observer:	Why did you call the police; why not an ambulance?
Citizen:	(no response)
Observer:	Did you call the police because you didn't want to pay for the ambulance service?
Citizen:	No man, that's not it at all; I wasn't going to pay no one, no how, anyway. I been down to the hospital before; this ain't the first time I got cut up you know. You let these ambulance people take you in and you sit out in the hall all night waiting to get service. These cops go walking their patients right in. You see this cut is hurting and when I go down there I don't want to sit in the hall all night. If I walk in with these cops, they will take me right away. No, man, I am not worried about the money because I ain't going to pay anyway. All I want is to get in there and get this arm sewn up again.

The citizen's observation about getting faster medical attention was accurate. The hospital tries to handle all the victims the police bring in as soon as possible because the police report requires a doctor's signature. This allows the police to get back on the street as soon as possible.

This citizen was, in effect, structuring the police into a linkage role. Because of the tacit agreement between the hospital and police department, in which the hospital does everything possible to get police officers out as quickly as they can, the citizen benefited from the simultaneous role the police played in both systems.

The role expectations a citizen has of patrol officers is but one facet of role expectations. Two others previously discussed were the role expectations police have of their own role; these can be referred to as role conception. The third aspect, norms and sanctions, was discussed because these, too, are built upon expectations of what is, in fact, proper police service.

The significant point is that the public itself is frequently confused about what to expect from police officers even when the public initiated the service call. Therefore, what we regard as police confusion as to the role the public expects of them may be more understandable when both sets of actors are viewed as having difficulty interpreting each other's roles.

MULTIPLE ROLE PHENOMENA AND METHODS OF RESOLUTION

The independent variable described as multiple role phenomena entails such areas as role conflict, role ambiguity, and role strain. These items will be described in terms of what was observed in the field during the patrol officer's role enactment.

The fifth independent variable, method of resolving multiple role phenomena, will be presented after each type of role conflict is identified. Special attention will be focused on the question of whether the conflict was resolved in favor of the organization, the client, a compromise, or whether officers attempted to avoid the situation.

The first situation described is that of role conflict encountered by patrol officers. Role conflict has been explained as when an officer encounters two sets of expectations, both expectations being mutually inconsistent. Essentially, four types of role conflict were observed in the field: organizational rules in conflict, organizational goals in conflict, linkage conflict, and norm conflicts.

A case illustrating the conflict caused by incompatible organizational rules occurred when a wino reported to police that he was robbed of $136. Both officers were somewhat apprehensive of the victim's statement because of his obviously low socioeconomic class and because the victim had had several drinks. The officers knew in reality that there was no chance of getting the victim's money back, and they attempted to point this out to the victim. The conflict arose over whether or not to fill out a police report, especially in view of the small chance of recovery. The organizational rules clearly called for a police report to be filled in this situation. Yet there is another organizational rule which suggests that police reports should not be taken from a person who is inebriated. The officers really did not want to waste their time on this case, yet the complainant was somewhat adamant about making a police report.

The manner in which this conflict was resolved was to take the police report, thus resolving the conflict in favor of the client. In this case, the officers would have been justified in asking the complainant to return when he was sober. The officers also had the option of avoiding the situation. This could have been done by merely getting a description from the complainant and suggesting that they go out and search for this suspect, knowing full well that on the basis of the information the complainant had given them, this response would have amounted to little more than a "kiss off" of the call.

Perhaps the most important type of role conflict observed revolved around the conflict of organizational goals. This has specific relevance to police resistance to police–community relations.

In short, the police organization is submitting two incompatible goals when it emphasizes the nature of desiring fine, aggressive patrolmen to do effective police work in terms of apprehension of criminals. The second goal, often highly espoused by police departments, is strong expectations for each officer in the area of police–community relations. To be an aggressive law enforcement specialist conflicts with the sensitivity, compassion, and empathy required for a strong police–community relations orientation. Furthermore, to be a law enforcement specialist requires a considerable degree of impartiality or noninvolvement in police–citizen interaction. On the other hand, to be effective as a police–community relations officer requires a great deal of involvement, but not necessarily the loss of any impartiality. The last point is itself a rather contradictory position, for how does one really become involved without becoming partial? It appeared as though most of the officers observed resolved this conflict in the form of a compromise, thus retaining the flexibility necessary to invoke either role orientation.

The third form of conflict observed can be titled linkage-role conflict. This is again defined as positions that simultaneously involve the individual in two different systems. Perhaps the situation that best illustrated this linkage role conflict was a case in which an officer received a call to pick up a shoplifter at a local department store. To appreciate fully the structural nature of this situation, it is important to note that the police department finds it is beneficial to cooperate with the department store security guards, as it reduces to a degree their workload and, if nothing else, the pressure to have detectives periodically check the premises. On the other hand, it is beneficial to the department store to have an officer come in and assist the security officer, as it seems to legitimatize the role of department store security guards by association, if nothing else. Additionally, police officers do convey the suspects off store premises, usually to police headquarters.

In a particular case, an officer found himself immersed in two systems. Two suspects were pleading for the officer to give them a break, while the store security guard asked the officer to please take the girls downtown as a personal favor because he felt the girls had a poor attitude. However, the officer talked with the girls and thought they had a fine attitude. He later confided to the observer that normally he would have interceded on their behalf and would have tried to talk the security guard into changing his mind; but in this instance, he was reluctant to do so because the security guard specifically asked the officer to carry through on the case.

The officer resolved his conflict by conforming to the security guard's desires. This action resolved the conflict in favor of the organization. The question is: Which organization? Certainly not the police organization, because when the juvenile detectives interviewed the girls, they asked the officer to call back and see if the guard still wanted to press charges. Now the patrol officer was receiving conflicting expectations from both organizations; the officer resolved this dilemma by stating that the security guard would consider it a special favor if these girls were processed.

The only other linkage-role conflict observed was in the earlier case of the citizen who was stabbed and called the police in order to be taken to the hospital. The officers, not wishing to burden the already busy ambulance crews, but also wanting to keep the lid on community relations, resolved that conflict in favor of the citizen, although they clearly resented the dilemma in which they were thrust by the citizen. In this particular case, the norms that conflicted were those of the patrol officer subculture and those of the administration as articulated by the police radio dispatcher.

The situation was that twice in one evening, particularly dangerous calls were assigned one patrol car, with the normal assist or backup car also assigned. This particular officer, not assigned to the call, felt very strongly that there should be another car sent because the area was very rough, and the circumstances of the situation were such that this officer felt he should also assist. When he called the dispatcher to inform the dispatcher that he was going over to cover, the dispatcher replied, "Negative," and assigned another call to the car. The officer was then clearly in a conflict situation. Should he adhere to the organizational norms and follow the dispatcher's orders; or should he cover the call not assigned to him? This is how patrol officers look after each other. The officer resolved the norm conflict in favor of the patrol officer subculture and went over to cover the other officers.

Along with the essential four types of role conflict observed in the process of role enactment, there was one important intervening variable that helped patrolmen in not only resolving many conflict situations, but also in preventing conflict situations from fully manifesting themselves. This intervening variable was the patrol officer's use of discretion.

One of the clearest examples of discretion occurred in a two-car auto accident with a fatality. In this case there were two officers, one having almost nine years' experience, the other a rookie with 11 months' experience, still in his probationary period. The circumstances surrounding the accident were very vague because there were no witnesses to the accident. It appeared as though each driver thought he had the right-of-way because the accident occurred in the middle of the intersection. Neither driver had attempted to brake his car. This was ascertained by the absence of skid marks and the admission of one driver. The driver of the second car was killed and the party riding with him was in such a state of shock that she could not speak. In short, neither driver saw the other.

The car in which the driver died had four open cans of beer, one can with half the contents remaining. The driver of the other vehicle freely admitted to the officers that he had had a couple drinks and that the accident might well have been his fault, since at the time he entered the intersection, his attention was diverted by the passenger in the back seat, who had dropped a lighted cigarette on the floor, and the driver was looking behind the seat trying to locate the cigarette. Furthermore, he went on to state that he was not entirely certain he had a green light; however, he did add that he was quite sure he did not run a red light. All occupants in his car thought that perhaps the traffic light was amber, just changing from green to amber.

Before describing the officers' perceptions, it should be stated that the senior officer had a very strong orientation toward police–community relations. The rookie officer, although certainly appreciating police–community relations, placed greater emphasis on enforcement of the law.

Both officers were fully aware that their police department placed an important emphasis on the enforcement of laws while placing an equally important emphasis on maintaining good police–community relations. Thus, they were faced with a conflict situation. The senior officer, in attempting to train the rookie officer, asked the rookie a series of questions as to the cause of the accident. As their conversation proceeded into what action to take, the nature of the role conflict and its relationship to the intervening variable became apparent.

Senior Officer:	Well, what action would you take if you were out here by yourself?
Rookie Officer:	I would give both drivers a ticket for running a red light.
Senior Officer:	How do you know they both ran the red light? Do you have any witnesses to that effect?
Rookie Officer:	Well, no.
Senior Officer:	Then why write them both up for running a light? Anyway, maybe one of the cars had a green light and only the other car blew the light.

As the conversation proceeded, it was quite evident that the senior officer respected the honesty of the one driver. In fact, the officer suggested that the driver, who was only nineteen years old, should call his father for advice on whether or not he should take a Breathalyzer exam.

Meanwhile, it occurred to the rookie that the one driver could be booked for vehicular homicide since on his own admission he wasn't paying attention to his driving. However, as the interaction between the police officers and the boy and the boy's father developed, the rookie's attitude changed visibly. He was deeply moved by the father's honesty and admonition to the son to "cooperate and tell it just as it happened, no matter what the consequences are."

The driver did decide to volunteer to take the Breathalyzer test and when informed that he had passed it, a loud cheer emerged from both officers. In fact, the senior officer stated: "I bet you didn't know you had so many people pulling for you." Both officers later told the observer that "they respected the kid's honesty and attitude; anyway, he was a good clean kid."

In short, the officers employed their use of discretion to write the driver the least serious ticket they could. This way they reduced the conflict of having to be rough on someone who cooperated to the fullest possible extent. Although they knew they were giving this driver a "break," both officers felt that they still were conforming to one of the police department goals, that of leaving the citizen with a good impression. What is of importance is that the officers resolved their conflict through the use of discretion on the basis of citizen attitudes.

The empirical observations of the study suggest that patrol officers systematically and quite pervasively relate to citizen attitudes before enacting their role as patrol officers. In short, it appears as though there is a definite relationship between an officer's use of discretion and citizen attitude. So to this degree, the police hypothesis "that people get treated the way they ask to be treated" is perhaps quite accurate.

Not all role conflict occurs along the lines of the restricted definition of two incompatible organizational expectations. Furthermore, not all role conflict is resolved by the use of discretion. There are situations where the use of discretion to resolve role conflict for one person may intensify or create role conflict for another person. For example, one evening while an officer of six years' experience and a rookie of five months' experience were being observed, the rookie took action in a case which completely infuriated the senior officer to the extent that he informed the rookie, "Never ever pull a stunt like that again or you are through working with me."

The "stunt" to which this officer referred was pulling over a drunken driver who was weaving in and out of three lanes; moreover, the driver was so drunk that he fell asleep or passed out twice while the officer was speaking to him.

So far, this certainly doesn't appear to be a "stunt" but simply good police work. However, the circumstances of the evening will not only explain the senior officer's attitude, but perhaps will also suggest the degree to which previous calls can influence a role enactment.

This particular squad car was exceptionally busy the entire evening; in fact, one of the calls to which this car responded that same evening was earlier described under the role-acquisition variable; this was the call of the "lost old man." The important point was that with all the frustration experienced that evening, the senior officer was looking forward to the end of the shift. At 2:00 A.M., one hour before the shift was to end, the officers received a hit-and-run call. The senior officer was furious to receive this call, especially as it was not even their beat, but that of another patrolman, who, in the words of the senior officer, "is so busy trying to impress the detectives that he does not do any police work—he just goes around trying to be a detective and everyone else has to do his work for him. That is why we got stuck with the call tonight."

The officers arrived at the scene, and the senior officer worked as hard as he could and finally got the report and the case finished at 2:50 A.M. He was exuberant at completing the call so quickly. There was just enough time to make it back to the station.

The officer's words were interrupted by a drunk driver pulling in front of them, almost hitting the squad car. Almost simultaneously, the senior officer stated, "Pass that guy and let's get out of here." However, the rookie had already turned the red emergency light on and was in the process of pulling the driver over. The senior officer exclaimed to the rookie: "Oh no, if we have to take this clown in, we will be around half the night. Whatever you do, kiss the guy off and I don't mean maybe."

While the rookie was out of the squad car admonishing the drunken driver, the senior officer told the observer, "Brother, these rookies! I spend most of my time watching them; hell, I do everything but wipe their noses for them."

Clearly, the senior officer was emotionally drained over the entire evening's calls; at the same time, a clear violation of the law had occurred right in front of them. The senior officer, through his use of discretion as to when not to invoke the criminal process, resolved his role dilemma in that fashion. Concomitantly, it created a role conflict for the rookie officer. Here was a definite criminal violation, which according to the training academy, should be pursued. However, the rookie was clearly admonished to give this driver a "pass" and continue on to the station.

The rookie resolved his conflict by obeying the senior officer's admonitions, further evidence for the proposition that patrolmen form a subculture. The rookie clearly decided against the mandate of the law, an organizational goal, and all the instruction he received from the training academy. He did this for the sake of conforming to a subculture norm that requires rookie officers to follow the orders of more experienced and "wiser" patrolmen.

In essence, then, the use of discretion by senior officers can provide a source of conflict for rookie officers. Furthermore, the role enactment of a patrolman is affected as much, if not more, by previous interaction in other calls than by all the training received in the training academy.

The use and application of discretion will not always resolve conflicts for individual officers. Occasionally, the use of discretion will intensify a conflict. For example, one evening while patrolling a ghetto area, the officers observed a fight with about 75 youths milling around on the periphery. Instinctively, the officers stopped the car and proceeded to the area. All of a sudden, one officer yelled: "This looks like a setup to me; let's get the hell out of here." Once in the squad car, they debated the merits of calling assistance, but decided against that because the evening was so busy with other activities. Reluctantly, they decided it would be better judgment to leave the area.

This discretionary decision intensified their conflict because they could not visualize themselves backing down from a situation. On the other hand, they did not find it very appealing to walk into a trap. As both officers thought over their decision later, one said to the other: "Oh let's go back and get those guys, I don't care if it is a setup." However, when they did return to the area, it was quite peaceful.

Curious as to what might have caused the one officer to have the hunch that a setup was imminent, the observer asked the officer what caused him to feel that a trap was in the offing. The officer replied in the terms of suggesting that there was nothing definite, only a feeling that trouble was brewing:

Officer A: Hell, that's part of this job, being able to sense when something isn't just kosher.

Observer:	How did you develop this skill of being able to sense when something might be wrong, such as this "set up," for instance?
Officer A:	God, I don't know, I just picked it up; some guys do and others don't.
Officer B:	Part of this comes from service—experience, like this setup, though I can't really say it was a setup, but last month one of the cars had a call over here; thank God there were two officers because there were about ten studs inside waiting. All had baseball bats. I guess they were scared of two cops, though, the odds you know.
Officer A:	Well, I wasn't thinking about that incident; it just appeared to me as though we could have been walking into trouble.
Observer:	Well, what was it that made you uneasy; I mean, how did it occur to you that it might have been a setup as opposed to something else?
Officer A:	Well, for one thing, all those kids milling around. I mean like you look at those punks and all you can say is there goes trouble looking for a spot to occur at. . . . Hell, I don't know what it was; if I had the answers I wouldn't be working here. . . .

Patrol officers also experience situations in which their role is limited in terms of its enactment. Many of these situations can be incorporated under the definition of role strain, in which no matter what the police do or attempt to do, they will not be successful in meeting citizen expectations. This is simply because some citizen needs are beyond the police system or any member of the police system's capabilities of reaching needs. The police officer often encounters situations such as this during family disturbance calls. No matter what the officer would like to do, it is practically impossible to make any meaningful improvement in many of the situations officers encounter in family fights.

One of the distinctive characteristics of role strain, at least for the police, is that there is almost no possible manner in which role strain can be resolved. Perhaps this explains in part the patrol officers' great dislike for family disturbance calls. In short, role distance may be as much a part of the resistance as is the potential danger to an officer's safety.

An excellent example of role strain involved a 19-year-old youth who received threats against his life by a local motorcycle gang. In this case, both the citizen and the officer left the interaction quite dissatisfied. The officer felt there was really little that he could do, while the citizen expected the officer to make an arrest. The conversation that followed clearly indicated the frustration of both parties.

Officer:	Sure, I will make an arrest if you will sign a complaint.
Citizen:	I will sign the complaint.
Officer:	You know these guys aren't going to prison for this. They will

	be out on bond in 15 minutes, and brother I can tell you one thing for sure, you are the first person they will want to see.
Citizen:	Well, what can I do?
Officer:	Don't get me wrong. I am not trying to talk you out of this; I just want to be sure you know what the hell you are signing.
Citizen:	If I don't sign the complaint, they are going to get me anyway. What am I going to do?
Officer:	Why don't you make yourself scarce, leave town or something?
Citizen:	Why should I leave—after all, those guys are the criminals, not me.
Officer:	Look, you wanted advice, and I gave it to you; now if you want I can arrest these guys tonight, it makes no difference to me.
Citizen:	Oh, forget it.

The officer, feeling that a reprisal would be a virtual certainty, felt very frustrated over the position he had to take; but as he said: "Look, as much as we want, we can't put everybody to bed every night. Hell, there just ain't enough of us to give this kid the kind of protection he wants."

METHODS USED BY PATROL OFFICERS
TO PROTECT THEMSELVES FROM THEIR CLIENTS

One final comment before concluding this section on empirical observation of patrol officer's role-enactment process. This pertains to identifying the methods that police officers use or apply to protect themselves from the expectations of their clients. Although these methods were observed, they were extremely isolated. Therefore, generalization is not appropriate other than to note that organizational members of even a police agency find it necessary to protect themselves from the clientele they serve.

Of all the isolated methods of protecting oneself from one's clientele, the one adopted most frequently by patrol officers was to drive very slowly to a particular call from which they were seeking to protect themselves. In the case of officers seeking protection from family disturbance calls, it was felt that the people might cool off by the time the police arrived, thus allowing everyone to interact in a more rational manner.

A variation of this pattern was used by one officer in a linkage-role situation. The officer sought protection from the role being imposed on him by a department store that consistently prosecuted all shoplifters, took no interest in mitigating circumstances, and refused to use discretion where appropriate. This officer, first, did not agree with the policies, and second, did not see his role as that of apprehending shoplifters. Therefore, whenever he received a call to go to this particular store, he would make certain that it would take an hour to arrive, thus hoping that the security guard would either get tired of waiting and let the suspect go, or get busy and let the suspect go.

In another situation, an officer used the implication of legal culpability to evade a particularly involved and time-consuming call. In this case, a 23-year-old woman complained that her boyfriend beats her up, tortures her, and forces her to have sexual intercourse. The officers learned that the boyfriend was 15 years old. They promptly *neutralized* the complaint by suggesting that she is guilty of contributing to the delinquency of a minor, and if the police followed up her complaint, she would probably go to jail while her boyfriend, age 15 would be put on probation.

The same officer, when arresting a suspect, uses a completely opposite approach. Instead of stating that the subject is under arrest, he actually would deny it, saying that "only a few questions need to be answered and that's all." The officer maintains: "This way you don't have to fight so many of them."

Two rather embarrassing methods utilized by one officer occurred as follows. The first took place in a restaurant where an officer and observer were having a cup of coffee; an elderly lady walked up to the officer with a glass of milk and requested permission to throw it into another customer's face. The officer denied permission and the lady walked away. A waitress then approached requesting that the officer hang around, as she thought the lady was a bit disturbed. The officer immediately got up and informed the waitress that he was leaving, and that if there was a problem, make sure not to call him. Within 30 minutes the officer was called to a disturbance at the restaurant. In short, the role-resistance approach did not work.

The second case involved a woman who constantly called the police about prowlers. She was so bizzare, according to the police, that a squad car was placed in front of her house. She called the police informing them that a squad car was prowling. One officer finally tired of this game; every time she called the police and he responded, he would turn on the siren and light and drive around the short block on which her house was located three or four times at a speed of about 10 m.p.h. Evidently, the neighbors started applying pressure to the woman because according to the officer, it wasn't long afterward that her calls stopped coming in.

A final method observed of protecting oneself from citizen expectations was the case of a patrolman who made it a point to answer all citizens' questions with very short answers, and then only if he had to respond. When asked why he did this, the officer replied: "I hold my conversation down to a bare minimum on purpose so that some of these citizens can't find something else to bitch about."

To state that this adaptation, like the others, has an impact on the role-enactment process is to put it mildly. However, these adaptations were the exception, the isolated cases; what is of more significance is that policemen do have to protect themselves from the expectations of citizens, and this protection appears to be attained only through modification of the role performance.

In summary, the impact of independent variables on the dependent variable of role enactment not only has an appreciable effect upon the ensuing role enactment, but also on the proposition that patrol officers' role enactment is primarily that of a reactive role is also of crucial importance. In short, the enactment of a patrol officer's role will not only be dependent on such factors as size of the city, location of the police precinct within the city, activity of the precinct, type of clientele in that precinct, and the time of day or night an officer works, but also on the type of call to which the officer is called upon to respond.

THEORETICAL IMPLICATIONS OF ANALYSIS

The remaining portion of this chapter will focus attention on the theoretical relevance of the empirical observations, indicating how the independent variables affect the dependent variable of role enactment.

Individual and Organizational Resistance to Police-Community Relations

There appear to be *two distinct types* of police resistance to police–community relations; the first emerges out of individual resistance, whereas the second results from organizational resistance. Unfortunately, most attempts toward improving police–community relations have been concentrated toward the individual officer while completely ignoring the structure and environment within which an individual works. The most critical point, and one that has been completely ignored by writers in this area, is that both factors have a reinforcing effect upon the other.

In observing the role-enactment process of patrol officers, it appears that the primary source of individual resistance to the concept of police–community relations finds its genesis in the fact that police–community relations do not fit the role expectations or role conception of municipal police patrol officers. Perhaps the essential reasons for this center on the fact that the organismic involvement of patrolmen in their role is so intense in terms of the conflict between remaining impartial or uninvolved and the prescription that improvement in police–community relations will be realized only through a sense of involvement. Second, officers' inadequate preparation in locating their role and judging role complementarity is reinforced by the few number of roles they can adopt. A very important causal factor for this is related to the sanctioning influences of the patrol officer subculture; in effect, the subculture depicts what are and are not appropriate roles by the sanctioning power it retains over role performance and role behavior of the neophyte patrol officer. Finally, patrol officers' ability to manipulate the *preemptive-ness* of their role, combined with the reactive nature of the role itself, allows patrolmen in general, and the patrolmen subculture in particular, the latitude of not only defining, but also to a degree of structuring, their own role in the terms they find most meaningful.

Organizational resistance to police–community relations can be described by the role dilemma in which administrators are immersed; while desiring to improve police–community relations, the central dilemma revolves around control of the police force. The aim of outside pressures toward improving police–community relations is focused in terms of greater police responsiveness to citizen need; implicit within this is increasing the control and accountability of police officers. However, police administrators who attempt to introduce a sound police–community relations approach into their departments are immediately vulnerable to losing the one factor necessary and requisite to increasing police responsiveness to citizen needs—that is, *control* of the police department, particularly the patrol officer subculture. Therefore, in reality, police administrators have been structured into a very cautious and deliberate position, a position that members of the general community do not appreciate, and one they counter with more intensified demands.

Another part of the structural problem of police resistance to police–community relations is the philosophical perfection of the concept of "adversarial proceedings held by our administration of justice system." Thus, poor police–community relations are implicitly structured into the role of a police organization by the very nature of its linkage position to the larger administration of criminal justice system. Restated, this might well be one of the social costs invoked in terms of a community's accepting the legal philosophy of our administration of justice system.

Empirical observations of the patrol officer's conceptual notion of police–community relations do not encourage one to have any degree of confidence with regard to meaningful improvement being made in this area. The reason is that patrol officers are using the concept of police–community relations as a giant repository for all their grievances and complaints, both real and imagined. To support this contention, the following empirical observations are offered.

Patrol officers in the department observed, quite systematically and pervasively, were of the opinion that a substantial majority of the suspensions that patrol officers received were the direct result of police–community relations considerations emanating directly from a chief of police. This attitude suggests that it is a gross oversimplification and rationalization based on a high degree of emotional immaturity. Perhaps the department has not recognized the utility of changing behavior by a training program as opposed to the far-too-prevalent punitive philosophies. Two observations are in order. The first revolves around the problem of disciplining an officer, yet retaining the same officer as a useful member of the organization. The second observation relates to the organization's directly addressing this prevalent attitude within the organization.

Some officers handled calls and wrote reports of the calls that they clearly considered to be a waste of time; they subsequently wrote this frustration off as another one of the problems caused by police–community relations.

One evening while observing with a senior patrol officer and a rookie patrol officer, it was noted that the rookie, in expressing his opinion of why police resist police–community relations, stated the following:

Rookie Officer:	You know, if you come over too strong with this community relations jazz, people think you are afraid of them, and they will take advantage of your softness.
Senior Officer:	No, I don't buy that statement. Hell, there are some people this community approach works fine with; however, there are a certain portion of the people you have to "thump" to get their attention. They will listen to talk but until then you are going to have to kick the _____ out of them.

The senior officer then proceeded to make a point that has a great deal of merit to it and deserves further exploration.

Hell, don't kid yourself. These citizens resist police–community relations as much as policemen because they don't want to see a policeman around— period; whether he's an expert on police–community relations or simply a very aggressive, stern officer.

The point the officer is making is that although the community knows it needs a police force, it has not yet decided whether it wants one.

In another situation, one officer clearly portrayed the role distance of police in police–community relations programs. In discussing the merits of police–community relations, the point he consistently and quite adamantly made was: "Tell me one thing, does it help fight crime? No. Therefore to me it's not my job; I'm nice to people but I'm no preacher." The officer then proceeded to articulate what perhaps is the patrol officer's main resistance to police–community relations: "In my view police effectiveness includes being feared, as well as respected, but police–community relations diminishes the fear people should have of policemen and consequently they don't respect police."

Another officer's contempt for police–community relations emerged because, in his view, while they were in the academy "they were taught not to get involved with the public." This officer's perception clearly documents both the conflict that officers experience and the task that is facing police training academies, that is, distinguishing between proper officer involvement and improper officer involvement. In short, the role-acquisition process is crucial to the development of sound attitudes.

Another officer's observation, which not only documents the training academy's dilemma but also really suggests one of the important consequences of the patrol officer subculture, was as follows:

> The training academy is spending so much time on police–community relations that it doesn't teach the recruits what real police work is, so when they get on the job they are lost. Hell, many of them don't even know where to sign a report. This means I've got to spend all my time teaching these guys what real police work is.

Simply stated, police–community relations, if nothing else, serves patrolmen as a fine device for releasing their frustrations and *scapegoating*. On the same terms, this only documents the resistance that is encountered in attempting to "sell" patrol officers on this concept.

One of the initial questions that must be addressed is whether the police resist police–community relations per se, or whether they resist the role that police–community relations imposes on them. The distinction is of considerable importance because the question can then be rephrased as: Do police subscribe to improving community relations, and do they see this mission as their role? Police feel that it should be self-evident to the community that the police are trying as hard as possible to be accepted. In short, the police view police–community relations with considerable suspicion and role distance.

It appears that a great deal of police resistance to police–community relations is not resistance to creating good community relationships, but more a resistance to accepting responsibilities that police feel should be shouldered by the community. If this is the case, it is incumbent upon the police to identify this resistance as resistance to accepting the transfer of community responsibility as opposed to strict resistance to police–community relations itself. In those terms, resistance can be quite functional as long as both groups understand what is being resisted and why it is being resisted. This also presupposes a degree of consensus in terms of the object of resistance—a condition, perhaps, far too idealistic for our police organizations.

In a word, the patrol officer's resistance to police–community relations can be generalized from the police point of view as resistance to something they did not cause and cannot cure. Unfortunately, this attitude not only oversimplifies the complexity of the problem, but it also tends to legitimize police resistance to becoming even a participant in the remedial efforts designed to bridge the community's fears, ignorances, and far too often, justifiable concerns.

Police–community relations suggest that a partnership exists. Until both sides of the dichotomized position come to terms with this by offering to help the other side help itself, instead of exhibiting irresponsible criticism and emotional immaturity by numerous countercharges that often ignore the salient issues involved, there will be both police and citizen resistance to improving the entire community. For in the final analysis, police–community relations problems are nothing more than symptoms of a more pervasive malady.

FACTORS SUSTAINING A PATROL OFFICER
SUBCULTURE WITHIN THE POLICE SUBCULTURE

Although writers such as Niederhoffer, Skolnick, Banton, Bordua, and James Q. Wilson have pursued the study of police as a subculture, none has distinctly characterized the patrol officer as constituting a subculture. Although Niederhoffer talked of the socialization process of police recruits, his essay focused more on socialization of a recruit into the general police normative structure rather than the patrol officer's normative structure.

To conceptualize the police as merely one large subculture of society prevents many theoretical postulates and hypotheses from being formulated. All the fine discriminations that are apparent within a patrol officer subculture are lost in the vastness of the more overriding subculture.

To support the observation that patrol officers as a class represent a subculture within a larger police subculture, empirical observation has disclosed mores, norms, and values that are *peculiar* to the patrol officer group and not generally shared by the rest of the police. They are as follows:

1. Patrol officers are, as a group, confined to the lowest organizational position within the police structure. Accordingly, the tasks allocated to them are those associated with the least skill and prestige.

2. As a group, patrol officers are particularly visible by being uniformed or in the "bag," as some officers refer to the uniform.

3. An extremely high percentage of patrol officers have no route of "escape" from the position of patrol officer, because very few will be promoted, and even fewer assigned to the detective bureau, the only two routes of advancement for patrol officers.

4. The element of danger and violence to which patrol officers are more systematically exposed than any other occupational subgrouping within the police organization develops an espirit de corps shared only by other patrol officers.

5. Patrol officers as a group share the common frustration of having their good patrol work go unrecognized or, at most, must share their successes with other special units of the department.[1]

6. Patrol officers, more than any other component of the police organization, are consistently vulnerable to their use of judgment, whereas others within the organizational structure can rely on policy and not be as vulnerable to criticism or disciplinary reprisals. As a result of this, patrol officers do not look to the administration for acceptance, but to fellow patrol officers. In essence, then, patrol officers do not measure their performance by policy standards as much as they look to other patrol officers for approval, judgment, and acceptance.

7. Although the police administration generally opposes the use of discretion by patrol officers, the patrol officer subgroup finds it necessary for the effective enactment of its role.

8. The structural organization of our police departments facilitates the emergence of a subculture, especially one with a hierarchical structure and one-way flow of communications.

9. In our police organizations, solidarity is developed among patrol officers as a result of a form of reverse *role segregation*. In normal role segregation, the more the incumbents of a role differ from the mainstream of that system, the more likely it is that the role is set apart from that system. In police departments, the overwhelming majority of personnel are confined to the patrol officer position, yet the patrol officer's role eventually becomes set apart from the rest of the police organization because the status accorded special units of a police organization is generally higher, thus causing reverse role segregation.

10. The police organization relies on senior patrolmen to help train neophyte officers in a form of on-the-job training. However, it is this portion of the role-learning process that transfers the most role skills to rookie officers. Implicit within this role-acquisition stage is not only the transmission of role skills, but particularly, the transference of the patrol officer's value structure; street patrol officers rank the skills needed by recruits in terms of priorities that conform more to the patrol officer subculture than they conform to the organizational value structure.

Finally, the theoretical relevance of viewing the patrol officer as a subculture, as opposed to the more generic term "police subculture," will allow researchers the opportunity to further discriminate in their explorations of police organization while facilitating police administrators' understanding of their police departments, especially as to the value structure, mores, and norms, and as to why some changes are resisted and other changes vociferously resisted.

Summary

This chapter has provided empirical vignettes illustrating the role-acquisition process of patrol officers. The enactment of the patrol officer's role contains many interactions that present role conflict, role ambiguity, and role strain situations. The purpose of presenting empirical vignettes was to illustrate the strategies of resolution that patrol officers utilize in the multiple role phenomena they encounter daily. For example, patrol officers frequently use discretion to prevent role conflict situations from fully manifesting themselves. However, in the process of invoking discretion as a method of resolution, the patrol officer is in effect providing another source of conflict for the recruit or "rookie" officer, who is still very much in the process of becoming socialized into the patrolmen subculture.

The phenomenon of role strain for the patrol officer and the methods utilized by police officers to protect themselves from the clientele they theoretically exist to service is an important aspect of this analysis. In this sense one could define role strain as follows: No matter what patrol officers do or attempt to do, they will not be successful in meeting citizen expectations. In part, this phenomenon sometimes occurs because some citizen needs are beyond the capabilities of the police system's response. When this occurs, patrol officers may respond to the situation by role distancing from the citizen and citizen expectations. The implications of this for police–community relations programming are, of course, obvious.

The theoretical implications of the empirical vignettes in this chapter reveal both individual and organizational resistance to police–community relations programming. Most efforts toward improving police–community relations have concentrated on individual officers while virtually ignoring the organizational structure and environment in which the patrol officers work. Ironically, both factors have a reinforcing effect upon the other, and to date precious little has been done in terms of resolving organizational resistance to police–community relations.

Finally, factors that sustain a patrol officer subculture within the more overriding police subculture were analyzed with particular reference to resistance to innovation as well as to police–community relations.

End Note

[1] For further enumeration of these five factors, the reader is directed to Arthur Niederhoffer, *Behind the Shield: The Police in Urban Society* (New York: Doubleday, 1967).

4

POLICING AND THE COMMUNITY INTEREST

CHAPTER
ELEVEN

THE POLICING SYSTEM:
COMMUNITY CONTROL

CITIZEN PARTICIPATION

During the past two decades, great emphasis has been placed on the subject of citizen participation. To many, the concept of citizen participation is both amorphous and analytically treacherous. To others, it represents a viable means of involving citizens in the decision-making process of those governmental agencies that have an impact on their lives. To the extent that citizen participation can be seen as the forerunner of community control, it is worthwhile to briefly explore the concept from a historical perspective.

The concept of citizen participation is not new. To the contrary, it is probably as old as modern civilization itself. Indeed, the concept is embodied in the Constitution of the United States, and it is manifested in the tradition of minimum involvement of the federal government in local affairs. It was not until the emergence of the New Deal in the 1930s that this concept was ever seriously challenged. As a result, the federal government began to exercise more and more control over local governmental programs, particularly social service programs. The end of

World War II saw an acceleration of the lessening of local control. It was during this time that large numbers of people became concerned about the "lack of responsiveness of government." This led to a number of federal agencies adopting a policy which required that citizens, particularly the politically disfranchised poor and minorities, be allowed a voice in program operation. Following that point, we can identify three distinct stages of citizen participation.

The first stage, from 1949 to 1963, can best be categorized as involvement of nonindigenous citizens, where citizens were used as advisors to agencies and programs. Those who were appointed to the advisory panels were carefully selected. They served on "blue ribbon" committees that were only *advisory* in nature, and they had little or no influence on the official policies that were made.

The second stage ran from 1964 to 1968 and differed from the first stage in that indigenous citizens, mostly poor minorities, were given the actual opportunity to participate in policymaking positions. This came about primarily through federal programs funded by the Office of Economic Opportunity and Model Cities. It was during this period that the phrase "maximum feasible citizens' participation" was coined. The expressed intent was to give indigenous citizens a role to play in decision-making processes, so that they could operate, and they often did, in an advocacy position against an established governmental bureaucracy. The experience of two such programs, Community Action and Model Cities, is well documented.[1]

The third stage of citizen participation started in 1969 and continues to the present time. During this stage, citizen participation was directed toward regional decentralization, with the major emphasis toward citizen participation on area-wide planning councils and regional advisory councils. The formulation of councils of governments (COGs) is a good example of what was occurring during this stage. Also emerging during this period were programs such as neighborhood councils, town hall meetings, community development corporations, multiservice centers, little city halls, and so on. Each of these programs represented attempts to gain greater participation by citizens in governmental programs.

The point to be remembered from this brief history is that citizen participation has a long history in this country. It represents a philosophy, a concept, and a program.

THE PILOT DISTRICT PROJECT

In previous chapters we discussed the police–community relations program as a mechanism of obtaining citizen participation in policing agencies. A most ambitious program tried in Washington, D.C. deserves explanation because of its uniqueness. Originally called the Pilot Precinct Project, the program represented the nation's best-financed attempt to improve the police relationship with the community.

he project started in 1968 when Robert Shellow, a psychologist from National Institute of Health, obtained a $1.4 million grant from the fice of Economic Opportunity.[2] The stated intent of the program was) increase police efficacy in ghetto areas by:

- Bettering relationships between police and ghetto residents
- Increasing community support for police activities
- Lessening tensions between police and ghetto residents
- Improving police intelligence sources[3]

It should be noted that the project did not claim to have anything to do with community control; rather, it explicitly attempted to "improve police service." Nevertheless, it came under heavy attack from its very beginning. On the one hand, the police were fearful of the "community control" concept, even though it did not exist. The local citizenry suspected that the demonstration project would only mean more "law and order" or "stop and frisk"-type activities without regard for "law and justice."[4] *The fact that one of the goals of the project was to "improve police intelligence sources" was a major item of protest.*

The project proposed to achieve its goals by utilizing the following techniques:

- Community advisory committees comprised of representatives of the entire spectrum of ghetto residents
- Partial decentralization of police functions into neighborhood service centers
- Continuous in-service police training
- Use of paid youth patrols comprised of ghetto youth
- Increased utilization of minority-group police officers
- Use of civilian personnel recruited from the project area to accomplish clerical and other tasks usually undertaken by police officers
- Redefinition of the police officer's role, through the introduction of a new incentive scheme[5]

A prime role was granted to citizen participation in the form of safety committees for each neighborhood service center and a precinct advisory council.

The main segment of the program that caused conflict was the Citizen's Advisory Board. Differing opinions existed over what functions, power, and control the board would have in the program. Blacks felt that this project would create a spy network.[6] *Washington Post* columnist William Raspberry said: "The program gives the impression of trying to buy citizen informants in exchange for welfare services."[7] However, not all of the opposition came from blacks or ghetto residents. Many whites refused to acknowledge the program, mostly because they feared "ghetto control."[8]

The Pilot District Project, which at one time was originally called the Pilot Police Project, was located in the Third Police District. The boundaries of the Third Police District are: on the north, Howard Street; on the east, 4th Street, N.W., to Rhode Island Avenue to 7th Street down to L Street; and on the west, Connecticut Avenue. The Third Police District also constitutes a major portion of that part of the Washington, D.C., Standard Metropolitan Statistical Area defined as a poverty area by the Office of Economic Opportunity.[9] The area contains a large proportion of Spanish-speaking people in addition to a large number of blacks, many below the poverty level.

During its existence from June 1968 to July 1971, the Pilot District Project had two distinct periods of activity under five different directors. The first was the 20-month period (June 1968–January 1970) under its initial project director, Robert E. Shellow, when there was no elected citizens' board. The second 18-month period, from February 7, 1970 to July 31, 1971, began with the election of the citizens' board and continued with activities under Ross Morgan, a black police administrator on leave from the New York Port Authority. Morgan became the second project director in March 1970; Fred Lander III, a black lawyer from the D.C. Government Crime Analysis Division, was appointed by the board as the third director in September 1970. H. Watson, a black English teacher from North Carolina, was named acting director in April 1971; finally, Robert E. Craig was appointed by the board in April 1972 and stayed with the project until its dismantling in October 1973.[10]

The Pilot District Project did not fail because of a lack of funds; OEO and LEAA invested over $2 million into it. Actually, there were several major reasons for the project's failure:[11]

1. There was no directive from the mayor or the police chief that required policemen to cooperate with citizens in the project.
2. The project had much more intensive training for police than for civilians, and a markedly different pay scale—$3 per hour for civilians and $7 per hour for police.
3. Lack of stable leadership (i.e., five directors in five years).
4. All the responsibility for the success or failure of the program was put in the hands of the "grass-roots" people and they did not have the administrative or technical abilities to maintain a program of this type.

The likelihood of success in improving police–community relations when a hostile community has general control is about the same as when only the police have control—very low. If this OEO experiment and all the previous police–community relations projects throughout the country impart lessons to be learned, the chief lesson is that *both* the police and the community have to be involved. Both have to agree on goals as well as means, at least in a limited fashion.

In addition to this basic necessity, the research and experiments coming out of the Pilot District Project suggest that if the following five general recommendations are kept in mind, the likelihood of efforts to improve police–community relations might be enhanced:[12]

1. Recognize that in-service police training is not necessarily the best point at which to attack the problem of improving police–community relations.

2. Concentrate on services currently the responsibility of the police, but not being performed at all or performed ineffectively by them.

3. View police–community relations from a long-term view; short-term training and other experimental programs are likely to be trampled in the political controversy over who will control and operate them.

4. Examine what community people are saying. Stress changing the power relationship by means of influencing policies connected with police recruitment, residence, and promotions, with particular stress on recruitments.

5. Concentrate on citizens as well as the police. Educate citizens to assume responsibility in law enforcement and other police tasks.

COMMUNITY CONTROL

The demands for community control of the police are based upon the belief that the police are not responsive to certain segments of the community, especially the minority community. Indeed, the role of the police in minority communities has been under severe scrutiny since the civil disorders of the 1960s. Police departments are often looked upon by certain enclaves of the minority community as completely autonomous units of the criminal justice system, without any control or direction from within specific neighborhoods or communities.

In the eyes of many minority-group members, the emphasis on professionalism of the police has meant a simultaneous deemphasis on populism (community control) or minority representation on police forces. This results in law enforcement and other vital police services by persons unrepresentative of the community.[13] The populist argument is that the race, residential, and cultural background of policemen are *critical* to proper policing and police–community relations. This "heritage," the argument goes, is more important than the professionalism of the police, particularly in black ghetto areas. In a 1968 publication, George Edwards, a judge in the Sixth Circuit U.S. Court of Appeals and former Detroit police commissioner, expressed the opinion that the "residential absenteeism" of white police officers in the inner city was an important part of the problem.[14] Edwards notes, as does Taylor, that blacks often see police officers with white faces as representatives not only of the white man's current law, but also of the white man's earlier laws of slavery and segregation.[15] Taylor, a black professor at Federal City College in Washington, D.C., states that the racial, residential, and cultural disparities between white police officers and black communities necessarily lead to physical conflict.[16]

In the area of community control, Nelson Watson stated that it is especially irritating to some officers to suggest that citizens ought to have something to say about how the police and the police department are to be run.[17] According to Bordua, police hostility to interference in police affairs is an intrinsic part of the police concept of professional status. As with other professionals, the police argue that they alone must determine the standards by which they are to be judged.[18]

In a 1970 study on police–ghetto relations, Mast disagrees that professionalization, human relations, in-service training, and other current programs will lead to a solution of the police–community relations problem. He recommends that police forces be composed of ghetto residents and organized ghetto leaders. The major restructuring suggested focuses on a *gradual* transfer of the present municipal police role of a community *manager* to one of "community crime consultant."[19]

Mast's restructuring plan to give communities more control includes three basic changes in police processes: (1) felonies would call for close consultative relationships between municipal and indigenous police forces; (2) misdemeanors, which often involve discretionary decisions by individual police officers would be different—they would be *culture bound*; and (3) municipal police would cease their routine ghetto patrol and police stations would be turned over to the indigenous force. Mast feels that this process would enhance a sense of efficacy in the community. For the police officer as a teacher-consultant "to the ghetto, his traditional police role would be somewhat elevated to a higher status with also an accompanying prestige and rewards."[20]

Of course, it must be stated that there are many definitions of community control. One of these definitions is given by Alan A. Altshuler in his book, *Community Control: The Black Demand for Participation in Large American Cities.* He terms community control as

> the exercise of authority by the democratically organized government of a neighborhood-sized jurisdiction.
>
> There is no consensus on how neighborhoods should be defined. . . . Nor is there any consensus about the precise amount of authority that such a government would have to possess in any given police arena for the label "community control" to be justified. What the term clearly denotes is a category of proposed reforms; transfers of authority from the government of large cities to the governments of much smaller subunits within them. Such transfers would constitute political decentralization. At the same time, it should be emphasized that they would remain subject to modification by higher levels of government—just as are the charters of cities and suburbs today.[21]

Altshuler also tells of the motivations for citizen participation: "These claims seem to focus on three values: political authority, group representation in public bureaucracies, and the private income (wages and profits) generated by governmental activity."[22]

Riessman and Gartner, on the other hand, argue that the community control movement has a variety of objectives, including a redistribution of power, expansion of democracy, decentralization of public administration, and reorganization and improvement of human services.[23] They emphasize that these goals are often contradictory. From their analysis, they feel that the following contradictions must be resolved:

- An increase in the accountability of social services may be accompanied by a decrease in productivity or efficiency.
- Involvement, which has as one of its objectives the development of a sense of personal competency, can become a form of sociotherapy—participation for its own sake.
- Community control can degenerate into localism and infighting among local groups and competitive groups for some "piece of the action."
- There is always the danger of "peripheralism": that groups involved in decentralization may have no influence on central power where the real decisions on funds, resources, and basic policy continue to be made.

Reissman and Gartner conclude by arguing that the demand for community control (local) must be connected, clearly and with sophistication, to larger issues because the basic problems of our society originate, and the basic control of resources lies, at a national and centralized level.

Altshuler, on the other hand, would argue differently. He maintains, for example, that

1. Community control should be conceived of as a continuum rather than as an absolute,
2. Its degree will inevitably vary from one field of activity to the next.
3. Its degree may also vary from one dimension of any given policy arena to the next.[24]

In that context, according to Altshuler, "one might reasonably judge that community influence over the police should be less than over the schools...."[25]

Arthur Waskow presents a third perspective. He states that there are at least three possible directions in which to go to achieve the kind of change necessary to restore democratic civilian control over the police.[26]

1. Formal restructuring of metropolitan police departments into federations of neighborhood police forces, with control of each neighborhood force in the hands of neighborhood people through the election of commissions.
2. Creation of countervailing organizations (in effect, "trade unions" of those policed) responsible to a real political base, able to hear grievances and force change.
3. Transformation of the police "profession" and role so as to end the

isolation of the police and be able to require transfers out; discipline officers, with the concurrence of a city-wide appeal board and set basic policy on law enforcement priorities in the neighborhood.[27]

Waskow goes on to state that the possibility of control of the police through *countervailing* power is based on two recent models: the emergence of the Community Alert Patrols (CAP) in Watts and elsewhere as checks on the police, and the Community Review Board created by the Mexican-American community in Denver. They are both different from the conventional, supposedly neutral civilian review boards in that they are explicitly based not on a quasijudicial model, but on the necessity of having independent political power to confront that of the police forces. There is the assumption by both that the police are themselves either an independent political force or an arm of a powerful establishment, not a neutral peacekeeping body.

In the Denver case (the Community Review Board), Chicano organizations investigate charges of allegedly illegitimate or unjust police behavior and, where regarded as well founded, demand punishment of the officers and back up their demands with political pressure. The CAPs in Los Angeles used the endemic anger of young black men to check the behavior of the police in the black community.[28]

Richard Myren has stated that there is little direct citizen participation in the establishment of police policies and procedures in large cities of the United States. When such participation does occur, it will probably be in a city in which administrative decentralization has established a strong tradition of neighborhood team policing coupled with a practice of consulting with neighborhood groups as to how police operations can best serve community needs. A city with that kind of tradition might well opt for politically guaranteed community control. Broad policy could be set by an elected neighborhood council, with the team establishing procedures designed to implement the policies.[29]

James Q. Wilson sees some advantages in administrative decentralization with central command control, but criticizes democratic decentralization and political decentralization:

> A decentralized, neighborhood-oriented order maintenance patrol force requires central command to insure a reasonably common definition of appropriate order, a reduction in the opportunities for corruption and favoritism, and the protection of the civil liberties of suspects and witnesses.[30]

Albert J. Reiss, Jr., seems to come out with the same result:

> There is a substantial risk that local political control will become merely a substitute for central bureaucratic control. Neither central nor local control guarantees or thwarts broad citizen participation in governments or the nature of the agency to citizens.... In mass democratic societies, the central problem for citizens is how they may be brought closer to the centers of

political power that control the acquisition and allocation of resources, not whether administrative control is centralized or decentralized in the bureaucracy.[31]

An alternative view of complete political decentralization, and its merits, is strongly put forward by Karl Hess:

> Many who oppose decentralization are haunted by a specter of resurgent plantationism in the South. But local power there certainly need not mean Klan power over everyone. Rather, localism could mean a chance for black communities to have the sort of local identity which can defend against depredations by making the black community something more than just a niggertown appended to the white establishment's turf. . . .
>
> But it is in the cities that the neighborhoods have been most abused. They have been gobbled up by the urban imperialism of downtown rentiers. They have been insulted as ethnic or racial while the downtown Wasps milked them dry for votes or zoning. And yet they persist—occupied by strange police, harassed by criminals who have more connections downtown than any of the victims, impoverished by absentee landlords and tax collectors, abandoned by megalopolitan hospitals and treated like Skinnerian mice by visiting teachers.
>
> They need not take it. They do not need it. They should rise. They should secede.[32]

In July 1968, the Seminar on Violence conducted by the New York State Joint Legislative Committee on Crime, Its Causes, Control and Effect on Society in New York City began discussions on the wisdom of vesting political control of police working in a big city neighborhood in the people of that neighborhood. Less than three years later, the arguments of the professors gathered there for a quiet discussion were heard again, more stridently, in a political contest in Berkeley, California. The Black Panthers petitioned for an amendment to the city charter that "would rearrange city government to permit direct control of the police by the people in three administrative (and neighborhood) districts."[33] The charter amendment failed at the polls in April 1971.

Proponents of the Berkeley charter amendment argued that there was no effective citizen control of the city police department. They alleged that the theoretical authority of the city manager was not, in fact, exercised. Even had the manager been in control, the manager was insulated from citizen supervision by a requirement of a two-thirds majority in the city council to override all decisions by the manager. To overcome this situation, citizens advocated splitting the city into three neighborhoods.[34]

In the Berkeley community, Jefferson's "wards" are the three distinct areas defined by the Community Control Amendment: (1) the black community, (2) the campus/youth community, and (3) the middle-class Northside/Hill community. Of course, these are not completely distinct areas. The "black" community defined in the amendment was actually one-fourth white. The "hill" community contained different age groups. The "campus" community contained both students and long-time Berkeley residents. Nevertheless, the communities were distinct from each other, each with its common "handouts," common life-styles, common shopping and recreation area, and common problems.[35]

Under the proposal, each of the three communities was to be divided into precincts on a population basis. A precinct representative would be elected by the people of that area to sit on a District Police Council. Because of population differences, the black and middle-class communities were each to have two *distinct* councils and the campus/youth community one. Each district was to comprise 15 precincts, with its council being called the Council of Fifteen. Each of the councils would have elected a commissioner to a five-man police commission for the City of Berkeley. Other duties of the councils would include the following: continual review of all policies of the police department; formulation of recommendations to the police department; formulation of recommendations to the police commissioner for policy changes when the needs or will of the neighborhood they served were no longer being met by the policies; creation and operation of a grievance procedure to hear complaints against police in the 15 precincts of the district; and discipline of members of the police department for violations of law or policy in their district. Each Council of Fifteen was to be required to meet regularly at times when interested persons could attend. Council members would be subject to a recall election on petition of 20 percent of those who voted in the last precinct election.

Administrative coordination of the three essentially autonomous neighborhood police departments was to be vested in the five-member police commission, which would have assumed many of the functions of the current police chief. Responsibilities of the commission would include: setting policy for all city police; determining qualifications for employment in the police department; meting out punishment to police officers found guilty of violations of law or policy; entering into necessary agreements with other police departments and governmental agencies; and facilitating agreements among the three departments for the operation, maintenance, and staffing of facilities of common interest, such as weapons, vehicles, laboratories, and vehicle repair stations. Financing would have continued to be through appropriation by the city council, with the budget distributed to the three constituent forces on a population basis. Every police officer would have been required to live in the neighborhood in which he or she was assigned for duty.[36]

Although the Berkeley neighborhood policing charter amendment was defeated at the polls, it is probably only a matter of time before a similar scheme of political decentralization of the police department is tried in an American city. Cities with strong team policing under administrative decentralization are likely candidates.[37]

Summary

Although the police represent only one segment of the criminal justice process, attention has been given in this chapter to the impact of citizen participation and community control on policing in the United States. This seems defensible for a number of reasons.[38] First, it is in the police component where most of the criminal justice decentralization and citizen participation action has occurred. This is probably attributable to the fact that police action is often obvious to the residents of a neighborhood; its impact is often felt immediately and directly. Policing is also a governmental subsystem usually manned by persons without special preservice education; this fact leads ordinary citizens to believe they are qualified to comment on and to participate in police operations.

Second, what happens at the police level determines to a large extent what the balance of the criminal justice process can do. The primary sorting out of "criminals" from "ordinary citizens" is done by the police. Police officers determine, in one way or another, the limits of community tolerance in their exercise of discretion. Police administrators determine how limited resources for enforcement and other services are to be deployed. It is literally impossible for the police to enforce the law all of the time. Only those arrested by the police can be adjudicated by the courts and "rehabilitated" by corrections. Some of the most interesting experiments and social campaigns for both administrative and political decentralization are found in police operations. There is much less experimentation in both courts and corrections, although there are definite trends toward the decentralization of programs in the corrections field. However, in the future, both of these segments of the criminal justice system may be affected dramatically by decentralization experiments at the "system threshold"—that is, in police agencies.

End Notes

[1]See, for example, Edgar S. Cahn and Jean C. Cahn, "The War on Poverty: A Civilian Perspective," *Yale Law Journal*, 73 (1964), 1317; Lillian Rubin, "Maximum Feasible Participation, The Origins, Implications, and Present Status," in *Poverty and Human Resources Abstracts*, November–December 1967; John C. Donovan, *The Politics of Poverty* (New York: Pegasus, 1967); Daniel P. Moynihan, ed., *On Understanding Poverty: Perspectives from the Social Sciences* (New York: Basic Books, 1969); James L. Sundquist, ed., *On Fighting Poverty: Perspectives from Experience* (New York: Basic Books, 1969); Daniel P. Moynihan, *Maximum Feasible Misunderstanding: Community Action in the War on Poverty* (New York: Free Press, 1969); Dale Rogers Marshal, "Public Participation and the Politics of Poverty," in *Race, Change, and Urban Society*, ed. Peter Orleans and

William Russell Ellis (Beverly Hills, Calif.: Sage, 1971); Roland J. Warren, "Model Cities First Round: Politics, Planning, and Participation," *Journal of the American Institute of Planners*, 35 (July 1969), 245; Melvin Mogulof, "Coalition to Adversary: Citizen Participation in Three Federal Programs," *Journal of the American Institute of Planners*, 35 (July 1969), 225; Junius Williams, "The Impact of Citizen Participation," paper prepared for the National Academy of Public Administration, Washington, D.C., May 1970; M. Anthony Kline and Richard Lee Gates, "Citizen Participation in Model Cities Program: Toward a Theory of Collective Bargaining for the Poor," *The Black Law Journal* 44 (1971); Barlow Burke, Jr., "The Threat to Citizen Participation in Model Cities," *Cornell Law Review*, 56 (1971), 751.

[2]David P. Riley, "Should Communities Control Their Police?" in *Policing America,* ed. Anthony Platt and Lynn Cooper (Englewood Cliffs, N.J.: Prentice-Hall, 1974).

[3]Rita Mae Kelly et al., "The Pilot Police Project: A Description and Assessment of a Police Community Relations Experiment in Washington, D.C.," American Institute for Research, Kensington, Md., January 1972, pp. 37–38.

[4]Ibid., p. 3.

[5]Ibid., p. 70.

[6]*Washington Post,* June 29, 1968, sec. B-1.

[7]*Washington Post,* July 28, 1968, sec. B-1.

[8]Wanda B. Johnson, "A Study of Police–Community Relations Programs in Washington, D.C.," National Institute of Law Enforcement and Criminal Justice, Washington, D.C., Sept. 1972, p. 14.

[9]Kelly et al., "Pilot Police Project," pp. 342–43.

[10]Interview with Ira Stahman, former community service supervisor at the Pilot District Project.

[11]Ibid.

[12]Kelly et al., "Pilot Police Project," p. 342–343.

[13]Kelly et al., "Pilot Police Project," pp. 37–38.

[14]George C. Edwards, *The Police on the Urban Frontier* (New York: Institute of Human Relations Press, 1968), p. 27.

[15]Ibid.

[16]Andres Taylor, "Report on Law and Order Seminar," Federal City College, Washington, D.C.; as cited by Garmon West, Jr., in *Memorandum for the Record,* dated January 30, 1971.

[17]Nelson A. Watson and James W. Sterling, *Police and Their Opinion* (Washington, D.C.: International Association of Chiefs of Police, 1969), p. 7.

[18]David J. Bordua, *The Police: Six Sociological Essays* (New York: Wiley, 1967).

[19]Robert Mast, "Police–Ghetto Relations: Some Findings and a Proposal for Structural Change," *Race* (London: Institutes of Race Relations), 11, no. 4 (1970), 458.

[20]Ibid., p. 441.

[21]Alan A. Altshuler, *Community Control: The Black Demand for Participation in Large American Cities.* Western Publishing Co., Inc. Reprinted by permission of Bobbs-Merrill Co., Inc.

[22]Ibid.

[23]Frank Riessman and Alan Gartner, "Community Control and Social Policy," 52 (May–June 1970).

[24]Altshuler, *Community Control,* p. 44.

[25]Ibid.

[26]Arthur I. Waskow, "Community Control of the Police," *Transaction,* 7 (December 1969), p. 4.

[27]Ibid.

[28]Ibid.

[29]Richard A. Myren, "Decentralization and Citizen Participation in Criminal Justice Systems," *Public Administration Review,* 32 (October 1972), p. 727.

[30]James Q. Wilson, *Varieties of Police Behavior: The Management of Law and Order in Eight Communities* (Cambridge, Mass.: Harvard University Press, 1968), p. 293.

[31]For an expanded view of the impact of bureacracies on police organization, see Albert J. Reiss, Jr. "Professionalization of the Police" in *Police and Community Relations: A Sourcebook,* A. F. Brandstatter and Louis A. Radelet, Eds. (Encino, California: Glencoe Press, 1968), pp. 216–219; 222–223, 228.

[32]Karl Hess, "Breaking Up City Hall: Why Neighborhoods Must Secede," *New York Times,* January 31, 1972, p. 26.

[33]Cited by Myren, "Decentralization," p. 726.

[34]Ibid.

[35]The Red Family, *The Case for Community Control of Police* (Berkeley, Calif.: The Red Family, 1971), p. 3.

[36]Ibid.

[37]Myren, "Decentralization," p. 726.

[38]Ibid., pp. 732–733.

CHAPTER
TWELVE

STRATEGIES
FOR COMMUNITY
INVOLVEMENT
IN POLICE-COMMUNITY
RELATIONS

HISTORICAL EMERGENCE OF COMMUNITY PARTICIPATION AND CONTROL

Since the beginning of the republic, citizen participation in government has been synonymous with voting and holding office. Another traditional form of involvement has been service with civic groups. With respect to the federal government, the first three decades of the twentieth century witnessed the growth of other types of direct relationships with individuals which also were considered to be forms of participation. These included the role of tribal organizations in dealing with the Bureau of Indian Affairs and the Indian Division of the Public Health Service, the responsibilities of citizen members of Selective Service Boards, the relationships between the Department of Agriculture and farmer committees, and the activities of tenants' associations in low-rent public housing projects.[1]

Although these early federal-private relationships were important insofar as they firmly established the idea that citizens have a legitimate role to play in government policymaking, the real beginning of the citizen participation movement as we know it today can be traced to the immediate post-World War II period. Starting in the late 1940s and continuing for the next 20 years, the federal government assumed the leadership role in this area.[2]

Stenberg observes that between 1949 and 1963, the prevailing model was one of the nonindigenous citizen as advisor–persuader. Several federal programs enacted from the end of the 1940s through the beginning of the Johnson Administration had citizen participation components. Three of the most important were Urban Renewal, the Workable Program for Community Development, and the Juvenile Delinquency Demonstration Projects (excluding Mobilization for Youth). In general, nonindigenous citizens were involved in these programs in an advisory and persuading capacity. Most of the citizens were white planners, business managers, civic leaders, and representatives of various groups and interests in the community—retail and manufacturing, construction, real estate, finance, labor, taxpayers, religion, and education. They were city rather than neighborhood leaders, and their orientation was directed toward meeting communitywide needs, not neighborhood problems, through the federal program. For the most part, there was little or no direct participation by residents of affected areas. These nonindigenous, "blue-ribbon" citizens participated through belonging to city-wide citizen advisory committees (CACs) for a workable program or urban renewal project or through serving on the government board of a delinquency demonstration project. Membership was usually by virtue of the citizens' association with civic, business, educational, and similar groups, as well as with the political elite of the community. Appointment by the mayor was the usual method of selecting citizen representatives.[3]

The types of participation included studying the nature of the problems of the target area and alternative solutions, usually without staff assistance. Citizen members advised officials of these needs and recommended possible ways to meet them. However, their power, was limited to persuasion. A major purpose of this kind of citizen involvement, in the view of many federal and local officials, was often to promote community understanding of a controversial project and to build popular support for its implementation.[4]

With respect to the impact of citizen participation, residents of target areas were not generally involved in project planning and development. "Good government" types served as community, rather than neighborhood representatives on CACs or delinquency-demonstration governing boards. Public officials advised, recommended, and persuaded citizens as to the need for and design of a project—rather than vice versa—and this "educating" of citizen members usually resulted in long delays in planning and programming. In the final analysis, citizens had little or no influence on official policy decision. Their participation fulfilled the social or therapeutic areas and in terms of "selling" unpopular programs such as urban renewal.[5]

During the four-year period between 1964 and 1968, a new model for community participation emerged, which Stenberg described as the indigenous citizen as partner–adversary. In Stenberg's view, Model Cities and Community Action programs were departures from the previous model of community participation, in that the type of citizen changed, as well as the goals and strategy of citizen involvement.

"Citizens" were no longer predominantly affluent whites; instead, they were mainly poor, minority-group members. They were generally neighborhood- rather than city-wide-oriented. Federal legislation specifically encouraged "maximum feasible" or "widespread" involvement on the part of those served by these programs. In Community Action, however, this was further refined to require that at least one-third of the agency policy board membership be representatives of the poor.[6]

In both programs a formal citizen participation structure was established. Citizens were accorded a role in policymaking as well as serving in an advisory capacity. Neighborhood organizations and their representatives were considered to be partners with government agencies in a coalition relationship and, particularly with respect to CACs, they were often viewed as the controlling force in deciding which programs were to be funded in neighborhood areas. Several objectives were reflected in the Community Action and Model Cities citizen participation structures. Both federal officials and citizens sought generally to build black community identification and to develop indigenous leadership that could unite diverse groups of the urban poor and help increase the political efficacy of low-income people. Another goal was to "democratize" the bureaucracy by having formally organized representative neighborhood decision-making bodies serve as spokespersons for the poor and bargain with the power structure in their behalf.

Although several of the foregoing objectives have been realized, the impact of citizen involvement in Community Action and Model Cities has varied widely. In some cities participation has not amounted to actual shared decision making or resulted in citizens' having coequal status with public officials and bureaucrats. Collaboration and placation, rather than control and power, characterized the citizen role here. In other areas, power was shared with citizens, often as a result of their taking it rather than the city giving it to them. Confrontation produced a meaningful citizen role in decision making, but this adversary relationship rather than partnership or coalition relationship also tended to alienate the CAC, in particular from other city agencies.[7]

Stenberg suggests that the most recent model, which emerged in 1969 and is still in vogue today, is the regionalism-decentralization model. This model has been characterized by several types of administrative responses made by local jurisdictions to the problems of citizen alienation and remote government decision makers. "Meet your mayor" or "town hall" meetings and regular legislative body sessions have been held in neighborhood areas. A special telephone number has been designated for citizens to use in registering complaints, or an office has been established to act on or relay grievances to appropriate departments. Community-wide resident committees composed of citizen representatives have been created to advise public officials in such functional areas as police, schools, housing, recreation, and health and hospitals. Neighborhood councils representing residents have been formed. Community service officers, neighbormen, or ombudsmen have been appointed to answer inquiries and investigate complaints concerning deficiencies in public services and to perform liaison functions between city hall and neighborhoods. Little city halls and multiservice centers have been set up in neighborhoods to bring government closer to the people, and resident boards occasionally have been selected to advise the heads of these agencies.[8]

These experiments were premised on the belief that improved communications, coupled with decentralized delivery of services, would overcome "politicosclerosis," hardening of the arteries of political communication, and improve the delivery of services on the neighborhood level, thereby dissipating political alienation.[9] Administrative changes, we must point out, are ameliorative devices; they cannot end political alienation that is the product of an unrepresentative electoral system.[10]

Finally, Stenberg points out that the results of a survey taken in all cities over 25,000 population on citizen participation and decentralization of services conducted by the Advisory Commission on Intergovernmental Relations—in cooperation with the National League of Cities and International City Management Association—suggest that most top city chief executives or administrators consider these approaches to have been effective. Seventy-two percent of the replies from 226 mayors, city managers, and heads of planning, community development, and community relations agencies agreed with the statement that citizen participation–decentralization had been "a difficult but very worthwhile experience resulting in increased trust and understanding between citizens, city hall officials, and public administrators." Twenty-three percent of the responses, however, reported that it had resulted in very little change in citizen–city hall, official–public administrator relations. Only five percent indicated that it had led to a deterioration of these relationships.[11]

To comprehend fully the dynamics and complexities of citizen participation and advisory groups, James Riedel presents a very informative and provacative classification, which underscores the realities of the situation. Riedel observes that almost all agency-appointed groups are called "advisory committees," but that this stretches the word "advisory." It might be more accurate to put the groups in categories called (1) advisory, (2) supportive, (3) put-off, and (4) put-on committees. The categories obviously reflect political functions, the implicit motives of the appointing body, which can be described as follows:[12]

ADVISORY

Advisory I.   Perhaps one of the most common and legitimate advisory committees stems from the appointive agency not knowing specifically what to do, or the best way of doing it, and being willing to be directed by the group appointed.

Advisory II.   The appointing agency does not know what to do and wants the report of a creditable group to publicize alternatives in order to get a reading on public (or interest group) reaction. This is the familiar way of cooling "hot potatoes," as with the Kerner Commission.

Advisory III.   The appointing agency is not even sure of the dimensions of the problem, and needs to have the problem itself defined before proceeding to alternative solutions. One thinks of numerous commissions of inquiry or of local narcotics advisory boards.

Advisory IV.   The appointing agency has arrived at a conclusion, but at the suggestion of some resistance is willing to modify it if a stronger case can be made for another decision. This motivation also leads to the open-ended committee, formed by inviting all interested parties to attend an open hearing or to file rejoinders to a proposed order.

SUPPORTIVE

Supportive I.   The supporting agency knows what it wants in the face of significant opposition, and names a group, usually with some status in the reacting groups, that will come up with the acceptable conclusion, adding an aura of authority to the decision. Cynics will also note that the citizen group may also share in the responsibility for it. A blue-ribbon committee, reporting back to the Food and Drug Administration, announced that "government decisions on the safety of food and drugs are too often based on politics rather than good science," something the administrators could never have said publicly in their own behalf.

Supportive II.   The appointing agency knows what it does not want in the face of contrary pressure, and names a group expected to present only acceptable choices, rejecting explicitly that which is unwanted, thereby reordering the presumed public status of alternatives.

Supportive III.   The appointing agency enlists the occasional or periodic evaluation of an existing body of appointed citizens, reserving the option of keeping comment and recommendations private or making them public. Such "visiting committees" often serve as buffers for the appointing agency when administrative changes and criticism flow.

PUT-OFF

Put-Off I.   The appointing agency does not want to act now, or perhaps ever, but is under acute pressure from a significant portion of the public. Appointing tactics suggest some clues as to when this is the motivation. (1) Appoints a cross-section that will never be able to agree on the relevant facts, appropriate procedures, conclusions or recommendations. (2) Appoints a narrow-spectrum group whose findings will be unacceptable even to those generally in accord with the direction of proposed action, anticipating hostile public reaction to dispose of the report (and perhaps even the issue).

Put-Off II.   The appointing agency does not want to act now, and hopes to divert pressure by averting any public consideration of the problem until after a citizens' committee has completed its work and its report has been studied; hoping that in the interim pressure for action will be dissipated, or events will intervene to dispose of the problem at that level. This is a common tactic at the local level when there is the slightest prospect that the next session of the state legislature may take over the issue. Suggestive appointing tactics include: (1) Appoints prestigious persons, but none that has a personal stake or intense feelings with respect to any particular outcome, naming as chairman someone who can be counted on to serve the dilatory objective; (2) after announcement that the committee has been established, fills it out slowly, adding people from time to time, forcing much retracing of steps and occasional redirection; (3) gives the committee a vague and general mandate, or asks it to design its own and submit it for review before proceeding, and then makes discouraging modifications out of public view.

Put-Off III.   The appointing agency feels that it cannot act in the face of sharp cleavages in the relevant public, naming to the committee the leaders (or their representatives) of opposing factions, roughly in balance. The committee thereby performs in the function often formerly ascribed to political parties— concentrating the heat and responsibility for accommodation outside the official agencies of government. If and when issues are resolved within the citizens' committee, the report may become either advisory or supportive. Otherwise, inability to resolve their differences can be cited as justification for governmental inaction.

PUT-ON

Put-On I.   The appointing agency has already made, or knows that it will make a decision that will readily be identified as crassly partisan, or partial to a person or group. To soften, if not offset that appearance, a group not so immediately noted for its partisan bias is named, and dutifully arrives at the desired conclusion. This is a notorious ploy when selecting city or county managers, screening appointed officials, or site-selection for costly public projects.

Put-On II.   The appointing agency is badgered by an unorganized or poorly organized element in the public, clamoring for ill-defined "action." A committee is formed and fed a bewildering array of information from the appointing agency, designed to quiet the leadership by helping them convince themselves that the problem is too complex for easy solution. Such committees often recommend a massive public information program to solve the problem by "understanding," which may or may not be the optimal solution in fact, but makes the appointing agency look responsive. Early Community Action Programs had this appearance.

Put-On III.   The appointing agency knows it has a serious problem with which it is not immediately prepared to cope in the face of organized or articulate criticism. It appoints a blue-ribbon committee of leaders and intellectuals to do a prestige study. Some appointees may be known to believe that the problem involves other agencies and jurisdictions. The committee report can then be substituted for decisive action in light of the probable finding that intergovernmental cooperation is the only or best hope.[13]

In essence, when a public agency calls into being a "committee" of persons not a part of the bureaucratic hierarchy, it is an indication of some kind of uncertainty, which includes the willingness, capacity, appropriateness, or whatever, of the appointing agency to make the required decisions alone. This is citizen participation in which the appointing agency maintains some control over the group's output, and which reveals something about the relationship between the government movement and the governed from the perspective of the governors.[14]

Perhaps a useful model to use to compare the concerns for greater citizen involvement, participation, and control that are beginning to emerge in the criminal justice system would be that of the public school system. Many of the issues surrounding centralization and decentralization have been articulated by various groups and governmental agencies within our public educational field.

In 1967 the New York State Legislature responded to Mayor John V. Lindsay's request for additional school aid by passing a law—chapter 484—requiring the mayor to submit a school decentralization plan to the 1968 Legislature as a condition for the receipt of additional state aid. The mayor appointed an Advisory Panel on Decentralization of the New York City Schools and selected McGeorge Bundy, president of the Ford Foundation, to head the panel. In November 1967 the panel added impetus to the movement for community control of schools by recommending that the Legislature establish 30 to 60 community school districts, each to be governed by an 11-member board. Community control would be assured by having parents elect six members; the mayor would appoint the other five in order to achieve balanced representation of all groups in each district. Each board would be authorized to determine the curriculum and use of buildings, select classroom materials, hire and fire teachers, and grant tenure.

The Bundy Plan for greater public participation in the school system was attacked strongly by the Council of Supervisory Associations and the 55,000 member United Federation of Teachers (UFT), a union favoring administrative decentralization. Fears were expressed that professionalism would be undermined, racial segregation would be promoted, and black teachers would espouse antiwhite sentiments in classrooms.

The movement for grass roots control of schools received major support when the Ford Foundation in 1967 decided to fund three demonstration districts—Ocean Hill–Brownsville, Intermediate School 201 Complex, and Two Bridges—in ghetto areas, each district having approximately 9,000 students. Following their creation, the boards of the demonstration districts held to the position that they should control their own budgets, establish the curriculum, and hire and fire teachers. The citywide Board of Education replied that it lacked legal authority to delegate these powers.

The three districts, Ocean Hill–Brownsville in particular, were centers of controversy involving parents, militants, UFT, and others as tension ebbed and flowed. Friction between UFT and ghetto parents developed when the schools in the districts remained open during the citywide strike of teachers by UFT.

The attempt in the spring of 1968 by the governing board of the Ocean Hill–Brownsville demonstration district to oust without formal charges 13 teachers, five assistant principals, and one principal from the district was especially upsetting to UFT. The board's action prompted UFT to remove 350 members from the district to force reinstatement of the 19 who had been discharged. This dispute unfortunately fanned racial animosity, as the chiefly black and Puerto Rican district was pitted against what it labelled a repressive white power structure. And anti-Semitism reared its ugly head: a sizable number of teachers in the city are Jewish and UFT members.

The measure of success achieved by these districts prior to their absorption into larger districts in 1970 is a subject of considerable controversy. With respect to administrative personnel, six new principals were appointed by the Ocean Hill–Brownsville governing board, including the first Chinese and Puerto Rican principals to be appointed in the city. Some observers contend that the districts operated during a period of turmoil and it is impossible to measure the effect of the turmoil on the quality of education.

Following extended debate and political maneuvering, the Legislature in 1969 enacted a law—chapter 330—decentralizing New York City's school system by establishing a federated system with limited community control effective July 1, 1970. Representing a compromise between the existing system and independent community school districts, the law has been criticized for giving too much and too little power to local communities.

A district is governed by a community school board composed of nine unsalaried members elected at-large for a two-year term by proportional representation (PR). The community school boards have jurisdiction over public schools from the pre-kindergarten level through junior high school. Each board may hire and establish the salary of a district superintendent of schools, contract for repairs and maintenance up to $250,000 annually, determine the curriculum in conformance with city and state standards, recommend school sites, submit an annual budget to the chancellor, select textbooks from lists prepared by the chancellor, operate social centers and recreational programs, and appoint teacher aides.

The citywide Board of Education remains in charge of high schools and special schools not under the jurisdiction of community boards, and is authorized to suspend, remove, or supersede a community school board or remove any of its members. In addition, the Board of Education retains extensive financial and personnel powers, including the preparation of the capital budget, and the disciplining and licensing of teachers.[15]

In discussing public education, or for that matter any other governmental service, Zimmerman offers a very enlightening observation: "Professionalism and the tenets of the municipal reform are under attack in large American cities by populists who contend that institutional arrangements have maximized the wrong values by placing too much emphasis upon centralization of power in city hall, professionalism, economy, and efficiency, and paying too little attention to responsiveness as a criterion of democratic government."[16]

Having established sufficient background material surrounding the complex issue of community involvement, participation, and control, we shall proceed to address directly the concept of community control of police organizations.

Ostrom and Whitaker observe that two types of remedies are most frequently recommended for reducing overt antagonism, mistrust, and hatred of the police by many black citizens. One remedy involves increasing the "professionalism" of the police. According to James Q. Wilson, a "professional" police department is one governed by values derived from general, impersonal rules which bind all members of the organization and whose relevance is independent of circumstances of time, place, or personality. Professional departments are said to have attributes which include the following:

1. Recruitment on the basis of achievement.
2. Treatment of equals in an equal fashion.
3. Negative attitudes toward graft both within the force and in the community.
4. Commitment to training of generally applicable standards.
5. Bureaucratic distribution of authority.

In communities served by "professionalized" departments, law enforcement may be stricter, but it is thought to be more equally applied to all groups in the community than in nonprofessional departments. Reliance upon brutality as a means of social control is thought to be less within such departments than in nonprofessional departments.

However, tensions between black citizens and the police have not lessened in cities with police departments described as highly professionalized. Two of the departments most frequently characterized as "professional," Oakland and Los Angeles, have also been observed to take strong punitive actions against blacks.[17]

Ostrom and Whitaker suggest that police professionalism may have served more to insulate the police against external criticism than to reduce the level of discrimination by police against black citizens. James Q. Wilson, who has been a firm advocate of police professionalism, has argued that professionalism among police officers will differ from professionalism in other occupations in that the primary function of the professional code will be to protect the practitioner from the client rather than the client from the practitioner.[18]

The second proposal to alleviate the growing tension between black citizens and the police is community control of the police. Proponents argue that reducing the size of local police jurisdictions and bringing the jurisdiction under the control of citizens living in the community served will increase the capacity of local police to provide services needed by community residents. This may be expected to increase citizens' satisfaction with police.[19]

After analyzing some of the arguments surrounding the issue of community control of the police, Ostrom and Whitaker derived nine propositions to elucidate the theoretical issues involved in this problem.

The propositions are enumerated as follows:

1. Police officers and police administrators working in small sized police agencies will have better information about the area they serve and conditions in the field than their counterparts in larger agencies.
2. Citizens living in community-controlled jurisdictions will have more capability to articulate demands for service, will have better knowledge about the police and will provide more support for the police than citizens living in citywide controlled jurisdictions.
3. An increase in the capacity of citizens to articulate demands for service more effectively and an increase in their knowledge about the police will be associated with an increase in the knowledge that police officers and police administrators have of citizen preferences.
4. An increase in the citizens' knowledge about police will be associated with an increase in their support of police.
5. An increase in citizens' support of police will be associated with an increase in the levels of police output.
6. An increase in the knowledge of police officers about the area they are serving and about citizen preferences will be associated with an increase in the levels of police output.
7. An increase in the knowledge of police administrators of field conditions in their area will be associated with an increase in their effective control over actions of their department.
8. An increase in the effective control of police administrators over actions of their department will be associated with an increase in the levels of police output.
9. An increase in the levels of police output will be associated with an increase in citizen support for the police.[20]

To fully appreciate these nine propositions while sensitizing oneself to the parameters of the issues in the concept of community control of the police, the following section will specifically focus on arguments put forth that would either support or not support the general issue of community control.

PROS AND CONS OF COMMUNITY CONTROL

Among the arguments against community control are: it supports separatism; it creates balkanization; it enables minority-group "hustlers" to be just as opportunistic and disdainful of the have-nots as were their white predecessors; it is incompatible with merit systems and professionalism; and ironically enough, it can turn out to be a new Mickey Mouse game for the have-nots by allowing them to gain control but not allowing them sufficient dollar resources to succeed.[21]

Ostrom and Whitaker enumerate the arguments against community control as follows:

The first argument is that community control supports separatism. The assertion is made that given existing patterns of residential segregation, the population of local communities would be more racially homogeneous than the population of city-wide districts. Once boundaries were drawn, the tendency toward homogeneity of communities would be increased as citizens scurried to move out of areas where they were racially in the minority. The resulting pattern might lead to the establishment of legalized segregation with the police forces in each type of community much more oriented to abusing members of the minority race in that community than now occurs in the big city.

The second argument is that community control creates balkanization of public services and is more costly and less efficient. This is an old argument repeatedly presented by advocates of metropolitan-wide governments. Advocates of metropolitan government recommend the *elimination* of most of the currently established units of local government in metropolitan areas. Metropolitan reformers assume that economies of scale exist for all public services and thus urge the creation of one or a few large-scale public jurisdictions to serve an entire metropolitan area. Those associated with this movement would argue that decreasing the size of police agencies and increasing their number within a particular metropolitan area would increase the costs of service and lead to grave problems of coordination among diverse agencies.

The third argument against community control is that local decision-making within small communities may be more "undemocratic" than within larger units (Kristol, 1968; Perlmutter, 1968). Advocates of this position point to the record of larger jurisdictions to move more rapidly toward integration, especially in the employment of blacks in public agencies. They also point to the low turnout of voters and the ineffective bickering among "poverty representatives" in many of the early community action programs. Because of the relative homogeneity of an individual community, they also argue that there would be less orientation to challenge local leaders who may be more demogogic than leaders of large, heterogeneous city governments. The intimacy of the local community may lead to corruption and lack of uniform enforcement practice (Wilson, 1968b; Prewitt and Eulau, 1969; for a different argument, see Rossi, 1963, p. 12).

The fourth argument is that small, community controlled police departments will be less professional. It is assumed that a relatively large department is needed to be able to afford adequate salaries, good training facilities and sufficient levels in the bureaucracy to achieve meaningful advancement for the ambitious young officer (Altshuler, 1970, p. 39). It is frequently argued that small departments just cannot attract the caliber of employees equivalent to that of large departments.

Finally, it is argued that community control may be a futile strategy if significant re-allocation of resources were not also accomplished at the same time. Impoverished areas would remain just that—impoverished areas. Once separated from the rest of the city, black citizens would find it difficult to obtain from white citizens living in separate jurisdictions the resources needed for effective programs. Community control might prove to be a cruel joke. Those in "control" would not have sufficient resources to be able to accomplish their goals. (See Altshuler, pp. 53–54 for an overview of this argument.) Consequently, the long-run consequences of community control might be further bitterness, disillusionment and alienation among black citizens (Aberback and Walker, 1970, p. 1218).

THE RESPONSE OF PROPONENTS

Proponents of community control have counter arguments for each of the attacks against community control. As to separatism, they argue that segregation is a fact imposed on black citizens by the unwillingness of white citizens to allow integration in any meaningful form (Spear, 1967; Tauber, 1968). Community control would not appreciably increase the amount of segregation and racism currently in existence—it would give to those who had been denied open access to housing a greater opportunity to control what happens in their own neighborhood.

As to the charge that community control would create more small districts, proponents would argue that community control would enable blacks in the center city to have the personalized, small-scale service provided today to whites in the suburbs (Ferry, 1968). Suburban residents have vigorously fought against being included within large, metropolitan wide governmental jurisdictions. Why should black residents of the center city be the only ones who can't have small-scale public agencies willing to serve them? (Rubenstein, 1970; Babcock and Bosselman, 1967; Press, 1963.)

Some proponents of community control have also argued that economies of scale do not exist for such services as police and education and that, consequently, community control may not lead to an increase in the cost of local services. Many proponents of community control urge the continuance of large-scale agencies to provide such services as transportation, water, sewage, and to help provide some of the financing for smaller units within the larger unit.

As to the level of democratic government possible in small units, proponents of community control argue that once black citizens had genuine control concerning local affairs, participation levels would increase (Gittell, 1968). Participation in many programs in the past has been low. However, proponents would argue that it is unreasonable to expect participation to be high in newly organized arrangements whose potential benefits are highly nebulous. Many of the past programs have used "participation" as a therapy device rather than as a means to enable local people to control significant events affecting them (Mogulof, 1969; Arnstein, 1969). People do not learn to participate actively or constructively in a short time period. If meaningful control were placed in the community, individuals would begin to learn that it was worthwhile to participate and how to participate more constructively. Once community control were established, the effect of having local public officials sympathetic to the needs and aspirations of local citizens would decrease the general level of alienation among black citizens living within the ghetto of a typical large American city. The supposed openness of larger jurisdictions to more widespread employment of blacks has been considered a sham by many. "In no major American city does the police force approximate the ratio of Negroes in the community and at the officer and policy making levels, the disparities increase."

Concerning professionalization, proponents of community control argue that many of the consequences of "professionalization" have been to keep blacks from obtaining jobs due to false education requirements or middle-class biased examinations. The establishment of less bureaucratized forces with police living in the community they serve and sympathetic to the life style of the residents is seen as a benefit rather than a cost.

As to the argument that community control without redistribution may lead to more alienation and distrust in the long run, several counter-arguments are made. For some advocates, there is considerable doubt about the value of current levels of redistribution. As Altshuler summarizes:

> Many black leaders argue . . . that the apparent redistribution which now occurs within cities is of little value to the supposed beneficiaries. They contend, for example, that the police who are both white and indifferent to community wishes constitute more of a provocation to disorder and violence than a preventative (Altshuler, 1970, p. 149).

Secondly, many of the needs of poor areas are not solved by the mere infusion of more economic resources. Frequently, the need is to fit public services to the particular needs of a community. Milton Kotler describes the deliberation of a community corporation in a poor neighborhood of Columbus, Ohio concerning medical services. Doctors were proposing "fancy new clinics with interns rotating the work day by day." However, the people in the neighborhood corporation "said no, they didn't need anything as elaborate as a big clinic. What they needed was a night doctor. . . . Neighborhoods like this need doctors who work on a different schedule." (Kotler, 1968, p. 16). Many (but, of course, not all) of the problems of the ghetto relate to the need for services more tailored to residents' own needs (Itzkoff, 1969). In the third place, the financing of a public jurisdiction does not always have to come entirely from the area itself. It is possible to devise redistribution formulas which are related to larger units providing some of the funds for smaller units. Effective organization of the local community may enable sufficient pressure to be brought at the state or federal level to achieve significant redistribution of resources. Such resources could then be utilized in the way local residents prefer rather than as a result of decisions made by white, middle-class officials for them.[22]

Zimmerman elucidates the pro and con approach to community control by offering the thought that we must seek more empirical support if we are to meaningfully analyze the pro and con positions of community control issues.

Advocates of community control maintain that a system of neighborhood government will prove beneficial in ghetto neighborhoods by restoring a sense of community. Unfortunately, this conclusion has little empirical support. The highly mobile population and relatively large size of proposed neighborhood governments—a population as great as 250,000—would make impossible the development of a deep-felt sense of community. On the contrary, many ghetto residents have developed a sense of rootlessness. The theory of neighborhood government is based upon the assumption that there is a coalescence of common interests within a definable geographic territory. It is apparent, however, that conflict may be more prevalent in many neighborhoods than a commonality of interests. In New York City, for example, we find blacks and Puerto Ricans fighting for control of neighborhood corporations and Model Cities citizen committees.[23]

One would be on tenuous ground to conclude that neighborhood governments will revitalize democracy on the local level by dramatically increasing citizen participation. Such a conclusion is wishful thinking, as low citizen participation is a fact of political life in a day and age when there are many diversions, including television. As the locus of authority in the city becomes loci, with the devolution of political power, citizens hopefully will be able to identify more readily with neighborhood governments because of their smaller scale; this identification may take the form of greater citizen participation. We would be deceiving ourselves, however, if we concluded that idealized town meeting democracy could be replicated on the neighborhood level in large cities, as we know that disadvantaged citizens are relatively apathetic.[24]

There is little evidence to suggest that neighborhood governments would be more innovative or able to provide services more economically than the existing municipal governments; the latter are more likely to benefit from economies of scale. Although ghetto residents may be quite willing to try innovations, it is unlikely that they will be able, on the basis of their limited education and experience, to develop innovations that will be more beneficial than innovations developed by professionals.[25]

Riedel views the issue of community control not simply as a mechanical problem, but as an immense political problem. In his view, changing the forms of representation, or protecting the existing ones, are political questions because the outcome may shift control over enforced values and the distribution of scarce resources from one aggregation of groups to another. Without any intent to discourage anyone from any effort to advance worthy goals, even through gimmicks and euphemisms, it may still be useful to review some of the harsh political realities about citizen participation.

1. Even under the best of conditions, most people tend to *avoid* participation involvement.
2. Our political system favors group over individual action, coalitions of groups (parties) even more so, but most individuals are activated only by single issues and are turned off by coalitions.
3. Localizing control does not necessarily *increase* participation.
4. Resistance to action tends to increase with the seriousness of the problem.
5. Citizen groups working outside the "system" tend to handicap themselves.

6. Official and citizen views of participation tend to be inherently contradictory.
7. Officially sponsored citizen participation tends to be cooptation rather than representation.
8. Direct citizen action, forcing governmental response, although seemingly hostile to the system, has strong historic support.
9. In this pragmatic society, the appropriate form of citizen participation is the one that works.[26]

Riedel also offers several postulates which further impose political realities into the discussion and analysis of community control. Much of the talk and writing suggest that the primary resistance to greater citizen participation comes from a reluctant system—from government. The first postulate is that while the resistance is there, what is far more obvious is that most people do not want to become involved in public policy formation beyond the very impersonal (secret) act of voting. And among those who are willing to be even marginally involved, more seem to be willing to sit around and make big decisions than to exert themselves in the slightest to translate those decisions into effective administrative or political action. How can you build an administrative structure on the dubious supposition that the relevant public will have actively participated when only self-selected spokespersons step forward?[27]

A second postulate is that most people drawn into politics are activated by a single issue, and a few more by not more than two or three that are often related. The most unreliable people in any political party organization are those with single-issue orientation. When there is no opportunity for trade-off in which each of several interests can get something it wants, there is almost no hope of holding a (party) coalition together. The strength of groups within coalitions (parties) is their ability to deliver support to other-group objectives in the expectation of support for the home group's program. Groups working alone outside the party system are easily put off. Issues can be blurred. Leaders can be momentarily discredited at little cost. Any visible attention to the problem by a statusful official or relevant public agency, whether or not it leads to a solution, tends to placate supporters and reduce the bargaining power of leaders.[28]

The third postulate relevant to this discussion is that, although it may have been true in earlier times, decentralizing jurisdictions to keep government close to the people concerned produces less rather than more participation. The poorest voter turnout is found at school board elections despite the relatively large proportion of taxes consumed by education and the presumed critical value-formation and social-perception roles of employees of those boards. With rare exceptions, public attendance at school board meetings ranges from nil to inconsequential.[29]

The fourth postulate is that problems serious or big enough to require government intervention tend to meet resistance, sometimes characterized as nonresponsiveness, regardless of the unit of jurisdiction or the empathy and rationality of the officials concerned. Nearly every decision that can be made in such cases involves a reallocation of scarce resources—money, personnel, time, and materials—which means denying others something they think they need and are entitled to, in order to meet a more pressing claim on those resources. And that means trouble no matter which way one turns. What will more citizen participation add to this dilemma?[30]

Riedel's understanding of the current upsurge in participation interest is that many are not talking about representative participation at all. They are asking for a direct transfer or reallocation of political (governmental) power, without having to achieve it through the tedious requirements of the existing political system. This is the pursuit of a phantom. Insofar as any redistribution of power is likely to occur, it will be because such individuals and groups who succeed will have, whether wittingly or unwittingly, played the age-old political game and won.[31]

For those who use the euphemism "shared-power" for "participation," the appropriate literature for guidance is practical politics, not organization and management. People do not give up power to others unless they no longer need it, can no longer sustain it for personal reasons, or are forced to do so. If the power involved is transferable and useful, there is almost always an heir apparent in the wings. In this light, talking of community control groups as if the government were about to surrender anything more than nominal power is to entertain a dangerously false expectation. If the governmental agency does not know pretty well how that power is going to be used, and is capable of withdrawing it on short notice, it would be a most improbable transfer. If the recipients of such a grant of power are satisfied with those terms, they are settling for a license, a franchise to perform a limited function in a limited area, subject to conditions and terms set by the larger public. There is nothing new in that form of "participation" except new services covered by a very old principle. That should create no great problem for governments, and might well be a constructive outlet.[32]

CHALLENGE TO POLICE AND PUBLIC ADMINISTRATION THEORY

In light of the changes that have occurred since 1949—from nonindigenous to indigenous citizen representation, and from adviser-persuader to coalition-adversary decision maker—what types of citizen participation will emerge in the years ahead? What roles and responsibilities will the various levels of government assume? What problems will have to be surmounted in order to reach alienated citizens, reform unresponsive bureaucracies, and eliminate ineffective services? And what are the implications of the likely style of citizen participation in the 1980s for the teaching and practice of public administration?[33]

The citizen participation movement in the 1980s will be accompanied by demands for major changes in the values, training, and rewarding of public administrators. Increased pressure will be placed on bureaucracies and on schools of public administration to make their efforts relevant to the times. Less attention will be given to the conflict between citizen involvement and traditional public administration, and more concern will be directed to the ways in which their common purpose— effective delivery of services—can be achieved through cooperative action. Many public administrators will need to undergo certain attitudinal modifications, such as being more inclined to take to the streets to find out firsthand if public services are adequate for resident needs, and be more willing to tolerate delays, inefficiencies, and disruptions in planning and programming stemming from citizen participation. Rapport with clients is a critical, and too often neglected criterion that will need to be given a more important place in the administrative reward systems.[34]

These types of citizen involvement are commonly thought to be antithetical to much of public administration theory and practice. The idea of "clients" having a voice in the determination of such policies as service levels, staffing patterns, and budgetary priorities is often considered to be unacceptable to administrators. This is particularly the case if the clients happen to be low-income, minority, or uneducated, and if they desire to do more than merely offer advice or be informed of decisions. In this sense, there is built-in conflict between citizen participation and the middle-class values of bureaucrats, the objectives of the merit system, and the traditional principles of hierarchy and professionalism found in American administrative thought.[35]

Not only will public administrators have to increase their face-to-face contacts with the community and to share their authority with citizen representatives, but they might also have to recognize the relevance of the concept of advocacy, which has been receiving more and more attention in the planning profession. "Advocate bureaucrats" working for community groups would, among other functions, serve as grantsmen in identifying sources of funds and preparing the necessary applications, help residents gain access to key decision makers, cut red tape, and supervise the operation of neighborhood-controlled programs. More important, they would work within the bureaucracy as proponents of their client's views regarding community needs and the best ways to meet them.[36]

To sum up, citizens in large cities generally are interested only in the delivery of quality services. As long as quality services in adequate amounts are delivered on the neighborhood level, the average citizen will be little interested in community control of governmental institutions and functions.[37]

CHALLENGE TO DEVELOP EMPIRICAL ANALYSIS
OF THE COMMUNITY CONTROL CONCEPT

It appears that there are principally four very critical issues that must be addressed in this concept of community control of police organizations. Moreover, it is felt that it is unlikely that one could make an informed judgment on this question until these four critical issues are addressed by empirical field research.

What are regarded as the four critical issues, and what should not be viewed as being mutually exclusive of others, are as follows: first, the issue of how one ensures or restores meaningfully democratic civilian control over police organizations; second, how to realistically engage citizen involvement and participation to reduce police–community alienation, without unilaterally making decisions as to community control that might tend to exacerbate the polarization that presently exists; third, how might we propose to address the issue of representation which extends beyond police organization and into the very fabric of governmental structure; finally, as David Riley has observed, the issue concerning political control of our police organizations, not in terms of whether it exists or does not exist, but in the more realistic terms of who exercises the political control.[38]

In essence, the arguments for and against community control of police organizations will remain at a theoretical level until empirical research which addresses these critical issues has been tested. Moreover, we must also be aware of the vagueness and ambiguity that surrounds the concept of community control. As presently articulated by many persons, little is offered by way of definition to constitute a meaningful guide to the host of public policy considerations that must be made.

Finally, we must be sensitive to the fact that demands for greater community control indicate a strong vitality and interest in our police organizations. This should not necessarily be written off negatively, as it does replace the previous public apathy that confounded police administrators. Moreover, there are numerous situations with both police organizations and other components of our administration of justice system that could benefit from this greater public awareness and interest. For example, one frustrating paradox has been efforts by correctional administrators to gain greater community acceptance to the concept of community-based correctional centers. If criminal justice officials could channel some of the communities' demand for control of police organizations to include that of correctional facilities, perhaps the public's resistance to residential treatment centers would diminish while enlarging the area of responsibility and involvement in many more facets of our criminal justice system. Thus, not ascribing to a few the total responsibility for criminality and its control, but embarking on a much more realistic endeavor of mutual involvement, concern and participation in matters that affect the entire community should quite properly engage the entire community.

Furthermore, demands for greater community control of our administration of justice system in general, and police organizations in particular, reflect a continuing awareness and interest in the situations that confront our criminal justice agencies. We would be well advised to cultivate this community interest instead of resisting it. At the same time, those of us in the criminal justice field should own up to our own responsibilities; for example, we have designed and organized criminal justice agencies that have organizationally emasculated the citizen's interest and participation. How many police, court, and correctional administrators can state that their departments have structured and organizationally provided for definitive pathways and means in which it is possible to engage their citizens' or communities'... concern ... involvement... support ... and participation? In the authors' view, it is the absence of these structured pathways or channels that play a formidable role in the isolationism of our criminal justice agencies, the very issue community control is all about.

Summary

The purpose of this chapter was to explore innovative ways to reduce overt antagonism, mistrust, and sometimes hatred which greets not only our police departments but other agencies of our criminal justice system as well.

This chapter explored the historical emergence of community participation and control in terms of the development of useful models that have been suggested over the years for a variety of public service agencies. The concept of community control as it would apply to police organizations was discussed in terms of remedies to reduce the overt antagonism and mistrust that minorities hold for police organizations. Nine propositions to elucidate the theoretical issues involved were presented, as were the pros and cons of community control strategies. The harsh political realities centering on citizen participation strategies were also discussed.

Finally, the challenge to both police and public administration theory was discussed with reference to developing a more rigorous and empirical analysis of the community control concept.

End Notes

[1]Carl W. Stenberg, "Citizens and the Administrative State: From Participation to Power," *Public Administration Review*, 32, no. 3 (May–June 1972), 191.

[2]Ibid.

[3]Ibid.

[4]Ibid.

[5]Ibid.

[6]Ibid., p. 192.

[7]Ibid.

[8]Ibid., p. 193.

[9]Joseph F. Zimmerman, "Neighborhoods and Citizen Involvement," *Public Administration Review,* 32, no. 3 (May–June 1972), 209.

[10]Ibid.

[11]Stenberg, "Citizens," p. 193.

[12]James A. Riedel, "Citizen Participation: Myths and Realities," *Public Administration Review,* no. 3 (May–June 1972), 216–17. Reprinted from Public Administration Review © 1972 by The American Society for Public Administration, Washington, D.C. All rights reserved.

[13]Ibid.

[14]Ibid.

[15]Zimmerman, "Neighborhoods," pp. 205–6.

[16]Ibid., p. 201.

[17]Elinor Ostrom and Gordon Whitaker, "Black Citizens and the Police: Some Effects of Community Control," paper delivered at the 1971 Annual Meeting of the American Political Science Association, Chicago, Ill., September 7–11, 1971, pp. 2–3. Also see Ostrom and Whitaker, "Community Control and Governmental Responsiveness: The Case of Police in Black Communities," in David Rogers and Willis Hawley, eds., *Improving the Quality of Urban Management,* Vol. 8, Urban Affairs Annual Reviews (Beverly Hills, Calif.: Sage Publications, 1974), 303–34.

[18]Ibid.

[19]Ibid., p. 4.

[20]Ibid., p. 5.

[21]Sherry R. Arnstein, "A Ladder of Citizen Participation," *Journal of the American Institute of Planners,* 35 (July 1969), 224.

[22]Ostrom and Whitaker, "Black Citizens," pp. 6–10.

[23]Zimmerman, "Neighborhoods," p. 206.

[24]Ibid.

[25]Ibid., p. 207.

[26]Riedel, "Citizen Participation," p. 212.

[27]Ibid., p. 213.

[28]Ibid., p. 214.

[29]Ibid.

[30]Ibid.

[31]Ibid., p. 218.

[32]Ibid., p. 219.

[33]Stenberg, "Citizens," p. 194.

[34]Ibid., p. 96.

[35]Ibid., p. 190.

[36]Ibid., pp. 196–197.

[37]Zimmerman, "Neighborhoods," p. 210.

[38]David P. Riley, "Should Communities Control Their Police?" *Civil Rights Digest,* Fall 1969, p. 34.

CHAPTER
THIRTEEN

SUMMARY STATEMENT
AND
RECOMMENDATIONS

INTRODUCTION

If our task is, indeed, redesigning our police system to more clearly meet the social needs and public service needs, perhaps we can begin by creating a bridge between inner-city communities and police departments. Lisa Liebert identified the areas for which this bridge can be made as delinquency, bad housing, unemployment, family disorder, and direct criminal inclination. Since police work is intimately connected to and affected by these areas, what the police require is an area of action that will facilitate their being identified in a helpful role rather than in a punitive role.[1] In short, the punitive role in which the police are seen and the vast number of adversary contacts they experience with the public, by nature of their organizational structure, almost neutralize any aspirations of a police–community relations program.

POLICE AND CITIZEN ENCOUNTER

One of the more important reasons for minimizing the adversary contacts with the public and increasing beneficial contacts is in the interests of decreasing police subcultures.[2] Along these lines, the University of California report recommended that police techniques for interacting with the public be analyzed in terms of the manifest and latent effects upon police–community relations. The emphasis should be toward developing more positive police–public contacts, and one should begin by analyzing the following:[3]

1. The effect of uniform regulations, including the required items of equipment and those additional items which policemen are permitted to carry.
2. The effect of field interrogation and "frisking" practices.
3. The effect of deliberate personnel rotation policies.
4. The effect of policies involving a "show of force."
5. The effect of certain production evaluation measures.
6. The effect of deliberate racial integration of police tours.
7. The effect of motorization of patrol forces.
8. The effect of different enforcement standards.

In analyzing police–citizen interaction, these interactions generally occur in times of stress for either one or both parties. Therefore, the ensuing role enactment of the officer will be appreciably affected, more so than other routine public employee–citizen encounters.[4] Furthermore, police encounters with citizens from minority groups are filled with an extreme amount of uncertainty, for police officers have learned from experience that they must be alert for violence and resentment.[5]

> Policemen understand that the lot of minority people is unenviable, but they are put off by the assertiveness of minorities, possibly because restiveness can threaten social order which the policeman is charged with preserving. Finally, the policeman may resent minorities precisely because they demand so much of him, because they expose him to danger and self-doubt, because they threaten him and yet plead for his help, and because they continually expose police to public scrutiny and oftentimes censure.[6]

McNamara identifies another area that creates confusion for the police in terms of interacting with the public—the inconsistency between a favorable attitude toward the police, specifically when the police are increasing their "service function," and the far-too-pervasive view of the police as consisting of white oppressors. This inconsistency perceived by patrol officers results in uncertainty for implementing their duties, and in some cases, resistance to implementing any "service function" duties.[7]

Another source of uncertainty in police interactions with citizens is simply that police lack the training and knowledge of appropriate interpersonal skills that could be used by police officers in encounters with citizens.[8]

Skolnick identifies another area of uncertainty—when the police officer with good intentions tries to advise a "troller" to leave the area for his own protection. A "troller" is defined as a man walking or driving slowly about an area waiting to be propositioned or to proposition a prostitute. The police officer's motivation is frequently interpreted as acting on the basis of morality, in which case the citizen shows resentment. But in truth, most of the time the officer is more concerned that the man will be robbed or "mugged." The police officer therefore finds the "troller's" resentful response both irrational and confusing, and consequently becomes somewhat cynical and may either order the next troller out of the area quite harshly, or simply ignore the individual.[9]

It does not take too many ambiguous encounters before cynicism helps convince the police that all unfriendly citizens are their natural enemies, and that all citizens are unfriendly.[10] However, it is possible that what might appear to be an unfriendly citizen is nothing more than a defense mechanism being manifested. Unfortunately, the police often react with a defense mechanism of their own; thus both the citizen and the officer become alienated. This might well be founded on a silent misunderstanding, which if communicated, might have proven unfounded to either party.

> If the point of interaction between police officer and citizen is viewed as a confrontation in defense mechanisms, this may facilitate a clearer understanding of why police are regarded, particularly but not solely by minority groups, as an institution to be protected from rather than by.[11]

Frequently, problems of misunderstandings in police–citizen interactions occur primarily because of certain expectations by both parties. Often, there are no specific expectations to guide the police in a given situation; or expectations on either the part of a citizen or an officer are defined to be inappropriate or undesirable.[12] Of course, the problem is the frame of reference from which one looks at a given set of facts or circumstances. When dealing with cultures and subcultures as with police–citizen interactions, what may be an appropriate expectation to one group may be very inappropriate to another. Police–community relations programming must address this area of culture conflict and the part each plays. In these terms, resistance to police–community relations may be a very normal response to those members of the particular subculture whose norms and mores are in opposition to the opposing subculture.

"Assuming that police officers, like most other actors, prefer ordered and routine social encounters to disorganized and unpredictable encounters, then one level or sanction that is available to citizens in encounters with the police is their capacity to disrupt it, particularly to 'make trouble' by denying the legitimacy of police authority."[13] Reiss and Black's observation is most significant because it suggests that citizens can take some form of retaliation to more fully manifest a defense mechanism or to stipulate to police officers that the citizens have received what they consider to be an "inappropriate expectation." If order is to prevail within police–citizen transactions, it depends upon whether citizens are willing to accept police officers as having legitimate authority as much as it depends upon officers' judicious use of their authority. As Reiss and Black suggest, the next important question is: "In what kinds of face-to-face encounters then are citizens most likely to pose a threat to the order of the encounter? Put another way, in what kinds of situations is police–citizen conflict most likely to arise?"[14]

It is quite clear that several factors influence the behavior of both citizens and police officers in their encounters. Most of these factors emerge out of the role conception each has of himself and of the other. However, as Reiss and Black indicate, the type of mobilization situation and the department's policies and system of command and control also influence the police–citizen encounter. Because we lack a base of empirical studies in the area of police–citizen interactions, it is really not possible to assess the consequences of these encounters in our police organizations.[15] This much we do know—one of the patrol officer's most serious problems in police–citizen interaction is that of gaining control of a situation. This is especially critical because most of a patrol officer's duties are nothing more than the ordering of social situations. Related to this problem of social control is the problem of self-control, which Reiss and Black concisely summarize: "For the police officer on patrol, the human relations approach to transactions with citizens is likely to be seen as less urgent than the problem of social control but quite synonymous with the problem of self control.[16]

A most significant contribution of the University of Michigan report was its discovery of the reciprocal expectations of police and citizens. This paradox finds its genesis in the "businesslike," "routinized," or "impersonal" bureaucratic treatment citizens receive from police, or as Reiss and Black state:

> The citizen who treats the officer with civility may regard civility in the officer as a sign of disrespect. And, the officer who meets civility in the citizen may perceive it as a sign of disrespect. The paradox arises because of their reciprocal expectations. The citizen wants the officer to behave with more than civility; he wants to be treated as a "person" or with what has come to be termed a "human relations" perspective. The officer wants the citizen to behave with more than civility, to show deference to his authority.[17]

The dilemma this presents to the police is how to become more "involved" with their clients on a personal level and yet retain the impartiality that the police organization demands of them as professional officers. Police resistance to involvement with their clients cannot simply be addressed by "human relations" seminars, because resistance is embedded in the organizational structure of our police system more than it is in the personality structure of those working within the system, although this, too, is a factor.

Expectations for deference and for personal treatment lie outside a system of civil bureaucratic treatment. In part, this arises because the police continue to operate within a "traditional bureaucracy" where legitimate authority is at the center while the citizen increasingly demands a "human relations bureaucracy" where the "person" is at the center. Clearly the problem lies in the structure and operation of organizations.[18]

This, more than most commentaries, certainly illustrates the pervasive and systematic impact structural and organizational deficiencies can have on police–community relations considerations.

CONFLICTING DEMANDS MADE ON POLICE BY CITIZENS AND THE POLICE ORGANIZATION

Policing in a democratic society may well be a job of maintaining or resolving conflicting situations, because determinations as to when order becomes "disorder" or when social becomes "antisocial" are decisions frequently made by the police in their observance of guidelines; these also frequently incur various appeals from a public which itself is more than divided on many of these situations.[19]

Blum explains the genesis of much of the conflict experienced by the officer.

Perhaps the most serious of all problems that plague the policeman is public acceptance. Here is the root of much of his uncertainty and job-caused conflict. The public has not yet made up its mind that it really wants a policeman. . . . Part of the public's uncertainty is because of this American rebellion against authority. . . . The public knows it *needs* policemen, but actually *wanting* them is another matter.[20]

Moreover, the police themselves are the object of conflicting standards, for as James Q. Wilson states: "Society wants police officers who cannot be bribed but it also wants to bribe police officers."[21]

The dilemma of the police in their ghetto-patrolling activities is another formidable problem in conflicts. Since the police want to maintain order in the ghetto, they carry out the normal functions of their duties. However, the police are painfully aware that these same patrolling techniques can provide the spark to ignite a riot, for which the police will ultimately receive much blame.

Thus it is on the one hand understandable that police should engage in such encounters. On the other hand, this reluctance has the unintended effect of increasing the danger of ghetto living for the black man or woman who is leading a reasonably law abiding existence. Accordingly, the police come to be seen not as protectors of those who need assistance against the depredations of gang activity, but rather as those who fail in their essential task of maintaining public order.[22]

Another dilemma facing the police is that while they are responsible for maintaining peace and order in our cities, the laws on which their authority is founded are frequently incompatible with the methods by which the police guarantee the community the peace and tranquility that the community demands.[23] A significant conflict identified in the violence that occurred during the 1968 Democratic National Convention was that two of our fundamental American rights were in conflict. "How can we assure both a people's right to dissent and a community's right to protect its citizens and property?"[24] Even more significantly, how can a role be structured for the police which will protect both rights, yet enforce the law when one right is abused at the expense of the other?

Another conflict occurs regarding the changing nature of our democratic society, and as Frederick Routh suggests: "Hopefully, part of the role of the police department is to see that change remains orderly, and to see, too, that there is no interference with orderly change as it takes place."[25] This, however, is a difficult task for the police officer to accomplish since the police are defenders of the status quo by the nature of their job. "[Their] job is not to lead social revolutions or to militate for new laws. A person interested in vigorous social innovation would hardly adopt police work as a career."[26]

A more direct conflict pertaining to police–community relations units is simply: How can the unit effectively relate with the minority community without alienating itself from the rest of the police department? The corollary, which is to remain on good terms with the police department, frequently means the minority community will be alienated.[27]

Police administrators themselves are thrust into a conflict situation when they desire to be responsive to the complaints of a citizen over an officer's behavior. An administrator knows that the reaction of the force to this posture could very easily create internal management problems.[28] This, itself, might explain another reason for police resistance to police–community relations.

In summary, the problems of conflict that are manifested by many police–citizen interactions suggest that, once again, structural and organizational deficiencies are the real forum to address concerning police–community relations. In concluding this section on police–citizen interaction, perhaps Colin MacInnes best summarizes the police position and dilemma when he states

> They are doing the difficult and dangerous job society demands without any understanding by society of what their moral and professional problems are. The public uses the police as a scapegoat for its neurotic attitudes toward crime. Janus-like, we have always turned two faces toward a policeman. We expect him to be human and yet inhuman. We employ him to administer the law, and yet ask him to waive it. We resent him when he enforces a law in our own case, yet demand his dismissal when he does not elsewhere. We offer him bribes, yet denounce corruption. We expect him to be a member of society, yet not share its values. We admire violence, even against society itself, but

condemn force by the police on our behalf. We tell the police that they are entitled to information from the public, yet we ostracize informers. We ask for crime to be eradicated, but only by the use of "sporting" methods.[29]

Bayley and Mendelsohn, in *Minorities and the Police,* also offer meaningful suggestions toward improving police–community relations. Their approach to offering solutions to police–community relations problems is much like that proposed in the University of California report, in which one of the fundamental approaches is to fully appreciate the structural nature of the problem. In other words, "tension between police and minorities is not a function simply of malevolent personalities. It is a function of different social roles and positions. Solutions must, therefore, be founded on an understanding of the structure of the worlds of the police officer and the minority individual."[30]

Couched in these terms, one immediately perceives how empty and impractical the suggestion of a "breakdown in communication" is to a possible solution to the problem of establishing better police–community relations. "Communications have indeed broken down, but the very reasons that have led to this rupture reduce the chances that further talk can be fruitful."[31] To subscribe to the "breakdown in communications" theory presumes that there was once a flow of communications between the police and the community, a presumption that is not accurate.

The following recommendations are essentially what Bayley and Mendelsohn envision as meaningful ways to improve police–community relations:

Solutions to tension between police and minorities should not be overpersonalized. . . . One can no more achieve a solution to police–minority antagonism by weeding out prejudiced policeman than one can eliminate urban riots by seeking out "outside agitators."

Policemen sincerely want to ease the tension between themselves and minority groups. Policemen are aware of the ambiguous position they occupy; they are not insensitive to what minority people think of them. Solutions to police–minority problems must be built upon the policeman's own desire for eased relationships. He must be approached as a partner in the enterprise, and not as a rogue who must be reformed despite himself.

If reform is to work, policemen must not be talked down to. They are exceedingly knowledgeable not only about the requirements for successful police work but about minority problems and minority perspectives on the law. . . .

Policemen for their part must recognize the hollowness of the dictum that their exclusive duty is to enforce the law and not to become involved with social reform. . . . If police–minority relations are going to be improved, it will only be if policemen admit among themselves and then to the public that sensitivity to social problems is a prime ingredient of successful police operations.

Policemen must begin openly and creatively to study and discuss the discretionary aspects of their work. . . . It is in society's interest and theirs, not that discretion be eliminated, but that it be employed intelligently, sensitively and foresightedly. . . .

They [the police] must not fall too quickly into the habit of treating all relations with minorities as being of an adversary character. Most importantly of all, they must not turn a deaf ear upon minority grievances just because they are couched in the language of demands. And they must not assume that a gain for minorities is a loss either for the police or the majority community.

The police cannot be expected to eliminate urban violence. They may not even be able to contain it successfully. The majority community must not become so preoccupied with meeting violence with a police response that it overlooks the deep, pervasive causes of violence.[32]

Bayley and Mendelsohn feel that it is a "profound mistake to conceive of policemen as being adamantly opposed to change in their relations with the community. In many ways, there is nothing they want more."[33]

Whether police are as "pathetically amenable to rehabilitation" as Bayley and Mendelsohn envision is a matter of conjecture, especially in the area of police–community relations.[34] However, the authors are quite accurate in their observation of the police officer's desire for improvement. Yet what the police officer's perception of improvement is and in what areas these needs are centered are probably different from what academicians would consider as appropriate needs of the police.

It is quite clear that police departments must begin to be more creative, more malleable, because these, indeed, are new times and the police are naive if they believe that business can go on as usual.[35]

The responsibility cannot and should not be placed solely with the police. For the police and minority groups are both products of society, and "unless that society is willing to inaugurate changes in patterns of living that touch everyone—dominants as well as minorities—policemen will remain locked with minorities in a relationship of antagonism which neither created, but from which neither can escape."[36]

Michael Banton adds further clarification to this point in his book, *The Policeman in the Community*:

The over identification of the police with responsibility for the maintenance of public order distracts attention from the public's responsibility. It would be advisable to investigate, more carefully than anyone has yet done, what the barriers are to increased public participation in the maintenance of order, and the ways in which other social institutions might be modified to facilitate such participation.[37]

As society is guided in assuming more responsibility, this will ultimately require the entire police system to reexamine its role and to reorganize and restructure its functions so that it becomes something more than a malfunctioning anachronism.[38]

An appropriate way to summarize the points at which police resistance to police–community relations manifests itself would be to conceptualize the main areas from which the points of resistance originate.

Essentially, this research has focused on two areas of police resistance to police–community relations: those of the individual police officer and the police organization. As a result, the following areas have been identified as having a major impact on police resistance to police–community relations.

Areas Under the Individual Police Officer

1. Role conception entails officers' perception of their duties, obligations, and perceived expectations. Of prime concern are those areas that police officers believe to be antithetical to their role perceptions or that seem to undercut their preferred role, such as social worker responsibilities.

2. Police–citizen interactions is an area where patrol officers are exposed to conflicting demands or expectations by both the citizen and the police organization. Of equal importance is the citizen's desire to be treated a "person" or with a human relations perspective, while officers expect more deference to their authority.

3. The patrol officer subculture offers the individual patrol officer membership in a distinct subculture within the larger police subculture. Of essential importance within this area is the normative value structure of the patrol officer subculture and its capacity for manifesting resistance to administrative policies, norms, and other value structures.

4. Individual officers have the ability to manipulate the preemptiveness of their role definition, usually toward a more pronounced law enforcement orientation. This is illustrated by patrol officers' aspiration of gaining more esteem and acceptance from the community. Therefore, the logical adaptation has been a more pronounced law enforcement orientation based on the premise that the community will, of course, accord this role the appropriate prestige and esteem patrol officers seek. Unfortunately, patrol officers have not been prepared for the total frustration they encounter when they find out that the community wants law enforcement-oriented police even less than it wants peacekeeping police.

5. This point comprises the small degree to which role taking or empathy is valued by individual officers and other associated points revolving around a basic confusion between impartiality and involvement. Of special interest is the manner in which patrol officers protect themselves from citizens with whom they are interacting. For example, in many instances officers specifically project a very impersonal bearing or attitude, not so much because they are against improved police–community relationships, but more as a defense from the client (e.g., to protect themselves from role conflict, role strain, or some other role dilemma or frustration to which a different role enactment would make them vulnerable).

6. Individual patrol officers manifest a role distance to the demands for which improved police–community relations programming calls. The training needs of individual patrol officers and police officers as a group are of interest in this regard. More often than not, officers perceive the

need for additional training in police–community relations in other officers with whom they have worked, as opposed to their own individual or overall department needs. Furthermore, the attitude of "police–community relations is an important area—but not really my job" deserves further analysis.

Areas Under the Police Organization

1. Administrative styles of management and leadership place emphasis on managerial efficiency as opposed to the consideration of individuals. This is exemplified by the police organization's orientation to the protection of the total community to such a degree that its members lose sight of the fact that the community is composed of nothing more than individuals.

2. Ideological values and philosophies of the police organization. For example, the value that no special favoritism be accorded anyone or any group frequently encounters difficulty when minority groups manifest political power and influence to make the police organization more responsive to their needs. Another area within this ideological dimension is the trend toward professionalism. This trend deserves extensive research simply because some of the characteristics of a professionally oriented police department might well generate more police–community relations problems than those it would hope to eliminate.

3. The limitations of organizational and structural deficiencies are of special importance to the unintended resistance to police–community relations. Although our research enumerated 16 areas where organizational deficiencies and limitations contributed to police–community relations resistance, this does not suggest that the list is all-inclusive.

4. The socialization process, the way in which the police organization recruits, trains, and rewards its members, plays a prominent role in the police organization's resistance to police–community relations.

5. The identification or absence of specific goals and objectives structures to a large degree police resistance to police–community relations.

6. The police organization either defines its clientele or maintains that it is a service organization without a client. This is an area that induces police resistance to police–community relations, and as such, requires immediate research.

Since a police organization and its members do not operate in a vacuum, this analysis also suggests various dimensions from which the public or general community influences resistance to police–community relations.

Areas Under the General Community

1. The view of the police as pariahs, in which the community suggests that the job of the police is important while it withholds appropriate prestige, status, and esteem. Police–community relations improvements will not occur simply because of a focus on the police alone; the general community also has an important responsibility.

2. The employment of individuals as police does not relieve the community from its responsibilities toward maintenance of law and order. In fact, this dimension will require innovative approaches of transferring back to the community and other social institutions their responsibility for the peacekeeping function.

3. An all-too-obvious area is that there appears to have been far too much presumed consensus; this is the dilemma of the community coming to terms with its admitted need of police organizations but not its desire to have these organizations.

4. Another area entails the overreliance on the police department as an agency of social control, while not providing additional impetus for an inquiry into problems that cause and create a need for a social control agency in the first place.

5. The community shares a responsibility with the police organization for maintenance of social order. Until the community fully acknowledges these responsibilities, there is little hope that police alone can do the job.

6. Perhaps the most devastating dimension, not only for police organizations, but also for minority groups, is simply the refusal of the general community to voluntarily become involved in the plight of the less fortunate members of society who do not share in the overall affluence and hopes that the majority of the white community possesses, or at least to which it has access.

These are but a small number of areas around which many specific points of resistance to police–community relations can become manifest. However, it is hoped that this research has projected areas for future research and insight into the extreme complexity of the problem of police resistance to police–community relations.

The problem of police resistance to police–community relations is simply not that of a group of people prejudiced toward minority groups, although this may well be a dimension of the problem. The complexity of the problem cannot be properly addressed by sensitivity training for police, although this may possess some remedial value. The problem of police resistance to police–community relations cuts across all lines, and as such, will require a total reevaluation of our municipal police departments and their functions and mission. Above all, it will require an involvement by the public to such a degree that a complete inventory must be taken of a community's responsibility, not only for the maintenance of order, but more important, for the reintegration of less fortunate members of society who are living in exile within the most affluent nation in all civilization.

End Notes

[1]Lisa Liebert, "Police–Community Relations and the Role of the Non-professional," unpublished paper for the New Careers Development Center, New York University, January 1968, p. 10.

[2]Ben Whitaker, *The Police* (Harmondsworth, Middlesex, England: Penguin Books, 1964), p. 170.

[3]Joseph D. Lohman and Gordon E. Misner, *The Police and the Community,* President's Commission on Law Enforcement and Administration of Justice, Field Survey IV, Vol. 2 (Washington, D.C.: Government Printing Office, 1966), pp. 313–14.

[4]David H. Bayley and Harold Mendelsohn, *Minorities and the Police: Confrontation in America* (New York: Free Press, a division of Macmillan Publishing Co., Inc., © 1968), p. 85.

[5]Ibid., p. 169.

[6]Ibid., p. 169–70.

[7]John H. McNamara, "Uncertainties in Police Work: The Relevance of Police Recruits' Backgrounds and Training," in *The Police: Six Sociological Essays,* ed. David J. Bordua (New York; Wiley, 1967), p. 167.

[8]Ibid., p. 168.

[9]Jerome H. Skolnick, *Justice without Trial: Law Enforcement in a Democratic Society* (New York: Wiley, 1966), p. 99.

[10]International City Managers' Association, *Municipal Police Administration,* 5th ed. (Chicago: The International City Managers' Association, 1961), p. 457.

[11]Thomas A. Johnson, "Police–Community Relations: Attitudes and Defense Mechanisms," *Issues in Criminology,* 4, no. 1 (1968), 76.

[12]McNamara, "Uncertainties in Police Work," pp. 172–73.

[13]University of Michigan, *Studies in Crime and Law Enforcement in Major Metropolitan Areas,* vol. 2, report of a research study submitted to the President's Commission on Law Enforcement and the Administration of Justice (Washington, D.C.: U.S. Government Printing Office, 1967), pp. 10–11.

[14]Ibid., p. 12.

[15]Ibid., p. 13.

[16]Ibid., p. 27.

[17]Ibid., pp. 57–58.

[18]Ibid.

[19]Eleanor Harlow, "Problems in Police–Community Relations," *National Council on Crime and Delinquency,* 1, no. 5 (1969), 19.

[20]Richard H. Blum, "The Problems of Being a Police Officer," in *Police Patrol Readings,* ed. Samuel Chapman (Springfield, Ill.: Charles C Thomas, 1964), pp. 44–45.

[21]James Q. Wilson, "The Police and Their Problems: A Theory," *Public Policy,* 12 (1963), 204.

[22]Jerome H. Skolnick, *The Police and the Urban Ghetto,* Research Contribution of the American Bar Foundation, No. 3 (Chicago: American Bar Foundation, 1968), p. 8.

[23]Skolnick, *Justice without Trial,* p. 234.

[24]Ibid.

[25]Frederick Routh, "The Police Role in a Democratic Society," in *Police and Community Relations: A Sourcebook,* ed. A. F. Brandstatter and Louis A. Radelet (Encino, Calif.: Glencoe Press, 1968), p. 277.

[26]Bayley and Mendelsohn, *Minorities and the Police,* p. 28.

[27]Skolnick, *Police and Urban Ghetto,* p. 20.

[28]President's Commission on Law Enforcement and Administration of Justice, *Task Force Report: The Police* (Washington, D.C.: U.S. Government Printing Office, 1967), p. 20.

[29]Whitaker, *The Police,* pp. 170–71.

[30]Bayley and Mendelsohn, *Minorities and Police,* p. 203.

[31]Ibid., p. 205.

[32]Ibid., p. 198–202.

[33]Ibid., p. 56.

[34]Ibid.

[35]Ibid., p. 206.

[36]Ibid.

[37]Michael Banton, *The Policeman in the Community* (New York: Basic Books, 1964), pp. 267–68.

[38]Eleanor Harlow, "Problems in Police Community Relations," *National Council on Crime and Delinquency,* 1, no. 5 (1969), 31.

APPENDIX
I

INVENTORY
OF POLICE–COMMUNITY
RELATIONS PROGRAMS

The term "police–community relations" has been interpreted in various ways by different police agencies. This can account, in part, for the diversity of programs developed by police departments to deal with their community relations problems. This also suggests that articulation of the definition of police–community relations will influence an agency's programmatic approach.

In its broadest context, the term "police–community relations" refers to all contacts between the members of a police agency and the residents of the community it serves. In general, a community consists not only of individuals but also of organizations and institutions to which those individuals belong."[1] Members of a police department can be defined as all of the agency's sworn personnel, from the top administrator to the patrol officers. Defining police–community relations in the context of these two definitions, it would describe all contacts that any member of the police agency has with individuals or groups in the community, whether the contact is formal or informal.

Such a definition can be graphically illustrated by a three-level scheme

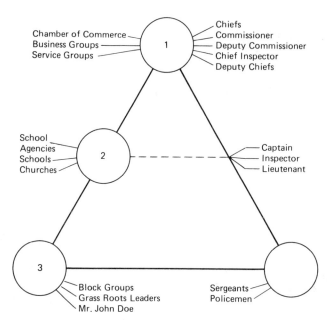

FIGURE A-1 How Police Departments Relate to the Community

showing how all ranks of a police department relate to all segments of the community[2] (see Figure A-1).

Such a scheme is not meant to restrict the upward and downward relationship outside the three-level structure. It is readily recognized that chiefs of police have as much responsibility to establish relationships with "grass-roots leaders" and "Mr. and Mrs. John Doe" as they do with chambers of commerce and business groups. By the same token, it is recognized that sergeants and patrolmen should not be restricted from exposure to categories at level 1.

Accepting such a definition implies that every member of a police department is a community relations officer. However, the turmoil of the 1960s caused many police agencies to realize that what was considered to be everyone's duty turned out to be no one's responsibility. As a result, many police departments proceeded to establish specialized police–community relations units for the purpose of dealing with the pressing problems surrounding the police relationship with the community.

A survey conducted in 1967 revealed that 237 of 1,129 cities responding had an ongoing police–community relations program (see Table A-1.[3])

The fact that such a large number of cities did not have a police–community relations program prompted Michigan State University, after completing a national study on police–community relations, to make the following recommendation to the President's Commission on Law Enforcement and Administration of Justice:

> It is recommended that police agencies develop extensive, formal, and comprehensive community relations programs. Two points deserve special emphasis in this regard: (1) The vital importance of developing effective liaisons between the police agency and all significant population elements in the community served by the agency, especially with groups known to be unfriendly or hostile toward the police; and (2) a really meaningful police and community relations program in a police agency saturates the entire organization, at every level. Ideally, it is total orientation, permeating every facet of police operations: policy, supervision, personnel practices, training and education, planning and research, complaint machinery, and of course, the community relations unit itself, whatever it may be called. A police administrator does not establish a community relations program entirely by activating a special unit, or by adding a few hours of special instruction in police training courses. Community relations must permeate the entire fabric of the organization and in a meaningful manner, not merely as "the current kick" in the department or as a matter of "window dressing."[4]

Although one city reported that it established its police–community relations program as early as 1930, the vast majority of the programs were established during the mid-1960s, as shown in Table A-2[5].

The structure of police–community relations programs differs from city to city. It is, however, possible to illustrate the difference between a structured and a nonstructured program, as indicated in Table A-3.[6]

An examination of ongoing programs shows that programs in police–community relations have been developed in three broad areas: (1) the general public, (2) youth, and (3) special-interest groups.

TABLE A-1 Cities with Police-Community Relations Programs

Population Group	Number of Cities Reporting	Community Relations Programs	
		Number	*Percent*
Over 500,000	25	18	72
250,000–500,000	27	12	44
100,000–250,000	86	34	40
50,000–100,000	180	63	35
25,000–50,000	264	43	16
10,000–25,000	547	67	12

TABLE **A-2** Year Police-Community Relations Programs Organized

Population Group	Number of Cities Reporting	Earliest	Lower Quartile	Median	Upper Quartile	Latest
Over 500,000	17	1950	1956	1964	1966	1966
250,000–500,000	11	1945	1948	1965	1966	1966
100,000–250,000	32	1955	1961	1964	1966	1966
50,000–100,000	50	1948	1962	1964	1966	1966
25,000–50,000	38	1930	1959	1963	1963	1966
10,000–25,000	63	1950	1960	1963	1963	1966

I. General public
   A. Recognition for those who show an interest in or assist law enforcement
   B. Speakers bureau
   C. Open house
   D. Police–community relations seminars
   E. Programs by the police and citizens
      1. Seat-belt clinics
      2. Crime prevention pamphlets
      3. Public education programs (e.g., radio and television programs)
   F. Neighborhood meetings
   G. Personal contact by police officers
   H. Vacation checks
   I. Distribution of information to new residents
II. Youth
   A. Athletic programs
   B. Sponsorship of youth groups
   C. School programs
   D. Juvenile bureaus
   E. Tutorial programs
   F. Tours with on-duty officers
III. Special-interest groups
   A. Conferences on regular basis
   B. Recruitment of minority police officers
   C. Regular contact with minority press
   D. Assistance in locating employment
   E. Attend meetings of minority-group organizations
   F. Open-door policy to discuss problems
   G. Programs such as summer camps for minority youth
   H. Acceptance of complaints about the department

POLICE AID PROGRAMS

In categorizing the many programs operated under the title of police–community relations, the following definition of police–community relations was used:

TABLE **A-3**   Structured and Nonstructured Police-Community Relations Programs

Structured	Nonstructured
A full-time command officer is assigned to the program	A sergeant is assigned part-time to community relations functions.
A full-time staff consisting of civilians and officers is assigned to the program	No staff. In some instances officers may volunteer off-time for participation in projects.
Formal channels of communication into the community are established	Contact with the community is informal and may filter through such individuals as church leaders, school officials, etc.
Clear identification of the role of the community relations unit vis-à-vis the rest of the department is established.	No clear departmental image of community relations function. Entire department becomes informally involved at various stages.
Establishes program goals in specific target areas.	No specific goals, just the establishment of "healthy community attitudes."
Materials such as newsletters, special reports, etc., are regularly published and distributed in specific neighborhoods.	Materials may be periodically published and dispersed throughout the entire community.

Police–community relations is defined as the process by which the police work in conjunction with the community to identify the problems that cause friction between the two groups and the working together to solve those problems.

If a program has built into it a mechanism whereby there is a meaningful relationship between the police and the citizens designed to identify problems and then work together to solve these problems, it was classified as a police–community relations program. The essential and basic ingredient in making this determination was: Through a particular program, are the citizens given the opportunity to make an input into the policies and procedures of the police agency, or is the program designed simply to arrest a social problem?

Community relations is not selling the police product. If the product is salable you wouldn't have to have community relations. Most of the programs today are public relations oriented. The police are there to tell the people, "these are the laws, and please help us do our jobs." This is the surest way of scuttling a community relations program.[7]

Using the preceding definition, many of the programs that are operated under that title of police–community relations do not fit. Consequently, it is necessary to list them under appropriate categories: public relations, crime prevention/safety education, youth programs, police-community relations training, and police-community relations. Thus, five different categories are used to describe the area of concentration of the various programs rather than one term (police-community relations) which is all-encompassing, vague, and often misleading. By using the definition of police-community relations given previously, the various programs identified are categorized according to their purposes and objectives. For example, if a program has as its basic objective reducing the incidence of crime, it was categorized as a crime prevention program. It is necessary to develop these categories for two reasons: (1) because of our definition of police-community relations, and (2) to avoid confusion. Regarding the latter reason, Winston-Salem, in their program evaluation, discovered an inconsistency as follows:

> There still seems to be some ambiguity in the basic foundation of the program. The program has elements of being a crime-prevention program, and elements of being a community-helping program. Which of these two goals, if either, is to take precedence in the organization and operation of the program is not clear. The program is operating in a schizophrenic fashion. The very basic nature of these goals would seem to point toward an explicit attempt to give precedence to one or the other or an explicit attempt to integrate them in a consistent manner that might reduce some of the uncertainty about the program.[8]

It should be kept in mind that no attempt was made to identify the many police-community relations training programs that are in operation throughout the nation. The category of police-community relations training is included here merely because some of the programs operated under the title of police-community relations are in fact training programs. Mention should also be made of the many storefronts that are operated and listed by many agencies as a police-community relations program. They have not been categorized as such because the establishment of the physical facility in itself does not meet the criteria of a police-community relations program; rather, it is what happens in the center that is important.[9]

Similarly, a program entitled "Operation Mobile Precinct" has been proposed by the Greensboro, North Carolina, Police Department as a police-community relations program and not listed as such here, for the same reason as that given for the storefronts. However, the program is mentioned because of its innovative concept. Under this program a van will be converted into an office for the use of the police-community relations officers. The program serves as an extension of the centralized police facility while directing its major emphasis toward the community relations aspect of the police operation. The major objective of the program is to "prevent riots, civil disorders and violence by eliminating the opportunity and causes which precipitate the emergence of such conditions." Methods of achieving this objective will consist of planned, comprehensive, and constructive efforts on the part of the police agency to hear complaints and grievances from the community and take appropriate action, encourage maximum community involvement in resolving problems that create conflict, and promote understanding between the police and the community for the purpose of eliminating sensitive and tension-developing situations which often lead to acts of violence and destruction. The program employs the "storefront" concept through the use of a van as a mobile precinct station for the purpose of hearing and handling problems and grievances relating to the police function on a neighborhood level, directed primarily at minority groups in the community.

Of a similar nature, the New York Police Department operated a program entitled "Precinct Receptionist Program." Under this program, the police precinct serves as a connecting agency for residents who were in need of community services. The purpose of the program was to make the precinct station a welcome place to visit. This goal was accomplished by having volunteers from the local neighborhood maintain a desk at the precinct station. The volunteers were given training as to what they could and could not do. They then served as interpreters for those who could not speak English, offered counseling, and listened to problems. If the person was in need of some other community service, they were referred to the appropriate agency offering that service.[10]

Under the definition of police-community relations, seminars may or may not be classified as a police-community relations program, depending upon the format. For example, some seminars allow for citizen input, whereas others are merely a process of the police and/or other speakers projecting a message to the participants. Many such seminars are held in conjunction with other organizations; an example is a police-community relations seminar sponsored by the San Jose, California, Police Department. In conjunction with the local office of the National Conference of Christians and Jews, the department sponsors an annual police-community relations seminar. The purpose of the program is threefold:

1. To bring police and members of the community together in a continuous relationship in order to reduce suspicion, misunderstanding, hostility and to discover their mutuality of interest and responsibilities.

2. To assist in the professional education of police officers with emphasis on the social, psychological, and essentially human dimensions of police work.

3. To introduce citizens at large to police problems, the role of law enforcement agencies, and the total community responsibility for law enforcement.

Several cities list liaisons with other organizations as an ongoing police-community relations program and label it "Liaison with Organizations."[11] Such details maintain liaison with groups, agencies, and organizations for better understanding of police functions and cooperation in general.

Liaison is also kept with "riot-prone" groups in order to effect proper police action when necessary.

San Jose operates another program entitled "College Liaison Officer." Under this program, the police department assigns one officer to work in uniform as a liaison officer between the police and the college community. This officer has the responsibility of working with all campus organizations (e.g., fraternities, sororities, dormatories, student clubs, faculty, and administrative groups). The purpose of this program is to have the officer associate on a formal and informal basis with the college community in an effort to control problems without taking official action.

San Diego has two liaison programs, one called "Constant Communication Projects," and the second, "Military Liaison." Under the Constant Communication Project, police–community relations officers maintain personal contact with both the professional persons and "grass-roots" leaders on a continual basis. Group interest represents racial, political, civil rights, labor, and representatives of government at all levels. The purpose of the program is to maintain open lines of communication. Under the "Military Liaison" program, members of the police–community relations unit establish a line of communication with the various military organizations and personnel in the city. The purpose of the program is to disseminate, through meetings, talks, and group discussions, information regarding current changes in matters relating to law, police procedures, and practices.

Los Angeles operates a program entitled "Teacher Institutes." Under this program, the police department sponsors annual sessions for teachers to expose them to topics that are currently of concern to the police and the board of education (e.g., juvenile procedures, narcotics, laws that apply on and off campus, police procedures, law enforcement, social change, etc.). This program assists in curriculum development and furnishes teachers with current information on handling school matters and classes.

Although not listed as a specific police–community relations program, the Chicago Police Department has a human relations section which works closely with the minority community. The purpose of the section is to coordinate the department's human relations activities by establishing and maintaining communications with racial, religious, and nationalistic groups in the community. The section serves as a source of information as to the legal requirements of any demonstration or group gathering, conducts in-service training sessions in human relations, and maintains continuous contact with racial, religious, and nationalistic groups in order to be aware of their attitudes and the influence of their actions.

Other programs operated under the title of police–community relations, although not categorized here are: (1) a proposed program by the Winston-Salem, North Carolina, Police Department entitled "Footpatrol in Poverty Areas" (police–community relations officers in uniform would walk in the poverty area in an effort to establish rapport), (2) "Family Crisis Unit," operated by the New York City Police Department, and (3) several "Rumor Control Clinics," Los Angeles, California, being one example. What follows, then, is a list of the many programs that have been developed and operated by police departments under the title of police–community relations.

PUBLIC RELATIONS PROGRAMS

Police–Community Relations Award[12]

Each spring, the police–community relations section sponsors a ceremony where framed letters of thanks are presented to each active member of the police–community relations executive committee. In the fall, the division presents letters of thanks to citizens who have contributed to the success of police–community relations programs.

Citizen Citations[13]

Under this program, "citizen citations" are presented to individuals by the police commission for meritorious acts brought to the attention of the public affairs division in the form of "a letter of appreciation from the chief of police" or a "police commission citation." The formal presentation includes full news coverage. The purpose of the program is to publicly acknowledge citizens who assist the police.

Ride-A-Long Program[14]

Under this program, citizens are allowed to ride in the patrol car with officers while they perform their normal patrol and police duties. The purpose of the program is to allow the citizen to see firsthand the job of police officers.

Citizenship Awards[15]

Promotional ceremonies are sponsored and awards presented to students who have demonstrated outstanding acts of good citizenship. The purpose of the program is to promote good citizenship.

Chief's Breakfast[16]

This is a program whereby the chief of police hosts breakfasts with selected groups and council members. The purpose of the program is to allow the chief to converse on matters of mutual interest.

Law Enforcement Assistance Award[17]

Every three months the police–community relations section sponsors a ceremony to honor citizens who have contributed the most to aid law enforcement. Framed certificates are given to each nominee and the winner is presented with a plaque. A plaque is also presented to individuals who have saved a life.

"Meeting Your Police" Program[18]

The purpose of this program is to establish better rapport between patrolmen and citizens of the community. Groups and organizations are encouraged to meet and become acquainted with police officers working in their area. Upon request from a group or organization, arrangements are made by the police–community relations unit for the beat cruiser to attend a meeting or function.

Citizen Committees[19]

Members of the police department serve on various citizen-type committees that have as their goal the betterment of the community. The purpose of this program is to show the public that the police are interested in the community as a whole.

Police–Community Relations Clergy Program[20]

Members of the clergy are organized and allowed to ride along with patrol units and observe the actual police operations. The clergy who participate in this program are given identification cards and a badge.

Jaycee Award Program[21]

This program is coordinated with the junior chamber of commerce. The purpose is to honor police officers who have done an outstanding job. The awards are given every three months. The winners are presented with a framed certificate.

Clergy Meeting[22]

Quarterly meetings are held with clergy on the precinct level. Once a year a city-wide meeting is held between the police and the clergy.

Police Buses[23]

Buses donated by the local transit company are used by members of the police–community relations division to provide free service to groups needing transportation to such events as picnics, tours, and sporting events.

Uniform Modification[24]

The purpose of uniform modification is to soften the visual effect of police officers by projecting a less military appearance. The traditional police uniform is replaced with a blazer type of uniform. The officers' firearms, handcuffs, and other equipment are hidden under the coat. A crest identifying the police department and the officer's nameplate are located in the area of the left breast pocket.

Movie Program[25]

During the summer months, members of the police-community relations division show outside movies to persons in low-income housing project areas. The movies cover such topics as athletic events, cartoons, and travelogs.

"Know Your Police Department" TV Series[26]

With the cooperation of a local TV station, the police-community relations division produces a weekly one-half-hour television program which spotlights a particular division of the police department each week.

Movies in the Street[27]

This is a summer program wherein the police use vans and trucks to show movies in the community.

Brochures[28]

The police-community relations division prepares and distributes a variety of brochures which are used by the department.

Police-Community Relations Information Program[29]

The police-community relations division promotes a special program on a local radio station. The aim of this program is to inform the listening audience about police operations.

Public Appearances[30]

The police-community relations detail makes public appearances as speakers, panelists, and resource persons covering the full spectrum of police work and addressing all levels of the educational establishment and civic organizations, social groups, and government agencies.

Mobile Narcotics Exhibit[31]

This is a public information program whereby a mobile unit goes to street corners in heavily stricken narcotic areas, schools, and public meetings with a narcotics exhibit.

The Commissioner Reports[32]

This is a bimonthly television program in which the police commissioner informs the public of recent developments within the department and also responds to questions called in by the viewing audience.

State Fair[33]

The police–community relations division produces and mans an annual police exhibit at the state fair.

Policemen Are People[34]

The purpose of this program is to humanize the image of the police officer by developing projects designed to enable the public, particularly young people, to "view the police officer as a friend, father, and fellow citizen."

Street Festivals[35]

A number of precincts have sponsored street festivals featuring intercultural entertainment, contests, and games. At such festivals, displays are erected by other city departments so that the residents can obtain a panoramic view of police, fire, health, welfare, recreation, and other services available to them.

Understanding the Policeman's Lot[36]

The purpose of this program is to give community leaders an opportunity to listen to, and ask questions of, the officers who patrol their neighborhoods.

Mass-Media Programs[37]

This program is directed primarily to the minority news media, wherein the police establish and maintain liaison with minority newspapers.

Mobile Booth[38]

This is a mobile law enforcement public relations display which is rotated throughout the city on a systematic basis (e.g., state fair, conventions, neighborhood meetings, and various business enterprises).

Tour of Police Headquarters[39]

Interested citizens are given a tour of police headquarters. The tours are conducted by police cadets, police officers, or community relations officers.

Senior Band[40]

The police department has a band that is coordinated by a full-time assigned officer. It performs at junior and senior high schools, large parades, civic events, academy graduations, and department functions.

Police-Community Relations News Bulletin[41]

Under this program the police-community relations unit prints and distributes throughout the community a monthly news bulletin. The purpose of this bulletin is to further the growth of communication, understanding, and cooperation between the police department and the community. The bulletins cover a wide range of subjects deemed to be of interest to the public.

Radio Spots[42]

Spots with a direct comment on police work or crime prevention are broadcast in English and Spanish during Crime Prevention Week, National Police Week, and at other selected times throughout the year.

Police-Community Relations Video-Tape Program[43]

The police department received a mobile closed-circuit television van from the Packard Bell Corporation for use in community relations. With this equipment, video tapes are prepared for presentation at community meetings. Following this, discussions are held and recorded by video-tape camera for viewing by the group to permit them to see themselves on television. Significant filming of groups is retained for use by the department to obtain community impressions of departmental policies and procedures.

Police Displays[44]

Displays of narcotics, communications, emergency vehicles, films, tours, dog demonstrations, and related units are presented during Crime Prevention Week, the county fair, and National Police Week. Full use is made of recruiting pamphlets, general information materials, and crime prevention flyers.

Radio Broadcasts[45]

Weekly broadcasts in Spanish and English present to the people information about new laws, police problems, advice on crime prevention, and other matters of mutual interest.

Visiting Officers Program[46]

Out-of-town police officers are hosted by the police–community relations division. They are oriented on the history and structure of the police–community relations division.

Ask the Sergeant[47]

A police sergeant has a weekly column in a local newspaper and the public submits questions to him regarding police matters.

Wave at a Cop[48]

Through advertisements on radio, television, and billboards, the public is encouraged to "Wave at a Cop. He's Human, too."

In addition to the above, most police departments operate a speakers bureau, which is generally coordinated by the community relations unit. Some departments (e.g., Richmond, California, and St. Louis, Missouri) prepare the department's news releases.

CRIME PREVENTION/SAFETY EDUCATION

Volunteer Parents[49]

Under this program, the police department works closely with groups of volunteer parents who assist the department by controlling the activities of young people at various problem areas, such as schools, dances, and parks. The approach of the volunteer parent is one of suggesting and urging peaceful and lawful conduct of the group.

Building Security Program[50]

This program is designed to assist local business owners in the security of their business and buildings. The merchants are contacted by a member of the department and advised about store security, shoplifting techniques, alarm systems, check-passing techniques, safes, and the placing of night and safe lights.

Stamp Out Crime Crusade[51]

This program is a joint venture of the police department and the Independent Insurance Agents Association. It is designed to attack the crime problem by destroying public apathy and making the public aware of the problem, the seriousness of the problem, and their responsibility to assist the police. The program involves public recognition to citizens who assist the police; publicizing the program through all the news media, including billboards; and personal appearances before civic clubs and other organizations.

Self-Defense Program[52]

Under this program self-defense classes for women are conducted by members of the police–community relations division. The class consists of several hours of instruction (e.g., films, lectures, and demonstrations). The purpose of the program is to create awareness on the part of women in the community, thereby lowering the risk of personal attack through preparation.

Shoplifting Lectures[53]

Lectures on the "shoplifting picture" are given to high school students and in the evening to community organizations such as PTAs and civic groups.

Theft Prevention Lectures[54]

Lectures on robbery, grand theft, bunco, burglary, and shoplifting are presented to citizen groups, students, PTAs, and merchants. Pamphlets on each subject organized, written, and printed by the detail are used with the lectures. Guest lectures by experts presently in the field are incorporated into the program.

Business Contacts[55]

Community relations officers make individual contacts with merchants in an effort to determine if there are police problems that may affect either the business or the area. One objective of this program is to explain to community representatives the procedures that are used by the police department and the reasons for them.

Operation Involvement[56]

Under this program, the police department uses various census tracts and attempts to make the people (every household in that tract) aware of the crime picture in the particular neighborhood. Letters are sent out announcing that on a certain date a meeting will be held at a school within the census tract sponsored by the police department and the Citizens Crime Prevention Committee. At the meeting, a film is shown and the main theme of the remainder of the program is that the police alone cannot handle the crime problem. During the week following the meeting, new recruits, new careerist, and regular officers are used to make a personal contact at every house in the census tract to talk with residents about the program and to drop off a package of material.

Residents' Council[57]

A nucleus of 50 members serve on residents' councils, which are established in various housing projects, plus others who participate in its activities. The councils concern themselves with such problems as gambling, prostitution, narcotics, traffic, juvenile delinquency, and other problems within the confines of the housing projects or the surrounding area.

Information on New Legislation[58]

This program was implemented by precinct council members who visit shopkeepers to inform them of the legal restrictions on the sales of plastic glue to youngsters and to ask them for their cooperation in eliminating the practice of glue sniffing.

Operation Safe Streets[59]

This is a crime prevention program whereby literature is distributed to the community containing tips on crime prevention (e.g., how to prevent burglaries, robberies, etc.).

Block Watcher Program[60]

The purpose of this program is to reduce crime, particularly daytime burglaries, and to improve the relationship between street officers and citizens. The program is designed to organize neighborhoods so that neighbors watch each other's homes for suspicious occurrences.

Tension Area Patrol[61]

Under this program, personnel from the community relations division maintain a patrol in those areas within the city that have demonstrated a tendency toward complicated law enforcement problems. The purpose of the patrol is to maintain close liaison with the residents of the areas in an effort to identify quickly any situations that are potentially disruptive.

Theft Prevention Survey[62]

Under this program, a survey is conducted by use of a checklist for merchants to point out weaknesses in a store's security against shoplifting and other thefts. Store managers are advised to make certain changes to prevent thefts.

Light the Night[63]

Under this program, the police work with the local real estate board on a publicity campaign in an attempt to encourage people to light their homes at night.

Community Radio Watch[64]

This program is sponsored by the police department with supplies and format supplied by the Motorola Corporation. Under this program, all businesses (e.g., trucking companies, taxis, etc.) are requested to assist the police by calling their dispatcher, who will in turn call the police, when they see a crime being committed or see any suspicious circumstances.

Shoplifting Seminars[65]

A city-wide seminar is sponsored and organized each year for merchants and their personnel to learn the latest laws, arrest procedures, theft techniques, and related information. Ample use is made of visual aids and actual demonstrations. On request, seminars at the shopping center level are conducted during the year. Yearly seminars are also put on for police officers to teach them techniques of detecting shoplifters.

Partners in Crime[66]

This program was devised by a precinct detective squad, in conjunction with a precinct council, and dramatized in a one-act play on how citizens can help prevent apartment burglaries. The play, written and acted by detectives and citizens, portrays how burglars ply their trade and how the public actually helps them through negligence.

Businessmen's Program[67]

Police–community relations officers meet periodically with businesspeople in their district to discuss methods of preventing crime.

Citizen's Against Crime[68]

Citizens Against Crime cards are distributed throughout the city to organizations and citizens. The purpose of the program is to obtain citizen cooperation in reporting crime and/or suspicious circumstances to the police.

Community Education Materials[69]

This program involves the distribution of messages of interest to the public such as advice on the dangers of narcotic addiction, hints on safeguarding property, and tips to women on protecting themselves.

Ministerial Alliance[70]

Initially, this program originated in the black community, but has expanded to include religious leaders throughout the city. The purpose of the program is to have a group of influential ministers serve to enlighten the police department and their congregation regarding matters of mutual concern (e.g., crime, delinquency, and disorder).

One of the first, and probably the most publicized crime prevention program is Chicago's Operation Crime-Stop. This program was launched April 13, 1964. It was established to increase public cooperation in reporting suspicious events occurring in and around business places, homes, streets, alleys, and parks.[71]

YOUTH PROGRAMS

Operation Blue Star[72]

The purpose of this program is to provide a feeling of safety for school children and to actively involve a significant segment of the community in keeping an eye out for occurrences that require police attention. Blue Star Home parents are recruited by the police department through local PTA organizations. The applicants for the program are screened by the police department. When a home is accepted as a Blue Star Home, a distinctive blue star sign is placed in the front window of the home so that it is prominently visible from the street. Each Blue Star Home resident is made aware of the importance of reporting any questionable incidents to the police. Children on their way to and from school can go to the Blue Star Home if they have a problem (e.g., lost child, injured child, molesters, gang fight, etc.). The goal of the project is to provide an effective method of relaying information regarding molesters and other neighborhood crime.

Police-Youth Discussion Groups[73]

The purpose of this program is to establish communication between the police and youth, to improve understanding and relations, and to direct the energies and efforts of youth toward constructive activities. Discussion groups are held for 6 to 12 weeks, meeting once a week. Special emphasis is placed on youth who are (or have been) on probation or parole, those who have a delinquent background, and those who could be categorized as "hard-core" youth. The meetings are designed to provide a setting whereby the youth will have an opportunity to confront police officers (verbally) frankly and release hostilities through speech rather than through physical action.

Citizenship Program for First Offenders[74]

Under this program, first offenders between the ages of 9 and 15 come to the police department one night a week for four consecutive weeks. They spend two hours with a police officer, who discusses the law, why the laws exist, and their responsibilities. The youngsters must be accompanied by one or both parents or guardians.

"Policeman Dan" Program[75]

The "Policeman Dan" program is a presentation geared to the primary grades in the elementary schools. The purpose of the program is to relate to the children a better image of the police officer by allowing them to meet and talk with an officer. For this reason, the officer who visits the school speaks to the children in the classroom rather than in an assembly. It is a response-type presentation encouraging youngsters to participate by using individual students in various examples. These techniques help the officer establish a close and friendly relationship with the children.

The program starts with a movie which gives a simplified explanation of police work for 5- to 10-year-old students. The movie, which lasts approximately 15 minutes, is followed by the officer showing the children his uniform and equipment. The officer than takes the class out to the playground, where various equipment on the police car is demonstrated.

To end the presentation, the officer has a question-and-answer period, after which he leaves with the teacher the "Policeman Dan" pamphlets. The teacher is encouraged to use the material in class discussion and is given enough pamphlets for each student to take one home.

The pamphlet contains a word–cartoon series showing the police officer as the child's friend. Included is a message to the parents with helpful hints on teaching the children the dangers of playing in the streets, talking to strangers, and so on.

The long-range goal of the program is to build a better relationship with the community and gain more support for the police department.

Community–Police Service Corps[76]

This is a police-sponsored organization consisting of young people between the ages of 10 and 18 who are supervised by adults and advised by police representatives. The purpose is to involve youth in positive relationships with the police through recreation or service projects to dispel negative feelings. Through contributions from various service clubs and business organizations, uniforms were designed and purchased for the corps. The youths represent their community and the police department by appearing as a marching group in various parades and other public events.

Citizenship Course[77]

This program is presented in the junior high schools as part of the students' social studies program. It consists of a 10-hour block of instruction which covers: (1) history of law enforcement, (2) inception of laws, (3) specific laws, (4) court procedure, (5) organization of police department, (6) tour of police department, (7) current police problems, and (8) panel discussions. The instructing is done by police officers. The objective of this program is threefold:

1. To develop an understanding of the police officers' role and their functions in the community.
2. To instill an attitude of community responsibility in students through an understanding of laws and their meaning, and to develop a positive attitude toward law observance through a proper understanding of enforcement and the judicial process.
3. To create a better relationship between the police and students through this personal teacher–learning experience.

Law Enforcement Scholarship Program[78]

The community relations unit established a citizens committee for the purpose of raising funds to give scholarships to needy students who wish to enter or continue in a law enforcement program at a local college. This program is designed to assist students in financial need and to encourage young people from the Mexican-American and black communities to enter the law enforcement field.

Junior Crime Prevention Program[79]

This program is geared for the fourth-grade level. It involves a uniformed police officer visiting a classroom four times each school year with visual aids and handout material to tell about crime prevention, juvenile delinquency, and the consequences of criminal acts. The purpose of the program is to provide students with an appreciation of the role of the police and their own responsibilities as good citizens.

Annual Boys' Day in Safety[80]

This program is sponsored by an automobile club in cooperation with the police department. Under the program, selected students are given an opportunity to spend a day with police officers. The program consists of a film on traffic safety and a tour of police facilities. The boys then participate in a program at the police academy, which includes an exhibition of police equipment. Each boy is hosted at lunch and presented with a citation for meritorious service in safety.

Law Enforcement Explorer Program[81]

The purpose of this program is to interest young men in a career in law enforcement and to develop an awareness of civic responsibility. The motto is "Learning to Protect and to Serve." Members are selected through a process similar to that employed in the selection of regular police officers. The Explorers are trained in the basics of law enforcement procedures which prepare them for participation in various police-related activities. Although chartered by the Boy Scouts of America, the program is law enforcement-oriented and emphasizes good citizenship and character development.

Policeman Bill[82]

This is a school program designed for the first, second, and third grades. It involves a police officer going into the classroom and discussing the history of the police and the role of the police in current society. Photographs and other visual aids are used in the presentation. One student is designated "Policeman's Helper" and wears a large replica of a police badge. The "talking police car" is demonstrated with detailed explanation of equipment. Other points stressed are "Traffic Safety" and "Dangerous Strangers."

Gun Safety Program[83]

This program is for youth under 16 years of age. It involves instruction on the use of firearms by police personnel. The program was initiated as a public service after the passage of a state law requiring youth in that age bracket to attend such a course prior to being issued a hunter's license.

Annual Boys' Day in Government[84]

This program is designed to give students throughout the city an opportunity to occupy various positions in government, including the police department, for one day. The purpose of the program is to inform students about the operation of city government and to develop a favorable relationship between youth and the public.

Annual Student Leadership Symposium on Law and Order[85]

This program is sponsored by the city's junior chamber of commerce in conjunction with the police department and involves student leaders from various high schools. Police personnel participate in the presentations, discussion groups, and social hours.

Summer Camping[86]

Summer camping consists of four one-week sessions, Monday through Friday, which include swimming, archery, canoeing, and fishing. Instruction in handicrafts includes woodwork, leatherwork, and wood burning. Additionally, campfire activities, singing and skits, movie nights, horseback riding, nature hiking, and night pistol team demonstrations are provided. Athletics include volleyball, horseshoes, basketball, and track meets. Discussions of problems that involve youth and the community are part of the "talk sessions."

Junior Band[87]

The police department sponsors a band for boys 12 to 20 years of age. They are taught concert and marching music, marching techniques, and participate in community and state-wide festivities, concerts, parades, and state and national junior band concerts. The purpose of the program is to give boys who are musically inclined a meaningful character-building experience in a high-quality marching and concert band.

High School Office Hours[88]

Weekly office hours are held at a local high school for the benefit of students who want to discuss any problems or seek information about the police department.

Send a Kid to Camp[89]

This program, sponsored by the Schlitz Brewing Company, involves sending underpriviledged children to camp. The police–community relations officers are involved in the selection of the children. Each child that is sent to camp receives tee shirts and toilet articles that have been donated for this purpose to the police–community relations division.

Police Partners[90]

This is a program involving sixth-grade students (boys and girls) designed to accomplish:

1. A positive attitudinal change of the police-partner group toward the police.
2. Enlargement of the knowledge of police functions, responsibilities, and services.
3. To implant a latent desire for, as well as knowledge of, the many and varied vocational opportunities for young men and women in a police department.

The goals of this project are pursued by a series of a classroom sessions and field trips once a week over a 14-week period.

Police–Community Relations Youth Council[91]

The Youth Council is composed of the presidents of each grade level in each high school, plus a representative from the student newspaper of each school. The purpose of this program is to advise police on any matters involving teenagers in an attempt to bridge the gap between youth and the police. The Youth Council meets once a month at police headquarters. At each meeting there is a program which consists of a speech and/or a demonstration.

Say Hi Program[92]

"Say Hi" cards are distributed to elementary school children by members of the police–community relations section. The purpose of this program is to encourage youngsters to wave and say hello to police officers.

Teen Post[93]

A community relations officer is assigned to each Teen Post in the city. The officer assists in an advisory capacity and provides communication with the police department. The officer also helps in obtaining needed equipment or services when possible. The purpose of the program is to develop rapport between officers and youths through informal and friendly discussion of problems confronting young people and the police.

Talk-A-Long Program[94]

Under this program an officer is assigned on a rotating basis to each high school in the city one day per week during the lunch hour. The officer is there to meet, talk, and listen to the views of the students. The students who participate in this program do so on a voluntary basis. The purpose of the program is to improve communication between the police and high school students and to allow students to meet officers in a situation other than field work.

Bicycle Rodeo Program[95]

Under this program the police teach young people safety methods and how to ride their bicycles legally. Safety checks are performed, handout material is distributed, and licensing is done. This program is an attempt by the police to come into contact with the younger members of the community.

Police Summer Fishing Group[96]

This is a summer program where every Wednesday police officers take a group of disadvantaged youth on a fishing trip.

School Contact Program[97]

Under this program community relations officers speak before students in every junior and senior high school in the city. The officers speak to small groups, two classes at maximum. They appear in uniform and, for the first 15 or 20 minutes of the class period, discuss the police department and its organization, authority, and responsibilities. Then for the remainder of the class the officer asks the students to "put me on the spot: Why do police officers do what they do?" The purpose of the program is to give students an understanding of the purpose and function of their police department and to answer any questions they have about law enforcement.

Boxing Program[98]

This program is for boys 10 years of age and up. Each day after school and during the summer months the kids report to the police gym, where a ring and a workroom are installed. There they are given boxing lessons by members of the police–community relations division.

Basketball Teams[99]

The community relations unit sponsors basketball teams which are entered in intercity leagues.

Talent Contests[100]

Each year the community relations division conducts a summer search for talent. Utilizing a portable stage built on the trailer of a large truck, the talent truck is moved into the poverty areas of the city. Prior visits to the areas to solicit talent are made by members of the police–community relations division. The program is concluded at the end of the summer with a talent show in which all the area winners compete for the city championship. Winners of the show receive savings bonds, trophies, plaques, and other gifts are donated to the police–community relations division.

Air Flights[101]

With the cooperation of an airline, children are taken for a jet flight by members of the police–community relations unit.

Rumor Clinic[102]

This program consists of a brief skit based on a routine traffic enforcement situation involving both students and police officers. The purpose of the program is to point out the fact that a rumor can potentially be the most disruptive social phenomenon facing our cities and towns today. The skit depicts how a rumor can start and analyzes the resulting exaggeration.

School Educational Program[103]

The program involves the presentation of programs regarding safety and informational-type presentations to all students of the city school system. Generally, safety programs are conducted in the elementary schools, while the informational-type programs are directed to the junior high and high school levels. The purpose of this program is twofold:

1. To present to students information in certain areas which may prove to be of value to them.
2. To promote a better relationship between students and the police and to provide the students with an understanding of the police role.

Youth Protection Lectures and Slides[104]

Under this program lectures are given to junior high and high school students on "Youth and the Law." The subject matter is about what juveniles can do to keep out of trouble and how their parents can prevent or assist in keeping them out of trouble. The goal is to bring law enforcement information to students and to improve their image of the police.

Summer Recreation[105]

Each year during the summer months, additional officers are detailed to the police–community relations division from the various police districts. These officers are used as sports supervisors in various poverty areas of the city. Through this program, officers organize softball games and other sports activities.

Boxing in the Street[106]

Under this program members of the Police Athletic League put on boxing exhibitions in the community. This is also a summer program.

Community Service Officer Program[107]

The community service officers are temporary employees (summer months) of the police department (young men between the ages of 17 and 25). To be eligible for the program, the young men must be unemployed and unemployable under police standards and qualifications. They are assigned to the crime prevention bureau to work in high-crime and high-poverty communities. Their duties are to render assistance in the neighborhood in any matter in which they may be of help. During their tour of duty they visit various facilities and activities in their assigned area (e.g., poverty centers, schools, play areas, youth centers, clubs, parks, etc.). The community service officers work in uniform but are not regular police officers. They do not carry a weapon and do not have the power of arrest.

Amusement Park Program[108]

By obtaining complimentary tickets, the police–community relations division takes a group of low-income kids to an amusement park. Metal police badges are given to children who participate in this program.

Special Sporting Events[109]

Tickets for special sporting events are donated to the police–community relations division, such as all-star high school basketball and football games. Members from the division invite young people from poverty areas to attend, transport them to the event, remain as supervisors, and on occasion, provide refreshments.

Neighborhood Helper Program[110]

This program is run in conjunction with a church community house and the police–community relations officers act as agents for youth by assisting them to obtain employment (e.g., cutting yards, baby sitting, etc.). The purpose of this program is to get the youth employment in their own neighborhood, thereby creating trust between youths and residents of their neighborhoods. The police–community relations officers are contacted by potential employers and the job is then referred to the community house, which sends the youth out on jobs.

Operation Little Sweep[111]

Boys between the ages of 10 and 13 are employed by the police-community relations division (on the district level) to sweep sidewalks and pick up bottles. The boys work three hours per day, four days per week, and receive 50 cents per hour. The funds for this program are supplied by businesspeople in the districts. The purpose of this program is to keep the boys out of trouble and at the same time give them some spending money.

Portable Swimming Pools[112]

During the summer, the police department purchased portable swimming pools and erected them in the low-income areas. The purpose was to provide a place for children of that area to swim on hot summer days.

Know Your Police Department Program[113]

The purpose of this program is to acquaint schoolchildren with police services. A long-range objective of this program is police recruitment. School classes visit police department facilities and police officers visit the schools. In the school assemblies the children are shown slides of police activities, and a talk is given by a uniformed officer. As a souvenir, each child receives an identification card containing a pledge of respect for law and order.

Operation Partnership[114]

The purpose of this program is to expose officers on post to the attitudes and problems of youth on their posts. This is accomplished by visiting youth activities, chatting with youngsters, and a challenge to the league-winning basketball team.

Adolescents Against Addiction[115]

This program is a peer approach designed to combat narcotic addiction among youth between 13 and 18 years of age. Boys and girls are recommended by their schools and trained to tell other teenagers about the dangers of narcotics and dangerous drugs. The youngsters attempt to accomplish these goals through skits, exhibitions, group discussions, and informal contact with local young people.

Officer Friendly Program[116]

This program is operated in the elementary schools and is designed to promote respect and understanding for law enforcement among students. The goal of the program is to have children view the police as their friends and as people they can turn to in need. The program is operated in conjunction with the board of education and consists of three visits by "Officer Friendly" to each participating elementary school:

1. The first visit is one-half hour in length and consists of a short talk by "Officer Friendly" about the role of a police officer.
2. The second visit includes a discussion of safety rules and hazards, an introduction to "Stranger Danger," and a demonstration of police equipment. A letter is sent to each child's parents explaining the program and encouraging discussions of law enforcement in the home.
3. The last visit is a review of what was presented previously. The officer also poses questions for individual response.

Police and Schools Programs[117]

This is a college-level course designed to familiarize teachers with police operations so that they will be better prepared to discuss them in their classrooms.

Summer Youth Program[118]

This is a two-phase program for youth which is city-wide. The first phase of the program involves police personnel recruiting youngsters between the ages of 7 and 18 to participate in district-sponsored athletic and recreational activities. The second phase involves the location of jobs for teens. This is done by community service officers who solicit support and cooperation from local businesspeople.

The purpose of this program is to prevent juvenile crime by providing youngsters with some creative activity. Another purpose is to bring youth and the police together in an informal situation and give them the opportunity to relate to each other on a person-to-person basis. The youth are involved in such activities as field trips, camping, fishing, sports, swimming, choral groups, musical groups, and picnics.

Youth Dialogue Programs[119]

Under this program 30 youths, ages 16 to 19, spend two days with the police officers at a camp. The purpose of the program is to establish a means of communication and understanding between youth and the police. The two-day program is held in a relaxed, informal, country-like atmosphere where all participants are given the opportunity to express their viewpoints. The goal of the program is to reduce any tension that may exist between youth and the police by making each group aware of the other on a personal basis.

Law Observance Program[120]

The purpose of this program is threefold:

1. To educate the children to the police role in the community and through them to reach their parents.
2. To improve understanding of the problems of the police and to create an opportunity for two-way communication between students and the police.
3. To prevent juvenile delinquency by exposing pupils to the facts that a police record reduces job opportunities.

This is a three-day program which consists of (1) pre-tour lecture about police work, (2) a tour of police headquarters, and (3) a post-lecture with the showing of a film and the answering of questions.

Headstart Program[121]

Members of the police–community relations unit visit each Head Start program in the city and teach pedestrian safety.

School Visitation Program[122]

Police–community relations officers visit all elementary schools in the city and present a police program. Police films are used to supplement the oral presentation. The program is coordinated with the board of education.

Junior Youth Council[123]

The council is composed of youth between the ages of 14 and 16, who serve in the same capacity as adult precinct community councils.

Visitation Program[124]

Under this program, members of the police–community relations division make regular visits to neighborhood youth centers and recreation grounds. The purpose of these visits is to assist youth in their problems (e.g., education, employment, and other personal problems).

Hangout Patrol Program[125]

Under this program, members of the community relations division maintain a regular patrol of areas that are known to be frequented by youths (e.g., pool halls, recreation rooms, movie houses, and carryout shops). The purpose of these patrols is to make contact with youth and attempt to direct them to the facilities and resources available within communities. At the same time, an attempt is made to identify potential trouble-producing situations (or individuals) and take appropriate remedial action.

The Squires[126]

Officers in the community relations section are involved in a program with a group of inmates from San Quentin Prison called "The Squires." This organization was formed to constructively counsel and assist delinquent-prone youths. Groups of youths are taken to San Quentin Prison for three consecutive Saturday mornings, where members of the Squires counsel and advise the young men on how to avoid the pitfalls of crime. Two police–community relations officers accompany groups of 15 to 20 youths. The purpose of the program is to provide confrontation in order to benefit the community, the police department, the youth, and the inmates.

Youth Discussion Groups[127]

The original concept of this program was to institute discussion groups made up of youth who were high school dropouts with criminal records. However, the program was expanded to include all youth in the community. The groups are largely composed of youth from existing organizations such as the Y.M.C.A., school clubs, Neighborhood Youth Corps, fraternities, sororities, and religious youth clubs.

Narcotic Education Lectures and Films[128]

This program entails lecturing to junior and senior high school students on the hazards of drug abuse. Duties also include speaking to PTA groups, home and school clubs, youth groups, service clubs, and the like during the evening hours.

Programs for Youth No Longer in School[129]

The police–community relations division participates in a variety of projects designed for young adults who are no longer in school. The aim of these projects is to provide an atmosphere conducive to the formulation of relationships of trust and understanding between police officers and youths.

Community Athletic League[130]

On the district level, police–community relations officers conduct a variety of juvenile programs. For example, youngsters are taken to ballgames, movies, and other entertainment shows by community relations officers.

Cruiser Tours[131]

Teenagers are given a tour of the district station or police headquarters and then ride in unmarked cars in the field.

First Aid Program[132]

This program, conducted in cooperation with the American Red Cross, is geared for youth who are no longer in school. The program consists of conducting a standard first-aid course and upon successful completion, the youths are employed by the recreation department to work at swimming pools throughout the city as pool aides and lifeguards.

School Counseling Sessions[133]

Under this program police–community relations personnel participate in sessions at various schools which are aimed at aiding students in matters of social adjustment. The purpose of this program is to allow officers and teachers to pool their talents in an attempt to aid the students in arriving at workable solutions to their personal problems.

Career Counseling Program[134]

In conjunction with school authorities and representatives of the Kiwanis Club, members of the police–community relations division participate in a Career Day Program in the schools. This program consists of a series of assemblies during which representatives from private industry and different governmental agencies introduce the youth to the benefits and requirements for entering various fields. The police officers discuss the opportunities available to youth in the field of law enforcement.

School Tour Program[135]

This program is designed for students at the junior and senior high school level. A three-day format is utilized. On the first day an officer pays a brief visit to the school, introduces himself to the faculty and students, and briefly outlines what the students are to see the following day. The second day is devoted to an extensive tour of the police station. The tour is concluded with a round-table question-and-answer period.

The third and final day is devoted to a demonstration of police equipment and procedure, plus the answering of questions generated by the program.

Classroom Visits Program[136]

This program is structured primarily around senior and junior high school sociology and government classes. The purpose of these classroom visits is to engage students and faculty in a discussion of police matters and to answer their questions about the police and their activities, goals, and methods. Efforts are made not to lecture to the students; rather, techniques such as group dynamics "rumor clinics" and "role playing" are used to involve students in the program.

Student Trips[137]

Through this program, trips are provided for high school students to state correctional facilities and other police-related institutions where youths hear crime prevention speeches from inmates and see the hardships involved in serving sentences. On occasion, needy youths are taken to professional ballgames.

Senior High Program[138]

This program is operated in conjunction with the required course on American government in the local high schools, wherein one block of the program concerns itself with the administration of justice. Each class is taken on a tour of police headquarters and spends two hours with a judge. The judge explains his or her role, the baliff's, the prosecuting attorney's, and the defense attorney's. The judge then takes the class into a courtroom to watch a criminal jury trial in action.

Prenatal Program[139]

Members of the police–community relations section visit all prenatal clinics in the city and conduct a program for expectant parents. The purpose of this program is to inform expectant parents of the need for properly educating their children and their attitude toward the police role.

Housing Authority–Police Youth Program[140]

This program is designed to reach youth within housing projects where concentrated populations present inordinate living complications. Off-duty police officers are paid by the city housing authority to form and supervise sports leagues and coordinate tours to athletic events and other points of interest.

Police–Student Councils[141]

Police–student councils are organized at various junior and senior high schools throughout the city. The program is coordinated with the board of education. The purpose is to involve students and the police in a joint effort toward finding solutions to school problems that are of a criminal nature.

The Police in the Classroom[142]

Under this program uniformed officers present a series of five lectures in the eighth-grade classrooms covering various topics (e.g., drug abuse, freedom and laws, responsibility of students, and the role of the police in our society). The purpose of the program is to narrow the gap of communication and understanding between youth and police and to establish positive contacts between both groups.

Operation Work[143]

This is a summer program operated by the precinct community council with the cooperation of a number of unions and local business firms. The purpose of the program is to locate employment for "hard-to-place" youth.

Let's Get Acquainted[144]

This is a school program designed for the sixth-grade level. It consists of a discussion of questions from the class, together with a display of the police uniform and equipment, drug charts, and other visual aids. "The Role of the Police," "Good Citizenship," "Rights of Students," and "Traffic Safety" are also discussed.

Stop on a Dime[145]

This program is presented in all elementary schools and sponsored jointly by the board of education and the police department. The purpose of the program is to show, through demonstration, that pedestrians, bicycles, and vehicles cannot "stop on a dime."

You and the Police Officer[146]

This program is designed for the eighth-grade level and involves a police officer, wearing a business suit, going into the social studies classrooms. The purpose is to permit discussion of "Good Citizenship," "Police Brutality," "Traffic Laws," "Narcotics," "Curfew," and "Sex Laws." The students suggest the topic by questioning the officer in these areas.

Police-School Cadet Program[147]

This program is designed for later-elementary, junior, and senior high school students. It is designed to involve the students in a structured, police-oriented club activity. The purpose is to show youngsters that conformity need not be stifling, that there are other achievements more satisfying than delinquent acts, and that they themselves are capable of choosing and reaching acceptable goals based on pride of accomplishment through community service. Senior high school and community college students who meet the requirements may enroll as police cadets. The cadets work 20 hours per week and the work schedule is arranged around their school classes.

Police Youth Service Corps[148]

The primary objective of this program is to improve police–youth relationships. As such, its purposes are as follows:

1. To offer youth and police a reciprocal opportunity for exposure to the development and improvement of youth attitudes toward law enforcement.
2. To improve youth's sense of belonging and sense of accomplishment by providing various work experience placements throughout the city, under the supervision of assigned group leader aides.
3. To demonstrate that effective and meaningful changes of attitudes and improved self-image are not only possible, but will lead to improved acceptance of individual youth-citizenship responsibilities and police responsibilities to youth.
4. To contribute to the reduction of juvenile crime.

This is a summer program whereby selected youths are employed, under police supervision, for 20 hours per week. Those selected are 14 or 15 years of age, show signs of dropping out of school, show antisocial behavior patterns or are already in trouble with the police. For 16 hours per week the youth perform quasi-police-type street patrol (e.g., reporting abandoned cars) and four hours a week is devoted to informal discussion groups.

Elementary School Child Safety Program[149]

The objective of this program is to impress upon elementary school children the need and value of pedestrian and bicycle safety, the danger of child molesters, and the training of safety patrol boys. The program is conducted in the classroom by uniformed police officers.

In addition to the preceding programs, Richmond has a "Tutoring Program," whereby police tutor school children; San Francisco operates an "Officer George Program" for elementary school children, plus a program in the high schools; Oakland sponsors an annual "Junior Olympics"; New Orleans, Philadelphia, Atlanta, and other cities operate a "Sprinkler Program," whereby sprinklers are attached to fire hydrants for children to play in during the summer months; and several departments have printed coloring books as handout material.

Police–Community Relations Training Programs Operation Handshake[150]

This is a police–community relations training program for new police officers. Under this program new officers who have just graduated from the police academy are taken on a "handshaking" tour of the city. The purpose of the program is to expose rookie officers to the multitudes of situations which will broaden their experience and make them more conscious of police–community relations. The new officers are taken on visits to such places as federal housing units, shopping centers, tot lots, recreation fields, business associations, NAACP headquarters, the Young Great Society, Black Coalition offices, and the Concilio (Council of Spanish-Speaking Organizations). The ultimate goal of the program is to break down barriers of suspicion by giving the new officers a chance to meet a variety of people representing all social stratas and religious, ethnic, racial, and economic backgrounds.

Coffee Klatch Program[151]

Under this program a few couples from a given neighborhood are invited to an informal evening gathering for coffee and conversation. Police officers responsible for patrolling that particular area are brought to the meetings and given the opportunity to present the department's views on law enforcement. Afterward, the couples are given the opportunity to ask questions, make known their personal expectations regarding law enforcement, and to air their complaints about police service. The basic purpose of this program is to open the lines of communication between police officers and citizens on their beat through personal contact. A second objective of the program is police–community relations training for the officers. This is accomplished by "planting" a couple who are members of a little theatre group in the meeting to agitate the officer by expressing "anti-police" attitudes. This is done to teach officers that they must eliminate personal defensiveness. The ultimate goal of this program is to make each officer a police–community relations officer.

In-Service Training[152]

The detail sets up a teaching curriculum for the police academy on matters involving community relations and writes the bulletins for in-service personnel.

Community Relations Officers Meetings[153]

Regularly scheduled meetings are held to bring together community relations officers, detectives, traffic and patrol representatives, and the director of community relations into a casual conference atmosphere for problem solving, policy discussions, exchange of information, and to assure consistency and effectiveness in community relations program.

Citizen Service Reports[154]

This program is designed to give an officer's supervisor an idea of what type of service the officer is giving the community. Under the program, a supervisory officer chooses at random several cases that the officer has handled during the month and sends the citizen a letter and questionnaire for an evaluation of the service received on a particular call and to allow citizens to offer suggestions on how they believe police service could be improved. A secondary objective of this program is to illustrate to the citizen that the police department cares about the type of service the citizens of the community are receiving.

Community Relations Training[155]

All new police officers who are hired are assigned to the crime prevention bureau until the police training school is ready to accept them. Through this program, young officers are sent into the community with an experienced crime prevention officer and familiarized with the people and their problems. In addition to serving as a training function for new officers, this program is designed to afford superior officers an opportunity to evaluate the performance of new patrolmen and to determine whether they will become good police officers. Upon completion of this training phase, if the evaluation points out any bias or prejudice on an officer's part, the officer can be discharged before becoming a liability to the department.

Police-Community Relations Training[156]

Members of the police–community relations division conduct recruit and in-service training in human relations. In addition, patrol sergeants are assigned to the police–community relations division for five days of orientation in police–community relations activities.

Community Relations Orientation for Police[157]

This is a program designed to establish a direct relationship between police–community relations officers and patrol officers. This is accomplished by having patrol officers meet with a police–community relations officer in a small group setting (no more than four patrol officers at a time). The content of such a meeting ordinarily includes a detailed exploration of the functions of the police–community relations division; a discussion of police professionalism, stressing that every officer should strive to obtain this goal; and the importance of good appearance. In addition, the patrol officers are allowed to offer suggestions and recommendations regarding problems that confront them.

Administrative Seminars[158]

Periodic seminars involving top administrators are held away from police facilities to assist in the development of new ideas and to assure consistency throughout the department in the administration of the community relations program as established by the chief of police. Seminars are also held for the levels of middle management, supervisors, and line officers.

Radio Blibs

Under this program, periodic short blibs dealing with police–community relations are announced over the police radio. The purpose of this program is to continually keep field officers thinking about good community relations. A secondary purpose is to express to the officers the administration's concern for good community relations. "Courtesy pays dividends" is an example of the announcements made.

Spanish Classes[160]

Classes in conversational Spanish are conducted for officers who work in predominately Mexican-American divisions to assist the police in overcoming the language barrier in those communities.

In addition to the programs listed above, Richmond, California, incorporates into their in-service training program a course in black studies.

POLICE–COMMUNITY RELATIONS

Economic Opportunity Council Liaison[161]

Under this program, police–community relations officers are assigned to Economic Opportunity offices located throughout the city. Their work in these offices is as follows:

1. To initiate communication and appropriate exchange of information with agencies regarding specific police cases of persons who might benefit through referral for agency services.

2. Follow-up investigation at the staff level of police contacts resulting in the arrest or citation of persons enrolled in area development programs.

3. To provide short-term counseling for persons whose lack of motivation relates to factors of police contact or involvement with other legal authorities.

4. To evaluate and interpret police records in terms of employment and educational opportunities, and to aid area development personnel in referral, screening, and placement of applicants.

5. To help develop employer awareness of the problems of persons who, by virtue of their juvenile or adult records, are termed "unemployable."

6. To aid in evaluating and interpreting police records where remedy is sought through procedures of record "sealing" and to advise and assist persons whose criminal records may be subject to sealing or expungement under existing laws, whenever such cases come to the attention of the police–community relations officers.

7. To take an active role in creating understanding on the part of the police department with respect to the peculiar problems of persons who have had police contact. This will be, in part, accomplished by periodic visits with district station commanders so that they are better informed concerning progress being made by the area poverty board.

Police-Community Relations Workshop[162]

Monthly community workshops are held in each district, involving the district commander, district police personnel, and interested citizens. The purposes of these monthly meetings are:

1. To develop a sense of community responsibility by having the citizens of a district become involved in the solution of local problems.

2. To provide an opportunity to arrive at solutions to community problems by bringing them into the open in an informal atmosphere.

3. To increase communication between all citizens within the established community structure.

4. To provide citizens with an insight into their district's police problems and operations in order to gain support and cooperation in the law enforcement effort.

Community Services Unit[163]

The purpose of this unit is to better the understanding between the police and the public by bridging the gap of misunderstanding, friction, and estrangement and by establishing and maintaining lines of communication between the police and the public. The primary purpose of the unit is to render service; however, community services unit personnel also enforce the criminal ordinances and statutes. The purpose and function of the community services unit can be summarized as follows:

1. To find people in need.
2. To direct them to those agencies or community resources where their needs can be met.
3. In addition, the community services unit has responsibility for juvenile delinquency control efforts, investigation of delinquency-producing conditions, and investigation of juvenile offenders and offenses committed against juveniles. The casework method is used to accomplish the objectives of the Unit.

Community Councils[164]

A community council is established in each police division. The councils are composed of community leaders who work with the divisional community relations officer in the development of programs and the two-way transmittal of information between the police and the public. The councils involve themselves in such activities as workshops, dinners, anticrime campaigns, motorcades, and parades in support of law enforcement.

Citizen's Advisory Committee[165]

This is a committee composed of various representatives of the community and established so that the police department could have the advantage of counsel from a distinguished group of citizens informally representing many segments of the community.

Police-Community Relations Area Councils[166]

This program is sponsored by the police department in conjunction with the local antipoverty community action program. The purpose of the councils is to allow the police to work with various neighborhood service centers in working with residents of low-income areas in an effort to emphasize the mutual interdependence of the police and the community in seeking solutions to neighborhood problems, and to develop mutual respect and understanding between the police and the public by promoting an atmosphere conducive to greater public cooperation.

Arrest Record Interpretation[167]

Under this program, members of the police–community relations unit make arrest-record interpretations to employers for prospective employees. The purpose of doing so is based on the knowledge that there exists a tendency on the part of employers to automatically disqualify prospective employees because they have arrest records. The police act as a mitigator to allow persons with police records to receive equitable consideration and not be unnecessarily excluded from employment.

Community Relations Volunteer Program[168]

This program is designed to take the fullest possible advantage of resources in the community which are capable of assisting in the area of police–community relations. It is designed to identify and organize these resources to bear upon questions of police–community relations and to produce concrete results. Interested individuals representing as broad a base as possible are invited to join the program. They are issued identification cards and members of the police–community relations division visit them frequently. During these visits, emphasis is placed on identifying potential trouble areas and soliciting advice on what steps should be taken to solve the problems of their neighborhood. Emphasis is placed on encouraging citizen participation within the total law enforcement effort.

Employment Centers[169]

Through facilities donated by merchants, employment centers are staffed by personnel from the police–community relations division (and volunteers) in low-income areas. The purpose of this program is to recruit persons from poverty areas in an effort to encourage them to seek employment with the city government in job openings that are generally not known.

Liaison with Poverty Programs[170]

Officers from the community relations section are assigned to work in Economic Opportunity centers throughout the city. The main objective of the officers is to build better relations between the police department and the general public. The Economic Opportunity centers were chosen because of the close contact between the centers' activities and the residents of poverty-stricken areas of the city. By working out of the centers, the officers acquaint themselves with the problems of the communities by attending meetings and speaking before various community groups. The officers also assist in organizing new groups which will help to improve the neighborhood; assist in recreational programs for the residents in their area; turn on sprinklers from fire hydrants for children during the summer months; counsel school dropouts; receive complaints from citizens regarding any other city service; handle missing person reports; and handle hardship cases (e.g., people who need food, clothing, or shelter). The officers drive station wagons equipped with speakers and a turntable. This allows the officers to go into the community, block off a street, and let the people relax by having a street dance.

Operation Friend[171]

This is a threefold project that focuses primarily on the relationship of the Puerto Rican population and the police:

1. Instructions for police personnel in the language, culture, and mores of Puerto Rico.
2. Meetings for local Puerto Rican leaders with the police to plan discussions of mutual problems.
3. Classes for neighborhood youths of minority groups to prepare them for entrance examinations for the police force. Also, ten police officers visited Puerto Rico to learn their customs and habits, which was reciprocated by having Puerto Rican children visit the homes of the officers.

Committee on Human Rights and Law Enforcement[172]

The purpose of this committee is to maintain a two-way street of communication between the police department and other law enforcement agencies and educational, church, ethnic, social, and professional groups, whereby the police department and the community can jointly discuss community conditions and problems. The committee meets monthly except during the summer months, when it meets biweekly. In addition, special meetings can be called as deemed necessary to attempt to solve any problem or condition critical to the good of the community.

Precinct Community Council Program[173]

The purpose of the precinct community councils are to promote support for law enforcement efforts, encourage and increase cooperation between the police and the public, and to develop specific programs in accordance with true needs, interests, and resources of the local community that will support the maintenance of law and order and the prevention of crime and delinquency. There are 76 councils, one for each police precinct. The activities of the councils focus on attaining the overall goals and objectives of police–community relations, and their activities fall into several general categories:

1. Crime prevention
2. Orientation to the department's structure and operation
3. Interpretation of police powers and limitations
4. Cultural exchange programs focusing on differences and similarities in race, religion, language, and traditions
5. Community education on narcotics and other harmful conditions
6. Neighborhood problem-solving directed at dangerous, unhealthy, and unsightly conditions

7. Information exchange regarding available community services, programs, and resources
8. Sponsorship and direction of youth activities as part of the department's delinquency prevention program

Elementary School Community Council Representatives[174]

The elementary school community council is composed of police officers, educators, business and professional people, members of the clergy, and citizens who are employed near or live within a school boundary. This includes school-related organizations such as scouts, men and women's clubs, child study groups, homeroom mothers, and block club organizations. The specific purposes of the council are as follows:

1. Offer an opportunity for all people to cooperate in their efforts to understand, analyze, and solve community problems.
2. Promote cooperation among organizations and individuals in making the community a better place in which to live and work.
3. Collect and give to members and others complete and accurate information concerning the community needs and the resources available for meeting these needs.
4. Secure democratic action in meeting local needs through existing agencies, organizations, and institutions.
5. Take all necessary and advisable civic measures to develop qualities of leadership for community betterment.
6. Maintain and improve mutual understanding between the schools and other integral parts of the community.
7. Work together in each school area and to cooperate with neighborhood organizations for the promotion of good human relations.

Case Work[175]

Chronic police problems in neighborhoods are investigated by this detail when referred by the chief of the division. Cases of an assorted nature are handled, settled, and referred to civil agencies when police action cannot solve the matter.

Neighborhood Sessions[176]

Under this program sessions are arranged by the police–community relations detail for beat officers to meet with citizens in a neighborhood to discuss neighborhood problems and other matters of concern and to allow the citizens to get to know the police. Sessions are arranged with adults and with juveniles. The purpose of this program is to identify problems on the neighborhood level that create friction between the police and the residents.

In addition to the programs listed above, the St. Louis Police Department operates two programs designed to arrest problems that occur on an ad hoc basis. The first one is called the "Helping Hand Program." Under the program, clothing and toys are donated to district community-relations officers, who in turn give them to families in need (e.g., people who remain homeless due to fires and other emergencies). The second program is entitled the "Christmas Basket Program." Through this program, merchants from the community are solicited several weeks before Christmas for donations of food and toys. Members of the community relations division then distribute food baskets to persons and families in low-income areas.[177]

End Notes

[1] While police organizations have typically been associated with police-community relations problems, one should not discount the fact that other components of our criminal justice system experience similar problems.

[2] Allen B. Ballard, "Police Working in the Neighborhood," *Police and Community Relations: A Sourcebook,* ed. A. F. Brandstatter and Louis A. Radelet. (Encino, California: Glenco Press, 1968), p. 356.

[3] J. Robert Havlick, "Police–Community Relations Programs," *Management Information Service,* Report No. 286 (Washington, D.C.: International City Managers' Association, 1967) November 1967, p. 5.

[4] Michigan State University, *A National Survey of Police and Community Relations,* report submitted to the President's Commission on Law Enforcement and Administration of Justice (Washington, D.C.: U.S. Government Printing Office, 1967), p. 3.

[5] Cutlip and Center, *Effective Public Relations: Pathways to Public Favor* (New York: Prentice-Hall, Inc., 1952), p. 2.

[6] Ibid., p. 6.

[7] Dante Andreotti, "Our War Was with the Police Department," *Fortune,* 1966, p. 195.

[8] Winston-Salem Police Department, *Community Services Unit: First Report and Preliminary Evaluation,* July 1967, p. 30.

[9] The New York City Police Department operates a program entitled "Police–Community Center," which is a storefront located in central Harlem.

[10] Two similar programs are operated by the New York City Police Department: (1) "Interpretation Program," where volunteers are called upon to serve as interpreters, and (2) "Citizen Advisory Service," where volunteers are at the station house to confer with citizens on nonpolice matters. The Washington, D.C., Police Department has a similar program called "Volunteer Aid Program," where volunteers run information and referral desks in precinct station houses.

[11] This program is operated by the San Jose, Ca., Police Department.

[12] St. Louis, Missouri, Metropolitan Police Department.

[13]Los Angeles, California, Police Department.

[14]Novato, California, Police Department. Many other departments operate similar programs (e.g., San Jose, California; New Orleans, Louisiana). A similar program called "Operation Observation," is conducted by the Richmond, California, Police Department.

[15]New York City Police Department.

[16]Los Angeles, California, Police Department.

[17]Ibid.

[18]Flint, Michigan, Police Department.

[19]In almost all cities that operate a police–community relations program, members of the unit serve on various community committees.

[20]Philadelphia, Pennsylvania, Police Department.

[21]St. Louis, Missouri, Metropolitan Police Department.

[22]New York City Police Department. A similar program is operated by the St. Louis Police Department and the Los Angeles Police Department.

[23]New Orleans, Louisiana, Police Department.

[24]Novato, California, Police Department. Two California law enforcement agencies (Riverside Sheriff's Office and South San Francisco Police Department) have evaluated citizens' reactions to uniform changes.

[25]New Orleans, Louisiana, Police Department.

[26]Ibid.

[27]Philadelphia, Pennsylvania, Police Department.

[28]Almost all police departments have developed a variety of printed material for distribution in the community.

[29]St. Louis, Missouri, Police Department.

[30]Almost all cities with a police–community relations program engage in this type of activity.

[31]New York City Police Department.

[32]Ibid.

[33]St. Louis, Missouri, Police Department.

[34]New York City Police Department.

[35]Ibid, and the San Jose, California, Police Department.

[36]New York City Police Department.

[37]Ibid.

[38]Des Moines, Iowa, Police Department.

[39]Almost all cities operate this program.

[40]Los Angeles, California, Police Department.

[41]San Jose, California, Police Department. Several other cities publish periodic newsletters (e.g., San Francisco, Winston-Salem).

[42]San Jose, California, Police Department.

[43]Los Angeles, California, Police Department.

[44]San Jose, California, Police Department.

[45]Ibid. San Jose and many other departments (e.g., Los Angeles, St. Louis) sponsor radio programs.

[46]St. Louis, Missouri, Police Department.

[47]Chicago, Illinois, Police Department.

[48]Portland, Oregon, Police Department.

[49]San Diego, California, Police Department.

[50]Novato, California, Police Department.

[51]San Jose, California, Police Department and those of several other California cities.

[52]New Orleans, Louisiana, Police Department.

[53]San Jose, California, Police Department.

[54]Ibid.

[55]Novato, California, Police Department.

[56]Oakland, California, Police Department.

[57]Los Angeles, California, Police Department.

[58]New York City Police Department.

[59]Ibid.

[60]St. Louis, Missouri, Police Department. A similar program entitled "Block Parent Program" is operated by the Santa Clara, Ca. Sheriff's Office and the San Jose, Ca., Police Department.

[61]Washington, D.C., Metropolitan Police Department.

[62]San Jose, California, Police Department.

[63]Oakland, California, Police Department.

[64]This Motorola-sponsored program is operated by many police departments throughout the nation.

[65]San Jose, California, Police Department.

[66]New York City Police Department.

[67]St. Louis, Missouri, Police Department.

[68]Ibid.

[69]New York City Police Department.

[70]Los Angeles, California, Police Department.

[71]"Citizens Helping Eliminate Crime" (CHEC) is a similar program operated by the Flint, Michigan, Police Department. Other programs of a similar nature are (1) "Town Watch," Philadelphia Police Department; "Signal Ten," Washington, D.C.: "Crime Stop," Richmond, California.

[72]Des Moines, Iowa, Police Department. (This program could also be classified as a crime prevention program.)

[73]Richmond, California, Police Department.

[74]Oakland, California, Police Department.

[75]San Jose, California, Police Department.

[76]Los Angeles, California, Police Department.

[77]Mountain View, California, Police Department.

[78]San Jose, California, Police Department.

[79]Los Angeles, California, Police Department.

[80]Ibid.

[81]This particular program is operated by the Los Angeles Police Department; however, many other cities have similar programs (e.g., St. Louis, Des Moines, San Jose, New York, Oakland, Philadelphia, San Diego).

[82]Los Angeles, California, Police Department.

[83]San Jose, California, Police Department.

[84]Los Angeles, California, Police Department.

[85]Ibid.

[86]Ibid.

[87]Ibid.

[88]San Jose, California, Police Department.

[89]New Orleans, Louisiana, Police Department.

[90]Philadelphia, Pennsylvania, Police Department.

[91]St. Louis, Missouri, Police Department.

[92]Ibid., and Fairview, Oklahoma, Police Department.

[93]San Diego, California, Police Department.

[94]Novato, California, Police Department.

[95]Ibid.

[96]San Diego, California, Police Department.

[97]Ibid.

[98]New Orleans, Louisiana, Police Department.

[99]Ibid.

[100]Ibid.

[101]Ibid.

[102]Washington, D.C., Police Department.

[103]Greensboro, North Carolina, Police Department.

[104]San Jose, California, Police Department.

[105]New Orleans, Louisiana, Police Department.

[106]Philadelphia, Pennsylvania, Police Department.

[107]Atlanta, Georgia, Police Department.

[108]New Orleans, Louisiana, Police Department.

[109]Ibid.

[110]St. Louis, Missouri, Police Department.

[111]Ibid.

[112]New Orleans, Louisiana, Police Department.

[113]New York City Police Department.

[114]Ibid.

[115]Ibid.

[116]Chicago was one of the first cities to establish this program and it has been evaluated by the board of education. Other cities (e.g., Oakland; Washington, D.C.; Richmond, Va.) operate similar programs under the same title.

[117]New York City Police Department.

[118]Chicago, Illinois, Police Department.

[119]New York City Police Department.

[120]Washington, D.C., Police Department.
[121]St. Louis, Missouri, Police Department.
[122]Ibid.
[123]New York City Police Department
[124]Washington, D.C., Police Department.
[125]Ibid.
[126]San Francisco, California, Police Department.
[127]San Diego, California, Police Department.
[128]San Jose, California, Police Department.
[129]Washington, D.C., Police Department.
[130]St. Louis, Missouri, Police Department.
[131]Ibid.
[132]Washington, D.C., Police Department.
[133]Ibid.
[134]Ibid.
[135]Ibid.
[136]Ibid.
[137]San Jose, California, Police Department.
[138]Oakland, California, Police Department.
[139]St. Louis, Missouri, Police Department.
[140]Los Angeles, California, Police Department.
[141]Ibid.
[142]Richmond, California, Police Department.
[143]New York City Police Department.
[144]Los Angeles, California, Police Department.
[145]Ibid.
[146]Ibid.
[147]Flint, Michigan, Police Department.
[148]Pontiac, Michigan, Police Department.
[149]Flint, Michigan, Police Department.
[150]Philadelphia, Pennsylvania, Police Department.
[151]Covina, California, Police Department.
[152]San Jose, California, Police Department. In addition, many other departments' community relations officers conduct in-service training programs in human and community relations.
[153]Los Angeles, California, Police Department.
[154]Novato, California, Police Department.
[155]Atlanta, Georgia, Police Department.
[156]St. Louis, Missouri, Police Department.
[157]Philadelphia, Pennsylvania, Police Department.
[158]Los Angeles, California, Police Department.
[159]Philadelphia, Pennsylvania, Police Department.
[160]Los Angeles, California, Police Department.

[161]San Francisco, California, Police Department. Under a program entitled "Economic Opportunities Commission Liaison," the San Diego Police Department also assigns officers to local community action councils, but not on a full-time basis.

[162]Chicago, Illinois, Police Department. Several other cities (e.g., Philadelphia, Des Moines, Los Angeles, San Jose) operate similar workshops.

[163]Winston-Salem, North Carolina, Police Department.

[164]Los Angeles, California, Police Department.

[165]San Jose, California, Police Department.

[166]Ibid.

[167]Ibid.

[168]Washington, D.C., Police Department.

[169]New Orleans, Louisiana, Police Department.

[170]Atlanta, Georgia, Police Department.

[171]New York City Police Department.

[172]Ibid.

[173]New York City Police Department.

[174]Flint, Michigan, Police Department.

[175]San Jose, California, Police Department.

[176]Ibid.

[177]The San Diego Police Department operates a similar program called "Police Department Christmas Program."

APPENDIX II

EVALUATION OF POLICE–COMMUNITY RELATIONS PROGRAMS

Donald Campbell is a noted authority in the field of social action research and evaluation. As such, he recognizes the need for special methodological tools for the assessment of programs already implemented or completed. He is not only credited with the development of quasi-experimental designs for social action research and evaluation, but is also applauded for his encouragement of "qualitative knowing" in this field.[1] The latter is an alternative to the quantitative-experimental approach to evaluation. In a lecture address to the Society for the Psychological Study of Social Issues, he drew the following distinction between qualitative and quantitative research-evaluation methods:

> These terms are shorthand for a common denominator among a wide range of partially overlapping concepts; for *quantitative* read also scientific, scientistic, and *naturwissenschaftlich;* for *qualitative* read also humanistic, *geisteswissenschaftlich,* experimental, phenomenological, clinical, case study, field work, participant observation, process evaluation, and common sense knowing.[2]

*The authors wish to express their appreciation to C. Sheila Misner for her suggestions on this appendix.

Campbell certainly does not advocate the use of qualitative methodology exclusively, but rather the combination of qualitative and quantitative tools. Often, however, social scientists and program personnel lack sufficient, accurate, and appropriate data to perform quantitative evaluations. This is particularly true when thought is given to the matter of evaluation only after actual implementation of the program. In some cases, quantitative evaluation is not possible or appropriate, or is simply too expensive. (It makes little sense to spend $100,000 to evaluate a program costing only $10,000 to implement!) For these types of programs, qualitative assessment is the only method available. According to Campbell, legitimate tools to develop qualitative evaluations of programs can take several forms.

It can involve the social scientist's own qualitative experiences, as in a single time sample in the *site visit,* or over an entire social action experience, including a preprogram period, as in *participant observation* and non-participant observation. But still more common in qualitative social science is the expert's role in recording and collating the participant's experiences, as through informant interviews, opinion surveys, or the *experience interview* of the Committee on Community Interrelations.[3]

In Appendix I, we presented an inventory of the variety of programs developed by police agencies around the country that are operated under the title "police–community relations." In presenting these brief descriptions of some programs, no attempt was made to evaluate quantitatively and scientifically the effectiveness of those programs. That is, there was no assessment of what the programs actually contributed to better police–community relations, nor what elements within programs were most successful in developing effective police–community relations. Such a task would depend on the availability of quasiexperimental methodological requirements. It would require, for example, a clear and concise definition of program goals and objectives; reliable and consistent recording of data related to programs, experimental control; and so on.[4] The police–community relations programs surveyed throughout the country failed to provide, or were unable to provide, these essential elements for evaluation.

The content of this chapter relies exclusively on qualitative descriptions and assessment of police–community relations programs. We recognize that there is no valid and reliable data base from which to determine the actual success of programs. One should recognize that there is no professional agreement as to what constitutes success in police–community relations programming!

Material for this chapter is based primarily on interviews with selected police department personnel or on reports from agencies operating various programs. Hence, any bias in using such information for evaluative purposes would probably be in favor of the reporting agencies. In addition, the content of this appendix undoubtedly contains some unintended but unavoidable biases on the part of the authors, especially those relating to assumptions of what constitutes, or is conducive to, successful police-community relations programming.

THE NEED FOR EVALUATION

Police-community relations programs have as their basic goal betterment of the relationship between the police and the public. Although simply stated, the core of goal achievement is massive. Cities have spent millions of dollars developing and implementing police-community relations programs. The proliferation of specialized units in police-community relations throughout the nation attests to the willingness of the city government to support the concept of programming in order to improve this relationship.

Although the major efforts devoted to police-community relations have been to develop action programs, there has been an increasing demand for a means by which the effectiveness of the programs can be assessed. Both those who are sincere about police-community relations and those who are critical of such programs are equally persistent in their demands for program evaluation. Interestingly enough, police-community relations is one of the few, if not the only, operational unit within the police department that is being asked to prove its effectiveness. It is one, if not the only, unit within the police department that is being asked to justify its existence.

This singling out of police-community relations units as a police function that has to justify its continuous support can be attributed to two causes. First, all other units of police departments, because of time, are generally accepted as serving a legitimate purpose just because they exist. At one time, for example, juvenile units were asked to prove their effectiveness and justify their continual support. Now, however, such units are accepted as being an indispensable unit of a police agency. Today, one would no more think of doing away with a juvenile unit than doing away with the patrol division. Time obviously brought about acceptance.

Second, many social-service-type agencies in the country today are being asked to prove their effectiveness. Is education accomplishing its purpose? What results came from the "war on poverty?" Is religion relevant? Police-community relations, established to deliver a social service, is caught up in the current public demand being made to all social institutions to prove their worthwhileness.

Basic changes are occurring in the society. The resistance to these changes has resulted in ferment, and for good reason demands are being made on the police to evaluate their police-community relations program to determine if they are meeting the needs of the community in an ever-changing society. The needs for program evaluation can be seen in the following developments.

Problems Change

The problems that cause abrasive police–community relations are directly related to socioeconomic problems that exist in the wider community. This suggests that abrasive police–community relations that exist in one segment of the community (e.g., the black community) have a direct bearing on police–community relations in the entire community. Just as the problems of inadequate education in the black community can be attributed to inequities in the total educational system, abrasive police–community relations in the black community can also be attributed to inequities in the police department. Thus, the problems of police–community relations cannot be attributed solely to individual estrangement or alienation. Rather, estrangement and alienation should be looked at in a different light. That is to say that the social institutions, including the police, might very well be estranged and alienated from the people. Rather than attempting to change the public's attitude toward the police, reforms within the police department are called for. Hence, there is a need to continually evaluate the policies, procedures, and activities of the police to assure that they are not, themselves, the causes of abrasive public attitudes toward the police.

Furthermore, the socioeconomic conditions of a community may change. Since police–community relations are influenced by those conditions, the focus of the programs must address itself to the same conditions. Changing patterns in socioeconomic problems call for evaluation of police–community relations programs.

Changing Police Role

Not only has the nature of police work changed, so have the public expectations of the police. Whereas the police once constituted an ultrasecretive organization, more and broader community participation in determining police policies and procedures is being demanded. No longer can the police define their role in strict and narrow terms of "law enforcement" and interpret that to mean "crook catcher"; they must now broaden that interpretation to include their service function and crime prevention responsibilities. Undoubtedly, the day will come when the police will consider their entire existence to be a service organization for the community, enforcement of the law being only one aspect of those services, and a small one at that.

Such a redefinition of the police mission will undoubtedly result in changes in the recruitment, training, and organizational structure of police departments. A reallocation of priorities, enlargement in both the scope and nature of services, and changes in activities will require evaluation on a continuous basis. Paramilitary organization structures as we know them today may be replaced with new categories that reflect a "new police." As police work approaches the status of becoming a true profession, as the educational and training level of the police increase, there will become an awareness of the need for critical self-evaluation.

Changes in the Community

The development, implementation, and operation of any police-community relations program must have as an integral ingredient citizen input and participation. When such programs were first started, there was general agreement that they were needed; consequently, they were accepted on face value. It is becoming increasingly clear today, however, that the need for police–community relations programs and the effectiveness of police–community relations programs are not synonymous. The public, and rightfully so, is no longer willing to support the programs on faith alone. Whereas it was once possible to develop programs, and correspondingly volunteers would participate, a more sophisticated public is now demanding proof that their time and efforts are bearing fruit. Continuous citizen participation, similar to continuous fan support of a baseball team, is contingent upon success. That is, if police–community relations are to continue to maintain citizen interest and participation, they must produce empirical evidence of their effectiveness.

The directions in which police agencies are moving are self-evident. More and more emphasis will be placed on the service aspect of policing or, if you prefer, police–community relations. Thus, after the novelty of a new approach to policing wears off, the demands for evaluation comes naturally as the next stage. This normal sequence of evaluation receives its impetus from (1) change in the problems within the community, (2) changes in the role of the police, and (3) changes that occur in the community.

THE STATE OF THE ART

A police department may orient its specialized community relations program to one of four general approaches. Each approach represents the development of a group of programs that the department feels will better the relationship between the agency and the public. The distinction that we will make is an analytical one. Although we will identify four departments as being illustrative of our four types, probably no department is governed exclusively by the orientation we shall describe. In other words, one department may have, in addition to its primary orientation, characteristics of one or all of the other three types. It is important for the reader to understand that our typology identifies only the operating style of an agency and suggests only certain characteristics in an abstract form. The four types identified here are: (1) externally oriented, (2) youth-oriented, (3) service-oriented, and (4) internally oriented.[5]

EXTERNALLY ORIENTED PROGRAMS

In developing their community relations program, some police departments have placed a heavy emphasis on implementing a wide variety of programs that are operated under the title of police–community relations. Such programs are generally developed by a specialized police–community relations unit and are directed toward the general public or various enclaves within the community. This approach we shall call "externally oriented."

The St. Louis Metropolitan Police Department is an example of an externally oriented department. St. Louis has a total population of about 720,000 people, 39 percent of whom are black. Similar to all other large cities, St. Louis has large poverty areas, which are characterized by "tension, frustrations and resentment toward police who apparently represent a tangible symbol against which poverty citizens can strike to relieve these frustrations. Also, in poverty areas, there is a high rate of crime considerably above the population proportion."[6]

Having established a public relations division in 1957, the St. Louis Police Department has developed numerous programs which have served as prototypes for other cities. "The basic objectives underlying the present St. Louis police–community relations program are to reduce and prevent crime in St. Louis through joint police–community cooperation and to improve intergroup relations in the community."[7]

To accomplish these objectives, the St. Louis Police Department has developed the following programs:[8]

1. Police–Community Relations Youth Council
2. Headstart Program
3. School Visitation Program
4. Say Hi Program
5. Youth Activities Program
6. Pre-Natal Program
7. Special Youth Program
8. Explorer Post Program
9. Police–Junior Aide Program
10. Cruiser Tours
11. Jaycee Award Program
12. Law Enforcement Assistance Award

13. Police–Community Relations Award
14. Police–Community Relations Training
15. Sergeants In-Service
16. Police–Community Relations Council
17. Tour Program
18. State Fair
19. Citizens Against Crime
20. Police–Community Relations Information Program
21. Clergy–Police Program
22. Brochures
23. Police–Community Relations Film
24. Visiting Officers Program
25. Police–Community Relations Store Front Centers
26. District Committees
27. Communications Program
28. St. Louis Council of Police–Community Relations
29. Mass Media Relations
30. Speaker's Bureau
31. Lock-Your-Car Campaign
32. Convention Letters
33. Businessmen's Meetings
34. Police–Community Relations Newsletter
35. Law Enforcement Day
36. Sanitation Project
37. Protection Project
38. Whom-to-Call
39. Police–Community Relations Committee on Housing Project
40. Block Watcher Program
41. Neighborhood Helper Program
42. Operation Little Sweep
43. Community Athletic League

As illustrated by this list, the essential characteristics of an externally oriented department is its willingness to try various approaches to accomplish its goal. Consequently, such a department's community relations program will generally represent all of the program categories identified in Appendix I: for example, public relations, youth programs, crime prevention, training, and police–community relations. The structure of an externally oriented department is often flexible and accommodates changes and experimentation in devising programs designed to achieve its goal. The variety of programs are, in general, operated external of the police department.

YOUTH-ORIENTED

A youth-oriented department is exemplified by police departments that direct the majority of their efforts toward the youth of the community. Here we are referring to the efforts of the community relations section and not the total police department. The programs that are developed by the police–community relations unit are aimed primarily at the youth and the majority of the community relations officers' time is spent working with youth.

The New Orleans Police Department is an example of a youth-oriented department. The City of New Orleans has a population of about 660,000, with 40 percent being black. "With ten federal housing projects, as well as other low income areas scattered throughout the city . . . policing presents certain problems."[9]

The police–community relations program in New Orleans was established in April 1966. One of the major objectives of the program is to "attempt to reach the youth of the community, where else should we start?"[10] With this objective in mind, the New Orleans Police Department has developed the following programs:

1. Meetings
2. Career Days
3. Coloring Books
4. Saints Pro-Football Games
5. Headquarters Tours
6. Special Sporting Events
7. Movie Program
8. Christmas Baskets
9. Self Defense Program
10. Portable Swimming Pools
11. Swimming Program
12. Police Buses
13. Sprinklers
14. Amusement Park Program
15. Boxing
16. Basketball Teams
17. "Know Your Police Department" TV Series
18. Air Flights
19. Employment Centers
20. Summer Recreation
21. Talent Contests
22. Send a Kid to Camp
23. Officer Friendly Program

24. Citizen Participation
25. Special Programs
26. Seminars
27. New Careers
28. Additional Training
29. Security Detail
30. Investigations

Of this list of 30 programs, 19 are designed primarily for youth. This illustrates the essential characteristics of a youth-oriented department. It should be noted that the department also operates programs in the areas of public relations, crime prevention, training, and police–community relations. The primary emphasis, however, is upon the youth of the community.

SERVICE-ORIENTED

In developing their community relations programs, some police departments have emphasized the alleviation of social problems as their basic objective. In such cases, the defining characteristic of the department's community relations objective becomes the orientation of their specialized program. We shall call this type "service-oriented," using a term that describes what really should be the mission of the American police system.

Illustrative of a service-oriented department is the Winston-Salem, North Carolina, Police Department.

With a population of 143,000 . . . [Winston-Salem] has in miniature the big city problems of slums, crime and unemployment. In many ways a remarkable city—beautiful, historic, cultural, wealthy, compared with some other places in the South—it has felt the mark of poverty; 15 percent of the whites and 45 percent of the non-whites fall below the official boundaries of deprivation.[11]

In 1966, the Winston-Salem Police Department established a community services unit. The purpose of this unit is threefold:[12]

1. To find people in need.
2. To direct them to those agencies or community resources where the need can be met.
3. To search out those things that are conducive to crime and see that they are rooted out of the community.

The Police-Community Services Unit is a service organization dedicated to the cause of helping citizens who, for many reasons, cannot or lack the knowl-

Appendix II

edge to help themselves. In the day-to-day operations of the unit, its members act as "transmission belts" whereby those who have a particular problem are referred to an existing agency which is in a position to render the needed service.[13]

These objectives have been carried out in the following ways:[14]

1. Upon discovering a specific case, or even in the cases of apprehension, the first step for each officer is to ask the basic question, "why?"
2. It will next be the duty of the police–community services unit officers to investigate underlying causes and to assess all community resources available for the person and family, and to offer all possible means of protective service and aid, in order to give the person a new approach to his or her problems and a new outlook on life.
3. By working through the Experiment in Self Reliance, Inc.'s neighborhood service centers, and by becoming familiar with the entire area on a professional and friendly basis, the officers assigned to this unit have become closely related to and familiar with most of the neighborhood.
4. In many instances, this procedure has helped to prevent early criminal records for young offenders, and to give such young offenders a chance to solve their problems without going through court formalities.
5. One of the greatest services of the community services unit is the giving to the community a new image of the function of police regarding law and order, and instilling of new ideas in young people as regards to their respect for law and order.
6. Systematic case follow-up has been initiated to ensure the effectiveness of the service rendered.

The essential characteristics of a service-oriented program are its expressed concern and involvement in the socioeconomic problems of the community. Such a unit acts as a discovery and referral agency for ridding the community of varied problems. Such a program, although primarily concerned with socioeconomic problems, also concerns itself with activities identified with the four other categories identified earlier. For example, the Winston-Salem Police Department is concerned with public relations, which is evident by their use of a newsletter. They are concerned with crime prevention, which is evident in this statement: "In view of our past experience, we must look for other means of preventing crime and decreasing the rate of recidivism. We must delve deeply into the 'why' of crime."[15]

They are concerned with youth, which is evident by the fact their community service officers follow up on all cases involving juveniles. They are concerned with community relations training, which is evident by the extensive training program they have developed.[16] Their primary focus, however, is on *service*.

INTERNALLY ORIENTED PROGRAMS

Some police departments have not established a specialized community relations unit but are still very community relations-minded. Such departments operate on the premise that every officer is a police-community relations officer and attempt to involve all members of the agency in promoting good community relations. We shall call this type "internally oriented." The essential characteristic of an internally oriented program is the explicit realization that the officer on the beat creates community relations, be they good or bad.

The Covina, California, Police Department is an example of an internally oriented department. With a population of about 30,000 people, Covina has only a small number of black families. Police–community relations for the Covina Police Department is designed to involve the total police department. It does not have a specialized police–community relations unit, and if one is ever created, "it will only serve in a staff capacity."[17] The philosophy of an internally oriented community relations program is articulated by former chief Fred Ferguson:

> We believe in Covina that it is possible to do a good job with fewer people if they are the right people with proper values, skills and equipment. Some communities facing the same type of problems have used another approach. They have trained several employees as experts in community relations. These few in turn meet with the various community groups and attempt to acquaint them with law enforcement problems and hopefully gain their support. In a community such as ours, it seems more logical to have all our personnel understand the people with whom they deal.[18]

In pursuing this philosophy, Ferguson implemented some novel programs within the Covina Police Department. One, all of the police officers (including the chief) are attending college or are involved in some other continuing educational program. This endeavor is supported by both the police department and the city government. The department supports it by rotating work shifts around the school schedules, and the city supports it by paying for members' tuition and books.[19]

Second, Ferguson initiated a program whereby a citizen who registers a complaint against the police department is invited to ride for one evening in a patrol car with officers to see the problems of those concerned with law enforcement.[20]

Third, members of the department underwent an extensive police–community relations training program designed "to equip selected uniformed and non-uniformed members of the Covina Police Department with greater knowledge and skill essential to better understanding and dealing more effectively with members of the Covina Community, and their own department."[21]

The specific objectives of this police-community relations training program were the following:

1. To obtain knowledge about the traditional Judaic-Christian democratic view of man generally held in the United States, and the application of the view to police-community relations.
2. To acquire skills in interpersonal and intergroup relations.
3. To gain information from the behavioral sciences about the human individual, interpersonal and group relationships, complex organizations and the community as an environment.[22]

Fourth, the department developed and implemented a program called "Operation Empathy." This program is designed to give police officers a realistic, though brief, view of the world in which many of their "clientele" live. This is accomplished by "booking" Covina police officers into jail in a neighboring community for an evening.

Fifth, the department operated a program entitled "Coffee Klatch."

Sixth, the department implemented a program entitled "Operation Empathy—Skid Row." Under this program, Covina police officers spend time on Los Angeles' skid row. Ferguson explained this program as follows:

Our Covina officers who were willing to become skid row inhabitants, were carefully selected and conditioned for the role they were about to play. Each man was given three dollars with which to purchase a complete outfit of pawn shop clothing. The only new article of attire he was allowed was footwear—reject tennis shoes purchased for a few small coins. Among his other props were such items as a shopping bag filled with collected junk, and a wine bottle camoflaged with a brown paper sack.

Conditioned and ready, our men, assigned in pairs, moved into the Los Angeles skid row district. They soon discovered that when they tried to leave the area, walking a few blocks into the legitimate retail sections, they were told, "Go back where you belong!" Our men knew in reality they were not "bums," but they found that other citizens quickly categorized them and treated them accordingly. Some women, when approached on the sidewalk and asked for a match, stepped out into the street rather than offer a reply, much less a light for a smoke.

During the skid row experiment, our men ate in the rescue missions, and sat through the prayer services with other outcasts and derelicts. They roamed the streets and alleys, and discovered many leveling experiences. Some were anticipated, others were not.[23]

Seventh, the Covina Police Department has proposed a new program entitled "Exploring Criminal Justice as a Total System." This program was to be operated as follows:

The thrust of our proposal is to select two Captain rank police personnel and rotate them in a work experience training program with five different parts of the System which include the District Attorney's Office, the Court, Corrections, Probation-Parole, and Mental Health-Welfare. While Mental Health and Welfare are not traditionally thought of as part of the System, current legislative trends would indicate that we should begin to consider them as such. For example, there is a desire on the part of some legislators to remove certain social problems, such as alcoholism and homosexual activities between consenting adults, from the criminal statutes, Obviously, some other referral will take place. Wherever possible, we hope to receive an exchange person from these agencies. The two Captains will alternate one month of work with the training agency and one month to relate back to the Police Department. Desirably, the exchange counterpart from the various agencies will move into a staff position during his month with us. His influence will undoubtedly have a positive impact which will be reinforced as each Captain returns. Relatively, the same impact is expected on the parent agency.[24]

A final example of Covina's police-community relations efforts can be seen in their appointment of a college professor as acting chief during Ferguson's absence from the city. Under this experiment, Paul Whisenand, a professor in the Department of Criminology, California State College at Long Beach (a former Los Angeles police officer), served as chief of police for one month during Ferguson's absence.[25]

The development of a program to improve every member of a police department, thereby involving all officers in police-community relations, is the essential characteristic of an internally oriented department. Such departments express a willingness to experiment and accept citizen input as a stimulus for changing or modifying the department's policies and procedures.

COMMONSENSE PROGRAM EVALUATION

Essentially, the program operated by police departments under the title of police-community relations have been of limited value. Many were hastily established because it was "fashionable" to have one. Some were created to prevent riots. In both cases, the programs were given little, if any, direction and virtually no authority to deal with substantive issues of the community or the department. In other cases, the existence of the unit was contingent upon the condition that it not do anything— "don't rock the boat." In some places, the unit became a dumping ground for officers who were misfits in other units.

In developing their police-community relations program, most cities, made the mistake of viewing police-community relations as separate from the other operations of the police department. Consequently, such programs were looked upon as being of marginal importance to the overall police mission and in many cases they were viewed with hostility by other members of the police department. The latter concern can be seen in the comments made by members of the San Francisco Police

Department at a community relations conference held in that city in 1966:

> They (community relations officers) are not doing police work. We are out in the street dealing with the garbage. We see the real slum. Those guys wear their suits and make out like good guys. Hell, they are not policemen, they are just social workers.
>
> Community relations people are not doing anything for us. They devote all of their time to the community and totally neglect the police department. If it is really *police*-community relations, then they should be doing something for the police also. We need help, too.
>
> What do I know about our community relations unit? Nothing except what I read in the paper. I feel bad when our department starts a new program and I have to read about it in the paper. I think the policemen should be the first to know about a new police program. We shouldn't have to learn about it from someone else or the paper.
>
> They are a bunch of elusive people. We don't know what they are doing. They seem to have a secret operation.
>
> Community relations? They're out there trying to pacify those minority groups. They are catering to the same people that give us a bad time on the streets.
>
> It seems to me and a lot of other policemen that community relations people are just trying to solicit complaints against us.
>
> They're social workers. That's all, just do-gooders.
>
> Yea, I got called on the carpet once because some guy I busted complained to the community relations unit. I don't trust them.[26]

This conflict between the community relations officers and the other members of the police department was summed up in a statement made by a veteran police–community relations director:

> The police in general look upon community relations as something of minor importance. They regard it as something forced upon them by the Negroes, not as something they want to do out of their hearts. They want to be efficient. You can get technically efficient as hell, but if you are not effective with people, you might as well close shop. Our war was with the police department. We were never successful in getting the message down to the foot soldier: that community relations is the most important job.[27]

In developing their police–community relations programs, many police departments placed great emphasis on establishing city-wide or neighborhood committees that met regularly for the purpose of solving the problems that separated the police from the community. The community residents that served on such committees were carefully screened and selected by the police officials. As a result, often only those were selected who were considered "safe" by the criteria defined by the police officials. Thus, only those issues that were noncontroversial in nature were discussed. They devoted their attention to such matters as crime prevention and youth programs. In a few places, the community residents did raise issues that were of substance (e.g., abrasive police practices, policies, or procedures). At such meetings, the police officials often would be very patient, attentive, and at times even appear to be aggrieved. Such meetings often turned into a catharsis session. Often, however, when the meetings were over, it became clear that nothing had really changed. The problems that led to the creation of the committees in the first place were not resolved. Consequently, many residents who were sincerely concerned about the problems stopped attending the meetings.

The "Officer Friendly" program is probably the most widely adopted police–community relations program in the nation. Under this program, uniformed officers go into the elementary schools and attempt to convince children that police officers are their friends. Although the "Officer Friendly" program has favorable short-range effects upon children, its latent effect is to increase the credibility gap between the police and children. This occurs because the children soon discover that there is a difference between Officer Friendly who comes into the classroom and the officers they meet on the streets. This point is closely related to our earlier statement that a major defect in police–community relations programs was the separation of community relations from the overall operation of the police agency. As a result, Officer Friendly, in the minds of the uniformed officers, was responsible for maintaining favorable contacts with children, whereas they were responsible for "real police work."

A number of police departments, following a recommendation made by the President's Commission on Law Enforcement and Administration of Justice, implemented the community service officer program. Under this program, young men, generally members of minority groups, were employed by police agencies as paraprofessionals. They were assigned nonenforcement activities, such as working with youth and handling abandoned vehicles. This program has not been successful because police officials have erroneously mistaken shadow for substance. That is, there exists the illusion that the community service officer program was successful because it employed a large number of minority youths. Yet the authority of the police continued to rest in the person of the sworn police officer, not the community service officer. Consequently, the gap between the police and the community was not bridged by the employment of community service officers, regardless of the number hired.

For some departments, the major involvement in police–community relations consisted of incorporating community relations sessions in their training curriculum. Too often, this occurred only after a crisis situation had developed and often only after being prompted by community pressure. With a few notable exceptions, such training programs have tended to treat community relations as concerns separate from the total police organization and operations. Rather than being treated as an integral part of all aspects of police work, "community relations" was spotted throughout the curriculum and often taught by outside instructors who more frequently alienated the trainees than captured their enthusiasm.

It is not the intention of the authors to suggest that police–community relations have been an unqualified failure. Rather, the preceding have been cited as examples of how many programmatic attempts have neglected the substantive issues that brought about their existence.

In reviewing the variety of programs in operation throughout the nation, the authors feel that there are three concerns that must be taken into consideration: program relevance, program effort, and program impact. It is within this context that police–community relations programs have been evaluated.

RELEVANCE

Relevance refers to the degree to which the programs are designed to address issues that create problems between the police and the community. In general, most police–community relations programs score low on relevance. Rather than being designed to address the *real* problems of the community, examples being socioeconomic issues and abrasive police policies and procedures, most programs have been designed simply to improve the image of the police. Illustrative of this point is one department whose sole police–community relations endeavor consisted of sewing a replica of the American flag on officers' uniforms.

The Portland, Oregon, Police Department developed an expensive public relations campaign consisting of billboards, radio and television spots, and speaking engagements asking the public to "Wave at a Cop—He's Human, Too!" The Philadelphia Police Department implemented a program called "Operation Handshake." Under this program, new officers are taken into high-crime areas to shake hands with neighborhood residents. Both the Fort Worth and the St. Louis police Departments have developed packets of information which are handed out to conventioneers, providing information on the cities. Several police departments, particularly in California, have implemented the "Coffee Klatch" program. Under this program, officers meet in the home of a resident who invites neighbors over to meet the officer, watch films, and drink coffee.

Essentially, the major objective of the police–community relations programs is image building. For that reason, they have been rather disappointing relative to their relevance to substantive issues.

COMMITMENT

Commitment refers to the amount of effort devoted to the programs. This can be evaluated in several ways: (1) the support given to the program by the top police administrator, (2) the degree of efficiency with which the program is operated, and (3) the resources allocated to the program.

Since most police-community relations programs were started as a result of crisis situations, many police administrators looked upon their program as merely a means of dealing with a temporary situation. Once the crisis passed, the pressures for having a program lessened, as did the chief's commitment.

In other situations, police agencies have established police-community relations programs because it was fashionable to have. Not fully understanding police-community relations from a conceptual or programmatic standpoint, they were unable to distinguish public relations from community relations and thereby limited the degree of involvement of those assigned community relations activities. This is illustrated by one police-community relations officer, who said:

> We have a program, but we are not doing anything. The Chief doesn't support the program. We are a kind of "don't rock the boat" unit. By that I mean we can't do anything. I have submitted several programs to the Chief for his consideration but nothing ever happens. As long as we don't rock the boat, the Chief is happy. He can go to his meetings and say "I have a community relations unit."

The nature of police-community relations is such that the success of the program is directly related to the commitment to the program on the part of the chief of police. Unfortunately, this commitment, for whatever reason, has been lacking, and that has contributed to a relative low degree of success of police-community relations.

There are cases in which police-community relations units have achieved relative success because of the administrative posture of the director of police community relations. In those relatively rare cases, the unit has organized itself in such a manner as to be successful in achieving its objectives. Illustrative of this point is the San Francisco Police-Community Relations Unit under the leadership of Dante Andreotti. With the objective of "reaching the unreachables," the San Francisco program was able to establish relationships with many segments of that city that were generally alienated from the police department. That success was limited, however, because the community relations officers, not the police department, established those positive relationships.

In general, most programs have not operated at their optimum level. Rather than being active in the community, community relations officers spend the majority of their time in the office. Hence, their major contribution is limited to the development of pamphlets, brochures, and other literature, with limited personal contact in the community. The authors feel that with proper motivation on the part of directors of police-community relations programs, many programs would show much greater success.

The degree of commitment to police–community relations, to a great extent, can be measured by the amount of resources devoted to the program. The problems of many departments are directly related to the fact that the unit is not given adequate resources to accomplish its objectives. Resources, as used here, refers to human and fiscal. Most community relations programs are understaffed and given low priority in budgetary considerations. There are cases where police–community relations officers are expected to maintain contacts in the community, yet are not assigned vehicles. In other cases, the police–community relations units are not assigned office space. These conditions have adverse effects on police–community relations, thereby contributing to their limited success.

IMPACT

The most difficult element to analyze in police–community relations programs is the impact they have had on both the police department and the community. It is in this context that police–community relations programs have exhibited the least amount of success.

This conclusion must be made intuitively because rarely, if ever, have police departments clearly defined the objectives they wish to obtain through their police–community relations program; nor have they developed the criteria for assessing goal achievement. Yet there are several observations that can be made to support that conclusion.

First, the concerns that gave rise to the development of police–community relations programs still exist. The polarization that existed between the police and the community is just as prevalent today as it was before the widespread implementation of the police–community relations programs.

Second, few, if any, procedural and operational changes have occurred in police departments as a result of police–community relations programs. It is not fair to suggest that police–community relations have been an unqualified failure in this respect; if nothing else, they have often raised issues and thereby forced the police to recognize the legitimacy of the community's concern about police policies and procedures. The point is, however, that the police often have not responded positively to these concerns.

Finally, police departments have usually not involved the community in their operations. For all practical purposes, the police still remain a closed organization. Citizen input is minimal or nonexistent. This element of secrecy accounts for a great deal of the suspicion directed toward the police on the part of the citizenry.

Police–community relations programs have rarely delivered what they promised. This can be attributed to the failure of police departments to integrate community relations into their total operations, the failure of police administrators to give their full commitment to the programs, and the focus upon "race relations," to the exclusion of focusing upon abrasive police policies and field procedures.

NECESSARY PREREQUISITES FOR EVALUATION

Essentially, we see five necessary elements as being basic to the evaluation of police–community relations programs:

1. Clearly drawn and precise program objectives
2. Organizational commitment to evaluation
3. Identification of criteria
4. Development of a data base
5. Methodological competence

These elements of program evaluation can be explained in the following manner.

Program Objectives

It is all well and good to favor serene motherhood, a desirable quality of life, and a tranquil and neighborly community. If we are serious, however, about evaluating social programs related to these matters, it will be necessary to be a bit more precise than this! How do we measure the serenity of motherhood? Although they may not object to serenity per se, some "population zero" advocates may question the necessity of incipient motherhood at all! How do we measure changes from "serene," to "more serene," and then to "most serene." (Most social programs, after all, advocate some change in the social condition. So how do we go about measuring progress from social state A to social change B?) How do we measure the "quality of life" and changes—in either direction—in that quality? Will all of our "subjects" (i.e., citizens) agree that a particular quality of life is more desirable than another? How do we measure "tranquility?" Maybe one segment of one community will be tranquil *only* when all members of another community are locked up!

You see the point. Anyone can come with some pet nostroms about how to improve the social condition. Be they liberal or conservative, be they bureaucrat or citizen, everyone has some pet scheme for improving the social setting. This "brainstorming" itself takes no particular stroke of genius.

Genius, when it exists in this organizational realm, comes into play when someone conceptualizes a social program in terms of a set of concrete, precise program objectives. Casting a program in terms of "To improve police community relations in Neanderthal City" builds into that program an absolute impossibility of evaluation. There is no feasible way that such a program can be properly evaluated. On the other hand, the suggested program should not be vetoed solely on the basis of imprecise objectives. Rather, upon examining the conceptualization of the program, it may very well be that the program has merit *if* the program objectives can be rewritten in a more precise way.

We might recast these potential objectives in the following manner:

1. To increase the Spanish-speaking facility of members of the patrol division
2. To provide for elected citizen representation on (police) departmental personnel selection and promotion boards
3. To increase the awareness of the (police) department's rank-and-file personnel about the unique crime-related problem of mentally retarded persons
4. To make it possible for the police department and the department of employment security to periodically exchange rank-and-file personnel as a training endeavor
5. To provide the mechanism by which representatives of rank-and-file personnel may become members of (police) departmental policy boards

Without debating the relative merits of any of the objectives outlined above, you will agree that they are written in fairly precise language. They are all capable of some form of accurate measurement, provided that the organization is willing to make the measurements.

Commitment to Evaluation

Let's face it, it takes an unusually strong and secure program or departmental administrator to accept the concept of effective evaluation. Few of us are willing to say that some program we have been working on is of no benefit. This is particularly true of the person, sometimes an agency head, who dreamed up the idea in the first place. In the opinion of the authors, for example, much of the "flak" directed at the Kansas City patrol experiment funded by the Police Foundation is based upon this very thing. For generations, the police world in the United States has geared itself to the notion that there is such a thing as "preventive patrol." Many police administrators and academics have based their entire careers on the validity of the notion of preventive patrol. Obviously, there was going to be a storm of controversy when the report was released by the Police Foundation. Whole patrol divisions have been funded largely on the notion of crime prevention. Literally thousands of appeals to city councils for increased police department funding have been buttressed by claims about the value of a mobile, prevention-oriented patrol force.

This is not the place to debate the issue of preventive patrol. None of the authors have examined in detail the field data contained in the complete final report of the Kansas City experiment. We mention it only as a classic example of organizational—and entire professional association—resistance to the notion of careful experimentation and evaluation. No one likes to be made to appear silly.

Therefore, evaluation can be very threatening: to the person conceiving of the idea, to persons employed in a program, and to the agency that allowed the program to be initiated in the first place. This explains *something* about the general organizational resistance to new programs; it explains a good deal about administrative resistance to effective evaluation!

How effective are programs that provide police personnel with blazer jackets rather than more traditional field uniforms? How effective are the so-called "white hat" programs that have sprung up all over the country? How effective are the "coffee klatch" programs, or the assignment of police officers to unemployment centers? Every one of these programs was conceived of by someone who had a stake in the "success" of the program. It is the unusual administrator who can admit that a pet idea failed and should be discarded.

This is why we feel strongly that there must absolutely be a commitment to serious evaluation even prior to the "startup" of a new program. Since most new programs involve outside funding, we feel that it is imperative that funding agencies insist upon this commitment before they release funds to the applicant agency. In this regard, the funding agency can be of material assistance to the applicant agency by saying: "If you want to use our money for your program, we insist that you make a commitment to evaluate the operation and the results of the program." If this had been done in the early stages of the Law Enforcement Assistance program, we are certain that a large number of the L.E.A.A.-funded programs would have never been started.

Criteria To Be Used

Obviously, if one wishes to measure "change" or "progress," one has to have some notion about precisely how to do this. What criteria do you use to measure "improved community relations"? It is relatively easy to measure the increased fluency of police field personnel in the use of the Spanish language. There are standardized tests in this area, and one needs only to invoke the use of pretests and posttests to measure progress toward the stated objectives of the program. To measure the effect of "coffee klatches" or the use of the blazer jackets is much more difficult, however. But it is not impossible! Neither is it impossible to measure changes in the number of complaints against police officers, nor to measure the changes in truancy that took place over the time period allotted to using police officers as attendance counselors in junior and senior highschools.

The techniques for evaluating some programs are certainly more sophisticated than those needed for certain other programs. In many cases, a police department will find it absolutely essential to seek outside technical assistance in developing evaluation plans. This is a classic case in which academic communities and private research firms can be of material assistance to an operating agency.

A word of caution, however! Don't blindly accept the expertise of an outside person, without making "commonsense" judgments about the appropriateness of a particular technique. Some recommended evaluation methodologies may be so complicated and refined that the cost of the evaluation will exceed by 10 times the cost of the action program itself! Simple data collection and computer analysis may, in fact, "eat up" three-fourths of program staff time, leaving precious little time for the action program itself. Such a situation is so silly on its face that we naturally reject it. In spite of its silliness, however, such evaluation efforts have been attempted. Toward the end of a project, the evaluation plan has had to be discarded and the program was left with no evaluation at all.

Data Base

Obviously, to do an evaluation we need some sort of data base which is central and germane to the criteria being used in the evaluation. There is no sense at all, for example, in using a daily "anchovy count" in Monterey Bay (California) if one is attempting to make a comparison of the relative effectiveness of three different ski bindings! That example should be rejected for its obvious silliness. Unfortunately, the authors have seen comparably silly attempts to use a data base intended for one purpose for a completely irrelevant and incomparable circumstance. Among the questions to be asked are the following:

1. What social or organizational phenomena are we attempting to measure?
2. Are these phenomena affected only by circumstances wholly within the police department?
3. If they are not, then we must try, as well as we can, to accumulate adequate data about these external matters.

For example, if we are attempting to measure the increased effectiveness of foot patrol in an area, we must, as well as we can, collect data from comparable social areas. We must also go outside the police department to obtain some of these data, for we should know something about changes in residential and business populations. How can you measure the effectiveness of a new patrol mode unless you have data for a period prior to the initiation of the new mode, and data throughout the experiment? Are you prepared to measure effectiveness without being able to account for the removal of 155 businesses that used to be licensed in the area? How can you measure effectiveness without taking into account that six square blocks of dilapidated housing has been vacated since the start of the program and the land cleared for a new convention center? Crime may be down if an area has lost 155 businesses and 6,500 residents! Patrol may have been irrelevant!

The reader will say: "Of course, all of that is obvious!" The authors will reply simply that although it may be obvious, these fundamental, crucial, and commonsense errors are continually being made in program evaluation. In some cases, the situation is so confused as to suggest that it could have resulted only from a deliberate attempt to foul the data base and make evaluation impossible!

Methodological Competence

Finally, we should reinforce a point made previously. This has to do with tailoring the methodology to the evaluation plan and assuring that there is competence to do a particular type of evaluation. In many types of police–community relations programs, there may be no need for highly sophisticated evaluation plans. In others, it may be absolutely essential to have available the services of a highly skilled applied mathematician, an economist, or operations researcher. Programs that require such skills will be complicated massive programs, probably involving other departments and social agencies as well as the police department.

For some programs, anecdotal material and some basic rudimentary data may be all that is necessary to make a defensible evaluation of the endeavor. Inherent in any planned program are its own evaluation demands. The important point is to recognize these and to insist that the person or group conceptualizing the idea of the program recognizes and deals with the requirements for effective evaluation.

Summary

After nearly a decade of police–community relations efforts, we may have a national inventory of programs, but we have very little in the way of properly evaluated programs. This is too bad, for it leaves departmental administrators and citizen groups with very little in the way of validated programming. Partially, this is the result of "crisis funding," brought about by the social disorder of the mid-1960s and early 1970s. In large part, our governmental decision makers were "grasping at straws," willing to fund nearly anything that looked as if it had even a remote chance of succeeding. There was a good deal of this in police–community relations toward the end of the last decade.

Another reason has to do with the "state of the art." Program evaluation in the governmental sector is relatively new. Essentially, it developed as a field of study during World War II and the period immediately following. At first, it was an endeavor devoted toward discovering methods for analyzing the comparative value of alternative military strategies. After the war, the techniques were directed toward the civilian sector of government, attempting to develop methods by which to assess the relative value of flood control, recreation, education, and so on.

Unfortunately, the techniques were unknown in the criminal justice field until 1967. We suspect that the availability of large sums of money under the "Safe Streets Act" (L.E.A.A.) took some of the pressure off insistence on appropriate program evaluation. "After all, if there is enough money for most of us, why waste some of it on evaluation? Let's wait until 'the well begins to run dry.'" That is certainly a cynical approach, but we suspect that there is more than a kernel of truth in it.

End Notes

[1]See, for example D. T. Campbell and J. C. Stanley, *Experimental and Quasi-Experimental Designs for Research* (Chicago: Rand McNally, 1966), for an expanded analysis of evaluative research models.

[2]"The Kurt Lewin Award Address" Society for the Psychological Study of Social Issues, Meeting with the American Psychological Association, New Orleans, September 1974.

[3]Ibid.

[4]See, for example, Campbell and Stanley, *Experimental Designs;* Francis G. Caro, ed., *Readings on Evaluative Research* (New York: Appleton-Century-Crofts, 1967); Edward A. Suchman, *Evaluative Research* (New York: Russell Sage Foundation, 1967); Carol H. Weiss, *Evaluating Action Programs* (Boston: Allyn and Bacon, 1972); and Carol H. Weiss, *Evaluation Research* (Englewood Cliffs, N.J.: Prentice-Hall, 1972).

[5]We have not listed crime prevention programs as a specific type because each department considers crime prevention as an essential part of its police–community relations program.

[6]St. Louis Police Department, "Police–Community Relations Planning and Development Program," a proposal for funding submitted to the U.S. Department of Justice, Office of Law Enforcement Assistance, September 26, 1966, p. 5.

[7]National Conference of Christians and Jews, "Police–Community Relations in St. Louis: Experience Report 103," pamphlet prepared January 1966, p. 3.

[8]For a brief description of these programs, refer to Appendix I. Some programs listed have been initiated and subsequently dropped.

[9]New Orleans, Louisiana, Police–Community Relations Division, mimeo, n.d., p. 3.

[10]Ibid., p. 2.

[11]Winston-Salem, North Carolina, Police Department, "A New Approach to Crime Prevention and Community Service," mimeo, n.d., p. 1.

[12]Winston-Salem, North Carolina, Police Department, "Background Police Community Service Unit," mimeo, n.d., no page.

[13]Ibid.

[14]Ibid.

[15]Winston-Salem Police Department, "A Proposal for the Second Year Funding of the Community Services Unit," n.d., p. 2.

[16]See, for example, "Curriculum for Police Community Service Unit Personnel," conducted at the Winston-Salem Police Training Academy, by the Institute of Government of the University of North Carolina, mimeo, n.d.

[17]Interview with Ferguson.

[18]Kendall O. Price and Kent Lloyd, "Improving Police-Community Relations through Leadership Training" (Inglewood, Calif.: Creative Management Research and Development, 1967), p 28.

[19]Interview with Chief Ferguson.

[20]Price and Lloyd, "*Improving Police-Community Relations*" (Inglewood Ca.: Creative Management Research and Development, 1967), p. 28.

[21]Ibid., p. 7.

[22]Ibid., p. 8.

[23]Ibid., pp. 22–28.

[24]"Exploring Criminal Justice as a Total System," an Application for Grant for Law Enforcement Purposes, submitted to the State of California Council on Criminal Justice, April 29, 1969.

[25]Interview with Ferguson.

[26]Comments made by San Francisco police officers at a 1966 Community Relations Conference held in that city.

[27]Dante Andreotti, "Our War Was with the Police Department," *Fortune*, January 1968, p. 196.

INDEX